Three
Pioneer Rapides Families

A Genealogy

By
GEORGE MASON GRAHAM STAFFORD,
A.B., M.D., F.A.C.S.

Baton Rouge
CLAITOR'S PUBLISHING DIVISION

Published and for sale by:
CLAITOR'S PUBLISHING DIVISION
3165 South Acadian at I-10, P.O. Box 3333
Baton Rouge, Louisiana 70821

Preface

THIS humble work is dedicated to the memory of Captain Peter Robert, Robert Tanner, and William Pearce, Sr. They were pioneers who left their homes at the dawn of the nineteenth century, and, traveling in ox wagons and flat boats, brought their families safely through the uninhabited wilderness of the great southwest to that section of the country in central Louisiana watered by Bayou Boeuf. When they first saw it there was little in the landscape to attract them. As far as the eye could see there were only dense cane brakes and impenetrable swamps. It was the character of the soil which induced them to settle there. For nearly a century and a half that soil has never failed to produce the most abundant cotton, corn and sugar cane crops in the whole Southland.

Captain Peter Robert hailed from Beaufort District, South Carolina, and was the fourth generation of his family in this country, being a great-grandson of Rev. Pierre Robert, the first Huguenot preacher to set foot on the shores of the New World. He came of that sturdy stock whose fearless spirit neither the cruelty of religious persecution nor the dangers of the ocean and the fear of the savage could intimidate or subdue. The descendants of our Louisiana pioneer are eligible to membership in the Daughters or Sons of the American Revolution, and also in the Huguenot Society of South Carolina.

Robert Tanner also came from Beaufort District, South Carolina, and was a son-in-law of Captain Peter Robert. He is said to have been a man of great force of character, was a surveyor and soon acquired prominence and wealth in his new surroundings. His forebears came from Virginia, so we believe, and he has left a numerous progeny, some of whom yet occupy the lands he first settled.

William Pearce, Sr., came from Screven county, Georgia, and his forebears from Virginia. He, like many others of his name, was a Revolutionary soldier. Two of his sons married daughters of Robert Tanner and Providence Robert. Thus the relationship of these three families is readily seen.

Numerous family Bibles preserved with care, and the old cemeteries of Cheneyville and Evergreen, Louisiana, tell the story of many generations of the descendants of these pioneers. There has been such frequent inter-marriage between them in the past century or more that at this period one of the present generation would make no mistake in calling one of the others "cousin."

Baton Rouge, La.
January 14, 1945.

Contents

PART ONE.

THE ROBERT FAMILY.

WE first find *our* Robert family appearing in America with the advent of Huguenot emigration to the colony of South Carolina in 1686. It is to be definitely borne in mind that the name is *Robert* and not *Roberts.* We are frequently prone to use the latter name when we intend the former. The two signify entirely different people. However, it is said within the family circle, that some members of the earlier generations in this country (through ignorance or carelessness) permitted an "*s*" to become attached to their names and have thus eventually been lost to the family where they rightfully belong.

Prior to the American Revolution that branch of the Robert family dealt with in this work was confined to the limits of South Carolina. Since then a few have drifted to the northern and western States of the Union, but large numbers followed the southwestern tide of emigration and settled in Mississippi, Louisiana and Texas. It can be said of them that wherever they went they became outstanding citizens in their community. They were ever a prolific people—sterility was never known among them—and today the blood of the first emigrant of that name courses in the veins of several thousand individuals.

We are particularly interested in that branch of the family which stopped in Louisiana in the early days of the nineteenth century and made their home in the central part of the State. The greater part of this work will be taken up with them and their descendants, but before doing so we will give a brief account of their South Carolina forebears, endeavoring to treat the subject in such a manner that those of the present generation will have no difficulty in tracing their descent back through the two hundred and fifty years of the past to the Rev. Pierre Robert, that earnest and fearless Huguenot preacher who led his flock from the persecuted valleys of France to the freedom of the wilderness in the Western Hemisphere. It is to be regretted that we have such meager knowledge of the life of this great and good man, and that we know almost nothing of his forebears. Such services as he rendered are worthy of more notice than it is possible at this remote period to accord them.

Tradition tells us that the Robert family originated in Wales and that several hundred years ago it was spelled *Rhobert.* Sometime after 1598 when Henry IV of France proclaimed the Edict of Nantes, thus giving religious freedom to his subjects, it is said that members of our Robert family left Wales and emigrated to France in order to take advantage of the blessings offered by this act.   They located in the Piedmont valley within the borders of what is now Switzerland, and it is there that we meet the first Robert whom we can definitely name.   He was Daniel and was born at Basle, Switzerland, in 1625.   He was very probably the second generation of the name born in a foreign land.   We have very little information about him; however, we do know that he lived at St. Imier, Switzerland, and that his wife was named Marie.   It was their son, Pierre Robert, who was the first of the name to emigrate to America.

PIERRE ROBERT.

Pierre Robert, the first generation of the family in the New World, was (as far as we know) the only son of Daniel and Marie Robert of St. Imier, Switzerland.   He is usually known as the *Rev. Pierre Robert.*   He was born in St. Imier, Switzerland, in 1656.   There is some reference to him in the early Swiss records as a Doctor, but this was probably an ecclesiastical title.   The following item from the church records in Basle, Switzerland, verifies his ordination:—

"Ce Dimanche, 19 Fevrier, 1682, le St. Pierre Robert de St. Imier a recu l'imposition des mains."

A glimpse of the early Robert genealogy has been left us by the Rev. William Henry Robert of Centerville, Mississippi, who was a son of James Jehu Robert and his second wife, Phoebe McKenzie, and a grandson of John Robert and Elizabeth Dixon of Robertville, South Carolina.   This information was left in an article in his own handwriting entitled "My Christmas Musings," which we will here insert in full: —

A few days since I met these two words as contrasted in their meaning; I have been thinking of times and things away back beyond my own personal being.   I have felt like Paul when he was induced to speak of his ancestry. I have thought how the affection of the poor Welsh Christians must have driven them to the throne of grace.

When in 1285, under the reign of Edward II, Wales became an English principality the "H" was left out of the name Rhobert, and it became Robert. Many of the name, however, taking on an "S".

I have been full of the thought of that family (Robert) which went into France to enjoy the privileges of the Edict of Nantes (1598), how they suffered loss of all things, save the love they had for the Saviour. In my thinking I was forced to say:—'We'll glory in tribulation also, for it only worketh patience, experience, hope and boldness in the love of God shed in our hearts.' I was thankfully thoughtful that tho' in France they suffered so much, yet the despised Huguenots were blessed, the Testament and Psalms having been translated into French by Farel and Le Fevre, and that Pierre Robert was enabled to enjoy the religious instructions of his parents in his youth near Basle, Switzerland, and to labor in the Piedmont valley as a pastor of the Waldensian Church until the Revocation of the Edict of Nantes in 1685, when by that cruel act of Louis XIV, he was forced to leave his home or be sent to the galleys.

Rev. Pierre Robert came with a colony of French and Sweedish refugees to Santee, South Carolina, being only thirty years old, with his wife Irania Buyser Robert* and their only son Pierre II, then five years old. When he, Pierre Robert, died in 1715, and his wife in 1717, they left three sons, Pierre II, Elias, and John. The last two allowed the "S" to their names and thus were lost to our family. One, a Col. Roberts of the Revolutionary Army, a prominent Presbyterian, settled in Pendleton county† and from him a village and church were called *Roberts*. Although we may not be able to trace our connection with many of those who claim and use "S" in the name Roberts, yet it is very pleasant thinking (as was remarked to me by a Methodist minister the past summer) that most of the aged men whom he had known of the Welsh Robert family were men of great piety and prayerfulness.

Jacques (James) Robert, a son of Pierre II, was a man of large size, six feet high and quite fleshy, a man of scientific education, became wealthy, and at one time

---

* This should be *Jeanne Brayé Robert*. In the court house at Charleston, S. C., there is a record of the marriage settlement of Pierre Robert II in which is mentioned the wife of Rev. Pierre Robert as *Jeanne Brayé*.

† In West Virginia.

owned four plantations in Santee, South Carolina, and at the same time carried on a store. By imprudence in trade, and by loaning the use of his name as security to his friends, he lost most of his property and had to resort to the school room for a living. He went to North Carolina and took his eldest son James with him. From the falling of an old house during a cyclone James was killed. His father soon after returned and moved his family to Colleton District, South Carolina. He died and was buried at Stone Creek Church in 1774, leaving three sons, Peter, Elias, and John, and three daughters, Elizabeth, Judith and Sarah. In 1775 his wife, Sarah Jaudon Robert, with her brother Thomas Jaudon,* her sons Peter and Elias, and her daughters, Elizabeth Grimball and Judith Cheney, moved to Black Swamp and established the village, Robertville, which was a place of considerable importance until the late Confederate War when Sherman had it thoroughly destroyed—even the fine old oaks and hickories under which I played as a school boy—burning the church and school house and Sunday school, also the fence around the graveyard, wherein laid the bodies of my grandmother and a sweet little girl nine weeks old, as well as other relatives and friends. God be praised! war could not touch their souls, these were at God's right hand, having fullness of joy and enjoying their inheritance undefiled, and that will never fade away.

The compiler of this work feels that we are most fortunate in having the above information from the pen of the Rev. William Henry Robert, affectionately known to his many Louisiana relatives as "Cousin Billy." This same has been handed down to us through other sources—principally tradition—and we feel more secure in our genealogical position in having it from one who really knew. His statements definitely establish for us the names of the first three generations of our forebears in this country. Rev. William Henry Robert was a great grandson of Jacques (son of Pierre II) whom he mentions in his "musings." He himself was the grandfather of Dr. James Jehu Robert of Baton Rouge, Louisiana, one of the prominent physicians and surgeons there at this date (1945).

---

* Rev. W. H. Robert has evidently made a mistake in the first name of Sarah Jaudon Robert's brother. We can find no Thomas Jaudon of that period. Sarah, who was the daughter of Daniel Jaudon, had five brothers, Daniel, Noah, Elias, Matthew, and Paul.

PIERRE ROBERT II.

The second generation of the Robert family in America is represented by Pierre Robert II, eldest son of the famous Huguenot preacher and his wife, Jeanne Brayé. He was born in Basle, Switzerland, in the early part of 1675. The register of the old Waldensian church at Basle records his baptism as follows:

> Le Registre de l'Eglise Francaise de Basle ce Dimanche 9 de Mai, 1675:—a ete baptize un fils de St. Pierre Robert et de Jeanne Brayé, presente par le Sieur Rene Frey, le Sieur de Beaulieu, et Demoiselle Elizabeth Tudore,—Pierre.

Young Pierre Robert was eleven years of age when his parents brought him to America, and not *five* as was stated in the paper left by the Rev. William Henry Robert and already quoted in full. It was in the year 1686 that he first saw the shores of South Carolina where he was to spend the remainder of his days. He was twice married. In 1701 he married Anne Marie Louise le Grand, daughter of Louis le Grand, Esquire, Sieur de la Fresnaye, and his wife, Anne de Magneville. Her parents were from Caen, in Normandy, France. The records in Charleston, South Carolina, show that the marriage settlement was signed in the house of the bride's uncle, Isaac le Grand, Esquire, Sieur d'Anerville. It was executed before Henry Auguste on September 10, 1701, and was witnessed by Isaac le Grand and Jacques le Grand. The text of the marriage settlement began in this manner:—

> We, the undersigned, Pierre Robert, minister of the Gospel, native of St. Imier, Switzerland, and now living in the county of Craven on the border of the Santee river in the Province of Carolina, and Pierre Robert, native of Basle, Switzerland, son of myself—the said Pierre Robert, minister of the Gospel, and Jeanne Brayé, his wife, - - -

Pierre Robert II, and his first wife, Anne Marie Louise le Grand, had but one child, Pierre Robert III, who was born at French Santee, South Carolina, in 1704. It seems apparent that his mother died in giving him birth. This Pierre Robert III married Mary Lynch in 1728 and they had four children:— Lynch, Jonah, Mary, and Susannah. We have no further record of them but it is quite probable that some of these four children married and left descendants. Pierre Robert III died in 1740.

Pierre Robert II married his second wife in 1706. She was Judith Videaul, daughter of Pierre and Jeanne Elizabeth Videaul, and grand-daughter of Pierre Videaul and his wife, Magdalaine Burgand, both of La Rochelle, France—so we learn from Baird's Huguenot Emigration to America, Vol. I, page 297. Judith Videaul was born in South Carolina. In some family records her surname appears as *de Bordeaux*. We are unable to account for this dual name, except that it seems to have been a custom among the early French inhabitants of this country to sometimes use an additional name taken from the locality in France whence they came, thus accentuating their identity. Be that as it may, this name seems to have stayed in the family and three generations later we find a *Bordeaux Robert*. Three children were born of this second marriage:— Jacques (James), Magdalene, and Elizabeth Robert.

Magdalene Robert, the elder daughter of Pierre Robert II, was twice married. Her first husband was Archibald Hamilton and her second was William Gough. In the South Carolina Historical and Genealogical Magazine, Vol. XXIII, we find some interesting data on this lady. On page 112 we read:—

Magdalene Hamilton, widow, daughter of Peter and Judith Robert, French Santee, born there September 28, 1719, married William Gough, widower, May 7, 1749.
Elizabeth Hamilton, daughter of Archibald, a lawyer, and the said Magdalene, was born at North Carolina April, 1, 1740.
George Hamilton, son of the same, was born at North Carolina, August 19, 1742.

On page 103 of the same volume of the above mentioned magazine we find considerable data about William Gough, the second husband of Magdalene Robert. We read as follows:—

William Gough, Jr., son of William and Martha, born in London October 5, 1703, married in London January 19, 1727, Mary Bearsley, spinster. He died May 12, 1758, aged 55, of pleurisy. He married 2nd Susannah Le Fong, widow, at Savannah, October 24, 1735. He came and settled in South Carolina 1737 and there married May 7, 1749, Magdalene Robert, widow of Archibald Hamilton. They were married by Mr. Hutson.
Martha Gough, daughter by 3rd marriage, born March 24, 1750, baptized April 22, 1750.

(Page 104) Mary Anne Gough, daughter by 3rd marriage, born November 13, 1753, baptized April 17, 1754.

(Page 107) William Bearsley Gough, son of 3rd marriage, born April 15, 1756, baptized August 31, 1756.

Elizabeth Robert, younger daughter of Pierre Robert II, married Elias Jaudon, son of Daniel and Elizabeth Jaudon, Huguenot pioneers to South Carolina. From the best information obtainable it would appear that they had five children:— Elias, Jr., Sarah, Paul, David, and Elisha Jaudon. The eldest, Elias Jaudon, Jr., married Mary Hyrne Dixon whose grandfather was the Second Landgrave Thomas Smith, son of First Landgrave Thomas Smith, Governor of South Carolina. They left numerous descendants, some of whom married back into the Robert family, thus returning to the fold whence they came. Those interested in this line should read that chapter entitled "House of Landgrave Smith", in Mrs. Annie E. Miller's book, "Our Family Circle."

Pierre Robert II died in 1731, between March 9, and May 1. We do not know the exact spot where he was buried, but evidently it was in French Santee. The date of his second wife's death is unknown to us, but according to his will we know that she survived him. Fortunately for us the will of Pierre Robert II, written in French, is on record in South Carolina. It was published in both French and English in "the Transactions of the Huguenot Society of South Carolina," No. 29, in 1924.

The following is a true copy of it:—

In the name of God the Father, the Son, and the Holy Ghost! Amen!

I, Peter Robert, born in Basle, Switzerland, and now living in Craven county, South Carolina, being by the grace of God, of sound mind and understanding, but unwell in body, not knowing when and what manner it shall please God to take me out of this world, do declare to have drawn up this my Testament which I hereby order to be enforced and executed as being my last will.

I recommend my soul unto God my Creator who redeemed it by the blood of His Son Jesus Christ, beseeching Him to have mercy upon me and receive me on my leaving this life into His eternal Tabernacles. As to my body I commit it to the earth to be therein interred in such a place as my heirs shall see fit.

As to my worldly goods which shall be found in my possession at the time of my death, I order that all my debts shall be paid off first and prior to any legacy.

Secondly I give to Judith Robert, my dear wife, her bed and all of its appurtances, a press with all of the linen that shall be found in the house, a table, a warming pan, a chest and a mirror.

Thirdly, as my son, Peter Robert, has inherited my late father's property, therefore and in consequence of the heavy losses I have undergone for many years, moreover believing that I cannot possibly leave to my other children more than he inherited from my late father, I do give and bequeath unto my aforesaid son, Peter Robert, the sum of one shilling sterling, or the value thereof in currency of this country, for his portion and share in all present and future possessions without him or his descendants ever having any further claim under the pretext of primogeniture or under any other pretext to my plantation or any other real estates that might be found in my possession after my death.

Fifthly, I will and order that in case my herein aftersaid Executors deem it advisable for the best interest of the family to sell all our real estate if they could get a reasonable price, they should do it for the sake of my debts, and I by this Testament and last will do empower them to do so; but if on the contrary they could get only a very low price, then I will and bequeath those real estates unto my son James Robert and his heirs to enjoy them, and dispose of them as they please forever, but I also will and intend that my aforesaid son James Robert shall be obliged to deliver the price and therewith pay up my debts. However, if he could not pay the price and should prefer to give the real estates over to another, he is free to do so. But should my said heirs get reasonable price for a part of the aforesaid real estates or plantation and deem it advisable to sell it, I order and intend that they shall sell it and pay off my aforesaid debts with the price and in that case I order and intend that my said son James shall inherit the rest of my real estates without any reserve to enjoy them and dispose of them forever as he sees it fit, without being obliged to pay anything thereof unto my other heirs. It is my will that he should have them under those conditions should the aforesaid circumstances prevail.

Sixthly, I do give and bequeath unto my dear wife, Judith Robert, one third of what shall remain of my possessions after my debts have been paid up to dispose of as she pleases and the other two thirds I give and bequeath unto my son James Robert and my daughters Magdalene Robert and Elizabeth Robert, and all other children that I may have hereafter by my aforesaid wife, the whole being equally divided among them. Should any of them die before being twenty-one years of age, or intestate after the aforesaid age, or unmarried, they shall inherit one from each other with the reservation that my son Peter Robert shall have no claim thereunto; and if all should die before the aforesaid age, or unmarried, then my aforesaid dear wife shall inherit without any reserve, if she be still living, but if she be dead then the whole should revert to my son Peter Robert. But if my dear wife be still living she shall dispose of it as she pleases as well as of all that I have already bequeathed her.

I also recommend and order that my children shall obey their mother and show her every possible respect according to the precepts of the Gospel and God's commandments in order to draw upon themselves His blessing.

I order and intend that my aforesaid wife Judith Robert shall have the use of the home all of her life, if the plantation is not sold, on the condition that she shall not remarry.

I order and appoint both Judith Robert, my dear wife, and Mr. Gendron as Executors and Administrators jointly with my son James Robert, when he shall be twenty-one years old, that is to say, on the third of April, one thousand seven hundred and thirty-two, as it appears from the baptism certificate delivered by the late Mr. Peter Robert, Minister (my dear father).

I revoke and annul any other Testament heretofore drawn up, signing this with my own hand.

Done in Santee, this ninth day of March, one thousand seven hundred and thirty-one.

Pierre Robert.

Witnesses :—

Andre Rembert
Jean Robert
Pierre Guerry
Jean Baxott.   Proved May 1, 1731.

JACQUES ROBERT.

Our third generation in America of this good old Huguenot family is represented by Jacques Robert (mentioned in his father's will above as *James Robert*), eldest child of Pierre

Robert II and his second wife, Judith Videaul. He was born in French Santee, South Carolina, on April 3, 1711. This date is verified by a definite statement in his father's will which says that he would be twenty-one years of age on April 3, 1732, and that the time of his birth is given in a baptismal certificate furnished by the Rev. Pierre Robert. The only specific data we possess of Jacques Robert as a citizen and business man we gathered from the article written by Rev. William Henry Robert and which we have inserted on a previous page. He married Sarah Jaudon on August 26, 1735. She was a sister of Elias Jaudon who married Jacques' sister Elizabeth Robert, and was a daughter of Daniel and Elizabeth Jaudon of Craven county, South Carolina, early Huguenot pioneers. She was born there on February 24, 1719. Her father, Daniel Jaudon, came to South Carolina from the Isle of Ré, in the Bay of Biscay, near the coast of France, with his sister, Esther Jaudon, when he was about thirteen years of age. His father, Elie Jaudon, had died some years previous to their embarkation and his mother had married Pierre Michaud who brought her and her children to America.

After meeting with severe financial reverses Jacques Robert left French Santee with his family and moved to what is now Colleton county, near the Combahee river. This move was made about 1770. There he endeavored to retrieve his lost fortune but died in November, 1774. He was buried in the Stoney Creek churchyard, near Yamasee. The following year his widow, Sarah (Jaudon) Robert, moved with most of her children and other members of her family to Black Swamp, near the Savannah river, and there they founded the town of Robertville. She died there on April 26, 1779, and was buried in the vicinity. Seven children were born of this marriage, six of whom reached maturity, married and left numerous descendants. These children were:

1.—James Robert who went to North Carolina with his father when a young man and was killed there during a cyclone.

2.—Peter Robert, born in French Santee, South Carolina, in 1738, and died in Cheneyville, Rapides parish, Louisiana, about 1825. He married Anne Grimball, daughter of Paul Grimball and his third wife, Mary Samms. They had twelve children, all of whom settled in Louisiana. See Part Two of this book for a full account of them.

3.—Elizabeth Robert married John Grimball, son of Paul Grimball, and his third wife, Mary Samms, and some years after his death she married Rev. Alexander H. Scott. She moved with her second husband to Woodville, Mississippi, and after his death went to live with her son, Paul Grimball, in Rapides parish, Louisiana, where she died in 1818. She had children by both marriages. Her numerous progeny from these two unions has been extensively dealt with in Chapters XIX and XX in the compiler's work, *General Leroy Augustus Stafford, His Forebears and Descendants.*

4.—John Robert, fourth child of Jacques Robert and Sarah Jaudon, was born in French Santee, South Carolina, on July 15, 1742, and died at Robertville, South Carolina, on February 25, 1826. He was a soldier in the American Revolution and a man of wealth and education. On April 19, 1770, he married Elizabeth Dixon, daughter of Captain Thomas Dixon and Elizabeth Smith, and grand-daughter (on her mother's side) of the Second Landgrave Thomas Smith whose father was Governor of South Carolina under the Royal Government. Elizabeth Dixon was born on James Island, Charleston, South Carolina, on June 7, 1750, and died at Robertville in that State on November 15, 1820. We find an account of the marriage of John Robert and Elizabeth Dixon in the issue of THE SOUTH CAROLINA AND AMERICAN GENERAL GAZETTE of Friday, May 11, 1770. The brief notice of it reads as follows:—

> MARRIED:—Mr. John Robert, of Indian-Land, to Miss Elizabeth Dixon, daughter of the deceased Capt. Thomas Dixon, of James Island.

The paper mentioned was a weekly periodical published in Charleston, South Carolina. All marriages recorded in it from 1766 to 1782 have been compiled in book form by Mr. A. S. Salley, Jr., Secretary of the Historical Commission of South Carolina. John Robert and Elizabeth Dixon had ten children:— Mary Harriett, Elizabeth Anne, John Hancock, Thomas Smith, William Henry, James Jehu, Benjamin Nathaniel, Sarah Dixon, Lucia, and an un-named infant. Mrs. Annie E. Miller has written a splendid genealogy entitled "OUR FAMILY CIRCLE", published by the J. W. Burke Co., of Macon, Georgia, in which, commencing on page 239, she gives a full account of all the descendants of John Robert. We refer all those interested to that wonderful book. We would like, however, to mention here that the Rev. William Henry Robert referred to in the first part of this chapter was a grandson of John Robert and Elizabeth Dixon, his father being James Jehu Robert. This Rev. William Henry Robert's grandson, Dr. James Jehu Robert (as we have stated elsewhere) now resides in Baton Rouge, Louisiana, where he is an outstanding citizen and physician.

5.—Elias Robert, fifth child of Jacques Robert and Sarah Jaudon, married Mary Rue and had five children. We regret we have no further information about his descendants.

6.—Sarah Robert, sixth child of Jacques Robert and Sarah Jaudon, was born at French Santee, South Carolina, on February 6, 1755, and died at Robertville on October 5, 1839. She was married on March 18, 1773, to Joseph Lawton, Jr. They had eleven children, four of whom died young. The others married and left descendants, an account of whom may be found on page 323 in "Our Family Circle".

7.—Judith Robert, seventh child of Jacques Robert and Sarah Jaudon, was born in French Santee, South Carolina, about 1757. She was three times married. First to John Audebert, of Huguenot descent, by whom she had two children, John and Rachel Providence Audebert. Both of these children married and left descendants. The latter married Leroy Stafford of Beaufort District, South Carolina, son of Seth Stafford and Amanda Maner. Judith Robert's second husband was John Cheney, and her third was John Calliham. She had no issue by her last two marriages.

BIBLIOGRAPHY:—

Huguenot Emigration to America, by Baird, Vol. I, page 297.

Register of the Waldensian Church in Basle, Switzerland.

Document left by Rev. William Henry Robert.

Record of Marriage Settlement of Pierre Robert II on file in Charleston, South Carolina.

Will of Pierre Robert II from Transactions of the Huguenot Society of South Carolina, No. 29, page 38.

Our Family Circle, by Mrs. Annie E. Miller, pages 187, 195, 239, 323.

Robert Family Records furnished by Mrs. Evelyn (Brewer) Gray, of Lecompte, Louisiana.

Data on Robert Family furnished the compiler by Mrs. Mary Boyd Fleming of Nashville, Tennessee.

South Carolina Historical and Genealogical Magazine, Vol. XXIII, pages 103, 104, 107, 112.

PART TWO.

CAPTAIN PETER ROBERT.

CAPTAIN PETER ROBERT was the Patriarch of the Robert family of Louisiana. He came in the early days of the nineteenth century with his good wife and his six sons and his six daughters, and they pitched their tents on the banks of Bayou Boeuf in Rapides parish, near the present town of Cheneyville, and there today many of their descendants still reside. This old pioneer was the second of the seven children of Jacques (James) Robert and his wife, Sarah Jaudon, and was born in French Santee, South Carolina, between the years 1738 and 1740. His grandparents were Pierre Robert II and his second wife, Judith Videaul, and his great grandparents were the Rev. Pierre Robert and his wife, Jeanne Brayé. He was of pure Huguenot stock on both sides and it was only with his children that other blood began to course in the veins of a Robert. He first saw the light of day on the banks of the Santee and there he spent his boyhood and his young manhood, but when he reached maturity the roving spirit seemed to materialize in him and he was ever moving towards the setting sun. Sometime prior to the American Revolution, accompanied by his wife and children, his mother, his brothers and sisters, and several members of his mother's family, he moved to Black Swamp, near the Savannah river, and there they founded the town of Robertville which for many years was a thriving little metropolis. Some years before this move, about 1763, he married Anne Grimball, daughter of Paul Grimball and his third wife, Mary Samms, who was born in Colleton county, South Carolina, in 1747. Her father was a son of Thomas Grimball and was born on Edisto Island, Colleton county, where his grandfather, the Honorable Paul Grimball, had settled in 1682 and for many years was Secretary of the Proprietary Government and probably one of the best known and most important personages in the colony of his time.

The twelve children of Captain Peter Robert and Anne Grimball were born in South Carolina—some of them in French Santee but most of them in Robertville. This early pioneer to

Louisiana has always been styled *Captain* Peter Robert, and according to family tradition this title is derived from the rank he held in the South Carolina militia during the Revolution. However, the compiler has ɩ᷑en unable to verify this tradition by any official records. But that does not mean he did not hold such a title. Records were badly kept at the time and many of them have long ago been lost. Military titles in those days were not carelessly bestowed and usually meant service of some kind. We do know with certainty that Peter Robert aided the cause of the Revolution in at least one capacity. He conducted a tannery on his plantation and during the war furnished leather to the Continental Army. Mr. A. S. Salley, Jr., Secretary of the South Carolina Historical Commission, has compiled and published "Stub Entries to Indents for Revolutionary Claims." In Books U-W, page 149, we will find Indent No. 370, issued on August 1, 1785, to Mr. Peter Robert for L4-3-10 sterling, which states that this was in payment for tanning leather for military use in 1781. In recognition of this service the descendants of Peter Robert have been accepted for membership in such patriotic organizations as the Daughters of the American Revolution and the Sons of the American Revolution. Through his wife, Anne Grimball, all female descendants are eligible to membership in the Colonial Dames of America.

Soon after 1800 Captain Peter Robert, with his own immediate family, joined a large concourse of the Robert and Grimball families in an emigration movement to the southwest. There were ninety-seven persons in this pioneer expedition, and one of the prime-movers of it was Peter Robert's son-in-law, Robert Tanner. They left South Carolina and, traveling overland in ox wagons, made their way through a wilderness inhabited only by Indians, in search of the Tennessee river. There they constructed rude flat boats in which they traversed the Tennessee into the Ohio, and thence down that stream into the Mississippi, and on down that great river until they reached a place on the east bank about fifty miles below Natchez known as Fort Adams, in that section of the Mississippi Territory now known as Wilkinson county. In Biographical and Historical Memoirs of Mississippi their new location is mentioned as follows:—"The Tanner settlement of 1804 was made four miles southwest of Woodville." This not only gives us a definite date as to when they reached their destination but also indicates that Robert Tanner was an outstanding character in the new settlement. He was a surveyor and was engaged to lay off the present town of Woodville. Other friends and relatives from South Carolina joined these first pioneers later and soon a thriving colony was firmly rooted in that section of what was then known as West Florida, and which within a few years was to become the great commonwealth of Mississippi.

After about ten or twelve years of residence among the sandy hills of southern Mississippi Captain Peter Robert heard of more fertile lands beyond the great river, and calling his tribe together he crossed over and led them towards the setting sun. Scarcely a hundred miles did he travel when he reached the Bayou Bouef country, the most beautiful and fertile section of Rapides parish, in the State of Louisiana. He saw at the first glance that he need go no further, that he had reached the "Land of Promise" for himself and his children and their children, that he could now rest and spend the remainder of his years in peace and contentment. It was on the banks of Bayou Boeuf, near the present little town of Cheneyville, that his sons and daughters built their homes a century and a quarter ago, and there today many of their numerous progeny are to be found.

We have no record of the date of death of Captain Peter Robert or his faithful wife, nor do we even know the spot where they were buried. It is quite certain that they died sometime just prior to 1825, and as private graveyards were customary in those days it is likely they were buried near their home. Most of the private burying grounds of that time have now been completely obliterated by neglect and time. Captain Peter Robert and Anne Grimball had twelve children, all of whom reached adult life and married. They were:—

A.—James Robert.
B.—Grimball Robert.
C.—Peter Robert.
D.—Joseph Robert.
E.—Providence Robert.
F.—Anne Grimball Robert.
G.—Paul Jabez Robert.
H.—Sarah Catharine Robert.
I.—Esther Susannah Robert.

J.—Daniel Robert.
K.—Martha Robert.
L.—Mary Robert.

A

JAMES ROBERT

James Robert, eldest child of Captain Peter Robert and his wife, Anne Grimball, was born in French Santee, South Carolina, in 1766.   While living in Beaufort District, near Robertville, South Carolina, he married Elizabeth Naylor* and there their children were born.   He brought his family to Mississippi and later to Louisiana when his father emigrated to those places. We have been unable to obtain any information about his wife, Elizabeth Naylor, and only know that after his death she married a Dr. McMullen.   There was no issue by this latter marriage.   James Robert and Elizabeth Naylor had five children:—

1.—Margaret Robert.
2.—Esther Susannah Robert.
3.—Hadley Peter Robert.
4.—Eldred Grimball Robert.
5.—Moses Elias Robert.

1.   Margaret Robert, eldest child of James Robert and Elizabeth Naylor, was born in Beaufort District, near Robertville, South Carolina, and was brought to Mississippi by her parents when a young girl.   She was born about 1792 and was twice married.   Her first husband was James Fanner and her second was a Mr. Hooker.   There may have been descendants from both marriages but we have been unable to find any record of them, nor do we know anything further of her except that it is said she lived in Ouachita parish, Louisiana, where her death occurred very suddenly.

2.   Esther Susannah Robert, second child of James Robert and Elizabeth Naylor, was born near Robertville, Beaufort Dis-

---

* The Lodowick Tanner family records tells us that James Robert married *Betsey Barlow*.   We have been unable to find anything to substantiate this, but it is not improbable that *Betsey Barlow* and *Elizabeth Naylor* were the same person.   She may have been a widow when James Robert married her.   We only find her in the records of this branch of the Robert family as Elizabeth Naylor.

trict, South Carolina, on May 22, 1794. This date is substantiated by records now in the possession of one of her descendants, Mrs. Evelyn Brewer Gray, of Lecompte, Louisiana. When about ten years of age she was brought to Mississippi by her parents. She is sometimes recorded as *Susan Robert*. The old records in the court house at Woodville, Wilkinson county, Mississippi, show that a license to marry was granted to Joseph Rutledge and Susan Robert on January 16, 1815. This Joseph Rutledge is said to have been of the famous South Carolina family of that name. He was a son of John James Rutledge and Anne Owen. Sometime after their marriage in Woodville we learn that Joseph Rutledge and his wife moved to Wilkes county, Georgia, and there six of their seven children were born. In 1835 they left Georgia and came to Louisiana, settling in Rapides parish. On March 8, 1836, he purchased 37 acres of land from Joseph H. Boone, situated on Hurricane Creek, in the pinewoods west of Cheneyville, and near the property of Joseph Tanner and Randal Eldred used as summer homes. There Mr. Rutledge died on January 12, 1849. His wife survived him many years dying in July, 1870. These dates are among the valuable records in the possession of Mrs. Gray of Lecompte, Louisiana. The seven children of Joseph Rutledge and Esther Susannah Robert were:—

> i.—Margaret Jane Rutledge.
> ii.—Sarah Ann Providence Rutledge.
> iii.—Robert Kennedy Rutledge.
> iv.—Elizabeth Susan Rutledge.
> v.—Joanna Lawton Rutledge.
> vi.—Joseph Sadler Rutledge.
> vii.—William Owen Rutledge.

i.—Margaret Jane Rutledge, eldest child of Joseph Rutledge and Esther Susannah Robert, was born in or near Woodville, Mississippi, on December 6, 1815, and moved to Wilkes county, Georgia, with her parents when an infant. She was married in Wilkes county, Georgia, on December 6, 1830, to James Brown Moore who was born in that county and State on December 7, 1808. In 1835 they went with Joseph Rutledge and his family to Louisiana and settled near Cheneyville, in Rapides parish. At that time they had two children. Later Mr. Moore moved to the hill section of Rapides parish west of

Cheneyville, and resided on Hurricane Creek in the vicinity of the present village of Forest Hill. There he lived until his death which occurred on January 10, 1877. His wife, Margaret Jane Rutledge, survived him thirty years and died in Lecompte, Rapides parish, Louisiana, on March 1, 1907, at the advanced age of ninety-two. They had ten children, the last eight of whom were born in Rapides parish. These children were:—

    a.—John Glenn Moore.
    b.—Eldred Robert Moore.
    c.—Esther Susan Moore.
    d.—Sarah Elizabeth Moore.
    e.—Margaret Sophronia Moore.
    f.—Mary Ophelia Moore.
    g.—Eunice Catherine Moore.
    h.—Henry Scott Moore.
    i.—James Rutledge Moore.
    j.—Corilla Jane Moore.

a.—John Glenn Moore, eldest child of James Brown Moore and Margaret Jane Rutledge, was born in Wilkes county, Georgia, on January 9, 1832, and came to Louisiana with his parents when three years of age. He never married, entered the Confederate Army at the beginning of the Civil War and from the best obtainable information was captured and died in a Federal prison.

b.—Eldred Robert Moore, second child of James Brown Moore and Margaret Jane Rutledge, was born in Wilkes county, Georgia, on April 14, 1834, and died in Louisiana on September 14, 1836, when two and a half years of age.

c.—Esther Susan Moore, third child of James Brown Moore and Margaret Jane Rutledge, was born in Rapides parish, Louisiana, on August 21, 1837. She was married on March 6, 1856, to Daniel Brewer, a native of New York who had emigrated to Louisiana in 1851. Mr. Brewer was born in the State of New York in 1824 and was a son of Lewis Brewer and Mary McClure, both natives of that State. The wedding of Daniel Brewer and Esther Susan Moore took place at the home of the bride's parents, in that section of Rapides parish then known as Spring Hill. Daniel Brewer and his wife made their home on Bayou Boeuf in the present town of Lecompte, and there their fourteen children were born. Mr. Brewer died at his home there on May 18, 1898, and his wife on October 4, 1923. Their children were:—

  az.—Kenneth Brewer.
  bz.—Mary Jane Brewer.
  cz.—Jester Moore Brewer.
  dz.—Esther Susan Brewer.
  ez.—Sarah Alice Brewer.
  fz.—Daniel Brewer, Jr.
  gz.—Ralph James Brewer.
  hz.—John Glenn Brewer.
  iz.—Samuel Alexander Hull Brewer.
  jz.—Eunice Anna Brewer.
  kz.—Lilly Cornelia Brewer.
  lz.—Evelyn Scott Brewer.
  mz.—Octavia Brewer.
  nz.—Arthur Lewis Brewer.

az.—Kenneth Brewer, eldest child of Daniel Brewer and Esther Susan Moore, was born in Rapides parish, Louisiana, on January 4, 1857. He never married. The following notice of his death is copied from the LOUISIANA DEMOCRAT, an Alexandria, Louisiana, newspaper:—

> DIED:—At the residence of his father at Lecompte, Louisiana, on September 16, 1884, Kenneth D. Brewer, in the 28th year of his age. He was the eldest son of Daniel and Esther S. Brewer of Lecompte.

bz.—Mary Jane Brewer, second child of Daniel Brewer and his wife, Esther Susan Moore, was born in Rapides parish, Louisiana, on August 31, 1858, and died unmarried.

cz.—Jester Moore Brewer, third child of Daniel Brewer and his wife, Esther Susan Moore, was born in Rapides parish, Louisiana, on October 29, 1859, and died unmarried. The following item from the LOUISIANA DEMOCRAT chronicles his death.

> DIED:—At the family residence at Lecompte, Louisiana, on Wednesday, October 19, 1887, J. M. Brewer, son of Daniel Brewer, aged 28 years.

dz.—Esther Susan Brewer, fourth child of Daniel Brewer and his wife, Esther Susan Moore, was born in Rapides parish, Louisiana, on December 14, 1861, and died in 1918, unmarried.

ez.—Sarah Alice Brewer, fifth child of Daniel Brewer and his wife, Esther Susan Moore, was born in Rapides parish,

Louisiana, on September 28, 1863, and was married to James J. Huncilman. The following notice of her marriage appeared in an Alexandria newspaper at the time:—

MARRIED:—At the residence of the bride's parents at Lecompte, Louisiana, on Monday, October 31, 1887, Miss Alice Brewer to Mr. Jim J. Huncilman.

Mr. Huncilman was a native of New Albany, Indiana. Both have long since died, leaving no issue.

fz.—Daniel Brewer, Jr., sixth child of Daniel Brewer and his wife, Esther Susan Moore, was born in Rapides parish, Louisiana, on March 12, 1865, and died young.

gz.—Ralph James Brewer, seventh child of Daniel Brewer and his wife, Esther Susan Moore, was born in Rapides parish, Louisiana, on December 5, 1866. He married on December 19, 1895, Ava Wilcox. Two daughters were born of this union, Lucille and Leona Brewer. The elder, Lucille, was married to W. C. Sullivan of Monroe, Louisiana. They have no children. The younger, Leona, married first Robert Ferguson, and second Jack Grant. No issue by either marriage. Ava (Wilcox) Brewer died some years ago and Ralph James Brewer then married as his second wife Mrs. Louise Marthis. There are no children by the second marriage.

hz.—John Glenn Brewer, eighth child of Daniel Brewer and his wife, Esther Susan Moore, was born in Rapides parish, Louisiana, on July 24, 1868. He married on December 29, 1899, in Bowling Green, Kentucky, Alice Alexander, a daughter of Dr. Robert Alexander and his wife, Margaret Sterritt. Mr. and Mrs. Brewer now reside in Lecompte, Louisiana. Three children were born of this marriage:—Margaret Esther Brewer who died young; Agatha Alexander Brewer who married Rev. Ira Wright Flowers of Laurel, Mississippi, and now has two children, Jean Alice and Jack Glenn Flowers; and John Glenn Brewer, Jr., who is now a student at the Louisiana State University.

iz.—Samuel Alexander Hull Brewer, ninth child of Daniel Brewer and his wife, Esther Susan Moore, was born in Rapides parish, Louisiana, on February 7, 1870, and died at his home at Lecompte, Louisiana, on Friday afternoon, December 13, 1940. He was a high-toned gentleman and an outstanding citizen and business man in his community. He married on October 3, 1916, Nell Sharman of Magnolia, Arkansas. She was a daughter of Mrs. Mary Jane (Bayliss) Harvey by her first husband, R. R. Sharman of Magnolia. One daughter, Nellie Sharman Brewer, was born of this marriage on January 14, 1919. She was educated at Gulf Park College, Gulfport, Mississippi, and now resides in Lecompte with her mother.

jz.—Eunice Anna Brewer, tenth child of Daniel Brewer and his wife, Esther Susan Moore, was born in Rapides parish, Louisiana, on April 5, 1874. She was married on April 6, 1902, to James Cravens Cobb, member of the noted Cobb family of Georgia. They resided in Dodd City, Texas, for a number of years and it was there that Mr. Cobb died in August, 1925. They had no children. After the death of her husband Mrs. Cobb returned to Lecompte and resided with her sisters until her death on Friday, February 17, 1939, at 5:10 p. m. She was buried in the Lecompte cemetery.

kz.—Lilly Cornelia Brewer, eleventh child of Daniel Brewer and his wife, Esther Susan Moore, was born in Rapides parish, Louisiana, on August 9, 1876. This dear lady and "cousin" yet resides at the old Brewer home in Lecompte, Louisiana, where she first saw the light of day. She has never married.

lz.—Evelyn Scott Brewer, twelfth child of Daniel Brewer and his wife, Esther Susan Moore, was born in Rapides parish, Louisiana, on June 28, 1878. She was married on December 2, 1924, to Fluellen Hurst Gray of Lake Charles, Louisiana, a son of Dr. Reuben Flannagan Gray and his wife, Frances Chiles. Mr. Gray died some years ago and since that time his widow has lived in Lecompte, Louisiana, with her sister, Miss Lilly Brewer. She is the family genealogist, and it has been through her generous cooperation that this record of the descendants of James Robert and Elizabeth Naylor has been made available. The compiler wishes here to gratefully acknowledge his gratitude and indebtedness to her.

mz.—Octavia Brewer, thirteenth child of Daniel Brewer and his wife, Esther Susan Moore, was born in Rapides parish, Louisiana, on October 14, 1879, and was married on May 19, 1896, to George M. Fischer. She died two months later on July 12, 1896.

nz.—Arthur Lewis Brewer, fourteenth child of Daniel Brewer and his wife, Esther Susan Moore, was born in Rapides parish, Louisiana, on March 4, 1881. He married in 1928 Ruby Jarrell, daughter of Dr. H. W. Jarrell and his wife, Vera Meadows, of Mansfield, Louisiana. No children were born of this union. Arthur Brewer died at his home in Lecompte, Louisiana, on Saturday, June 10, 1939, at 10:20 p. m. He had been in ill health for some time. He was buried in the Lecompte cemetery.

d.—Sarah Elizabeth Moore, fourth child of James Brown Moore and Margaret Jane Rutledge, was born at Cheneyville, Rapides parish, Louisiana, on March 16, 1839, and was twice married, her husbands being brothers. She was first married to Nicholas Yeager who died soon afterwards leaving no issue. She was then married to Clement Yeager. They resided on the north side of Red river, a few miles beyond Pineville, in Rapides parish, Louisiana, where some of their descendants yet live. We have not the exact date of the death of Mr. Yeager but know that he died some years prior to his wife. Mrs. Yeager died on June 15, 1921. The following notice of her death appeared in the Alexandria Daily Town Talk:—

DIED:—At the family residence, near Pineville, at 8:40 p. m., on Wednesday, June 15, 1921, Mrs. Sarah Elizabeth Yeager, aged 82 years and three months. Mrs. Yeager had been in ill health for some time and her death was not unexpected. She was born near Cheneyville, Louisiana, on March 16, 1839 and had resided in Rapides parish practically all her life. She is survived by four children, as follows:—Miss Daisy Yeager and V. Glenn Yeager of Pineville; James N. Yeager of Lake Charles, and C. Scott Yeager of Alexandria. She also leaves one sister, Mrs. E. S. Brewer of Lecompte. Her brother, Mr. W. S. Moore, died only a few days ago. She was buried in the family graveyard near Forest Hill, La.

Mr. and Mrs. Clement Yeager had four children:—

> az.—James Nicholas Yeager.
> bz.—Clement Scott Yeager.
> cz.—Daisy Yeager.
> dz.—Van Glenn Yeager.

az.—James Nicholas Yeager married Molly Harrop of Lake Charles, Louisiana. They now reside in Houston, Texas, and have six children:—James, Clement, Benjamin Harrop,

Francis, John Glenn, and Rosemary Catherine Yeager. The only daughter, Rosemary Catherine, was married in 1941 to Richard Hammond Tubman of Pelham, New York.

bz.—Clement Scott Yeager is a prominent architect in Alexandria, Louisiana, and resides in a beautiful country home a few miles beyond Pineville on the Alexandria-Monroe highway. It is on a portion of the property owned by his father, and near the site where he was born. He married Grace Martin of Lake Charles, Louisiana, a daughter of William Martin and his wife, Jane Howell. Mr. and Mrs. Martin were natives of Michigan and came to Louisiana many years ago. Clement Scott Yeager and Grace Martin have four children:—Clement Scott, Jr., John Moore and William Martin (twins), and Grace Patricia Yeager.

Clement Scott Yeager, Jr., is now a lieutenant in the U. S. Army and married at Heflin, Louisiana, on Saturday, October 9, 1943, Winona Pace, daughter of Mr. and Mrs. Louie Pace of that place. She is a grand-daughter of Mr. and Mrs. W. H. Pace of Athens, Louisiana, and of Mr. A. F. Levins and the late Mrs. Levins of Mt. Lebanon, Louisiana. She is descended from Capt. Jesse Smith and Emily Antronette Bryan, pioneer settlers of Louisiana. Clement Scott Yeager, Jr., was educated at the Louisiana Polytechnic Institute at Ruston, Louisiana.

John Moore Yeager was educated at the Louisiana Polytechnic Institute at Ruston, Louisiana, and is now of the U. S. Medical Corps Reserve. He married in New Orleans, Louisiana, on December 27, 1943, Leila Clouatre, daughter of Mr. and Mrs. Felix Joseph Clouatre of that city.

William Martin Yeager graduated from the United States Naval Academy at Annapolis, Maryland, in 1941, and is now an officer on duty with the navy. He married Betsy Ellen, daughter of Mr. and Mrs. Hyland L. Hodgson of Scarsdale, N. Y.

Grace Patricia Yeager was married on Wednesday afternoon, April 8, 1942, at St. James Episcopal church in Alexandria, Louisiana, to Lieutenant William John Burleigh, U. S. A., a native of Petersburg, Virginia. They now have a daughter, Grace Rutledge, born Sunday, April 22, 1945.

cz.—Daisy Yeager, only daughter of Clement Yeager and his wife, Sarah Elizabeth Moore, has never married.

dz.—Van Glen Yeager was a prominent and most promising young physician and died unmarried before his career had scarcely begun.

e.—Margaret Sophronia Moore, fifth child of James Brown Moore and his wife, Margaret Jane Rutledge, was born near Cheneyville, in Rapides parish, Louisiana, on September 4, 1841. She was married to James Davis who was a native of Bienville parish, Louisiana, and a brother of John Fletcher Davis who married Eunice Catherine Moore. Mr. and Mrs. Davis lived in Rapides parish from the time of their marriage until their deaths. We have been unable to obtain the exact dates of their demise. They had two daughters:—

az.—Jimmie Davis.
bz.—Sarah Davis.

az.—Jimmie Davis was married to Jones Thomas of Bienville parish. She died without issue and her husband then married her sister, Sarah Davis, usually called Sally.

bz.—Sarah Davis was married to her brother-in-law Jones Thomas. They resided most of their married life in Boyce, Louisiana, and had the following children:—Arthur, Fanny, Florence, and James Thomas. Fanny Thomas was married to William Eversull of Boyce. Florence Thomas was married to S. S. Martin and had several children among whom are Gwendolyn, Ricardo, Eldon Keith, and Fanny Yvonne Martin. The eldest, Gwendolyn Martin, is a graduate of the nursing school of the Baptist Hospital in New Orleans, and was married on Sunday, September 8, 1940, at Boyce, Louisiana, by the Rev. R. L. Cook of Baton Rouge, to Cecil Hoyt Everitt, son of Mr. and Mrs. Pope Everitt of Marshall, Texas. They are making their home in Little Rock, Arkansas.

James Thomas married Laura James and they have several children, the eldest of whom is married and living in Shreveport, Louisiana. Two of the younger ones, Elizabeth and James Thomas, are students at the Louisiana State University.

f.—Mary Ophelia Moore, sixth child of James Brown Moore and his wife, Margaret Jane Rutledge, was born at the old Moore homestead near Forest Hill, Rapides parish, g.—Eunice Catherine Moore, seventh child of James Brown Moore and his wife, Margaret Jane Rutledge, was born at the old Moore homestead near Forest Hill, Rapides parish, Louisiana, on March 17, 1846. She was married to John Fletcher Davis of Bienville parish, Louisiana, who moved to Rapides parish and settled on Bayou Boeuf near Lamourie. They had seven children, two of whom died in infancy. Eunice Catherine Moore died soon after the birth of her youngest child. The LOUISIANA DEMOCRAT of Wednesday, April 21, 1880, records her death as follows:—

> DIED:—On Tuesday, April 13, 1880, on Elmwood plantation in this parish, Eunice Catherine Moore, beloved wife of John F. Davis. She was a native of Rapides parish, born on Bayou Boeuf, March 17, 1846, daughter of James and Jane Moore. A husband and seven children are left to mourn her loss.

After this wife's death John Fletcher Davis married on July 31, 1882, Mary Alice Robinson, widow of Samuel Levi Wells (a son of ex-Governor James Madison Wells of Louisiana). His second wife was a daughter of Andrew Jackson Robinson and Elizabeth Ann Jones, and was born in Amite county, Mississippi. There was one child born of this second marriage, Alice Davis, who was married to Q. T. Hardtner of Urania, Louisiana, and had a son and daughter. The five children of Eunice Catherine Moore and John Fletcher Davis who lived to adult life were:—

>   az.—Johnnie Cornelia Davis.
>   bz.—John Glenn Davis.
>   cz.—William Moore Davis.
>   dz.—Katherine Davis.
>   ez.—Ollie Davis.

az.—Johnnie Cornelia Davis was married to Ben Rougeou, a native of Rapides parish, and they had one son, Clarence Rougeou, who married Constance Abat of Boyce, Louisiana. This latter couple now reside in Alexandria and have no children.

bz.—John Glenn Davis is now residing in Dallas, Texas. He first married on March 13, 1890, Mary Averill of Salem, Massachusetts, by whom he had one son, Alfred Wood Davis.

After this wife's death he married a Miss Olsen. No issue by the second union.

cz.—William Moore Davis is now dead. He resided in Dallas, Texas, where he married but left no children.

dz.—Katherine Davis was married to John Jordan who at that time resided in Bunkie, Louisiana, where he was engaged in the mercantile business. They now reside in Baton Rouge and have three children:—Katherine Jordan who married Marshall R. Clements and has one son, Marshall R., Jr.; Donald Boyd Jordan who married Bernice Lee—no issue at this time: John Davis Jordan who married Sadie Lunsden and has one daughter, Martha Kate Jordan.

ez.—Ollie Davis was married to Dr. Sheerwood S. Robinson of Marble Falls, Texas. Both died there some years ago. They had three children, Davis, Earl, and William Glenn Robinson. The first two are married and living in Texas; the youngest is in the U. S. Navy.

h.—Henry Scott Moore, eighth child of James Brown Moore and his wife, Margaret Jane Rutledge, was born at the old Moore homestead near Forest Hill, Rapides parish, Louisiana, on September 26, 1847. He must have changed his name to *William Scott Moore* as he always signed as *W. S. Moore.* He was familiarly known to his friends and family as *Doc Moore.* He married the widow of Albert D. Lewis, who before her first marriage was Theodosia Williams, a daughter of Govan Williams. Mr. and Mrs. Moore never had any children.

i.—James Rutledge Moore, ninth child of James Brown Moore and Margaret Jane Rutledge, was born at the home of his parents on Spring Creek, near Forest Hill, Rapides parish, Louisiana, on February 11, 1849, and spent his entire life in his native parish, living to a ripe old age. He was a well known and highly respected citizen and liked by all who knew him. He made his home in the town of Lecompte, on beautiful Bayou Boeuf, and resided there for nearly half a century. He married Ruth Graham, a daughter of Robert Graham, descendant of a good old Scotch family who had emigrated to America during the previous century. Five children were born of this marriage:—

az.—Ella Moore.
bz.—John James Moore.

cz.—Robert Scott Moore.
dz.—Leona Moore.
ez.—Charles Clark Moore.

az.—Ella Moore, eldest child of James Rutledge Moore and Ruth Graham, married Frank Rougeou, a native of Rapides parish.

bz.—John James Moore married Alice Randolph, daughter of Thomas Edward Randolph and Arexene Barker. He died without issue and his widow then married James Willis of Forest Hill, Louisiana.

cz.—Robert Scott Moore married Clara Wittig of Galveston, Texas. We have no further information of him.

dz.—Leona Moore, fourth child of James Rutledge Moore and Ruth Graham, was twice married. Her first husband was John Fox Wood of New Orleans. They were divorced some years later and she then married Peter W. Harrison, formerly of New Orleans but at the time prominent in the cotton business in Alexandria. He is now dead. Two children were born of the first marriage:—Ruth Octavia Wood and John Sarber Wood.

The elder of these, Ruth Octavia Wood, first married on May 31, 1918, Donald de Grey Damorest of Garden City, Long Island, by whom she had two children:—Donald de Grey Damorest, Jr., born March 1, 1919, and Samuel Henry Damorest, II, born July 31, 1924. These two boys were educated in England and are now back home, both serving in the armed forces of their country. Donald is in the naval air force and Samuel Henry in the army somewhere in the South Pacific. Ruth Octavia Wood was divorced from her first husband and then married on June 5, 1932, Giraud van Nest Foster, a native of Lennox, Massachusetts. Mr. Foster has come to Louisiana and purchased the old David Pipes place near Clinton, one of the beautiful and historic land-marks of that vicinity. He has renovated and landscaped it and renamed it "Swing-a-long" Mr. Foster is at this time serving his country somewhere in the Pacific in the "Seabees."

John Sarber Wood, son of John Fox Wood and Leona Moore, first married Mable Burton. They had a son, Albert Baldwin Wood, born in 1929. Mr. and Mrs. Wood were divorced and he then married Frances Caroline Johnson, daughter of Albert Sumner Johnson and Susan Wright. Of this union one son, Ralph Wood, was born in August, 1933. Mr. and Mrs. Wood now reside in New Orleans.

j.—Corilla Jane Moore, always called "Lilly," tenth child of James Brown Moore and his wife, Margaret Jane Rutledge, was born on December 2, 1861. She never married and died on August 6, 1883.

ii.—Sarah Ann Providence Rutledge, second child of Joseph Rutledge and Esther Susannah Robert, and grand-daughter of James Robert and Elizabeth Naylor, was born in Wilkes county, Georgia, in 1817. She was there married to Anderson Leonard Chafin and soon afterwards moved with him to Louisiana. They settled in the southern portion of Rapides parish, as was indicated to the compiler in a recent letter from Mrs. John W. Keller of Avoyelles parish whose grandmother (Joanna Lawton Rutledge) was a sister of Sarah Ann Providence Rutledge. She wrote as follows:—"Anderson Chafin lived some place in this part of Louisiana, for his son, Winn Chafin, used to visit our home quite frequently." We regret exceedingly that our data on this branch of the family is so meager. We know, however, that Anderson Leonard Chafin and Sarah Ann Providence Rutledge had a number of children, among whom were, Emma, Winburn, Mary Susan, and Robert Chafin. The first of these, Emma Chafin, married Warren O'Neill, who at the time was a widower, and their daughter, Mary Ellen O'Neill, married Milton Calhoun of Rapides parish, Louisiana, and had several children among whom was a daughter, Luna Calhoun, who married William M. Cady, one of the most prominent and successful lumber manufacturers of his time in the southwest. He founded THE CADY LUMBER COMPANY of McNary, Rapides parish, Louisiana, and after cutting out all the timber owned by that concern he moved the plant and a train-load of employees to Arizona and there established another saw-mill town by the name of McNary. Some years later he located in Pasadena, California, where he died within a short time. His widow is now living there, and also her two children, William M. Cady, Jr., and Octo Cady (a girl), both of whom are married. Octo Cady was married to Christopher Bacon, a prominent attorney in Los Angeles. Mr. Bacon died at his home there on October 24, 1938, leaving no issue. Winburn Chafin, better known as

"Winn," married Martha Nugent. Mary Susan Chafin married Ezekial O'Quinn. We here insert the following notice of her marriage taken from THE LOUISIANA DEMOCRAT, an Alexandria newspaper, of the date of March 14, 1860:—

> MARRIED:—On Sunday, March 11, 1860, at the residence of her father, by William Randolph, Esq., Mr. H. E. O'Quinn of Thibodeaux, Louisiana, to Miss Mary Susan Chafin of Rapides parish, Louisiana.

This notice not only establishes the residence of Anderson Leonard Chafin as being in Rapides parish but also shows that he was living at that date. Robert Chafin, from the best information obtainable, never married. Mrs. Pearl Clugston of New Orleans is a grand-daughter of Anderson Leonard Chafin and Sarah Ann Providence Rutledge, being a daughter of their son, Winburn Chafin and his wife, Martha Nugent. Sarah Ann Providence (Rutledge) Chafin died sometime prior to June 21, 1856, as on that date her husband executed a legal transaction before a notary which shows he was then married for the second time. The following is a brief extract of the document:—

STATE OF LOUISIANA
PARISH OF RAPIDES

> Be it known that on this day before me John W. Pearce, a Notary Public duly commissioned and sworn, personally came and appeared Anderson Leonard Chafin and with him also came and appeared Mrs. Prudence Smith, his wife, who intervened and became a party to this act, when the said appearers declared to me the said Notary that for and in consideration of the sum and price hereinafter expressed they have bargained, sold, transferred and delivered unto Walter Bailey of the same residence the following named negroes, slaves for life, etc. . . This sale is made for and in consideration of the sum of two thousand dollars paid and payable as follows . . . . . . In testimony whereof the said parties have hereunto subscribed their names in presence of the undersigned competent witnesses and me the said Notary, this 21st day of June, A. D. 1856.

Witnesses:—   Prudence Chafin.
    Henry Butter   A. L. Chafin.
    Jas. B. Moore   Walter Bailey.
        Done and passed before me,
        John W. Pearce, Notary Public.

We know of no children by this second marriage. From our knowledge of the location of the homes of the two witnesses we would infer that Mr. Chafin at that time was living somewhere on Spring Creek in Rapides parish. We have no record of the dates of death of himself and his second wife.

    iii.—Robert Kennedy Rutledge, third child of Joseph Rutledge and Esther Susannah Robert, was born in Wilkes county, Georgia, in 1819. He married Susanna Brooks in Sumter county, South Carolina, and died on November 1, 1874, leaving five children:—

> Loula J. Rutledge.
> Joseph D. Rutledge.
> Esther M. Rutledge.
> Brooks Rutledge.
> Alice Rutledge.

We are indebted for the names of the above mentioned children and the meager information of them which follows to a letter from Joseph D. Rutledge (the second of them) written from Summerton, South Carolina, on October 1, 1910, to Mrs. Esther (Moore) Brewer of Lecompte, Louisiana. The letter tels us that all of the above mentioned children were living in 1910, except Esther who died in October, 1909. She and her sister Loula (the eldest) never married and lived with their brother, Brooks Rutledge, at Florence, South Carolina, where he was a prominent dentist. In 1910 Loula Rutledge was still keeping house for her brother Brooks who had lost his wife in 1898. He (Brooks) had one child, Robert D. Rutledge, who was fifteen years old in 1910. The letter also tells us that Alice Rutledge, the youngest of the five children, married Dr. L. D. Bass, a Baptist minister, and in 1910 was living in Mexia, Texas, and had six children—three boys and three girls. The eldest boy had just graduated in medicine and was married and located in Barry, Texas. Alice Rutledge and her husband later returned to South Carolina. Joseph D. Rutledge (writer of the letter) married on February 26, 1884, Minnie Lee Burgess of Macon, Georgia. They had five children:—Robert Kennedy Rutledge, born in 1885, and employed in a bank in Florence, South Carolina; Irwin Brooks Rutledge, born in 1889, a civil engineer; Annie Rutledge, born in 1892, married to A. B. Carson and living in Greenville, South Carolina; Joseph D. Rutledge,

Jr., born in 1894; William Burgess Rutledge, born in 1898. Joseph D. Rutledge, Sr., to whom we are indebted for the above information, died in 1923.

iv.—Elizabeth Susan Rutledge, fourth child of Joseph Rutledge and Esther Susannah Robert, was born in Wilkes county, Georgia, in 1821, and married about 1838 in Rapides parish, Louisiana, her cousin, Thomas Grimball Bettison, son of David Bettison and Sarah Catharine Robert. They lived near Cheneyville, Louisiana, until 1850 and then on Bayou Chopegue in Avoyelles parish until Mr. Bettison's death on January 7, 1873. Mrs. Bettison died in Texas on October 7, 1894. They had sixteen children. (See pages 146-147).

v.—Joanna Lawton Rutledge, fifth child of Joseph Rutledge and Esther Susannah Robert, was born at Milledgeville, Baldwin county, Georgia, on February 10, 1825. She was brought to Louisiana by her parents in 1835 and a few years later was married to Atkinson Augustus Brinkley, who was born in Raleigh, North Carolina, on January 5, 1818. Mr. Brinkley left North Carolina at the age of fourteen and went to Alabama. He lived there near Greensborough a few years and then in 1836 emigrated to Cheneyville, in Rapides parish, Louisiana. It was there he met and married Joanna Lawton Rutledge when she was about fourteen years of age. This young couple remained near Cheneyville until after the birth of their first child and then in 1843 moved to the vicinity of Plaucheville in the adjoining parish of Avoyelles. They left there in 1848 but returned in 1855 to remain the rest of their lives. One of Mr. Brinkley's grand-daughters writes that "he there cleared and operated a goodly sized plantation, owned a few slaves and practiced medicine." He died there in April, 1878, and his wife (Joanna Lawton Rutledge) on September 9, 1871. They had five children:—

        a.—Robert Lovel Aurelius Brinkley.
        b.—Edward Elias Brinkley.
        c.—Francis Marion Brinkley.
        d.—Atkinson Augustus Brinkley, Jr.
        e.—Joanna Minerva Brinkley.

a.—Robert Lovel Aurelius Brinkley was born October 15, 1841, and died February 21, 1869. He never married.

b.—Edward Elias Brinkley was born February 21, 1844 and died young.

c.—Francis Marion Brinkley was born in Avoyelles parish, Louisiana, on January 28, 1846, and died there December 27, 1915.   He married in 1869 Frances Sarah Vannoy, daughter of Joel Vannoy and his wife, Margaret Elizabeth Hathorn, of Big Cane, Louisiana.   They lived and died in Avoyelles parish, Louisiana, and there their nine children were born.   Francis Marion Brinkley's wife died on November 8, 1896.   Their nine children were:—

> az.—Alice Marian Brinkley.
> bz.—Edward Augustus Brinkley.
> cz.—Frances Joanna Brinkley.
> dz.—Margaret Elizabeth Brinkley.
> ez.—Horace Walden Brinkley.
> fz.—Walter Scott Brinkley.
> gz.—Francis Joel Brinkley.
> hz.—Vernon Irl Brinkley.
> iz.—Eva May Brinkley.

az.—Alice Marian Brinkley was born February 6, 1871. We understand she is living at this time but regret we have been unable to obtain any further data about her.

bz.—Edward Augustus Brinkley was born January 9, 1873, and is dead at this date.   We have no further data on him.

cz.—Frances Joanna Brinkley was born September 27, 1875, and is living at this time.   She was married on August 1, 1920, to John Wilson Keller who was born on September 1, 1866.   They now reside at Elba, Louisiana, and have no children.

dz.—Margaret Elizabeth Brinkley was born January 18, 1878, and died April 30, 1880.

ez.—Horace Walden Brinkley was born August 7, 1880, and now lives at Palmetto, Louisiana.

fz.—Walter Scott Brinkley was born January 11, 1883, and now resides at Palmetto, Louisiana.

gz.—Francis Joel Brinkley was born August 31, 1885.   He died at Simmesport, Louisiana, on May 15, 1943.   The following notice of his death appeared in the New Orleans Times-Picayune of that date:—

Simmesport, La., May 15—Frank Joel Brinkley, 55 years old, distributor of the Times-Picayune at Simmesport for the past four years, died at the family home after a short illness. Funeral services were held at the home, with Father Gremillion officiating. Interment was in the Christ the King cemetery.

Mr. Brinkley was a leader in his community and took an active interest in the progress of Simmesport.

Besides his widow he is survived by a son, Marion of Simmesport; a daughter, Mrs. Lee Couvillion of Baton Rouge; three sisters, Mrs. Johnnie Keller of Elba, Mrs. Charlie Keller of Bunkie, and Mrs. Albert Riche of California; three brothers, Vernon of Bossier City, Walter and Horace of Palmetto. Three grandchildren also survive.

hz.—Vernon Irl Brinkley was born November 2, 1888, and now resides at Bossier City, Louisiana.

iz.—Eva May Brinkley was born November 1, 1891. She is living at this date, is married but we have been unable to get any further information about her.

d.—Atkinson Augustus Brinkley, Jr., was born March 30, 1848, and died March 19, 1849.

e.—Joanna Minerva Brinkley was born May 13, 1850, and died July 28, 1888. She was married on December 9, 1869, to Amos Kendall Fisher who was born March 17, 1849. Five children were born of this marriage:—

az.—William Kendall Fisher.
bz.—Clarence Wilsford Fisher.
cz.—Edward Marion Fisher.
dz.—Amos Augustus Fisher.
ez.—Ela Fisher.

az.—William Kendall Fisher died about 1932. He married and left two daughters:—Oma Fisher who married Harold Clopton, son of Bettison William Clopton and Dora Havard, and Ura Fisher who married Jimmie Scott.

bz.—Clarence Wilsford Fisher died about 1917, leaving one son, Clarence Wilsford Fisher, who was born June 5, 1913.

cz.—Edward Marion Fisher lives in Lordsburg, New Mexico. He is married and has two daughters and a son.

dz.—Amos Augustus Fisher has been twice married. He had four children by his first wife and one by his second.

ez.—Ela Fisher was born March 20, 1882, and was married on January 24, 1900, to Ewell West who was born January 6, 1874, and died at his home in Bunkie, Louisiana, on Monday,

January 24, 1938. Mr. West was a son of Isham West of Evergreen, Louisiana, and his wife, Eliza Catherine O'Quin, a daughter of Rev. John O'Quin and Anna Allen. Mr. West's mother was born February 7, 1837, and her mother (Anna Allen) was probably a daughter of William Allen and Dorcas Ogden, and Dorcas Allen was very probably a daughter of John Ogden and Martha Robert (daughter of Captain Peter Robert and Anne Grimball). William Allen was dead prior to 1828 and a few years later his widow (Dorcas Allen) married Starky Barfield. Rev. John O'Quin (Mr. West's grandfather) was a prominent Baptist preacher and a successful planter of Avoyelles parish, Louisiana. He was born in South Carolina on January 1, 1808, and was a son of Ezekiel O'Quin and Mary Brockston. Rev. Ezekial O'Quin was one of the first Baptist preachers to cross the Mississippi river and enter the Louisiana Territory. For many years he was pastor of Beulah Baptist Church at Cheneyville, in Rapides parish, Louisiana, and died there April 23, 1823. He was a son of John O'Quin and Gracey Spivey of North Carolina and was born there February 18, 1781. Ewell West and his wife, Ela Fisher, had two children:—

Gladys Loula West, born September 7, 1904.
Eleanor Mae West, born January 1, 1919.

The elder of these, Gladys Loula West, was married on July 14, 1928, to Ralph Charles Allor. They reside in Bunkie, Louisiana, and have two children:—Ralph Herschel Allor, born April 30, 1929, and Charles Russell Allor, born November 29, 1937.

The younger daughter, Eleanor Mae West, after completing her education at the Louisiana State University was married at the Baptist church in Bunkie, Louisiana, on Saturday afternoon, December 7, 1940, to Frank Nelson Carroll of Beaumont, Texas, where they now reside.

vi.—Joseph Sadler Rutledge, sixth child of Joseph Rutledge and Esther Susannah Robert, was born in Baldwin county, Georgia, on April 6, 1827. He came to Louisiana with his parents when a small boy and was reared in Rapides parish. He married Catharine Nancy Cowan about 1854 and moved to Avoyelles parish where they lived for many years. She was born March 28, 1835, and died February 28, 1929. He entered the Confederate Army in the early part of the Civil War and was killed in battle. The fact that they were husband and wife and at one time resided in Avoyelles parish, Louisiana, is substantiated by the following legal document:—

STATE OF LOUISIANA,
PARISH OF RAPIDES.

Be it known that on this day before me, J. J. Robert, a Notary Public in and for the Parish of Rapides and State aforesaid, duly commissioned and sworn, appeared Catharine Nancy Cowan, wife of Joseph S. Rutledge, late resident of the Parish of Avoyelles and State of Louisiana, who duly authorized and assisted herein by her husband, did declare that Joseph S. Rutledge, her said husband, did, by notarial act passed by H. W. Robinette, a Notary Public of St. Landry and State aforesaid, on the 30th day of August, 1858, sell and convey to William M. Ewell of the Parish of Avoyelles, two tracts or parcels of land, containing two hundred and thirty-nine acres, more or less, bounded as follows:—north by land of A. A. Brinkley, east and west by lands of William M. Lambeth, deceased, and south by land of William Taliaferro. And the said appearer declared also that it is her right and intention to release in favor of the purchaser, etc. . . . .

In testimony whereof the said Mrs. Catharine Nancy Rutledge and W. H. Scott, authorized agent and attorney-in-fact for the said purchaser, William M. Ewell, have before subscribing witnesses signed their names hereto, this 5th day of October, 1858.

Witnesses:—   C. N. Rutledge
F. W. Marshall   (I authorize my wife) Jos. S. Rutledge
T. W. Robert   Wm. H. Scott,
                                    Attorney for Wm. M. Ewell.
               Done before me
               J. J. Robert, Notary Pub.

Joseph Sadler Rutledge and his wife, Catharine Nancy Cowan, had five children:—

a.—Joseph Malancthon Rutledge, born June 15, 1855.
b.—Ursula Catharine Rutledge, born October — ,1856.
c.—Alvah Mathias Rutledge, born January 9, 1858.
d.—Sarah Ida Rutledge, born July 27, 1860.
e.—Joseph Sadler Rutledge, Jr., born July 13, 1862.

a.—Joseph Malancthon Rutledge married and reared a large family. We have been unable to learn the name of his wife. Both are long since dead. Catharine, the eldest of their children, married a Jones and lived at Lapine, Ouachita Parish, La. It is our impression that she is still living at this time but it has seemed impossible to contact her. She had three brothers, Joseph, Edward and Samuel, all of whom lived near Lapine at one time.

b.—Ursula Catharine Rutledge, second child of Joseph Sadler Rutledge and Catharine Nancy Cowan, was born in Avoyelles Parish, La. She was married to a Mr. Mayes but we have been unable to get any additional data on her.

c.—Alvah Mathias Rutledge, third child of Joseph Sadler Rutledge and Catharine Nancy Cowan, was born in Avoyelles parish, La., and probably died young as we can find no further record of him.

d.—Sarah Ida Rutledge, fourth child of Joseph Sadler Rutledge and Catharine Nancy Cowan, was born in Avoyelles parish, La., and died unmarried.

e.—Joseph Sadler Rutledge, Jr., fifth and youngest child of Joseph Sadler Rutledge and Catharine Nancy Cowan, was probably born in Rapides parish, La. He was a posthumous child. His wife, who is living at this date (1944), recently wrote the compiler, "My husband was born three months after his father was killed." So this definitely places the date of Mr. Rutledge's death in battle as April, 1862. Joseph Sadler Rutledge, Jr., was a Methodist minister and for many years was a member of the Louisiana Methodist Conference. He was married at Bonami, Calcasieu parish, La., (now in Beauregard parish), by Rev. H. Armstrong, on March 17, 1903, to Sarah Tinie Kent, a daughter of James Thomas Kent and Mary Frances Heard. She was born July 1, 1877, and is now living at Walker, Livingston parish, La. Her grandfather Kent came to Calcasieu parish, La., from Georgia prior to the Civil War. Mr. Rutledge died April 11, 1933, and was buried at Denham Springs, La. Three children were born of this marriage:—

> az.—Pearl Dean Rutledge.
> bz.—Glenn Cowan Rutledge.
> cz.—Eris Kent Rutledge.

az.—Pearl Dean Rutledge was born January 12, 1904, at Dry Creek, Calcasieu parish, La., and was married in 1924 to Jesse Kline of Delhi, La., who was born in 1899 and was a son of Wilbur Kline. Mr. and Mrs. Kline are prominently connected with the teaching profession in Livingston parish where Mr. Kline is principal of the Doyle High School. They reside in Denham Springs and have three children:—Cecil, born July 31, 1930; Joseph, born March 17, 1934; Sarah Frances, born January 4, 1940.

bz.—Glenn Cowan Rutledge was born August 28, 1906, at Pine Grove, St. Helena parish, La., and was educated at the local public schools and the Louisiana State University. He selected journalism as his profession and was Associated Press Editor of THE DAILY' HERALD at Gulfport, Miss., for 14 years. Mr. Rutledge was actively connected with the Mississippi National Guard for many years and was Captain of a Machine Gun Company. In that capacity he entered the United States Army in 1940 just prior to the outbreak of the present World War and at this date (1944) is a Lieutenant Colonel of Infantry. He was stationed for some time at Camp Claiborne, La., and at Camp Howze, Texas. Presently he is commanding officer at Camp Joseph T. Robinson, near Little Rock, Arkansas. Col. Rutledge married on August 28, 1930, Wilmuth Saunders, born January 20, 1907, a daughter of John William Saunders and Lula McCarty of Charleston, Miss. They have two children:— William Saunders Rutledge, born September 22, 1931, and Eris Anne Rutledge, born August 27, 1933.

cz.—Eris Kent Rutledge, born August 12, 1908, at Pine Grove, La., was married July 2, 1938, to Monroe Edison Milton who was born April 30, 1907, and was a son of Walter Milton and Martha Stafford. Mr. Milton is employed by the Standard Oil Company. He and his wife now reside at Denham Springs, La., and have two children:—Rita Lynn Milton, born February 2, 1940, and Fred Edison Milton, born October 9, 1943.

vii.—William Owen Rutledge, youngest child of Joseph Rutledge and Esther Susannah Robert, was born in Baldwin County, Georgia, about 1829. The only data we have of him is a very meager account obtained through the kindness of Mrs. Evelyn Brewer Gray, his great niece. In a recent letter she says, "Uncle William came to see grandmother and mother when we were small children. The only thing I remember is he lived in San Antonio, Texas, and married a Miss Armstrong. They must have had several children, but I remember one named Annie used to write to mother."

3.—Hadley Peter Robert third child of James Robert and Elizabeth Naylor, and grandson of Captain Peter Robert, was born in Beaufort District, South Carolina, about 1796. He left his native State with his parents when a mere boy and went with them to Woodville, Miss., and later to Cheneyville, Rapides parish, La., where they permanently located. There on July 22, 1824, he married his first cousin, Ann Eliza Bettison, daughter of David Bettison and Sarah Catharine Robert, who was born in Beaufort District, S. C., in 1802. The old notarial records for the Cheneyville section of Rapides parish show that Hadley Peter Robert was quite active in business affairs there, and we frequently find his name in the books kept by the notaries of those days. On January 1, 1828, he buys land on Bayou Boeuf from his first cousin Joseph J. Robert, and on January 28 of the same year he purchases land adjoining that mentioned above from Randal Eldred who had married his aunt, Esther Susannah Robert. Then two years later, on January 1, 1830, he sells both tracts to Randal Eldred. On October 25, 1845, he buys 26 slaves from his cousin Grimball Addison Robert for $15,750.00 cash. All through the records of that day we find his name appearing in various and numerous business transactions. In April, 1835, his home was on the left descending bank of Bayou Boeuf, in the vicinity of Cheneyville, as we learn from a description of land sold by John O'Quin and wife to Grimball A. Robert. About 1850, or thereabouts, Hadley Peter Robert and his family moved to Washington county, Texas. There he lived until his death which occurred on June 11, 1856. His wife died there November 27, 1866. These dates we obtained from the family Bible of Mrs. Irene Ethel (Tanner) Johns, a niece of Mrs. Robert, which is now in the possession of Mrs. Blanchard Iles of Oakdale, La., whose mother was a niece of Mrs. Johns.

Hadley Peter Robert and his wife, Ann Eliza Bettison, had the following children:—i. Sarah; ii. Benjamin R.; iii. Mary Margaret; iv. Cranmer Thomas; v. Hettie; vi. George; vii. Solon H.

i.—Sarah Robert was born in Rapides parish, La., about 1827. She never married.

ii.—Benjamin R. Robert was born in Rapides parish, La., about 1830. The year after his father's death we learn from the notarial records of Rapides parish that he returned to Louisiana to look after his mother's affairs. We find record of a sale passed before A. M. Kilpatrick, Notary Public, on February 3, 1857, in which "B. R. Robert, agent for Mrs. Ann E. Robert, both of the State of Texas, and Washington county," sells property on Bayou Boeuf to Peter Tanner (a brother-in-law and cousin of Mrs. Robert). Benjamin R. Robert married Susan Coonie Daniels and they had three children:—Hadley Peter, Lizzie, and Lula. The son, Hadley Peter, appears to have been the only one living at the time Mrs. Johns made the entries in her Bible, which was probably about 1890.

iii.—Mary Margaret Robert was born near Cheneyville, Rapides parish, La., in 1834. She was generally called "Maggie." In 1860 she was married at Independence, Texas, to Dr. Jesse Shivers Eddins, son of William Wellington Eddins and Julia Shivers. He was born in Greensboro, Alabama, on April 7, 1839, and died at Ingram, Texas, on February 4, 1924, at the age of 85. Mrs. Eddins died at Ingram on July 19, 1897. Dr. and Mrs. Eddins had eight children, six of whom are living at this date (1945). The six are:—a.—Annie; b.—Jessie Mary; c.—Emma; d.—Alice Haygood; e.—Julia; f.—Charlie.

a.—Annie Eddins was born near Independence, Texas, on September 9, 1864. She married Robert Morris in August, 1883, and they had seven sons:—az.—Clinton Pope; bz.—D. E.; cz.—Robert, Jr.; dz.—Roy; ez.—Carl; fz.—Ernest; gz.—Neil.

az.—Clinton Pope Morris was born May 22, 1884, and died October 16, 1938. He married Zollie ———— and left two children, Zollie D., and Elton K. He was a prominent Baptist minister and served as pastor in Texas, Arizona, California, Washington and Chicago. He graduated from Baylor University in June, 1911, and from Southwestern Theological Seminary in June, 1913.

bz.—D. E. Morris was born near San Antonio, Texas, on December 7, 1885. He received his education from Baylor University and married Eva Gulick near San Antonio. They have two children.

cz.—Robert Morris, Jr., was born May 12, 1888. We have no further data on him.

dz.—Roy Morris was born in 1890 and received his education from Baylor University.

We have very little information on the last three sons of Robert Morris and Annie Eddins. We only know that ez.—Carl Morris was born in 1893. fz.—Ernest Morris was born in 1895; gz.—Neil Morris was born in 1902.

b.—Jessie Mary Eddins, second daughter of Dr. Jesse Shivers Eddins and Mary Margaret Robert, was born near Independence, Texas, on September 9, 1864, and is living at this date (1945) in the State of Washington. She was three times married: 1st to Milburn P. New, 2nd to Will Clark, and 3rd to George Evans. Her 1st husband, Milburn P. New, was born June 24, 1861, at Goliad, Texas, and they were married at Junction, Texas, on December 25, 1885. He died near Pearsall, Texas, on November 21, 1891, leaving three children:—az.—Clara Milburn; bz.—Harvey; cz.—Robert Emmett. Jessie Mary Eddins married her 2nd husband, Will Clark, at Ingram, Texas, on May 3, 1896, and he died February 7, 1901, at San Angelo, Texas, leaving her with two sons: dz.—Louie Willard, and ez.—Willie, Jr. Jessie Mary Eddins and her 3rd husband had no children.

az.—Clara Milburn New was born in Kimball county, Texas, on June 17, 1887, and received her education at Baylor College. She was married December 14, 1907, to Alfred Clinton Anderson who was born February 9, 1886, in Hunt County, Texas. He was a son of William Allen Anderson and Virginia Charlotte Gantt. Mr. and Mrs. Anderson are living at this date (1945) near Pineville, Louisiana. They have had four children:—Alfred Clinton Anderson, Jr., born August 21, 1908, and married Daisy Beatrice Thompson—no issue; Virginia Clair Anderson, born May 27, 1911, and married Russell Stewart Connor who died at Miami, Florida, on February 21, 1945, leaving   dren, Melba Clair and Gloria Stewart; Donald Eddin: on, born September 13, 1913, married Elizabeth Cha: ller, and has one son, John Donald, born November 12,   ck Raymond Anderson, born January 17, 1917, and died

bz.—Harvey New was born January 8, 1889 and died at San Angelo, Texas, in 1903.

cz.—Robert Emmett New was born January 2, 1891. He married Wilma Capps of San Marcos, Texas. They have no children.

dz.—Louie Willard Clark was born January 20, 1897, at Ingram, Texas, and married Florence Taylor, born October 25, 1900. They have no issue.

ez.—Willie Clark, Jr., was born in 1899 at San Angelo, Texas, and married Goldie ————. They have two daughters, Phylis and Corlyss.

c.—Emma Eddins, third daughter of Dr. Jesse Shivers Eddins and Mary Margaret Robert, was born near Independence, Texas, on October 28, 1867. She was married March 12, 1890, to Joseph B. New, a brother of Milburn P. New. They have two children:—az.—Harold J., and bz.—Annie.

az.—Harold J. New was born December 22, 1893. He married 1st Irene White (now dead) in 1923 and had one child, Harold J.; 2nd Lola Skipworth in 1929—no issue.

bz.—Annie New was born May 24, 1898, and was married in July, 1917, to H. L. Bunch. They have six children:—Annie Lee, born November 27, 1918; Harold L., born October 29, 1922; Joe H., born January 18, 1924; Emma L., born October • 23, 1925; Lynn, born December 18, 1928; Gwynne, born December 9, 1933.

d.—Alice Haygood Eddins, fourth daughter of Dr. Jesse Shivers Eddins and Mary Margaret Robert, was born September 23, 1872. She was married May 29, 1890, at Junction, Texas, to Julius Augustus Heyman. He was born December 2, 1868, and was a son of William Frederick Heyman and Verena Balmer. They had six children:—az.—Alice Verena; bz.—Roscoe Merle; cz.—Julius Augustus, Jr.; dz.—Charles William; ez.—Charlotte; fz.—An un-named infant, born April 27, 1912.

az.—Alice Verena Heyman was born May 9, 1891, and was married October 17, 1916, to Thomas H. King, born December 6, 1888, son of Thomas King and Kate Easterland. They have had four children:—Verena Alice, Harvey Heyman, Milton (now dead), and Ruth.

bz.—Roscoe Merle Heyman was born September 13, 1893, and married Grace Kay on April 16, 1916. They have three children:—Roscoe Merle, Jr., James J., and Julius Augustus, III.

cz.—Julius Augustus Heyman, Jr., was born October 12, 1895, and married Alzade Knickerbocker. He is a member of the medical profession and a prominent surgeon.

dz.—Charles William Heyman died young.

ez.—Charlotte Heyman was born December 16, 1899, and was married to Fred L. Johnson of Georgia. She received her B. A., and M. A. from the University of Texas.

e.—Julia Eddins, fifth daughter of Dr. Jesse Shivers Eddins and Mary Margaret Robert, was born about 1874. She was twice married: 1st to Henry McNealy (now dead) in 1894, and 2nd to Lester Boyer. She had seven children by her first marriage:—Ralph, born 1895; Jennings, born 1897; Offa, born 1899; Kennon, born 1901; Wallace, born 1903; Velma, born 1905; Eddens, born 1908. By her second marriage she had two children:—Julia and Lester W.

f.—Charlie Eddins, youngest child and only son of Dr. Jesse Shivers Eddins and Mary Margaret Robert, was born in 1879. He married Maud Kane (now dead) in 1904. They had two children:—Carleton, born 1906, now dead; Mildred, born 1908, married to Joe Croom about 1929.

iv.—Cranmer Thomas Robert, fourth child of Hadley Peter Robert and Ann Eliza Bettison, was born in Rapides parish, Louisiana, about 1836. He went to Texas with his parents and there married Sallie Greer. They had three daughters and a son:—Annie Mallard, Minnie Stewart, Lula Mallard, and Hadley. The names *Mallard* and *Stewart* were evidently the daughters' married names.

v.—Hettie Robert, fifth child of Hadley Peter Robert and Ann Eliza Bettison, was born in Rapides parish, La., about 1838. She married Tom Mitchell. They had no children.

vi.—George Robert died single about a month before he was to marry Emma Beckham.

vii.—Solon H. Robert, born in 1845, was a soldier in Co. B, 15th Texas Volunteer Infantry, Confederate Army. His company was a part of General Polignac's Brigade. See pension record No. 6101, State of Texas.

4.—Eldred Grimball Robert, 4th child of James Robert and Elizabeth Naylor, was born in Beaufort District, South Carolina, about 1798. He married Dorcas E. Stafford in Rapides parish, La., daughter of James Seth Stafford and his wife, Ann Stafford. In January, 1845, we find Eldred Grimball Robert recorded as Clerk of the Spring Hill Baptist Church, which was on Spring Creek in the western pine woods section of Rapides parish. He evidently lived in that community. About 1850 he moved to Claiborne parish, La., and there he and his wife died, leaving a daughter, Christine, of whom we have no further record. Mr. and Mrs. Robert were living after July, 1855, when Mrs. Robert returned to Cheneyville in Rapides parish on business. The following extract from the notarial record kept by John W. Pearce bears this out:—

> Personally appeared before me, the said notary, Mrs. Dorcas E. Stafford, wife of Eldred G. Robert of the parish of Claiborne, State of Louisiana, and duly authorized and assisted by her husband represented by Leroy A. Stafford, Esq., of the parish of Rapides, State of Louisiana, by a duly authenticated power of attorney dated March 19th, 1855, ...

The two notarial acts which Mrs. Robert executed at that time were dated April 25, 1855, and July 6, 1855.

5.—Moses Elias Robert, fifth child of James Robert and Elizabeth Naylor, was born in Beaufort District, South Carolina, about 1800. He came to Woodville, Miss., with his parents when an infant, and later to Rapides parish, La. We have been unable to secure any information about him except that he married a Miss Arrants, nor do we know of any descendants or even where he lived. However, knowing the fertility of this family it would not be surprising if at some later date it was discovered there were many descendants.

B.

GRIMBALL ROBERT.

Grimball Robert was very probably the second of the twelve children of Captain Peter Robert and Anne Grimball, and was born about 1766 in French Santee, South Carolina. He later went with his parents to St. Peter's Parish, in Beaufort District, where we find him living when the census of 1790 was taken. At that date he was married, had one son and owned two slaves. It now appears quite definite that he did not leave South Carolina at the time that his father and other members of the family started out on their journey to the southwest, which was about 1804, but that he remained in his native State until after 1810. We learn this from a power-of-attorney on file in the court house at Woodville, Miss., and from a family record kept by his son Peter William Robert. The power-of-attorney was dated July 1, 1810, and was executed by his brothers Peter and Joseph Robert, then residents of Woodville, and directed "to Grimball Robert, planter, of St. Peter's Parish, Beaufort District, South Carolina" (see page 94). In the family record kept by Peter William Robert we are told that in 1809 he (Peter William Robert) obtained permission from his father (Grimball Robert) to leave South Carolina and go to the Mississippi Territory. We have every reason to believe that Grimball Robert was later a resident of Woodville, Miss., and at a still later date there are plenty of official records to show that he lived on Bayou Boeuf in Rapides parish, La. According to existing descriptions of property he owned we feel certain that his home was on the right descending bank of Bayou Boeuf a short distance above the present town of Cheneyville. Rev. W. E. Paxton in his History of Louisiana Baptists tells us in the following words that he was living in that vicinity:—

> Among these settlers on the Bayou Boeuf twenty-five or thirty miles below Alexandria, were Robert Tanner and his son Robert Lynn Tanner, the Elder Robert with his two sons, Baynard C. and Peter William Robert.

The *Elder Robert* referred to above was our Grimball Robert—this we know from the fact that he had two sons bearing names of those given in this quotation. Both of these sons became prominent Baptist ministers.

Grimball Robert married in South Carolina in 1788 Mary Sealey Cheney, daughter of William Cheney and Sarah Norris. Her father was a son of James Cheney and Mary Johnson, and a brother of John Cheney the father of the Cheney brothers who came to Rapides parish in the early days of the 19th century and founded the town of Cheneyville. The Cheney family came to New England in the first half of the 17th century, being represented by John, Thomas and William, probably brothers. Thence James Cheney, of a later generation, went to Virginia and there married Mary Johnson. Among their children were John and William whose descendants came to Mississippi and Louisiana. Grimball Robert's wife, Mary Sealey Cheney, died

sometime after the birth of their fifth child, probably about
1799. A few years later Grimball Robert married his second
wife. The old family Bible, now property of Charles Addison
Riddle (a lineal descendant) of Marksville, Louisiana, contains
the following record of this second marriage:—

> Grimball and Eliza T. Robert were married October
> 23, 1806.

This second wife was Eliza Tuzette Cook, a daughter of
Wilson Cook of Beaufort District, South Carolina, and his wife,
Judith O'Bannon, daughter of Thomas O'Bannon and Frances
Jennings (her descendants claimed she was one of the heirs of
the famous "Jennings' fortune", about which so much was published in the papers many years ago). The second Mrs. Robert
had two sisters, Nancy Cook who married Elijah Johnson, and
Rebecca E. Cook who married Tristram Verstile. There was a
Wilson Cook who married Providence Tuzette Tanner in 1823,
a niece of Grimball Robert. He was probably a grandson of
Wilson Cook and Judith O'Bannon. The census of South Carolina for 1790 shows Grimball Robert and Wilson Cook living
near one another in Beaufort District, S. C. Grimball Robert
married his second wife before coming to Louisiana as he did
not leave South Carolina until after 1810. It would appear
from official records now available that Grimball Robert's
second wife was the widow Tanner when he married her, and
had a son, Joseph Tanner. The following two records will bear
out this statement:—

STATE OF LOUISIANA,
PARISH OF RAPIDES.

> At a Family Meeting of five of the relatives and
> friends of the late *Grimball Robert and Eliza T. Tanner,*
> deceased, they mutually agree and advise that the negro
> man Horace belonging to the succession aforesaid be sold
> at public sale for cash and that the same will be to the
> interest of the heirs of said succession. This 21st day of
> December, 1825.

Witnesses:—	Joseph Robert
Branch Tanner	L. A. Robert
Joseph B. Robert.	Eldred G. Robert
	Hadley P. Robert
	Joseph Tanner.

> Done before me
> Silas Talbert, Notary Public.

STATE OF LOUISIANA,
PARISH OF RAPIDES.

Know all men by these presents that I, Joseph Tanner of the State and Parish aforesaid, planter, have in consideration of $315.00 the receipt whereof is hereby acknowledged, granted, bargained and sold, and by these presents do grant, bargain and confirm to Joseph Robert of the State and Parish aforesaid, a certain tract or parcel of land consisting of thirty-one acres and a half, more or less, situated in the State and Parish aforesaid, taken from the section of land purchased by Grimball Robert of John Stafford, extending one mile back. Bounded on the east by land belonging to Joseph Robert, and on the west by land of Grimball Addison Robert, *the same being the fraction of a tract of land partitioned agreeably to law among the heirs of Grimball Robert and Eliza T. Tanner, deceased, on the 11th of April, 1827, which fraction was allotted to me the said Joseph Tanner by experts appointed by the Probate Court to effect a partition of said estate.* To have and to hold the said thirty-one and a half acres to him the said Joseph Robert, his heirs and assigns forever. And lastly I warrant and by these presents will forever defend the said thirty-one and a half acres of land to him the said Joseph Robert, his heirs and assigns, from and against the claim or demand of all persons whosoever, the United States excepted. In testimony whereof I hereunto set my hand and seal this 10th day of May, 1828.

Witnesses:—
    Robert Tanner   Joseph Tanner
    J. J. Robert   Joseph Robert
           Done before me
           W. B. Pearce, Notary Public.

* * * *

The above deed certainly substantiates the statement that Joseph Tanner was an heir of the succession of "Grimball Robert and Eliza T. Tanner." He could only inherit from the latter by being her son, especially as she had Robert children. We know that John Stafford did not come to Louisiana until about 1815, so when Grimball Robert purchased the above mentioned property he was already married to Eliza T. Tanner, and consequently it became a part of their community interest. So when the Probate Court allocated a part of it to Joseph Tanner it did so because he was a natural heir of Eliza T.

Tanner. We know that when Joseph Tanner sold this property to Joseph Robert he was a mature man and the father of eight children, the eldest of whom was born before 1800. This would put the date of his own birth about 1778 or 1780, and his mother must therefore have been close to forty when she married Grimball Robert in 1806. According to the records in her son's Bible she had five Robert children and the youngest was born in 1812. This was rather unusual for one of her age but not at all impossible. The records of those early days were very faulty and a mistake of a few years in a date would make a big difference in computing the ages through several generations. Be that as it may, the deed given above definitely establishes Joseph Tanner as a son of the second wife of Grimball Robert.

The family Bible tells us that Grimball Robert died March 29, 1820, and that his second wife, Eliza T. Tanner, died March 20, 1824. His children by his first wife were:—

        1.—Peter William Robert.
        2.—Baynard Cheney Robert.
        3.—Sara Ann C. Robert.
        4.—Bayley T. Robert.
        5.—Joseph Jerediah Robert.

His children by his second wife were:—

        6.—Wilson Cook Robert.
        7.—Judith Rebecca Robert.
        8.—Elizabeth Elvira Robert.
        9.—Mary Ann Rebecca Robert.
      10.—Grimball Addison Robert.

The three daughters by the second marriage all died young. We find the following item in the family Bible relative to them:

    Judith Rebecca Robert died Sept. 25, 1817. Elizabeth Elvira Robert died Sept. 9, 1817. Mary Ann Rebecca Robert died Aug. 12, 1821. These were daughters of Grimball and Eliza T. Robert.

1.—Peter William Robert, eldest child of Grimball Robert and his first wife, Mary Sealey Cheney, was born in St. Peter's Parish, Beaufort District, South Carolina, October 15, 1789. He was a carpenter, a planter and a prominent Baptist minister. When about seventeen years of age, so he tells us, he persuaded his father to let him be apprenticed to Benjamin Themistocles

Dion Lawton for two years to learn the carpenter's trade. This Lawton was the son of Joseph Lawton, Jr., and Sarah Robert, and was therefore a first cousin of Grimball Robert. This was in 1806 and young Robert remained with his employer for the prescribed time. Later with his father's permission he emigrated to Wilkinson county, Mississippi, then a part of West Florida and usually called the "Mississippi Territory." The following account of him is taken from Paxton's History of the Louisiana Baptists:—

ELDER PETER WILLIAM ROBERT was distinguished among the early evangelists who labored in Southern Louisiana. He was a brother of Baynard C. Robert, and was born in South Carolina in 1798, and removed to Louisiana in 1818, and settled in St. Mary's parish, where he was converted under the preaching of Joseph Willis. He was licensed by Bayou Salé Church and ordained by Joseph Willis in 1821. Elder Robert was by trade a brickmason, and in 1833 removed to Jefferson, a suburb of New Orleans, where he remained eight years, engaged at his trade and preaching as best he could as opportunity presented itself. In 1837 he aided in the re-organization of the First African Baptist Church, and ordained two colored ministers, Sanders and Satterfield. In 1841 John O'Quin and others residing in St. Landry parish, desired to receive baptism, and P. W. Robert was sent for to perform the ordinance, there being no more convenient administrator. Mr. Robert came, and continuing some days preaching, he gathered the church of Bayou Rouge (now Avoyelles parish). Encouraged by his success, he continued two years or more to labor as an evangelist in the bounds of Louisiana Association, during which, as the fruit of his labors, four hundred and six were added to the churches. He then returned to Jefferson, where he continued a few years, but again returned to the Red River region, broken down in health, and settled in Rapides parish, where he died about 1847.

Of this brother, Elder John O'Quin, who knew him long and intimately, says:—"He had a good estate to begin life with, but was much engaged in preaching, and without any provision being made for a support, together with his great kindness of heart in giving away good books and helping the poor, he was much reduced in poverty at his death. He was a man greatly beloved, very catholic in spirit, but sound in faith. I have heard many great men, but never listened to a better one as a teacher of Christian-

ity. He was a natural orator. Under his ministry Elder
D. D. Forman and Elder D. H. Willis, and many others,
the most useful members of our churches, were brought in.
The wife of Brother W. R. Hargrove* of Sugar Town,
Rapides parish, is his only surviving child. In doctrine
he was not very *hard-shelled*, and by some he was called a
Campbellite, but he died a Baptist."

Mr. Ford claims that he endorsed the doctrine of
McCall, the Campbellite evangelist. But as he continued
with the Baptists until his death, it is probable that he
differed from his brethren in that he opposed the hyper-
Calvinistic and Antinomian views of many of his brethren,
without adopting the peculiar errors of Campbellism.

This good man left in his own handwriting a record of his
family which is now invaluable to us in giving a correct por-
trayal of his particular branch. This manuscript is now the
property of his great grandson, Matthew Leon Hargrove, of
Oakdale, La., who kindly permitted the compiler of this data
the use of it. Due to the importance of it we will here insert
the greater portion of it just as it was written:—

FAMILY RECORD KEPT BY P. W. ROBERT.

The following record is copied from my former record
which being injured caused me to copy it here this 16th
of February, 1821. In witness whereof I hereunto sign
my name.

(signed) P. W. Robert.

I Peter William Robert (according to my father's
record) was born 15th October, 1789, on Black Swamp, St.
Peter's Parish, Beaufort District, South Carolina. My
father's name was Grimball Robert. His mother's maiden
name (that is my father's mother) was Ann Grimball.
My mother's maiden name was Mary Sealie Cheney—her
father's name was William Cheney† and her mother's
maiden name was Sarah Norris.

I was married on the 27th July, 1809, to my cousin
Elizabeth Robert, daughter of Mr. Peter Robert, my
father's brother. Her mother's maiden name was Elizabeth Jaudon, daughter of Mr. Elias Jaudon and his wife

---

* This should be *M. V. Hargrove*—his son was W. R. Hargrove.
† William Cheney was a son of James Cheney and Mary (Johnson)
  Young and a brother of John Cheney who was the father of William
  Fendon Cheney, the founder of Cheneyville, Rapides parish, Louisiana.

Mary. We were married in Mississippi Territory, Wilkinson County, on Bayou Sarah, by the Rev. Moses Hadley. My wife according to her father's record was born 24th March, 1794, in the same neighborhood with myself, her father's parents were the same as my own.*

1st.—Our first child was a son, he died without bearing a name. He was born 22 October, in the year of our Lord 1810.

2nd.—Elizabeth Sealie Robert was born 12th July, 1812, about 11 o'clock at night on Bayou Sally, Attakapas, La., and named after her two grandmothers.

3rd.—Grimball Peter Robert was born 4th December, 1814, on Bayou Sally, Attakapas, La., at 9 o'clock in the morning, and named after his two grandfathers. Grimball Peter died 6th September, 1818—he measured 2 ft. 11¾ inches in length. He died with an illness of 7 days constant fever.

4th.—Sarah Carline Robert was born 13th December, 1816, about 11 o'clock at night on Bayou Sally, Attakapas, La.

5th.—Baynard Scott Robert was born January 29th, 1819, at 11 o'clock, on Bayou Sally, Attakapas, La.

6th.—Edmund Grimball Robert was born April 1st, Sunday morning, one hour before day, 1821, on Bayou Sally, Attakapas, La. This child was named by his grandfather Peter Robert.

7th.—Adlai Ann Robert was born January 13th, 1823, on Bayou Sally, Attakapas, La.

8th.—Bollever Washington Robert was born 13th September, 1825, in Franklin, St. Mary's Parish, La., at 3 o'clock in the morning on Tuesday. Bollever Washington died after an illness (the remains of influenza) of twenty days on 12th July, 1826, aged 8 months and 29 days.

9th.—Pamela Mistake Robert was born 1st December, 1827, at 10 o'clock on Saturday, near Franklin, St. Mary's Parish, La. Pamela Mistake died 2nd October, 1828, aged 10 months and 22 days.

---

* He means that her father's parents and his father's parents were the same persons.

She died of the billious fever of six days continuance without abating.

10th.—Retep* Esther Robert was born 5th November, 1829, at 10 o'clock p. m., near Franklin, St. Mary's Parish, La.

11th.—Mailliw† Louisa Robert was born 27th September, 1831, at 10 o'clock a. m., at Franklin, St. Mary's Parish, La.

Elizabeth Sealey Robert was married to Mr. John Hiram Waddle of Virginia on the 9th August, 1831, at lower Bayou Salle, St. Mary's parish, La. Clear fine weather and a large company of friends. The celebration was by the Elder Baynard C. Robert of said parish.

Sarah Carline Robert was married near Franklin, St. Mary's parish, La., by Elder Baynard C. Robert to Mr. Thomas Henry Adams (of Virginia) on 25th December, 1832. Very rainy weather but a large company of friends in attendance.

John H. Waddle died 12th June, 1832, by the breaking of a blood vessel inwardly (as supposed by Doctor Settleton), three miles below Franklin, St. Mary's parish, La. He was a worthy young man and an affectionate husband, and a kind and respectful son-in-law, and a smart intelligent man.

Elizabeth Sealey Robert Waddle, widow of John Hiram Waddle, was married to Mr. William Henry Hurst 6th December, 1838, the celebration by Judge Elliott, City of Lafiatte, La., parish of Jefferson, after being the widow of J. H. Waddle six years, five months, and twenty-four days. Bad weather, not many in attendance.

Grimball Peter Robert died 6th September, 1818, aged 3 years, 9 months and 2 days. He measured 2 ft., 11¾ inches in length. He died with an illness of 7 days fever without intermission.

Edmund Grimball Robert died 13th September, 1823, with an illness of 23 days remitting fever. He measured 2 ft., 9¾ inches in length and was 2 years, 6 months and 5 days old.

Baynard Scott Robert died 16th December, 1832, with an unknown disease that contracted his limbs and brought

---

* Retep is Peter spelled backward.

† In the instance of his youngest child's name Mr. Robert carried out a similar idea and called her Mailliw, which is William spelled backward. It is pronounced *May-Lou*.

his head and knees together. He was a moral good child, beloved by all the neighborhood. He was 12 years, 10 months and 18 days old, and I think pious before God. He was orderly in all his conduct.

Retep Esther Robert died 10th February, 1833, with scarlet fever, aged 3 years, 3 months and 4 days.

Adlai Ann Robert died of yellow fever at City of Lafiatte, La., on the 26th September, 1837, aged 14 years, 8 months and 13 days. This child was highly esteemed by the Sunday School teachers and they have honored her memory. She was to have been a teacher in Sunday School in the following year.

William Henry Adams, son of my daughter Sarah Carline Robert, was born 23rd April, 1834, at Bayou Sale, St. Mary's parish, La., at her uncle's, B. C. Robert, at 3½ o'clock, p. m.

W. H. Adams died near Franklin, La., the 29th February, 1837.

Dick Asaph, son of my daughter Sarah Carline Robert, was born 15th November, 1839, at 2½ o'clock in the morning, City of Lafiatte, La., Jefferson parish.

William Robert Hurst, son of my daughter Elizabeth Sealey Robert, was born 2nd April, 1840, at 8½ o'clock, City of Lafiatte, La., Jefferson parish.

The foregoing record comes to us out of the past and speaks with a voice of authority which none can gainsay. Would that all our genealogical material were based on such a solid foundation. The story Mr. Robert tells is surely a pathetic one. Out of his eleven children only three reached adult life, and they were girls, none of his boys lived to carry on his name. In the Hargrove family Bible it is recorded that Peter William Robert died December 25, 1849 (and not 1847, as Rev. W. E. Paxton tells us), and that his wife, Elizabeth Jaudon Robert, died October 4, 1867, aged 73 years, 6 months and 10 days. The date of his death is further confirmed by the records in the Bible of his half brother, Grimball Addison Robert. The item referring to this reads:—"Peter William Robert, half brother of mine, and eldest son of my father, departed this life December 25, 1849. He was my friend and brother."

Elizabeth Sealie Robert, eldest daughter of Peter William Robert and his wife, Elizabeth Jaudon Robert, was married (according to her father's record) on August 9, 1831, to John Hiram Waddle who died in less than a year. Apparently there was no issue. Then six years later she married William Henry Hurst. Mr. Robert in his record tells us of one son, William Robert Hurst, born April 2, 1840. If there were any other children we have been unable to find any mention of them in later family records. Whether or not this son reached adult life we are unable to say. It seems probable that he died young.

Sarah Carline Robert, fourth child of Peter William Robert and his wife, Elizabeth Jaudon Robert, was married (so her father tells us) near Franklin, Louisiana, on December 25, 1832, to Thomas Henry Adams. Her first child, William Henry Adams, died at the age of three years. Her second son, Dick Asaph Adams, was born November 15, 1839. There has remained no trace of him, so it is probable that he also died young.

Mailliw Louisa Robert, youngest child of Peter William Robert and his wife, Elizabeth Jaudon Robert, was born at Franklin, St. Mary's parish, La., at 10 o'clock a. m., on September 27, 1831. It was left to this lone little girl to transmit the blood of her parents down through the generations, and well has she fulfilled her task. She was unmarried at the time of her father's death so we find no mention of her marriage in his "family record," but in the Hargrove family Bible we find that "Matthew Vernon Hargrove married Louisa Robert on July 11, 1850." We shall designate this gentleman as *Matthew Vernon Hargrove, Sr.*, since we are to meet this name so frequently in the generations following him. He was born (so the good old family Bible tells us) on November 22, 1830, and was a son of William Hargrove and his wife, Mary Elizabeth Vernon. William Hargrove was born in North Carolina and died in Louisiana on August 15, 1850. His wife (Mary Elizabeth Vernon) died on October 9, 1848. She was a daughter of William S. Vernon who died December 12, 1836, and his wife, Elizabeth Keller, who died June 26, 1836. Matthew Vernon Hargrove, Sr., died in Oakdale, Allen parish, La., on December 25, 1908, aged 77 years, and his wife (Mailliw Louisa Robert) died there on October 19, 1918, at the age of 87 years. Both were buried in the Oakdale cemetery. They had twelve children, seven of whom died in infancy. The births of these twelve children and the deaths of the seven infants are recorded in the family Bible as follows:—

BIRTHS.
  i.—Mary Elizabeth Hargrove, born October 10, 1852.
 ii.—William Robert Hargrove, born March 15, 1854.
iii.—Eliza Ann Hargrove, born April 22, 1856.
 iv.—Stephen Quirk Hargrove, born July 18, 1857.
  v.—Matthew Vernon Hargrove, Jr., born March 1, 1859.
 vi.—Mailliw Louisa Hargrove, born August 2, 1861.
vii.—George Griffin Hargrove, born February 28, 1866.
viii.—Washington Lee Hargrove, born March 27, 1868.
 ix.—Jaudon Hargrove, born January 17, 1869.
  x.—Ophelia Esther Hargrove, born January 19, 1870.
 xi.—David Charles Hargrove, born April 16, 1872.
xii.—Thomas Jackson Hargrove, born September 2, 1873.

DEATHS.
Mary Elizabeth Hargrove, died November 22, 1854
Eliza Ann Hargrove, died September 5, 1859.
Matthew Vernon Hargrove, Jr., died Sept. 6, 1859.
Stephen Quirk Hargrove, died Sept. 13, 1859.
Washington Lee Hargrove, died May 22, 1869.
Jaudon Hargrove, died January 17, 1869.
David Charles Hargrove, died May 16, 1872.

ii.—William Robert Hargrove, second child of Matthew Vernon Hargrove, Sr., and Mailliw Louisa Robert, was born at Washington, St. Landry parish, La., on March 15, 1854, and died at Oakdale, Allen parish, La., on June 17, 1931. He lived during a great portion of his adult life at Sugartown, then in Calcasieu parish, La., but now in the new parish of Beauregard. He was ever a zealous member of the Baptist church and was ordained to the full work of the ministry on Sunday, October 8, 1893. He was married at Sugartown, old Calcasieu parish, La., on May 2, 1878, by John W. May, Justice of the Peace, to Effie Kazar Elizabeth Jane Watson who was born at Sugartown on December 19, 1858, and died at Oakdale, La., on March 1, 1932. Both were buried in the Oakdale cemetery. She was a daughter of Andrew Jackson Watson (died at the age of 80) and Louellen Reeves (died about the age of 80). Louellen Reeves was the daughter of Elizabeth Dunn and her first husband —— Reeves. Elizabeth later married a Talbert and died when about 90 years of age.   Rev. William Robert Hargrove and his wife had eleven children:—

        a.—May Liw Hargrove.
        b.—Matthew Vernon Hargrove, III.
        c.—Jennie Hargrove.
        d.—John Everette Hargrove.
        e.—William Robert Hargrove, Jr.
        f.—David Merwyn Hargrove.
        g.—Edward Lee Hargrove.
        h.—Jackson Cedric Hargrove.
        i.—Benny Hill Hargrove.
        j.—Paul Hargrove.
        k.—Landry Hargrove.

      a.—May Liw Hargrove was born at Sugartown, old Calcasieu parish, La., on Monday, May 19, 1879, and died there on Sunday, September 21, 1890, at the age of eleven.   Her name, as given above, is thus recorded in her father's Bible, tho' we know she was named for his mother, Mailliw Louisa Robert.

      b.—Matthew Vernon Hargrove, III, was born at Sugartown, old Calcasieu parish, La., on Monday, November 22, 1880. He graduated in medicine from the University of Tennessee in 1909 and is now practicing his profession in Oakdale, La., where, assisted by his son, he operates a private hospital of twenty-five beds, well and favorably known as the Hargrove Clinic.   Dr. Hargrove has been most successful in his life work and is generally recognized as a man of ability and skill by the profession in his native State.   He was married by his father, Rev. William Robert Hargrove, at Oakdale, La., on December 4, 1904, to Jennie Lawson Rigsby who was born July 11, 1883, at Calmesmeil, Tyler county, Texas.   She was a daughter of James Monroe Rigsby and Mildred Ann Crenshaw who were married September 13, 1865.   Mr. Rigsby was born September 13, 1843, at Woodville, Tyler county, Texas, and died July 14, 1914, at Oakdale, La.   He was a son of Lewis Johnson Rigsby and Mary Foster (whose mother was a Miss Lawson before marriage).   Mildred Ann Crenshaw was born in Alabama on September 10, 1849, and died at Oakdale, La., on June 20, 1920. Dr. and Mrs. Hargrove have had three children:—

        az.—Sidney Branch Hargrove.
        bz.—Matthew Vernon Hargrove, IV.
        cz.—William Rigsby Hargrove.

az.—Sidney Branch Hargrove was born at Oakdale, La., June 24, 1906, and died the same day.

bz.—Matthew Vernon Hargrove, IV, was born at Oakdale, La., on Wednesday, February 16, 1910. He is a pharmacist by profession and now owns and operates a drug store in his native town. He was married at the home of his parents in Oakdale, La., by the Rev. J. L. Barrett (Baptist minister), on December 24, 1934, to Mildred Elizabeth Corley, born at Winnfield, Winn parish, La., on October 10, 1913. She is a daughter of Isham Allen Corley, born in Grant parish, La., August 27, 1874, and Cora Lou Walker, born July 11, 1884, at Pollock, La. Mrs. Hargrove's paternal grandfather was J. F. Corley, born July 24, 1852, in Scott county, Miss., and died May 25, 1932, at Oakdale, La. Her paternal grandmother was Nancy McCarty, born October 13, 1856, near Flat Creek, Winn parish, La., and she was a daughter of Allen McCarty, born in North Carolina, and Mary Peters, born in South Carolina. Mrs. Hargrove's maternal grandparents were Wiley and Martha Walker. Mr. and Mrs. Hargrove have a son, Matthew Vernon Hargrove, V, born Wednesday, May 15, 1940, at the Hargrove Clinic, Oakdale, La.

cz.—William Rigsby Hargrove was born at Oakdale, Allen parish, La., on February 3, 1912. He graduated in medicine from Tulane University, New Orleans, La., and is now a prominent physician and surgeon in his native town where he is associated with his father in operating the Hargrove Clinic. He was married at the home of his parents in Oakdale, La., on February 15, 1942, by the Rev. E. C. Harris (Baptist minister), to Jewell Letaine Knowles who was born at Grant, Allen parish, La., on February 16, 1923. She was a daughter of Vernon Earl Knowles, born in Wolfe City, Texas, and died in January, 1925, and Thelma Gertrude Andrews, born July 26, 1898, and died June 18, 1932. Mrs. Hargrove's paternal grandparents were Rice and Bell Knowles of Texas. Her maternal grandfather was Dempsey Andrews, born February 25, 1874, and died June 26, 1941, a son of Samuel Solomon Andrews. Her maternal grandmother was Dellar Simmons, born November 6, 1877, and died August 6, 1925. Dr. and Mrs. Hargrove have one child at this date, Jenny Letaine, born March 6, 1945, at Baptist Hospital, Alexandria, La.

c.—Jennie Hargrove, third child of Rev. William Robert Hargrove and Effie Kazar Elizabeth Jane Watson, was born at Sugartown, old Calcasieu parish, La., on Saturday, January 27, 1883. She was married at Sugartown on December 27, 1903, by Rev. Daniel T. O'Quin, to Thomas Walter Guy Carrol who was born at Merryville, Beauregard parish, La., on October 3, 1883. They had four children:—

> az.—Portis Lowell Carroll.
> bz.—Eunice Lorena Carroll.
> cz.—William Thomas Ray Carroll.
> dz.—Mary Effie Carroll.

az.—Portis Lowell Carroll was born at Merryville, La., on October 3, 1904, and died in Baton Rouge, La., in April, 1921.

bz.—Eunice Lorena Carroll was born at Merryville, La., on January 7, 1907. She now resides in Baton Rouge where she is well known in insurance circles, having the agency of the Mutual Life Insurance Company of New York. She was married 1st on August 29, 1924, at the home of her grandparents in Oakdale, La., by her grandfather Rev. William Robert Hargrove, to James Ivy Seals who was born at Oakdale on October 18, 1902. He was a son of James Adolphus Seals, born near Opelousas, La., December 11, 1879, and Malinda Elizabeth Monk, born at Oakdale on June 1, 1881. James Adolphus Seals was a son of Alford Seals and L. Perry. Malinda Elizabeth Monk was a daughter of David C. Monk and Amelia Dunn. Mr. and Mrs. James Ivy Seals had one son, Robert Alton Seals, born at Oakdale, La., on October 12, 1926, who is now in the Marine Corps and serving over seas. Eunice Lorena (Carroll) Seals was married 2nd on November 6, 1933, to Harry Farwell Bush. There are no children by the second marriage.

cz.—William Thomas Ray Carroll was born at Merryville, La., on March 12, 1908. He married Edna Walker on January 1, 1937. They have no children.

dz.—Mary Effie Carroll was born at Merryville, La., on May 29, 1916, and was married October 15, 1938, to William Bryant Parker. They have one son, Phillip Carroll Parker, born November 24, 1942.

d.—John Everette Hargrove, fourth child of Rev. William Robert Hargrove and Effie Kazar Elizabeth Jane Watson, was born at Sugartown, old Calcasieu parish, La., on Saturday,

August 23, 1884. He was a school teacher and died near Oakdale on Saturday, July 18, 1903, from accidental drowning in
the Calcasieu river. He was buried beside his sister,. Mailliw
Hargrove, in the Camp Ground cemetery.

e.—William Robert Hargrove, Jr., fifth child of Rev. William Robert Hargrove and Effie Kazar Elizabeth Jane Watson,
was born at Sugartown, old Calcasieu parish, La., on Saturday,
March 6, 1886. Mr. Hargrove has been prominent in business
circles in his community for many years and is at present
Manager of the Hargrove Funeral Home of Oakdale, La. He
married at Alexandria, Rapides parish, La., on October 28,
1910, Daisy Irene Flowers, better known to her family and
friends as "Rena." The ceremony was performed by Rev. H.
R. Singleton, Methodist minister, at the home of the bride's
father. Daisy Irene Flowers was born at Gloster, Amite
County, Miss., on December 27, 1888, and was a daughter of
Milburn Watkins Flowers and Rebecca Annie Miller. Mr.
Flowers was born June 13, 1860, at Union Church, Miss., and
died at Alexandria, La., on November 25, 1938. He was a son
of Ephram A. Flowers and Mary Griffin. Mrs. Flowers
(Rebecca Annie Miller) was born July 21, 1869, at Springfield,
Livingston parish, La., and died at Alexandria, La., on Febru-
ary 25, 1901. She and her husband were buried in Pineville,
La. She was a daughter of Zachary Taylor Miller, Sr., born
October 25, 1848, at Springfield, La., and died January 24,
1891, at Greenville, La., and his wife, Mary Jane Gordon, born
July 2, 1849, at Springfield, La., and died June 13, 1901, at
Centerville, La. Zachary Taylor Miller, Sr., was a son of
Joseph D. Miller, born April 22, 1792, in Scotland, and died at
Centerville, La., and his wife, Elizabeth Rhodes, born May 20,
1806, in Mississippi, and died in April, 1906, at Clio, La. Mary
Jane Gordon was a daughter of Thomas Gordon, born 1815, at
Gillsburg, Amite county, Miss., and died in the summer of 1855
at Springville, La., and his wife, Rebecca Ann Wall, born April
26, 1822, at Springfield, La., and died September 15, 1891, at
Clio, La. William Robert Hargrove, Jr., and Daisy Irene
Flowers had seven children:—

> az.—Effie Annie Hargrove.
> bz.—Infant son who died at birth.
> cz.—Infant son who died at birth.

dz.—Nedra Fay Hargrove.
ez.—Infant son who died at birth.
fz.—Bobbye Rena Hargrove.
gz.—Joy Hargrove.

az.—Effie Annie Hargrove was born at Oakdale, Allen parish, La., on Thursday, August 2, 1911. She is a mortician by profession and is at present Office Manager of the Hargrove Funeral Home at Oakdale, La. It has been principally due to the kindness and untiring efforts of this gracious lady that we have been able to include in this work the voluminous amount of data presented here on the descendants of the Rev. Peter William Robert. She is the real historian of her branch of this pioneer family and the compiler of this book wishes here to express his gratitude for her most valuable assistance. Those in future generations who are infected with the "genealogical bug" will loudly sing her praises and the more enthusiastic ones among them will "rise up and call her blessed."

dz.—Nedra Fay Hargrove was born at Oakdale, La., on Monday, May 3, 1915, and died there on January 28, 1919, aged 3 years, 8 months and 25 days.

fz.—Bobbye Rene Hargrove was born at Alexandria, La., on Friday, April 2, 1919, and is by profession a Social Welfare Worker. She was married June 23, 1941, by Rev. J. L. Barrett, Baptist minister at Oakdale, La., to Murphy Collier Smith, born at Oakdale, La., on Saturday, January 26, 1918. He is a son of Oscar Franklin Smith, born September 21 1890, at Pinebluff, Jefferson county, Arkansas (son of Daniel Webster Smith and Julia Ann Fike), and Minnie Maude Hinson, born January 2, 1897, at Beaver, old St. Landry parish, La. now, Evangeline parish (daughter of Pinkney Rollen Hinson, born March, 1867, and Barcelona Morris, born June 7, 1872, at Lake Cone, Avoyelles parish, La.). Barcelona Morris was a daughter of William Thomas Morris, born on Pearl river, in old Washington parish, La., and died in 1918, and his wife, Jane Thomas. Murphy Collier Smith and Bobbye Rene Hargrove have three children:—William Robert Smith, born Monday, March 16, 1942; Lona Maude Smith, born Thursday, March 4, 1943; Murphy Collier Smith, Jr., born Monday, March 27, 1944. All were born at the Hargrove Clinic in Oakdale, La.

gz.—Joy Hargrove was born at the Baptist Hospital in Alexandria, La., on Wednesday, February 17, 1926. She was married in Alexandria, La., on June 4, 1944, to Ewing Frank Sherrill, son of Mr. and Mrs. C. E. Sherrill of Jefferson, Texas.

f.—David Merwyn Hargrove, sixth child of Rev. William Robert Hargrove and Effie Kazar Elizabeth Jane Watson, was born at Sugartown, old Calcasieu parish, La., on Saturday, April 20, 1889. He married at DeRidder, Beauregard parish, La., on April 16, 1914, Georgia Clark who at the time was the widow Blackwell with two children (J. T. and Mae Blackwell). She was born at Bunkie, Avoyelles parish, La., on February 10, 1893, and was a daughter of Thomas Nathaniel Clark (born May 21, 1860, and died November 25, 1943, at Oakdale, La.) and Aramenta Dormer Barron (born February 28, 1865, at Crystal Springs, Simpson county, Miss.), who was a daughter of Samuel Madison Barron and Aramenta Dormer Bowie. Mr. and Mrs. Hargrove have no children.

g.—Edward Lee Hargrove, seventh child of Rev. William Robert Hargrove and Effie Kazar Elizabeth Jane Watson, was born at Sugartown, old Calcasieu parish, La., on Tuesday, January 29, 1891. He was married at Alexandria, La., in the lobby of the Rapides Hotel, by Rev. W. J. E. Cox, Baptist minister, on October 1, 1913, to Lois Velma Gray who was born November 27, 1895, at Forest Hill, Rapides parish, La. She was a daughter of John Hillory Gray (born December 3, 1871, at Amite, Miss., and died November 3, 1936, at Long Leaf, Rapides parish, La.) and Alice Ruth Sermons (born April 16, 1871, at Dunnville (now Oakdale), Allen parish, La.). Edward Lee Hargrove and Lois Velma Gray have three sons:—

az.—Edward Lee Hargrove, Jr.
bz.—Johnnie Cedric Hargrove.
cz.—James William Hargrove.

az.—Edward Lee Hargrove, Jr., was born at Oakdale, La., on October 30, 1914, and is at present in the military service of his country. He was married at his father's home in Jonesboro, Jackson parish, La., by J. M. Shows, Justice of the Peace, on May 3, 1939, to Verda Lou Black who was born April 20, 1915, at Liberty Hill, Bienville parish, La. She was a daughter of Allen Titus Black and Minnie Bell Kemp (daughter of John Kemp and Frances Elizabeth Williams).

bz.—Johnnie Cedric Hargrove was born at Oakdale, La., on November 28, 1915, and now resides near Long Leaf, La. He was married by the Rev. V. L. McKee, Baptist minister, on June 7, 1936, in Homer, Claiborne parish, La., at the residence of the bride's sister (Mrs. J. G. Edwards), to Evelyn Brinson who was born August 25, 1919, at Bienville, Bienville parish, La. They now have a son, Johnnie Cedric Hargrove, Jr., born at Jonesboro, Jackson parish, La., on February 8, 1938.

cz.—James William Hargrove was born at Long Leaf, Rapides parish, La., on November 28, 1919. He is now in the military service of his country and was recently home on a furlough after serving more than a year overseas. He was married in the Methodist parsonage at Ruston, La., by Rev. J. L. Hicks, on December 13, 1937, to Felcie Elizabeth Hays who was born February 9, 1920, at Arcadia, Bienville parish, La. She is a daughter of Andrew Ward Hays and Gladys Pauline McGuire (daughter of W. H. McGuire).

h.—Jackson Cedric Hargrove, eighth child of Rev. William Robert Hargrove and Effie Kazar Elizabeth Jane Watson, was born at Sugartown, old Calcasieu parish, La., on Tuesday, October 25, 1892. He died June 11, 1905, at the age of about twelve years.

i.—Benny Hill Hargrove, ninth child of Rev. William Robert Hargrove and Effie Kazar Elizabeth Jane Watson, was born on Saturday, March 16, 1895, at Sugartown, old Calcasieu parish, La., and died July 5, 1940, near Glenmora, Rapides parish, La. He was buried in the Oakdale cemetery. He was married 24, 1914, at Oakdale, La., by the Rev. J. B. Herndon, at the Baptist parsonage, to Mae Blanchard who was born February 25, 1894. They had two children:—

az.—Benny Hill Hargrove, Jr.
bz.—Carlton Hargrove.

az.—Benny Hill Hargrove, Jr., was born June 2, 1915, at Oakdale, La., and married in 1935 Allie Lovelady who was born October 18, 1916. They now reside in Baton Rouge, La., where Mr. Hargrove is in the employ of the U. S. Government. They have two children:—June Yvonne Hargrove, born at Taylor's Hill, near Glenmora, La., on June 8, 1936, and Gail Annette Hargrove, born October 30, 1943.

bz.—Carlton Hargrove was born at Oakdale, La., on November 6, 1916, and died there in January, 1917.

j.—Paul Hargrove, tenth child of Rev. William Robert Hargrove and Effie Kazar Elizabeth Jane Watson, was born at Sugartown, old Calcasieu parish, La., on Tuesday, June 1, 1897, and died at Oakdale, Allen parish, La., on October 3, 1935, and was buried in the cemetery there. He never married.

k.—Landry Hargrove, eleventh child of Rev. William Robert Hargrove and Effie Kazar Elizabeth Jane Watson, was born at Sugartown, old Calcasieu parish, La., on Monday, April 3, 1899. He was married 1st, at Oakdale, La., by Rev. Sullivan, Baptist minister, on January 4, 1920, to Dessie Mae Phillips, daughter of James Charlton Phillips (born March 14, 1875, and died September 3, 1943) and Mary Ellen Coker (born June 6, 1875, and died July 2, 1926). Mr. Phillips was a son of Zachariah Phillips (born January 5, 1853, and died in December, 1943) and Sarah Gatsie Raimer (born in 1847 and died March 16, 1903). Mary Ellen Coker was a daughter of Thomas and Fannie Coker. Landry Hargrove and Dessie Mae Phillips had three children:—

az.—Landry Phillip Hargrove.
bz.—Robert Vernon Hargrove.
cz.—Mailliw Ellen Hargrove.

Landry Hargrove married 2nd, Winnie D. Honeycutt who was born February 18, 1913. They had one daughter:—

dz.—Mildred Elizabeth Hargrove.

Landry Hargrove married 3rd, at Kinder, Allen parish, La., on May 13, 1942, Cecelia Cooper who was born March 26, 1921. She was a daughter of Frank Ross Cooper (son of John and Mollie Cooper) and Elizabeth Veronica Duncan (born January 4, 1880, and died October 18, 1942). They have one child:—

ez.—Leonard Cooper Hargrove.

az.—Landry Phillip Hargrove was born at Oakdale, Allen parish, La., on November 27, 1920, and married Florine Johnson, born November 11, 1918, daughter of A. Eula Johnson who was born December 1, 1892, at Pine Prairie, Evangeline parish, La. Landry Phillip Hargrove is now in the U. S. Army and is presently stationed at Rapid City, South Dakota.

bz.—Robert Vernon Hargrove was born at Oakdale, Allen parish, La., on July 7, 1922, and was married June 13, 1942, at the First Baptist church, Oakdale, La., by Rev. E. C. Harris, to Edith Mavis Leggett who was born November 4, 1918, at Beaver, Evangeline parish, La. She was a daughter of John D. Leggett (born February 5, 1891, at Beaver, La.) and Emma Wagner, (born September 20, 1897, at Pollock, La.). Mr. Leggett was a son of John Wesley Leggett (born in Miss., January 26, 1857, and died November 28, 1936, at Beaver, La.) and Elizabeth Hinson (born in Alabama, March 23, 1847, and died at Beaver, La., January 29, 1939). Elizabeth Hinson was a daughter of Duncan Hinson (born in Alabama and died at Beaver, La., about 1912) and Nancy Cooper who died at Ten Mile, La. Emma Wagner was a daughter of Thomas Jefferson Wagner (died at Pollock, La., October 27, 1916, at the age of 65) and Minerva Maxwell (died at Pollock, La., at the age of 43) who was a daughter of William and Jane Maxwell. Thomas Jefferson Wagner was a son of William and Mary Dean Wagner. Robert Vernon Hargrove is now in the U. S. Navy.

cz.—Mailliw Ellen Hargrove was born at Oakdale, La., on June 23, 1924, and is yet unmarried.

dz.—Mildred Elizabeth Hargrove, daughter of Landry Hargrove and his second wife, Winnie D. Honeycutt, was born at Oakdale, La., on October 25, 1932.

cz.—Leonard Cooper Hargrove, son of Landry Hargrove and his third wife, Cecelia Cooper, was born on Monday, March 14, 1943, at the Hargrove Clinic in Oakdale, La.

vi.—Mailliw Louisa Hargrove, sixth child of Matthew Vernon Hargrove, Sr., and Mailliw Louisa Robert, was born in St. Landry parish, La., on August 2, 1861, and died March 20, 1900. She was married on Thursday, May 22, 1884, at Sugartown, old Calcasieu parish, La., by Rev. Warren Hamilton, to John A. Perkins of DeQuincy, La. He was a son of Ivan Perkins and Ernestine Lyons, and died October 28, 1940. Both he and his wife were buried in Orange Grove cemetery, at Lake Charles, La. They had six children:—

a.—Charles Wilmer Perkins.
b.—Pearl Perkins.
c.—Matthew Ivan Perkins.

d.—Ernestine Louise Perkins.
e.—Addison Robert Perkins.
f.—Martha Effie Perkins.

a.—Charles Wilmer Perkins was born near Sugartown, La., on December 8, 1886. He married Ada Self in Lake Charles, La., and they had three children:—El, Charles and Ned Self Perkins.

b.—Pearl Perkins was born near Sugartown, La., on June 19, 1888. She was married in Oberlin, La., to L. C. Rushton. They now live in San Antonio, Texas, and have three children: —Lonnie Conroe, Martha Louise, and Jack Rushton.

c.—Matthew Ivan Perkins was born in Calcasieu parish, La., on February 5, 1890, and was married in Kinder, La., by Rev. Leeds, to Lew Hollingsworth.

d.—Ernestine Louise Perkins, known to her family as "Tiny," was born in Calcasieu parish, La., on August 3, 1892. She was married in Lake Charles, La., by Father Walsh, on June 1, 1914, to Walter Leo Fitzenrieter who was born November 18, 1885. He was a son of Charles Fitzenrieter (born in New Orleans on December 3, 1840) and Barbara C. Goos (born in New Orleans on December 20, 1847, and died in Lake Charles, La., on July 12, 1921). Barbara C. Goos was the eldest daughter of Captain Daniel C. Goos of Lake Charles, La. Mr. and Mrs. Fitzenrieter have two children:—

az.—Mildred Ruth Fitzenrieter.
bz.—Walter Leo Fitzenrieter, Jr.

az.—Mildred Ruth Fitzenrieter was born at Bel, Allen parish, La., on September 16, 1923, and was married at Rawlins, Wyoming, on June 11, 1943, to Dual C. Eubanks of Monroe, La.

bz.—Walter Leo Fitzenrieter, Jr., was born at Bel, Allen parish, La., on July 13, 1926.

e.—Addison Robert Perkins was born in Calcasieu parish, La., on March 19, 1894, and married Margaret Foster. They have two children:—Albert and William Perkins.

f.—Martha Effie Perkins was born in Calcasieu parish, La., on May 17, 1896, and married a Wimberley. Two children were born of this marriage:—

az.—John Wimberley.
bz.—Virginia Wimberley.

az.—John Wimberley was born in Lake Charles, La., in 1918, and was married in 1941, at DeQuincy, La., by Rev. Price of the Baptist church, to Lucille Young.

bz.—Virginia Wimberley was born at Bel, Allen parish, La., in 1921, and was married in 1941, by Rev. Grimes, to George Lee Koonce.

vii.—George Griffin Hargrove, seventh child of Matthew Vernon Hargrove, Sr., and Mailliw Louisa Robert, was born in St. Landry parish, La., on February 28, 1866, and died near Sugartown, La., on November 10, 1884. He was evidently a promising young man as is indicated by the following news-paper clipping which was found in the family Bible:—

HARGROVE:—At his father's residence, near Sugar-town, Calcasieu parish, La., George, son of M. V. and M. L. Hargrove, aged 18 years, 8 months and 12 days. Wash-ington (La.) Argus please copy.

It seems strange that Death should pass by so many whose heads are grey and whose steps are tottering, to seize upon this young life, so full of hope and future promise, as his prey. In claiming this boy, he seized upon "a shining mark." George was beloved by all who knew him. His usual gentleness and kindness endeared him to all his circle. On all sides one may hear him spoken of as without an enemy. But his active and earnest espousal of good, far outshone his negative qualities. The Sabbath school has lost a regular and faithful attendant; temper-ance an earnest champion, a living exemplar; society a youthful model, cherishing virtues, disdaining vices. He who doeth all things well, seems to have fitted him by the repressing power of peaceableness and the stimulating power of love to meet his end. Peaceful was thy life. Peaceful was thy death. "Rest in peace." I heard his mother say, "he spent his young life in trying to serve his God." This was the consoling thought. It was sufficient.

M. E. S.

x.—Ophelia Esther Hargrove, tenth child of Matthew Vernon Hargrove, Sr., and Mailliw Louisa Robert, was born at Washington, St. Landry parish, La., on Wednesday, January 19, 1870. She was affectionately known to the family as "Auntie." She was married to William S. Perkins who died January 5, 1900. They had no children.

xii.—Thomas Jackson Hargrove, twelfth and youngest child of Matthew Vernon Hargrove, Sr., and Mailliw Louisa Robert, was born at Washington, St. Landry parish, La., on Tuesday, September 2, 1873, and died at Oakdale, Allen parish, La., on February 15, 1943. He was buried in the Oakdale cemetery. He married May 23, 1900, Gracie Magdoline Tate, born February 11, 1881, and died July 24, 1942. She was a daughter of Leon Tate and Emily Savant. Thomas Jackson Hargrove and Gracie Magdoline Tate had five children:—

    a.—Matthew Leon Hargrove.
    b.—Mae Vivian Hargrove.
    c.—Otto Ernest Hargrove.
    d.—Estelle Bessie Hargrove.
    e.—Esther Louise Hargrove.

a.—Matthew Leon Hargrove was born at Oakdale, Allen parish, La., on April 30, 1901. He is Assistant Manager of the Hargrove Funeral Home of Oakdale, La. He married at Oberlin, Allen parish, La., on June 20, 1935, Claudine Thigpen, born August 24, 1914. She is a daughter of Van E. Thigpen who is a son of Benton Thigpen and Vina Skinner (daughter of Frank Skinner and Mary Lanier). Mr. and Mrs. Hargrove have been unfortunate with their children. They have had three and lost the first two at birth or soon afterwards. The first was an un-named son, born March 8, 1936. The second, Merwyn Leon Hargrove, was born August 23, 1937, and lived but a few hours. The third, Anita Louise Hargrove, born September 19, 1939, at Oakdale, La., is living at this time.

b.—Mae Vivian Hargrove was born at Oakdale, La., on August 24, 1903, and died there on March 6, 1939. She was married by her uncle, Rev. William Robert Hargrove, at his home in Oakdale, La., on October 11, 1927, to Clifton Waldon, born October 6, 1903, son of Sam and Alice Waldon. They had no children.

c.—Otto Ernest Hargrove was born at Oakdale, La., on December 24, 1905. He was married at Oakdale by his uncle, Rev. William Robert Hargrove (at the latter's home), on November 9, 1929, to Jessie Ann Riser, born May 29, 1911, a daughter of Luther Riser and Rosella Edwards (daughter of Mitchell Edwards and Julia Hilbern). They have four children:— Larry Lee Hargrove, born June 10, 1931, at Oakdale;

Thomas David Hargrove, born December 9, 1932, at Oakdale; Marlea Ann Hargrove, born May 12, 1938, at Hargrove Clinic in Oakdale; Judith Grace Hargrove, born April 8, 1940, at Hargrove Clinic in Oakdale.

d.—Estelle Bessie Hargrove was born at Oakdale, La., on September 6, 1908. She was married to John Campbell Gaffney, born May 4, 1909, at Bonham, Fannin county, Texas. He is a son of John Aloysius Gaffney, born at Texarkana, Texas, April 5, 1882, and Johnny Lessie Ives, born at Little Rock, Arkansas, March 1, 1890. His grandparents were Harry Gaffney, born in Providence, Rhode Island, and Alice Elizabeth Quinn, born in Birmingham, Alabama. Mr. and Mrs. John Campbell Gaffney have three children:—Jack Aloysius Gaffney, born in Shreveport, La., March 6, 1933; Harry Quinn Gaffney, born in Bossier City, La., February 10, 1935; Martha Sue Gaffney, born in Shreveport, La., May 7, 1938.

e.—Esther Louise Hargrove was born at Pitkin, Louisiana, on July 11, 1912. She was married May 5, 1934, to James Luther Mitchell, born January 25, 1902. He is a son of Martin Mitchell and Matilda McGhee. They have one child:—Gracie Lou Mitchell, born December 7, 1942, at the Hargrove Clinic in Oakdale, La.

2.—Baynard Cheney Robert, second son of Grimball Robert and his first wife, Mary Sealey Cheney, was born in St. Peter's Parish, Beaufort District, South Carolina, about 1791. He, like his elder brother Peter William Robert, was a noted Baptist divine. We regret that outside of his religious activities we have no information about him. He settled on Bayou Salé, in St. Mary's parish, Louisiana, and it is quite probable that he married and left descendants but we have been unable to procure any data on this phase of his life. His brother, Peter William Robert, in his "record book," makes the following entry which leads us to believe that he was married:—

William Henry Adams, son of my daughter Sarah Carline Robert, was born 23rd April, 1834, at Bayou Salé, St. Mary's parish, La., at her uncle's, B. C. Robert, at 3½ o'clock, p. m.

It is not likely that she would have been confined at the home of a *bachelor uncle*. The reasonable impression given by the above quotation is that Baynard C. Robert was a married man. On page 503 of Paxton's History of the Louisiana Baptists we find the following sketch of him:—

ELDER BAYNARD C. ROBERT:—Among the most intelligent and efficient of the pioneer ministers, who planted the Baptist cause in Louisiana, may be mentioned Baynard C. Robert. He was born in South Carolina in 1800.* He came to Louisiana in 1818, and settled in Rapides parish. He subsequently removed to St. Mary's parish, and in 1820 united in the formation of the Bayou Salé Church. The year following he and his brother, Peter W. Robert, at the request of the Bayou Salé Church, were ordained to the Gospel ministry. The Presbytery appointed for this purpose consisted of Isham Nettles and Joseph Willis. Nettles having failed to attend, Willis proceeded with the ordination alone. Baynard C. Robert at once entered upon that active career in the ministry which he had come to regard as his great life-work. From his residence in St. Mary's parish he traveled far and near. In 1824 he was chosen Clerk of the Association, to which position he was frequently re-elected, and even when others were chosen he was often requested to aid in preparing the minutes for the press. In 1833 he was Moderator of the Executive Board, a position to which he was frequently re-elected. The war swept away his property and he was reduced to poverty, but his labors never abated and his zeal never cooled. He died in 1865, full of years and good works, ripe for the reward above.

3.—Sarah Ann C. Robert (the C probably was for Catharine—she had an aunt named Sarah Catharine), third child of Grimball Robert and his first wife, Mary Sealey Cheney, was born in St. Peter's Parish, Beaufort District, South Carolina, about 1795. She was married to John C. Cook and the only official record we have of them shows they were living in St. Mary's parish, La. Whether her husband was related to Wilson Cook who married her first cousin, Providence Tuzette Tanner, or to Eliza Tuzette Cook who was her father's second wife, we are unable to state with any degree of certainty, but we are strongly inclined to believe he was related to both. We can find no record of any descendants from this marriage. The

---

* Baynard C. Robert was undoubtedly born before 1800. His elder brother, Peter William Robert, was born in 1789 and he himself is usually listed as the 2nd child, which would make his birth about 1791.

following deed tells about all we know of her husband and herself:—

STATE OF LOUISIANA,
PARISH OF ST. MARY.

On this 31st day of December, 1829, before me, Joshua Baker, Parish Judge and ex-officio notary public in and for the said parish, personally came and appeared Sarah A. C. Robert, wife of John C. Cook of this parish, who declared and confessed that she had with the advice and consent of her husband who is here present for the purpose of advising and assisting his wife to bargain sell alien set over and deliver unto E. L. Briggs of the parish of Rapides and by these presents the said Sarah A. C. Robert doth bargain sell alien set over and deliver unto said Briggs, his heirs and assigns forever a certain tract or parcel of land lying and being situated on both sides of the Bayou Boeuf having so much front on both sides that by running back forty arpents on both sides of said bayou so that the tract will contain one hundred and twenty-five superficial acres, bounded above by land of William Allen's heirs and below by Joseph J. Robert, with warrants of title against or claims of all persons whomsoever. This present sale, transfer and delivery is made for and in consideration of the sum of one thousand dollars cash in hand paid, the receipt whereof the vendor doth by these presents acknowledge. In witness whereof the said Sarah A. C. Robert hath hereunto signed in presence of Seth Lewis, Jr., and Joel Coe, subscribing witnesses, and me said Judge and Notary, on the day and year first written.

Sarah A. C. Cook

(I authorize my wife to sign)   John C. Cook

Witnesses: —
   Seth Lewis, Jr.
   Joel Coe.

Admitted to record
      S. Talbert, Notary Public.

4.—Bayley T. Robert, fourth child of Grimball Robert and his first wife, Mary Sealey Cheney, was born in St. Peter's Parish, Beaufort District, South Carolina, about 1797. He lived in Rapides parish, La., and died there unmarried sometime before March 7, 1827. The time of his death and his marital status are determined by a legal document on page 49 in the notarial record book of Silas Talbert, one of the early notaries for Rapides parish, and bearing date of March 7, 1827. In the proceedings we find the following item:—

> And the said Peter William Robert, further declares that his brother, Bayley T. Robert, has died intestate without relations in the ascending or descending line, and that he is one of the legal heirs of the said deceased. . . . .

On page 50 in the same book, bearing date of January 9, 1827, we find the following:—

> Be it remembered that I, Sarah A. C. Robert, wife of John C. Cook of the parish of St. Mary, State of Louisiana, and one of the legal heirs of Grimball Robert and Bayley T. Robert late of the parish of Rapides in this State, deceased, have with the aid and authorization of my said husband named, constituted, appointed and ordained my brother, Baynard C. Robert, my true and lawful attorney-in-fact, etc.

5.—Joseph Jerediah Robert, fifth child of Grimball Robert and his first wife, Mary Sealey Cheney, was born in St. Peter's Parish, Beaufort District South Carolina, about 1799. His mother evidently died in his infancy as we know that his father (Grimball Robert) married his second wife (Eliza T. Cook) in 1806. His status as a son of the first marriage is substantiated by the following transfer of property:—

> Joseph J. Robert on November 20, 1834, for $2,500.00 sells to Hugh Carlin "a certain parcel or fraction of land consisting of fifty-three American acres, more or less, taken from land purchased by the said *Joseph J. Robert from his half brother Wilson C. Robert*, situated in the parish of Rapides, State of Louisiana, bounded on the north by land claimed by the heirs of W. W. Chambers, deceased, south by public lands, east by land now owned by Margaret Briggs."
> Witnesses:—P. W. Robert and S. V. Randon.

Joseph Jerediah Robert came to Woodville, Mississippi, with his father when a small boy and later to Rapides parish, La., where he spent the remainder of his days. His middle name is variously given in the records as *Jediah, Jeddiah*, and *Jerediah*, the last being the one most frequently used. From our knowledge of the names of the characters in the Old Testament we are inclined to believe his parents intended his name to be *Jedediah*. He married his first cousin, Rosella Ann Robert, daughter of Joseph Robert and Mary Hyrne Jaudon.

They were married some time before 1834, as during that year she signs a deed as his wife. It is our surmise that they were married at least ten years before that date. His name appears frequently in the records of the legal transactions of that day and from July 28, 1858, to May 9, 1860, he was a notary public for Rapides parish in the Cheneyville neighborhood. He died prior to February 28, 1866, as we find a deed in which *Joseph S. Robert* sells to Linn Tanner "his undivided interest of his deceased father's property in the village of Cheneyville" on that date. Then later, on March 13, 1866, we find where Martha L. Robert sells to Linn Tanner "her undivided interest in her mother's, Rosella Ann Robert, deceased, property situated in the village of Cheneyville." The description of the property in the two sales is exactly the same, and since we know that Rosella Ann Robert was the wife of Joseph Jerediah Robert, we are justified in the conclusion that he and his wife were dead before the dates given in the deeds, and that the two vendors were their children. However, there were more than two children. This is substantiated by a letter of March 21, 1852, written by Thaddeus S. Robert (brother of Rosella Ann Robert) to his brother-in-law Frank Myers. He says:—
"I have letters from Bro. J. J. and *several* of his young ones." He always mentioned his brother-in-law Joseph J. Robert in his letters as "Brother J. J." Frank Myers, Jr., who resided with Joseph J. Robert and his wife while his father was in California makes the following statement in a letter to his uncle Thaddeus Robert:—"Uncle Joseph and Aunt Rosella, Zette, Rose and all are very kind to me." Then we find a deed which tells us of another child of Joseph J. Robert and his wife. It was passed before M. R. Marshall, Notary Public, on February 6, 1867. The following extract is taken from it:—

> Personally came and appeared Madam Mary E. Robert, wife of Edwin Epps and by him authorized, both residents of Avoyelles parish, who declared etc. . . . she has bargained sold etc. . . . to Alexander M. Haas her undivided interest in the property belonging to the estate of Joseph J. Robert and Rosella his wife, her parents, situated in the village of Cheneyville, etc.

The probate court records at Marksville, La., Book E, 1866 and 1869, show that on March 3, 1867, Mary Elvina Robert was appointed Natural Tutrix to her children:—minors Edwin, Robert D., Virginia A., Mary C., William, and Henry G. Epps. The same records show she died a short while after her husband's death. We regret we have been unable to contact any of the above children or their descendants. The above Edwin Epps is one of the principal characters in the book, "Twelve Years A Slave", by Solomon Northrup, written in 1854.

It would appear quite evident from the data given above that Joseph J. Robert and his wife, Rosella Ann Robert, had at least six or seven children.

An old copy of THE LOUISIANA DEMOCRAT of the date of Wednesday, January 4, 1860, contained the following item:—

Succession sale, Wednesday, January 11, 1860. Estate of Rosella A. Robert.
J. J. Robert, Administrator.

We know definitely from this succession sale that the wife of Joseph J. Robert died before January 11, 1860, and from this and data on the preceding page it would seem that he outlived her several years.

6.—Wilson Cook Robert, eldest child of Grimball Robert and his second wife, Eliza Tuzette (Cook-Tanner) Robert, was born in St. Peter's Parish, Beaufort District, South Carolina, about 1807. He came to Louisiana with his parents when a small boy and was reared on Bayou Boeuf, near Cheneyville in Rapides parish. Towards middle life he moved to the adjoining parish of Avoyelles and there occupied himself with his profession which was that of a civil engineer. In 1854 we find him recorded as a "Deputy United States Surveyor" in Avoyelles parish. We regret that our knowledge of him is so sparse. The most definite information we have of him in his later life comes to us from his will which is recorded in the court house at Marksville, La., in Will Book "B", page 539. In it he makes the following very unusual bequest:—

I give and bequeath unto my disobedient and cruel wife, Sarah Caroline Robert, a certain parcel of land, etc.

He also bequeaths property to his daughter, Sarah Estelle Robert, and to two aunts, Rebecca E. Verstile and Nancy Johnson. The probate records show that after his death his wife was appointed natural tutrix for his minor daughter, Sarah Estelle Robert. The records in Avoyelles parish show nothing further of this daughter or whether she ever married, so it is not unlikely that she died young. This is the view entertained by the family in that vicinity. The two aunts mentioned in his will were his mother's sisters, daughters of Wilson Cook and Judith O'Bannon. In regard to one he has this to say :—

> I give unto my beloved Aunt Rebecca E. Verstile who in my lonely orphan state proved to me a kind friend and Foster Mother.

In the probate proceedings of the above succession of Wilson C. Robert we find Peter Tanner (his first cousin) making an affidavit that "he saw Wilson C. Robert dead and that he knew that he had been buried." He further stated that he died *about* June 9, 1862. Mr. C. A. Riddle of Marksville in writing to the compiler of these records states, "I have been rather reliably informed that Wilson C. Robert was found dead in a field near Evergreen, La., and that probably accounts for Peter Tanner stating in his affidavit that he died on or about the date he gives, showing that he was not sure of the exact date of death."

10.—Grimball Addison Robert, youngest child of Grimball Robert and his second wife, Eliza Tuzette (Cook-Tanner) Robert, was born December 27, 1812, very probably near Cheneyville, Rapides parish, La., and died in Avoyelles parish, La., on December 30, 1854. This latter date is substantiated by his family Bible which tells us that "Grimball A. Robert departed this life December 30, 1854, forty-two (42) years of age." We find the following record of a family meeting held in Rapides parish, La., to emancipate him :—

> We the members of a Family Meeting appointed by the Probate Court for deliberating on the application of Grimball Addison Robert for Emancipation do solemnly swear in the presence of Almighty God that we will decide agreeable to the best of our knowledge and belief on the said application.
>
> Joseph J. Robert   Joseph Robert
> Peter R. Eldred   Hadley P. Robert
> L. A. Robert
>   Sworn to before me,
>   W. B. Pearce, Notary Public.

A Family Meeting of five of the relatives of Grimball Addison Robert.

At a Family Meeting of five of the relatives of Grimball Addison Robert, minor, appointed by the Probate Court they mutually agree that it will be to the interest and advantage of the said Grimball Addison Robert, minor, to be Emancipated, believing him to be capable of managing his own property.

State of Louisiana, Parish of Rapides, October 8, 1831.

Witnesses:—

J. G. Pearce
P. W. Robert

Joseph Robert
Joseph J. Robert
Hadley P. Robert
L. A. Robert
Peter R. Eldred

Sworn to before me

W. B. Pearce, Notary Public.

It was a few months before this transaction that Grimball Addison Robert married Lavinia Murphy Hoggatt, the elder daughter of William Hoggatt and Lucy Calliham. His marriage probably precipitated the emancipation proceedings. They went to the home of Rev. George Anderson Irion at Eola, in Avoyelles parish, La., a prominent Baptist minister of that period and were there married by him on December 20, 1830. We find this date recorded in the family Bible. A slab in the Cushman cemetery at Marksville, La., tells us that Lavinia Murphy Hoggatt was born May 13, 1815, and died December 3, 1879. Her death is also recorded in the family Bible of her son as follows:—"Mrs. Lavinia M. Hoggatt, wife of Grimball A. Robert, departed this life December 3, 1879, aged 62 years, 11 months and 24 days. One of the best mothers that lived and Christian, and is at this time an angel in Heaven." Lavinia M. Hoggatt was a grand-daughter of John Calliham and his wife, Lucy May. John Calliham, a son of David Calliham, Sr., and his wife, Elizabeth Calliham, lived for many years in Edgefield county, South Carolina, before coming to Louisiana. His father left Lunenburg county, Va., about 1770 and moved to South Carolina. After the Revolutionary War he (David, Sr.) moved to Washington county, Georgia, where he died about 1790. John took an active part in the American Revolution on the side of the colonists (see page 41, Books U-W, Stub Indents to Revolutionary Claims, by A. S. Salley, Jr.). He died in Rapides parish, La., prior to December 12, 1825. He had two sons, David May and John Calliham, neither of whom married. His three daughters married and left descendants. They were, Joyce Calliham who first married James Howard and second John Havard; Lucy Calliham who married William Hoggatt; Elizabeth Susan Calliham who married Leroy Stafford and was the mother of General Leroy Augustus Stafford who was killed at the battle of the Wilderness during the Civil War.

Grimball Addison Robert and Lavinia Murphy Hoggatt appear to have lived in Rapides parish most of their lives. We have in our possession a notarial transaction bearing date of October 2, 1854, showing they were residing there at that date. The following extract from it reads:—

Grimball Addison Robert of the parish of Rapides, State of Louisiana, and his wife, Lavinia M. Hoggatt, sell to William M. Glenn now on the way to the State of Texas, a certain negro man named William, aged about 21 years, for the sum of $775.00, etc.

Grimball Addison Robert died three months after the date of the above transaction and was buried in Marksville, in the adjoining parish of Avoyelles. His son was living there at the time and he either died at the home of that son or was brought there for burial. He and his wife had one son, Berlin Addison Robert, who was their only child.

Berlin Addison Robert, only child of Grimball Addison Robert and Lavinia Murphy Hoggatt, was born on Bayou Boeuf, in Rapides parish, La., on September 24, 1833. In the old records of Rapides parish there has been an error in recording his name. That given above is undoubtedly as it should be. When he was quite an infant his father made two purchases of slaves in his name and it was in these deeds that his name was incorrectly stated. As a matter of record we will here insert a copy of one of those deeds:—

Before me W. B. Pearce, Notary Public in and for the Parish of Rapides, State of Louisiana, and the undersigned witnesses came in person Hadley P. Robert inhabitant of the aforesaid State and Parish who acknowledged that for the consideration of $1,600.00 in hand paid, the receipt of which is hereby acknowledged, to have bargained sold transferred and delivered unto AUSTIN BERLIN ROBERT, the minor son of G. A. Robert, three certain slaves towit, man Henry aged 21 years, woman Sally aged 20 years and her child Julia aged 4 years, slaves for life, to have and to hold the above slaves to him the said A. B. Robert his heirs and assigns forever against the claims of himself his heirs or those claiming by from or under him and against the claims of all persons whatsoever.

In testimony whereof the said H. P. Robert and G. A. Robert here present and accepting hereto subscribe their names before me the said Notary and witnesses, 21st November, 1834.

Witnesses:—

Wm. Hetherwick	Hadley P. Robert
Winder Crouch	G. A. Robert

Done before me
W. B. Pearce, Notary Public.

Berlin Addison Robert settled in Avoyelles parish, Louisiana, near the town of Marksville, on his plantation which he named "Fig Grove," and there he lived the greater part of his life. His wife was Mary Virginia Peyton who was born in Barnwell county, South Carolina, August 8, 1836. She was a daughter of William H. and Frances C. Peyton of that place. Mr. Robert met her while visiting his relatives in South Carolina and after the wedding remained there until their first child was born and then returned to Louisiana. Their marriage is recorded in the family Bible as follows:—

Berlin A. Robert and Mary V. Peyton (daughter of Wm. H. and Frances C. Peyton) were married on the evening of the 21st day of October, 1852, by the Rev. W. S. Johnson, Baptist Preacher, at Boiling Spring, Barnwell County, South Carolina.

Berlin Addison Robert died at his home near Marksville, Avoyelles parish, La., in 1913. The family Bible gives the following record of his wife's death:—

Mary V. Peyton, wife of B. A. Robert, departed this life on the 8th day of March, 1897.

Berlin Addison Robert and Mary Virginia Peyton had eight children:—

1.—Lucy Frances Robert.
2.—Helen Lurenia Robert.
3.—Elizabeth Linnie Robert.

4.—William Hoggatt Robert.
5.—James Addison Robert.
6.—Maccie Haas Robert.
7.—Jennings O'Bannon Robert.
8.—Carrie A. Robert.

1.—Lucy Frances Robert was born at Boiling Spring, Barnwell county, S. C., on August 10, 1853. She was married to Glenn Clarence Riddle at Marksville, La., on November 8, 1871. According to the story handed down in the family their marriage was tinted with quite a bit of romantic glamour. It seems that Berlin Addison Robert once took his eldest daughter, Lucy Frances, with him on a visit to relatives in South Carolina. On the return trip they met a young man from North Carolina who was on his way to Texas where he intended to locate. Mr. Robert gave him such a glowing account of Louisiana and its wonderful possibilities that the young man became quite interested and before the journey was over he was invited to stop in Louisiana and see something of the country. He readily accepted and was so pleased with what he saw that he spent a year with Mr. Robert on his plantation. In the meantime something besides the landscape and the fertility of the soil attracted him. He fell in love with Lucy Frances and they were eventually married. This young man was Glenn Clarence Riddle who was born in Salisbury, North Carolina, in 1849. The family Bible records tell us the following about the marriage:—

> Glenn C. Riddle and Lucy Frances Robert, daughter of Berlin A. Robert and Mary V. Robert, were married on the evening of the 8th of November, 1871, by Rev. John O'Quin at Marksville, Louisiana.

Mr. Riddle died in Marksville, La., on December 15, 1903 and his wife on August 8, 1935. They had eight children:—

a.—Flora Emma Riddle.
b.—Mary Ann Riddle.
c.—James Clarence Riddle.
d.—Charles Addison Riddle.
e.—Daniel Murphy Riddle.
f.—Virginia Etna Riddle.
g.—Alvis Robert Riddle.
h.—Clifton William Riddle.

a.—Flora Emma Riddle was born at Marksville, La., on February 16, 1873. She was married to Benjamin Franklin Voinche and they have had nine children:—

> az.—Wilber Voinche married Lilly Saucier and has one son, Merville Adrian Voinche, born in Marksville about 1916.
>
> bz.—Jimmy Voinche was never married. He was killed in 1917 during the 1st World War.
>
> cz.—Valley Voinche married but has no children.
>
> dz.—Frances Voinche married K. E. Chaze and has one son, Rene.
>
> ez.—Frank Voinche married Hazel Edwards and has four children:—Martha Benita, Mary Frances, William Frank, Patricia Jane.
>
> fz.—Myrtle Voinche married Moore Normand. No issue.
>
> gz.—Willie Benita Voinche married Sterling Herman. No issue.
>
> hz.—Flora Voinche married Robert Nelson and has one daughter, Susie.
>
> iz.—Benjamin Franklin Voinche, Jr., married Lena Landina and has two daughters, Anne and ———.

b.—Mary Ann Riddle was born in Marksville, La., on February 9, 1874, and was married there on February 18, 1891, to Robert Miller Guillot who died on February 28, 1933. Mrs. Guillot is living at this date (1944). They had seven children:—

> az.—Addie Annie Guillot was born in Marksville, La., on October 24, 1892. She was married on March 23, 1914, to Robert Ashton Holloway of Bunkie, La. He died in Monroe, La., on November 28, 1942. They had one son, Robert Ashton Holloway, Jr., born April 29, 1916, and married June 29, 1938, Polly Anna Shotwell of Monroe, and they have a daughter, Susan, born January 31, 1943.
>
> bz.—Clarence Miller Guillot was born in Marksville, La., on May 10, 1894. He married Ruth Linsey of Neadland, Alabama, on February 25, 1921. They have one son, Robert Miller Guillot, II, born January 2, 1922, who is now in the military service of his country and is presently stationed at Marietta, Georgia.
>
> cz.—Daniel Herbert Guillot was born in Marksville, La., on May 31, 1896, and married Pearle Brown of Alexandria, La., on October 22, 1921. They now reside

in New Orleans and have one daughter, Doris Ann, born November 21, 1935.

dz.—Louis Creath Guillot was born in Marksville, La., on July 14, 1898. He married Esther Self of Robeline, La., on July 10, 1921. They have had two children: Louis Creath, Jr., born March 31, 1925, and died April 8, 1925; Thomas Edward, born August 24, 1926.

ez.—Vera Etna Guillot was born in Marksville, La., on April 14, 1901, and was married to Harvey Charles George of that town on March 31, 1923. They now reside in Bunkie, La., and have one daughter, Geraldine Gladys, who was born March 22, 1924, and was married to Clyde R. Spears on June 14, 1943.

fz.—Max Alveber Guillot was born in Marksville, La., on May 20, 1903. He married Hersilie Smith of Meridian, Miss., on October 27, 1928, and they have two sons:—Max Alveber, Jr., born July 24, 1929, and Robert Creath, born August 28, 1933.

gz.—Iola Rena Guillot was born in Marksville, La., on June 30, 1906. She was married on August 14, 1923, to Lemoine Moise Couvillion of Cottonport, La. They now reside in Bunkie, La., and have two sons:— Ralph Lemoine, born July 9, 1926, and Herbert Harvey, born November 8, 1932.

c.—James Clarence Riddle was born at Marksville, La., in 1876, and died when quite young.

d.—Charles Addison Riddle was born at Marksville, La., on May 1, 1879. He is a prominent attorney in the place of his nativity and for several years represented his parish in the State Legislature. He married on Friday, June 13, 1913, at Ruston, La., Margaret Robinson who was born in Claiborne parish, La., October 9, 1890. In speaking of the date of her marriage Mrs. Riddle says:—"We were not afraid of Friday or the 13th either." Her parents were Benjamin Franklin Robinson of Claiborne parish and Indiana Sowell of Henry county, Alabama. Mr. and Mrs. Riddle have three children:—

az.—Margaret Thelma Riddle, born March 29, 1914, at Marksville, La., was married in Washington, D. C., on February 25, 1937, to Glenn Foster Hardin of Greenwood, Miss., who was a famous athlete at the Louisiana State University a decade ago and familiarly known as "Slats" Hardin. He won the 400 meter hurdles in the Olympic games held in California in 1932, and again he won the same in 1936 at Berlin. His records still hold. He was recently inducted into the U. S. Navy. He and his wife have two sons:— Glenn Charles Hardin, born in New Orleans on March 5, 1938, and William Foster Hardin, born in Shreveport on January 13, 1942.

bz.—Audrey Inez Riddle was born June 2, 1915, at Marksville, La., and was married at New Roads, La., on August 31, 1935, to Mike John, Jr., of Monroe, La., who is now a 1st Lieutenant in anti-aircraft artillery, U. S. Army, and stationed at Camp Hulen, Texas. They have two daughters:—Gwendolyn Hope John, born in Monroe, La., on December 20, 1938, and Audrey Gail John, born in Monroe, La., on January 22, 1943.

cz.—Charles Addison Riddle, Jr., was born July 19, 1917, and has been associated with his father in the practice of law under the name of RIDDLE AND RIDDLE at Marksville, La. He married Alma Rita Gremillion of Marksville on December 18, 1943, at Norfolk, Virginia. He is at present a Lieutenant (J.G.) in the U. S. Naval Reserve.

e.—Daniel Murphy Riddle was born at Marksville, La., on September 25, 1881. He received his education at the Marksville High School and the Chamberlain-Hunt Academy at Port Gibson, Miss. He is principally engaged in the lumber business. He married Cora Elmatine Saucier at Marksville on January 18, 1910, a daughter of Fremont Henry Saucier and Rachel Rebecca Lanius, who was born at New Era, Concordia parish, La., on February 22, 1888. She was educated at the Southern Female College at West Point, Miss. Mr. and Mrs. Riddle have had four children:—

az.—Daniel Murphy, Jr., was born at Marksville, La., on September 12, 1910. He attended the Marksville High School and Asbury College at Wilmore, Kentucky, and received a B. A. degree from Louisiana College at Pineville, La., and his Master's from Louisiana State University. While serving as Secretary to Congressman Leonard Allen he studied law at George Washington University. He is unmarried at this time and is a Major in the U. S. Army, being presently in Germany in the Intelligence Service.

bz.—Arville Elwood Riddle was born in Marksville, La., on November 9, 1913. She was married on September 9, 1938, in Pineville, La., to Daunton Woodrow Kees who was born September 9, 1912, at Verda, La. They now reside in Marksville and have two children:—Madeline Helaine Kees, born in Natchez, Miss., on March 20, 1942, and Daunton Woodrow Kees, II, born in Alexandria, La., on November 29, 1943.

cz.—Beverly Fae Riddle was born in Marksville, La., on December 14, 1920. She is unmarried at this time and is now employed at the Recruiting and Induction Station at Fort Humbug, near Shreveport, La.

dz.—Glenn Clarence Riddle, II, was born in Marksville, La., on December 25, 1922, and died there in March, 1923.

f.—Virginia Etna Riddle was born in Marksville, La., on October 22, 1885, and died at her home there on Monday, April 10, 1944, at 7 p. m. She was married in Marksville in 1903 to Henry E. de Nux, son of Dr. Emeric de Nux of Auch, France, where he was born in 1842, and his wife, Annette Derivas, native of Louisiana. Dr. de Nux came to Avoyelles parish about 1870 and practiced his profession there until his death. He was a son of Emeric de Nux and Berthe Gardere. Henry de Nux is yet living. He and his wife had five children:—

az.—Alton Rine de Nux, successful member of the dental profession, mayor of his native town of Marksville, member of the Avoyelles parish school board, and now a member of the state legislature, married Esther Martin of New Orleans and they have two daughters:—Wanda Lee and Connie de Nux.

bz.—Virginia de Nux married Richard Ewing of Abbeville, La. They have one daughter, Jacqueline Lucy Ewing.

cz.—Gertrude Constance de Nux married Pias P. McNeely of St. Francisville, La. They now reside in Marksville and have three children:—Patricia Ann, Pias P., Jr., and Gertrude Constance McNeely.

dz.—Henry de Nux, Jr., better known as "Billy," now resides in Marksville and married Juliette Barbin of that town. They have two daughters:—Glenda and Sandra de Nux.

ez.—Glenn Clarence de Nux, generally called "Pete," is unmarried at this time and is serving in the armed forces of his country, being presently stationed at Fort Benning, Ga.

g.—Alvis Robert Riddle was born in Marksville, La., where he still lives. His birth occurred on March 6, 1888. He is yet unmarried.

h.—Clifton William Riddle was born in Marksville, La., on July 17, 1893. He still lives there and is unmarried.

2.—Helen Lurenia Robert, second child of Berlin Addison Robert and Mary Virginia Peyton, was born near Cheneyville, Rapides parish, La., on June 5, 1853. She was married on February 24, 1875, to Gilderoy H. Griffin by Judge Louis J. Ducote. The ceremony was performed at "Fig Grove," the home of her parents near Marksville, La. They had no children.

3.—Elizabeth Linnie Robert, third child of Berlin Addison Robert and Mary Virginia Peyton, was born near Marksville, Avoyelles parish, La., on May 4, 1861. She was married at "Fig Grove" on March 4, 1878, to Washington Page White. They had no children.

4.—William Hoggatt Robert, fourth child of Berlin Addison Robert and Mary Virginia Peyton, was born at "Fig Grove," near Marksville, Avoyelles parish, about 1864. He married Lilly Lemoine but as far as we know they had no children.

5.—James Addison Robert, fifth child of Berlin Addison Robert and Mary Virginia Peyton, was born at "Fig Grove," near Marksville, Avoyelles parish, La., on November 10, 1866. He appears to have been three times married but we only have a record of two of his wives. The family Bible shows that he married Maggie Victory on November 17, ——, at Leggett, Polk county, Texas. Then on June 8, 1927, we know that he married Velma Lee Harris. He is now dead. When last heard from in this life he was living at Aransas Pass, Texas. As far as we know he left no descendants.

6.—Maccie Haas Robert, sixth child of Berlin Addison Robert and Mary Virginia Peyton, was born at "Fig Grove," near Marksville, Avoyelles parish, La., on July 29, 1870. She was twice married, 1st to Abraham Frederick Kimball, and

2nd, to Richard Jennings Johnson. She had no children by either marriage.

7.—Jennings O'Bannon Robert, seventh child of Berlin Addison Robert and Mary Virginia Peyton, was born at "Fig Grove," near Marksville, Avoyelles parish, La., on March 5, 1879. He married at Pittsburg, Texas, on December 24, 1901, Iva Lightfoot of that place. She was born there April 16, 1888. They had ten children, some of whom are now living at Aransas Pass, Texas. Their children were:—

  a.—Morris Berlin Robert, born at Pittsburg Texas, March 7, 1903, married Annie Burroughs of Sidney, Australia. They now live in San Diego, California.

  b.—Earl Ward Robert, born at Pittsburg, Texas, on December 7, 1904, married Cortez Pearson at Linden, Texas, on December 3, 1923. They now reside at El Dorado, Arkansas.

  c.—Jennings Creston Robert was born a Haynesville, La., on March 12, 1907.

  d.—Crystelle Robert was born at Haynesville, La., on February 3, 1909.

  e.—Ollimoe Robert was born at Haynesville, La., on April 29, 1911.

  f.—Jewel Lightfoot Robert was born at Haynesville, La., on February 17, 1913.

  g.—Mary Virginia Robert was born at Haynesville, La., on August 6, 1915.

  h.—Charles O'Bannon Robert was born at Haynesville, La., on November 7, 1917.

  i.—Harold Dennis Robert was born at Haynesville, La., on December 5, 1920.

  j.—Dorothy Robert was born at Haynesville, La., on August 6, 1923.

8.—Carrie A. Robert, eighth child of Berlin Addison Robert and Mary Virginia Peyton, was born at "Fig Grove," near Marksville, Avoyelles parish, La., on December 14, 1880. She was married on December 28, 1903, to David Levi Goodman. They lived at Corsicana, Texas. Both are now dead, leaving no children.

*   *   *   *

C.

PETER ROBERT

Peter Robert, third son of Captain Peter Robert and Anne Grimball, was born in French Santee, South Carolina, about 1768. His family later moved to St. Peter's Parish, in Beaufort District of the same State, and it was probably there that he married. His wife was Elizabeth Jaudon, daughter of Elias Jaudon, Jr., and Mary Dixon (sometimes spelled *Dixson* and *Dickson*). The family tradition is that Elias Jaudon, Jr., was a captain in the Revolutionary Army. Whether he held that rank or not we are unable to prove by any official records. But irrespective of rank we do know that he served in that war of independence. A. S. Salley in Stub Entries to Indents for Revolutionary Claims, Books U-W, page 113 shows that a warrant was issued "July 22, 1785, to Elias Jaudon for twenty pounds for a horse lost in militia service." Mrs. McCall in her book, McCall-Tidwell and Allied Families, page 583, tells us that Elias Jaudon who married Elizabeth Robert was a "Revolutionary soldier." She has mistaken the father for the son. It was Elias Jaudon, Jr., who was a soldier. His parents were Elias Jaudon and Elizabeth Robert but his father was more than sixty years of age at the beginning of the Revolution.

Mary Hyrne Dixon, mother of Elizabeth Jaudon, was a daughter of Elizabeth Smith and Captain Thomas Dixon, and a grand-daughter of the Second Landgrave Thomas Smith who was the elder son of the First Landgrave Thomas Smith. The records show that the First Landgrave was born in Exeter, England, in 1648, and came to South Carolina in 1684. His son, the Second Landgrave, was born in Exeter in 1668. The elder Smith received in 1691 a patent of four baronies of land consisting of 48,000 acres and in consequence of such large holdings he was created a Landgrave. He was an important man in the colony and was commissioned governor on November 29, 1693. He died the following year and left two sons, Thomas Smith, Jr., and George Smith. The younger became one of the noted physicians of his day and left three children from whom many descendants are to be found in various parts of the country. The elder son, Thomas Smith, Jr., succeeded his father to the title of Landgrave, was twice married, and left innumerable descendants.

We have no record of the date of marriage of Peter Robert and Elizabeth Jaudon. Since she was born November 13, 1774, it is probable that the marriage took place about 1790. Soon after the dawn of the 19th century, about 1804, Peter Robert and his family went to Wilkinson county, Mississippi, in that great emigrant train of the Robert and Grimball families. It now appears certain that he did not move a decade later to central Louisiana when so many of his relatives located there. We are inclined to believe, however, that he lived for a while in the southern part of the State in the latter years of his life where his daughter, Elizabeth, resided. Among the old records of Wilkinson county, Mississippi, in the court house at Woodville, we find the following certificate signed by him:—

> This is to certify that I have no objection to a union between Mr. Peter Robert and my daughter, Elizabeth Robert.
> July 1, 1809.   Peter Robert.

This Peter Robert whom he mentions in the certificate was his nephew, Peter William Robert, who was the eldest son of his brother, Grimball Robert. A full account of this couple and their descendants will be found in previous pages of this work.

Among the same old records of Woodville, in Book I, pages 168-70, we find another document which tells us something of Peter Robert and his brother, Joseph Robert. It reads as follows:—

> Know all men by these presents that we, Peter Robert and Joseph Robert, of the Territory of Mississippi and county of Wilkinson, planters, for divers considerations and good causes we hereunto moving, have made, ordained, constituted, and appointed, and by these presents do make, ordain, constitute, and appoint our trusty friend Grimball Robert, of the State of South Carolina, in the District of Beaufort, St. Peter's Parish, planter, our true and lawful attorney for us in our names and to our use, to ask, demand, recover, or rescue of and from Elias G. Jaudon, Thomas D. Jaudon, and James B. Jaudon of Beaufort District of South Carolina, Executors to the last will and testament of Elias Jaudon, deceased, our full share and portion, agreeably to the said will of our father-in-law, Elias

Jaudon, which he bequeathed to his daughters, Elizabeth Robert and Mary Hyrne Robert, the former being the lawful wife of Peter Robert, and Mary Hyrne the lawful wife of Joseph Robert.

Given and by these presents granting to our said attorney our sole and full power and authority to take, pursue, and follow such legal courses for the recovery, receiving, and obtaining of the same as we ourselves might or could do were we personally present, and upon the receipt of the same appurtenances and other sufficient discharges for us and in our names, to make, sign, seal and deliver as also, one or more attorney or attorneys under him to substitute or appoint, and again at his pleasure to revoke and further to do, perform, and execute for us and in our names all and singular thing or things which are or may be necessary touching and concerning the premises as fully, thoroughly and entirely as we the said Peter Robert and Joseph Robert, in our own person ought or could do in and about the same. Ratifying, allowing, and confirming whatsoever our said attorney shall lawfully do or cause to be done in and about the execution of the premises, by virtue of these presents.

In witness whereof we have hereunto set our hands and seals the first day of July in the year of our Lord 1810, and in the 34th year of the Independence of the United States of America.

Signed, sealed, delivered in the presence of us,

Robert Tanner	Peter Robert
Robert J. Chisolm	J. L. Robert.

We have no record of the dates of death of Peter Robert and his wife. He evidently survived her and was living as late as 1821. On April 1st of that year his son-in-law, Peter William Robert, who was living on Bayou Salé, in St. Mary's parish, La., records the date of birth of his son, Edmund Grimball Robert, and makes the following comment in his record book:—"This child was named by his grandfather Peter Robert." This certainly means that Peter Robert was living at that time and it is not unlikely that his wife was dead and that he was residing with his daughter in St. Mary's parish. This daughter, Elizabeth Jaudon Robert, is the only child of Peter Robert of whom we have any definite knowledge. She married Peter William Robert and a full account of her is to be found in his family record on page 52 in this book. It seems fairly certain that Peter Robert and Elizabeth Jaudon had at least one son, Peter Hedekiah Robert. He was evidently a minor when his father died as we find in the record book of Peter William Robert the following item dated 1824:—

> Memoriam of P. H. Robert's property delivered him when he came of age, I having been his guardian.

Then follows a list of the property and the value of same. Among the various items we find the following which seems pertinent in identifying this son:—

> 24 arpents front of land, titles to be made to him hereafter, the purchase being made for him but wait his being of age to take title—the land in part he bought of his father and part of B. C. Robert, and gave them his notes for payment tho' not of age, and his note came in his inheritance of P. R. estate.

The *P. R.* above stands for *Peter Robert* who was undoubtedly his father as is definitely indicated by the fact that he inherited the note he had given his father when purchasing land from him while still a minor. In the Rapides parish notarial records we find further reference to this Peter Hedekiah Robert. On May 24, 1830, an appraisement was made of the property of Joseph Robert and in the proceedings we find the following item:—

> Amount of sales of thirteen negroes sold to Peter Hedekiah Robert of the parish of St. Mary's and State aforesaid. Price $7,612.50.

In an old graveyard on Bayou Salé, St. Mary's parish, we find two tombstones and the inscription on one reads:—

> Louisa Armstrong
> Consort of Peter H. Robert.
> Died March, 1832.

The inscription on the other reads:—

> Louesar Robert, daughter of
> Peter H. and Louisa Robert
> Who died May 9, 1833,
> Age 2 yrs. 1 mo. 26 days.

Whether Peter Hedekiah Robert married again or whether he left any descendants we are unable to say.

*   *   *   *

D.

JOSEPH ROBERT.

Joseph Robert, fourth son of Captain Peter Robert and Anne Grimball, was born in French Santee, South Carolina, about 1770. In the power-of-attorney inserted on a previous page which he executed with his brother Peter Robert, he signs his name *J. L. Robert.* It is quite likely that his middle name was *Leonidas.* One of his sons bore that name and it has been handed down through his progeny to the present generation. But that was the only instance among the many legal documents which he signed in which his name is not simply given as *Joseph Robert.* He married about 1798 Mary Hyrne Jaudon, daughter of Elias Jaudon, Jr., and Mary Hyrne Dixon. She was born in St. Peter's Parish, Beaufort District, South Carolina, on April 27, 1781, and was a younger sister of Elizabeth Jaudon who married his brother, Peter Robert, and a direct descendant of the Landgrave Thomas Smith who was one of the colonial Governors of South Carolina.

Joseph Robert and his wife left South Carolina about 1804 and came to Wilkinson county, Mississippi, settling on Bayou Sarah near Woodville. At that time they had three children. The location of their home is indicated in the following document:—

STATE OF LOUISIANA,
PARISH OF RAPIDES.

Personally appeared before the undersigned Notary Public in and for the Parish and State aforesaid Mary H. Robert of said Parish who acknowledged on an examination separate and apart from her said husband, that she did freely without fear, threats or compulsion of her said husband, relinquish and forever quit claim unto Prestwood Smith of the county of Wilkinson, State of Mississippi, his heirs and assigns forever, all of her right of dower in premises conveyed by her husband to the said Smith on the third day of December, 1817, by deed bearing date at that time, which said premises or tract of land is known and distinguished as follows:—Situated in the county of Wilkinson, State last aforesaid, on the waters of Bayou Sarah, beginning at a beach tree the south corner of the Bayou Sarah Meeting House lot, thence to the Bayou

Sarah Creek cornering on a stake in said Creek, from thence the Creek the line to the south corner three stakes in the Creek, thence west to Mather's line, thence on Mather's line and Morris' line to the meeting house road cornering on the black gum on the side of the said road, from here the road is the line to the commencement, containing 185 acres, more or less, the graveyard containing three fourths of an acre is excepted in the above grant.

Taken, signed, sealed and acknowledged before me this 2nd day of October, 1826.

Mary H. Robert.

Witnesses:—

  B. Q. Rigg
  Robert Cade.

Done before me
Silas Talbert, Notary Public.

The above transaction tells us that Joseph Robert sold his property in Mississippi in 1817. It was then that he came to Louisiana and settled on Bayou Boeuf in Rapides parish near the present town of Cheneyville. The earliest official record we have of him there is in a deed dated February 23, 1819, when he bought land on Bayou Boeuf from Stephen Jackson, which land the said Jackson had purchased from Walter Turnbull, attorney-in-fact for John Towles. We find frequent mention of him in the notarial records of Bayou Boeuf in the early days of that community. He was present December 12, 1827, when a "Family Meeting" was held in behalf of his minor children. On May 10, 1828, he bought a tract of 31½ acres of land on Bayou Boeuf from Joseph Tanner, which tract was "taken from the section of land purchased by Grimball Robert from John Stafford." On May 11, 1828, he bought 160 acres of land from Joseph J. Robert for $3,000.00 cash. On August 1, 1829, he sold a lot in Cheneyville to Martin Gibbons. On February 19, 1830, he bought a lot in Cheneyville from R. L. Taliaferro. On May 28, 1830, he was appointed one of the appraisers of the estate of David Bettison, deceased, his brother-in-law. On August 10, 1830, he sells slaves to Joseph J. Robert (his nephew and son-in-law). On October 8, 1831, he took part in a "Family Meeting" for the emancipation of Grimball Addison Robert, minor. On May 24, 1830, an appraisement of his holdings was made by Robert Tanner and

Stephen Pearce. The object of this was probably to make a settlement with his children as he was about to marry again. The transaction is of sufficient interest to our story to be recorded here in full:—

An Inventory and Appraisement of the goods and effects, rights and credits of Joseph Robert by Robert Tanner and Stephen Pearce, appraisers, before Silas Talbert, Notary Public in and for the parish of Rapides, State of Louisiana, this 24th day of May, 1830.

No. 1—Two adjoining tracts of land situate on the right bank of Bayou Boeuf in descending: one bought of Joseph J. Robert containing 160 acres, more or less; the other bought of Joseph Tanner containing 31½ acres, adjoining vacant lands below, and lands of Grimball Addison Robert above. Appraised at $3,000.00.

No. 2—An undivided portion $4,530.26½, that remains between said Joseph Robert and his children of the succession of his late wife, Mary H. Robert, deceased.

No. 3—One negro woman Silvia..............$600.00
No. 4—Negro man George 650.00
No. 5—Negro man Jacob 700.00
No. 6—Negro man Tom 750.00
No. 7—Negro boy Martin.......................... 450.00
No. 8—Amount of sales of thirteen negroes sold to Peter Hedekiah Robert of the parish of St. Mary and State aforesaid $7,612.50

As will show by a title given to the said P. H. Robert.

We the appraisers of the foregoing property after being qualified according to law have appraised it as it stands stated, this 24th May, 1830.

Robert Tanner
Stephen Pearce.

Witnesses:—
Isaac Lambright
William Henderson.
Done before me
Silas Talbert, Notary Public.

Joseph Robert's wife died prior to December 12, 1827, as on that date there was held a "Family Meeting of five of the friends and relations of Joseph Robert and his late wife, Mary H. Robert." Those composing it were:—Joseph J. Robert, Joseph B. Robert, L. A. Robert, Mary A. Robert and Tuzette Robert. Joseph J. Robert was his nephew and son-in-law, and was appointed under Tutor to the minor children. Joseph B. Robert was his eldest son, and L. A. Robert was his third son. Mary A. Robert was very probably the wife of Joseph B. Robert, and we know that Tuzette Robert was the wife of L. A. Robert. Joseph Robert died sometime between November 26, 1833, and May 1, 1837. On the first of these dates he signed a note with P. W. Robert (his second son) and Leroy Stafford, and on the latter date the note was protested. In the protest proceedings it was set forth that Joseph Robert and Leroy Stafford were dead at the time. Sometime during 1830 Joseph Robert married his second wife. She was Elizabeth Thomas, daughter of James Thomas and Elizabeth Calliham. She was born about 1790 and first married David Glover by whom she had at least one child, Mary Glover. She married again after Mr. Glover's death but we have been unable to ascertain the name of the gentleman she chose at that time. She then married Robert H. Marshall, and finally Joseph Robert. There do not appear to have been any children except by the first marriage.

Joseph Robert and his first wife, Mary Hyrne Jaudon, had at least seven children—there may have been more. Those we have a record of were:—

1.—Joseph B. Robert.
2.—Polhill Ware Robert.
3.—Leonidas Alonzo Robert.
4.—Rosella Ann Robert.
5.—Jane S. Robert.
6.—James Bordeaux Jaudon Robert.
7.—Thaddeus Sobieski Robert.

1.—Joseph B. Robert, eldest son of Joseph Robert and Mary Hyrne Jaudon, was born in St. Peter's Parish, Beaufort District, South Carolina, about 1799. His name is frequently found in the records of the business transactions of the Cheneyville section of Rapides parish where he came with his parents when a boy of eighteen. We find him recorded as one of those taking part in a "Family Meeting" held December 12, 1827, soon after his mother's death. On October 21, 1830, he buys a slave from Richard H. Allen of Giles county, Tennessee, for $400.00. On November 28, 1832, we find a record where "Evolina Griffin, alias Eldred, sells slaves to Joseph B. Robert, by and with the consent of her husband, Peter Robert Eldred, her interest as one of the heirs of the late James and Elizabeth Griffin." This lady's husband was a first cousin of Joseph B. Robert. On April 24, 1833, "Joel Coe of the Parish of St. Mary sells slaves to Joseph B. Robert." This Joel Coe may have been the husband of Jane S. Robert, one of Joseph B. Robert's sisters. She first married a Coe and then a Myers. We are not certain of the identity of Joseph B. Robert's wife, but she appears to have been the "Mary A. Robert" mentioned in the family meeting referred to above. We learn something of Joseph B. Robert from letters written by his youngest brother, Thaddeus Sobieski Robert, who went to California in 1849 where he lived the remainder of his life. We are fortunate in having obtained from the daughter of the latter who is yet living there some of his letters to his brother-in-law Frank Myers. The following quotation is from one written March 7, 1857:—

I received a letter yesterday from *Brother Joseph B.* He is in New London, Arkansas, and is in good health. He requested especially to be remembered to you and wants to know your office that he may write to you. You will answer me soon that I may let him know, or write him yourself. I was really glad to receive his letter. He went to Tennessee last fall to see his daughter Sarah who went there on a visit in company with Rosella Ann, and Rose while there married a dentist, and it seems he is a worthless man, a gambler and drunkard, and has ere this left her, thinking when he married her she was rich and, as he said, worth $35,000.00.

The Rosella Ann mentioned in the letter was a sister of the writer of it and had married her cousin, Joseph J. Robert, and the "Rose who married a dentist" was evidently her daughter. In a letter from young Frank Myers to his uncle Thaddeus S. Robert we get a glimpse of the family. He was living with Joseph J. Robert while his father was in California. He writes:—Uncle Joseph and Aunt Rosella, and Cousin Cette and Rose are all very kind to me." This substantiates the opinion we have already expressed that Rose was a daughter of Joseph J. and Rosella Ann Robert. "Cette" was evidently intended for Tuzette Robert, another daughter of the above.

The identity of Joseph B. Robert as a son of Joseph Robert is further established by a petition filed in the Rapides Parish

Court at Alexandria, La., on December 18, 1878. The substance of the petition is as follows:—

Captain Samuel Haas represented by Robert P. Hunter filed a petition in probate No. 327, Rapides parish Court, alleging that Joseph Robert died domiciled in Rapides about 1835; that he was owner at death of a tract of land of about 900 acres, lying partly in St. Landry and partly in Rapides, the larger portion being in Rapides, as was the family domicile; and that he left five heirs, to wit:— Joseph B. Robert, Mrs. Rosella Robert, Bordeaux Robert, Polhill Robert, and Alonzo Robert. That Joseph B. Robert was appointed administrator and succession was in process of administration when the court house was burned in May, 1864. That Joseph B. Robert died about 1870 without taking steps to revive the succession papers and nothing was done since. That petitioner is owner of 2/5 interest by purchase, has paid taxes, that some of his heirs are dead and represented by their heirs, that some of them are absent from Louisiana. . . . . Prays to be appointed administrator.

Appointed February 18, 1879. Qualified February 19, 1879.

A second petition was filed in connection with the above case in 1880 which throws additional light on the subject. It was as follows:—

On February 2, 1880, S. E. Parks* filed a petition stating she was one of the children of Joseph Robert† who died about 1860; that succession papers were burned, that the heirs have been in possession of the property from 1865 to 1879, that Haas was an inter-meddler, and praying that his claim be vacated. (There was no action taken on this petition).

The records show that this property was sold to pay debts on February 13, 1886, and that Haas filed his account on October 31, 1888. But even after the sale of the property there was another petition filed in 1888 which is interesting to us from a genealogical point of view. It was as follows:—

On November 10, 1888, Andrews and Hakenyos filed a petition for Mrs. Sarah E. Robert, femme sole, and

---

* This was Sarah Evolina (Robert) Parks, a daughter of Joseph B. Robert.

† This should have been *Joseph B. Robert*, who was a son of Joseph Robert.

Franklin A. Robert, residents of the parish of Avoyelles, alleging that they are legal heirs of Joseph Robert, inheriting by representation through their deceased father Joseph B. Robert "who recently died in the State of Arkansas;" that Sam Haas has filed an account which they oppose. That Joseph Robert* died about the year 1864 and that he left an estate of $5,000.00 which was duly administered, that the proceedings were destroyed by fire, that the estate was settled as required by law, that the acts of Haas are unwarranted. They pray that his account be rejected.

In the above case judgment was returned June 18, 1889, approving the account of Samuel Haas, administrator. It says in the preamble "the only opposition having been dismissed." How Sarah E. Robert in the above petition got to be "Femme sole" is quite a mystery to us as we know that she was three times married. There is a constant tendency in the above petitions to confuse Joseph Robert and his son Joseph B. Robert. It must be borne in mind that the former died about 1835 and the latter sometime between 1864 and 1870.

Joseph B. Robert left Rapides parish, La., about 1856 and moved to New London, Arkansas. This we learn from the letter we have already quoted from his brother Thaddeus Sobieski Robert. It seems quite certain that he remained there until his death. As far as we can ascertain he and his wife, Mary A. Robert, had but two children:—1.—Sarah Evolina Robert and 2.—Franklin Agrippa Robert. If there were any other children they must have died in infancy as we can find no record of them.

1.—Sarah Evolina Robert, daughter of Joseph B. Robert and his wife, Mary A. Robert, was born in Rapides parish, La., about 1823. She was a "muchly married" lady and according to available records she at least three times "plighted her troth." Her first husband was Joseph Addison Cocke, son of James Cocke and grandson of Joseph Cocke and Winifred Alston of Warren county, North Carolina. They had no children and Mr. Cocke was killed at Marksville, La., a few years after their marriage. We know none of the circumstances of his death. Her second husband was Willie Vernon

---

* This is intended for Joseph B. Robert.

by whom she had one daughter named Willie who married a Mr. Elmer and had one daughter, Maude Elmer. Her third husband was John Parks who must have died before 1888 as she appears to have been a widow at that time. In 1856 she was apparently living in Tennessee as we learn from a letter written in 1857 by her father's youngest brother. In speaking of Joseph B. Robert he says:—"He went to Tennessee last fall to see his daughter Sarah." The last official record we have of her was on November 10, 1888, when she with her brother Franklin A. Robert filed a petition in the District Court of Rapides parish.

2.—Franklin Agrippa Robert, son of Joseph B. Robert and his wife, Mary A. Robert, was born near Cheneyville, Rapides parish, La., in 1824, and died at Evergreen, Avoyelles parish, La., on January 12, 1902. We find his name listed as a student in the catalogue of the Spring Creek Academy for the year 1841. This was quite a noted educational institution in the early days of Rapides parish. It was located in the beautiful pine hills southwest of Cheneyville, on Hurricane Creek, a tributary of Spring Creek. Here in the early period of development of central Louisiana the settlers of Bayou Boeuf moved their famliies in the hot summer months from the lowlands to the higher and cooler pine hills where malaria was not so prevalent. There quite a settlement was formed and in the midst of it the Academy was built. Teachers of exceptional qualifications were procured and the Academy became famous as a high class institution of learning. Among the teachers was Hon. Michael Ryan, a highly educated Irishman who had just come to this country, and who afterwards was a prominent lawyer of Alexandria, La., and a judge of the district court. He was professor of ancient languages. It is said that Judge Ryan had been educated to be a priest before coming to America. Dr. Jesse D. Wright, one of the founders of the institution and a prominent physician and planter on Bayou Boeuf, was an enthusiastic advocate of higher education, being himself a graduate of Yale. He sent to Connecticut, his native State, to procure the services of two of his nieces, the Misses Kelsey, as teachers. The old Academy was long since burned to the ground but the site of it is well known and is still referred to in the neighborhood as "The Academy." After completing his studies in this famous local institution Franklin Agrippa Robert was sent to the University of Ohio. He then returned home and devoted himself to planting. About 1856 he married Ursula Matthews, daughter of M. M. Matthews and Narcile Cappel. Her father was born April 13, 1814, and died August 1, 1896. He was a son of John Matthews of South Carolina and Polly Bretheth of Richmond, Va. We have no record of Mrs. Robert's death but it occurred prior to 1866. She left two children:—

    i.—Willie Robert, born January 26, 1858.
    ii.—Anna Robert, born August 22, 1859.

About 1866 or 1867 Franklin Agrippa Robert married as his second wife, Julia Matthews, widow of John Paul Grimball*. She was a first cousin of Mr. Robert's first wife, being a daughter of Peyton and Adeline Matthews (Peyton and M. M. Matthews were brothers). Mr. Robert had four children by his second marriage:—

    iii.—Edward Bane Robert, born July 31, 1868.
    iv.—Sarah Robert, born May 22, 1871.
    v.—Maude Robert, born ————, 1872.
    vi.—Agnes Robert, born August 8, 1873.

    i.—Willie Robert, son of Franklin Agrippa Robert and his first wife, Ursula Matthews, was born near Evergreen, Avoyelles parish, La. He married Eliska Mary Gremillion who was born April 23, 1862, and died February 13, 1905. They had nine children:—

  (1) Clarence Robert, born 1883, died in infancy.
  (2) Arthur Robert, born 1885, died in infancy.
  (3) Carrie Robert, born August 25, 1887, married Arthur J. Calligari* on June 28, 1911. They had four children:—Bascom Vernon, born October 25, 1920; Janet Mary, born October 29, 1922; Dama Catherine, born December 23, 1923; Myra Eliska, born March 29, 1935.

---

* John Paul Grimball was a son of Paul Jabez Grimball who was a son of John Grimball, Jr., and Mary Robert (daughter of Capt. Peter Robert and Anne Grimball). He died before May 15, 1366, as on that date an inventory of his estate was taken at the instance of "Mrs. Julia

(Footnotes Continued on Next Page)

(4)   Lee Robert, born December 27, 1890, married Keely
       Pratt.   Their children are Velva, Verbie, Idel, W. A.,
       and Gloria Mae.

(5)   Nina Robert died young.

(6)   Anna Robert, born April 10, 1895, married Lemmie
       Ducote.   They have no children.

(7)   Joseph Robert died young.

(8)   Bascom Robert, born July 10, 1898, died unmarried
       on October 25, 1919.

(9)   Edine Robert, born September 25, 1901, married
       Alwin Calligari, brother of her sister Carrie's hus-
       band.   They had one child, Dorothy Dean Calligari,
       born July 26, 1920.

Willie Robert married as his second wife about 1909 Emma
Turner and they had three children:—

(10)   Earl Robert, died young.
(11)   Floyd Robert, born December 8, 1913.
(12)   Sadie Robert, born August 26, 1916.

Willie Robert married as his third wife Esma Guillot.
They have had no children.

ii.—Anna Robert, second child of Franklin Agrippa Robert
and his first wife, Ursula Matthews, was born near Evergreen,
Avoyelles parish, La.   She was married about 1879 to Luigi
Gremillion, a brother of Eliska Mary Gremillion, the first wife
of Willie Robert.   They had ten children:—

(1)   Mildred Gremillion, born October 5, 1881, married
       Bert Logan.   They had two children, Bert and
       Emmett.

(2)   Minnie Gremillion, born May 18, 1883, married
       Willie Thayer.   They had one child, Myrtle Thayer.

Grimball."   Mr. Grimball was a cousin of Franklin Agrippa Robert.
He left two sons, Charles and Luther Grimball, both of whom married
and left descendants.

* Mr. Callegari's ancestor, J. Callegari, was born near Rome, Italy, and
  educated at Venice.   He came to America when 30 years old and settled
  in Avoyelles parish, La., where he taught school many years, being
  Parish Superintendent of Education at one time.   He married Ellen
  Scallan in 1834 and died in 1887, aged 85.   His son, S. Callegari,
  prominent merchant of Cottonport, was born October 7, 1840.   He
  entered the Confederate Army in 1862, being in Co. F, 18th La. Infantry.   He married Irine Richi in 1875, and they had three sons and
  four daughters.

(3)   Calvin Gremillion married Clara Price. They had two children, Price who married and has a daughter, and Dorothy.

(4)   Oda Gremillion married Marile Armand and had two children, Oda, Jr., and Sidney.

(5)   Lee Gremillion married a Miss Haney of New Orleans and has two children, Bert and Mildred.

(6)   Bonnie Gremillion married Philomene Miller. They have six children. The eldest are Bonnie, Jr., and Margaret.

(7)   Carl Gremillion married Ethel Thompson of Grand Cane, La. They have two children, Carl, Jr., and Ellen.

(8)   Curtis Gremillion married Beatrice Watson of Baton Rouge, La. They have one child, Curtis, Jr.

(9)   Johnny Gremillion married Amelia Stromeye. They have two children, Johnny, Jr., and Elizabeth.

(10) Birdie Mae Gremillion married Lee Jordan of Kansas City and has one child, Lee, Jr.

iii.—Edward Bane Robert, son of Franklin Agrippa Robert and his second wife, Julia (Matthews) Grimball, was born near Evergreen, Avoyelles parish, La., on July 31, 1868, and died there September 10, 1914. He married November 19, 1892, Martha Davis who was born March 9, 1873, and died August 1, 1933. She was a daughter of Louis Taylor Davis and Mathilda Catharine Doyle, and her grandparents were John Wesley Davis and Nancy Carter, both of Mississippi. Mr. and Mrs. Robert had eight sons all of whom are living at this date (1944). They are:—

a.—Ford Mayo Robert.
b.—Vernon Mae Robert.
c.—Edward Bane Robert, II.
d.—Frank Aaron Robert.
e.—Willie Meade Robert.
f.—Peyton Charles Robert.
g.—Orlando Ulysses Robert.
h.—Louis Davis Robert.

a.—Ford Mayo Robert, eldest son of Edward Bane Robert and Martha Davis, was born at Evergreen, Avoyelles, La., on September 30, 1893, and still resides there. He has always taken a prominent part in the civic affairs of his community and has served for some years as Police Juror of Avoyelles parish from the ward in which he lives. He is now Mayor of Evergreen. He married in 1918 Julia Clopton, daughter of Bettison William Clopton and Dora Havard, and grand-daughter of Dr. William Franklin Clopton and Julia Foote. She was born in St. Landry parish, La., June 30, 1900, and died June 7, 1919. They had one son, Clopton Cecil Robert, born March 20, 1919. This son married Dorothy Ducote and they have a daughter, Caroline Julia, born October 18, 1942. He is at present in the armed forces of his country fighting for "The Four Freedoms of the Atlantic Charter." Ford Mayo Robert married as his second wife Lena Armand, born May 6, 1907, daughter of Leonard Armand and Alice Bordelon. They have had six children:—Alvin Lee, born September 21, 1927, and died October 15, 1929; Mary Fay, born June 14, 1929; Louise Nell, born August 18, 1931; Huey Drew, born March 23, 1936; Bobby Joyce, born May 10, 1939; Opal June, born December 2, 1941.

b.—Vernon Mae Robert, second son of Edward Bane Robert and Martha Davis, was born in Evergreen, Avoyelles parish, La., on October 24, 1895. He now resides in Homer, La., where he is postmaster. He married Martha Emma Collins, born April 26, 1896, daughter of William Dreaux Collins and Emma Jane Bartholomew of New York City. They have two children:—William Collins, born March 8, 1926, and Vernon Mae, Jr., born November 26, 1930.

c.—Edward Bane Robert, II, third son of Edward Bane Robert and Martha Davis, was born at Evergreen, Avoyelles parish, La., on October 17, 1898. He has been active in educational work most of his life in which he has reached a high degree of eminence and is at present Dean of the College of Education at the Louisiana State University. He obtained his Bachelor's degree from the Louisiana State Normal College at Natchitoches, and his Mastre's degree and Doctorate at Peabody, Nashville, Tennessee. Dr. Robert was in the armed forces of his country in World War I. He married August 6, 1923, Alberta de Blanc, daughter of Albert A. de Blanc and Emily Hacker of New Iberia, La. Dr. and Mrs. Robert have three children:—Barbara Jane, born July 18, 1929; Helen Emily, born August 20, 1932; Edward Bane, III, born November 10, 1934. All of these children were born in Natchitoches, Louisiana.

d.—Frank Aaron Robert, fourth son of Edward Bane Robert and Martha Davis, was born at Evergreen, Avoyelles parish, La., on June 18, 1901. He married Ethel Futral, born November 22, 1902, daughter of Sam Futral and Gertrude Dodd of Port Barre, La. They now reside at White Castle, in Iberville parish, La., where Mr. Robert is prominent in the public schools of that parish. He is now principal of a school in Plaquemine. They have four children:—Sylvia Marguerite, born September 1, 1928; Don Millard, born December 27, 1929; Frankie Merlene, born August 29, 1931; Dorothy Miriam, born February 18, 1936.

e.—Willie Meade Robert, fifth son of Edward Bane Robert and Martha Davis, was born at Evergreen, Avoyelles parish, La., on January 25, 1904. He married Ozite Manuel, born March 15, 1910. They live in New Orleans where Mr. Robert is in the employ of the Delta Shipyard, and have three children:—Carl Roland, born March 24, 1932; Willie Meade, Jr., born - - - - - - - -

f.—Peyton Charles Robert, sixth son of Edward Bane Robert and Martha Davis, was born at Evergreen, Avoyelles parish, La., on August 10, 1906. He was educated at the Louisiana State Normal College at Natchitoches and is now principal of the Doylene High School in Webster parish, La. He married December 27, 1929, Margaret Lacey Fort who was born March 21, 1910. She is a daughter of Arthur Fort and Alice Hill of Baton Rouge, La. They have one son, Peyton Charles, Jr., born January 3, 1932.

g.—Orlando Ulysses Robert, seventh son of Edward Bane Robert and Martha Davis, was born at Evergreen, Avoyelles parish, La., on January 10, 1909. He now resides in Houston, Texas, where he is Secretary of the Rutherford Oil Company. He married August 20, 1932, Eunice Irene Patterson, born April 1, 1914, daughter of Willard Henry Patterson and Irene Pullin of San Antonio, Texas. They have two children:— Orlando Ulysses, Jr., born March 9, 1934, ana Edward Patterson, born March 11, 1937.

h.—Louis Davis Robert, eighth and youngest son of Edward Bane Robert and Martha Davis, was born at Evergreen,

Avoyelles parish, La., on June 29, 1911. He received his Bachelor's degree from the State Normal College at Natchitoches, La., and his Master's at the Louisiana State University. At present he is teaching in the Cankton Junior High School at Sunset, St. Landry parish, La. He is as yet unmarried. He is much interested in genealogy and it was through his kindness and cooperation that the compiler of these chronicles obtained much of this data on the Robert family.

2.—Polhill Ware Robert, second child of Joseph Robert and Mary Hyrne Jaudon, was born in St. Peter's Parish, Beaufort District, South Carolina, about 1801. He came to Wilkinson county, Mississippi, with his parents when a small child and then later to Rapides parish, La., where he married Caroline Amanda Rowley. We find the record of a sale on December 16, 1834, which substantiates his wife's name. It reads in part:—

> This instrument of writing made between Polhill Ware Robert and his wife, Caroline Amanda Robert, on the one part, and George Keller of the other.

His wife was very probably a daughter of Job Rowley. We find his name in the South Carolina census of 1790 next to the names of Peter and Grimball Robert. They were neighbors living in St. Peter's Parish, Beaufort District. The names in the census of 1790 are not alphabetically arranged but are listed by the census taker in the order in which he came to them in his rounds. Thus it is easy to tell from it who lived in the same neighborhood. According to this census there were eight members in Job Rowley's family besides himself, three of whom were "white males under 16 years," which means that he had three sons. There were five "free white females," one of whom was undoubtedly his wife, and this would indicate that he had four daughters. We do not think Job Rowley ever came to Louisiana but his three sons, Henry C., James B., and John M. settled on Bayou Boeuf near Cheneyville in Rapides parish in the first quarter of the nineteenth century.

Polhill Ware Robert appears to have been quite prosperous at one time and lived in New Orleans where he was engaged in the commission merchant business. Later his prosperity declined. We learn this from a letter written by his young brother in California in July, 1851, to his brother-in-law Frank Myers. The following item from it is self-explanatory:—

A letter of April 12th brought the sad intelligence of the failure of Leckie, Robert and Co., who failed this spring. It is difficult to tell what Polhill will do now.

In another letter written March 21, 1852, he says:—

Polhill is a notary in New Orleans now.

Our information on the descendants of Polhill Ware Robert and his wife, Caroline Amanda Rowley, is unfortunately very sparse. We have been able to find authentic record of but one child, Mary Tuzette Robert, who in 1853 eloped with and married Charles Lafayette Pearce, son of Stephen Pearce, and his first wife, Sally Goodwin Bray. Charles Lafayette Pearce was born near Cheneyville, Rapides parish, La., on May 14, 1829, and he and his wife resided in that parish all of their lives. They had nine children, a list of whom will be found on page 396 We are told of the above marriage in one of the letters from Thaddeus Sobieski Robert (brother of Polhill) to his brother-in-law Frank Myers. In his letter of February 9, 1854, written from San Jose, California, he says:—

I received a letter from Polhill—all were well, and his daughter married to Charlie Pearce. They knew he intended to prevent it and they ran off to Natchez and were married, and returned the day before he reached Cheneyville. He would not see them. He hates it very much.

On May 18, 1854, Alma (Coe) Bennett, the step-daughter of Frank Myers, writes him:—

Uncle P. is still unforgiving towards Mary. I hope he will not continue so.

Whether Polhill ever forgave his daughter we are unable to say. We know nothing further of him and his wife beyond what is given above, but it seems probable that they continued to reside in New Orleans as there is no recorded evidence of them in Rapides after 1854. The members of the Robert family were very prolific and there may have been other children than the daughter already mentioned.

3.—Leonidas Alonzo Robert, third son of Joseph Robert and Mary Hyrne Jaudon, was born in St. Peter's Parish, Beaufort District, South Carolina, on May 4, 1803. He was brought to Wilkinson county, Mississippi, when an infant, and later to Rapides parish, near the present town of Cheneyville, on the Bayou Boeuf, in central Louisiana, where he grew to manhood. We find him there as late as January 11, 1836, when it is recorded that "Leonidas A. Robert of the parish of Rapides" buys three slaves. Some time after that date he moved to the adjoining parish of Avoyelles and settled on Bayou des Glaises where he spent the remainder of his life. He was twice married. His first wife was Tuzette Eliza Pearce, daughter of William and Elizabeth Pearce, born September 17, 1811, and died June 20, 1839. Whether her father was William Pearce, Sr., or William Pearce, Jr., is at this date a very mooted question. For more detailed information on this subject see that portion of Part Four of this book which deals with William Pearce, Sr. Leonidas Alonzo Robert and Tuzette Eliza Pearce were married February 4, 1827, and had four children:—

> i.—Leonidas Alonzo Robert, Jr.
> ii.—Mary Eliza Robert.
> iii.—William Columbus Robert.
> iv.—Samuel Henry Robert.

The second wife of Leonidas Alonzo Robert was Sarah H. Coffeen, daughter of Henry and Sarah Coffeen. They were married on July 13, 1841. He died on March 15, 1867, and some years later she married Joshua Pearce, a widower, by whom she had no children. She died January 15, 1884, in Cheneyville, La. Leonidas Alonzo Robert and Sarah H. Coffeen had four children:—

> v.—Catharine Ann Robert.
> vi.—Cornelia Tuzette Robert.
> vii.—William Henderson Robert.
> viii.—Ann Eliza Robert.

Mrs. Alice Robert Havard, grand-daughter of Leonidas Alonzo Robert, is now the owner of his family Bible and has kindly furnished us with a copy of the valuable old records it contains. All of the items from it listed below are in his own handwriting except the last two. We now insert in full an exact copy of them:—

BIRTHS.

Leonidas A. Robert, son of Joseph and Mary H. Robert, was born on the 4th of May, 1803.

Tuzette E. Robert, daughter of William and Elizabeth Pearce, was born September 17, 1811.

Leonidas A. Robert, son of L. A. Robert and his first wife, was born September 9, 1829.

Mary Eliza Robert my first daughter was born 19th of December, 1830, on the Lord's Day.

William Columbus, second son, was born on the 18th of September, 1832.

Samuel Henry, the third son, was born on the 25th of July, 1837.

Sarah H. Coffeen, daughter of Henry and Sarah Coffeen, was born in New York state, Jefferson county, Watertown, on the 15th of January, 1820.

Catharine Ann was born on the 22nd of July, 1842.

Second daughter, Cornelia Tuzette, was born on the 15th of July, 1845.

William Henderson, first son of my second wife Sarah, was born on the 13th of November, 1849.

Third daughter, Ann Eliza, was born on the 22nd of January, 1854, on Sunday night.

MARRIAGES.

L. A. Robert and his first wife, Tuzette E. Pearce, were united in marriage on the 4th of February, Sunday night, 1827.

L. A. Robert and his second wife, Sarah H. Coffeen, were united in marriage on the 13th of July, 1841.

DEATHS.

Tuzette Eliza Robert, my first wife, departed this life on Thursday the 20th of June, 1839, at 3 o'clock in the day.

William Columbus, 3rd child and 2nd son of my first wife, departed this life on the 8th of April, 1834.

(Recorded by his 2nd wife, Sarah H. Coffeen):

Departed this life on the 22nd of August, 1865, Catharine Ann Neal, eldest child of Sarah H. Robert and L. A. Robert, Sr.

Died on the 15th March, 1867, L. A. Robert, in the 63rd year of his age.

(Recorded by some later member of the family:—

Sarah H. Pearce, 2nd wife of L. A. Robert, Sr., died January 15, 1884, in Cheneyville, La., age 64 years.

i.—Leonidas Alonzo Robert, Jr., son of Leonidas Alonzo Robert and his first wife, Tuzette Eliza Pearce, was born in Rapides parish, La., on September 29, 1829, and died May 1, 1887, in St. Paul, Minnesota, where he had moved about 1872.

He married Eleanor H. Gurney in Louisiana about 1855, daughter of Asa Gurney, Jr., of Cunnington, Massachusetts. Savage in his Genealogical Dictionary of New England tells us something about the Gurneys who first landed in Massachusetts about fifteen years after the founding of Plymouth by the Pilgrims. In Vol. II, page 325 we find the following item:— "Richard Gurney, Weymouth, Mass., wife Rebecca, probably daughter of John Taylor." In Vol. IV, page 261 we find:— "John Taylor of Weymouth in his will of January 6, probated May 22, 1668, names wife Rebecca, daughter *Rebecca wife of Richard Gurney*, and son John who was made executor."

Mr. T. S. Gurney of Hart, Michigan, in a letter written May 19, 1908, to Miss Carrie Robert (daughter of Leonidas Alonzo Robert, Jr.), gives the following Gurney pedigree:—

    1.—Richard Gurney, settled in Weymouth, Mass.
    2.—Zacharia Gurney, born in Weymouth, Mass.
    3.—Nathan Gurney, born in Weymouth, Mass.
    4.—Benjamin Gurney, born in Abington, Mass.
    5.—Asa Gurney, born in Bridgewater, Mass.
    6.—Asa Gurney, Jr., born in Cunnington, Mass.
    7.—Eleanor H. Gurney, born in Cunnington, Mass.

T. S. Gurney states that Richard Gurney came to Weymouth, Mass., in 1636 and mentions him as *Richard I*, so he must have been the father of the Richard who married Rebecca Taylor.

Leonidas Alonzo Robert, Jr., lived in Avoyelles parish, La., on Bayou Chopegue, until 1872 when he moved to St. Paul, Minnesota. His wife had relatives in Ohio and Minnesota which probably accounts for this move. They had six children:—

    a.—Corwin Robert.
    b.—Marshall Oscar Robert.
    c.—Alonzo Beauregard Robert.
    d.—Edward Robert.
    e.—Carrie Mary Robert.
    f.—Tuzette Robert.

    a.—Corwin Robert was twice married but we only know that his first wife was named Ada and that they had a son Ralph who lives in North Dakota and has three sons.

    b.—Marshall Oscar Robert was born in 1859 and died in 1936. We only know that he married, that his wife was named

CAPTAIN PETER ROBERT 109

Mary, and that he left two sons, Raymond Graham and Howard Payne Robert who live in Washington, D. C.

c.—Alonzo Beauregard Robert was born on Bayou Chopegue, Avoyelles parish, La., on July 11, 1861, and died in New Orleans, La., on March 9, 1924. He was born just a few days before the Battle of Bull Run in the Civil War and it is likely that his middle name of Beauregard was given him in honor of the general of that name who was then in command of the Confederate forces in Virginia. As before stated, his father moved to St. Paul, Minnesota, in 1872, and there Alonzo Beauregard Robert grew to manhood and continued to live until 1890 when he moved to New Orleans where he spent the remainder of his life. He married in St. Paul on September 24, 1884, Alice Fonseca who was born in Baton Rouge, La., on February 22, 1858, and died in New Orleans on September 3, 1934. She was a daughter of ——————— Fonseca and his wife, Amelia LeBlanc, both natives of Baton Rouge. Alice Fonseca's father died a short while before her birth and her mother some time later married Colonel James B. Quinn of the U. S. engineers who graduated from West Point in 1866. After their marriage Colonel Quinn was stationed in St. Paul and there his stepdaughter met and married Alonzo Beauregard Robert. They had four children:—

        az.—James Marshall Robert.
        bz.—Alice Amelia Robert.
        cz.—George Romeo Robert.
        dz.—Alonzo Raphael Robert.

az.—James Marshall Robert was born in St. Paul, Minnesota, on June 20, 1885. He came to New Orleans when a boy with his parents and has lived there ever since. He is an engineer by profession and most of his life has been spent teaching. For some years he has been Dean of the College of Engineering and Professor of Mechanical Engineering at Tulane University in New Orleans. He married in that city on April 21, 1909, Gladys Roberta Kearney, daughter of Inskeep Kearney and Clara Roberta Jones. Mrs. Robert is a great-great-granddaughter of Judge Thomas Charles Scott, a native of Charlotte county, Virginia, who emigrated to Alexandria, Louisiana, when that town was a young settlement and became prominent in the legal profession there as well as in social, business and political circles. He was one of the early judges of Rapides parish and there married Marie Francoise Laulette LeDoux, a daughter of Pierre LeDoux and Eugenie Louise La Mothe. His eldest daughter married Governor James Madison Wells of Louisiana. Mrs. Robert's mother, Clara Roberta Jones, was the only daughter of Robert Byron Jones, Jr., and Maria Catharine Johnston. Her father was a son of Robert Byron Jones and Jennie Jones (cousins), both natives of Virginia. Maria Catharine Johnston was the second wife of Mr. Jones and married him in 1865. His first wife was Laura Susan Larche, whom he married in 1855, and they had one daughter, Mrs. Maude Beattie (now of New Orleans), and several sons all of whom are now dead. Mr. Jones was born in July, 1830, and died in New Orleans on July 21, 1866. Maria Catharine Johnston, his second wife, was a daughter of Dr. William J. Johnston and Maria Catharine Scott (daughter of Judge Thomas C. Scott), and was born in Alexandria, Rapides parish, La., on Monday, July 17, 1843.

James Marshall Robert and his wife, Gladys Roberta Kearny, have had four children:—

James Marshall Robert, Jr., born June 5, 1911.
Kearney Quinn Robert, born January 28, 1914.
William Douglas Robert, born December 31, 1915.
Gladys Kearney Robert, born October 29, 1919.

The eldest of these children, James Marshall Robert, Jr., died in New Orleans on Wednesday morning, March 6, 1940. He was unmarried and had been in ill health for some time. The youngest, Gladys Kearny Robert, died in New Orleans on November 5, 1925.

Kearny Quinn Robert, the second son, married Roslyn Lambright Thompson at Trinity Church in New Orleans, La., on August 24, 1940. She is a native of Atlanta, Georgia. Mr. Robert is an engineer in the exploration department of the Magnolia Petroleum Co., and due to the transitory nature of his profession his place of residence is being constantly changed. He and his wife have a son, Kearny Quinn Robert, Jr., born June 12, 1943.

William Douglas Robert, the third son, is at this time an officer in the aviation corps of the United States Army. He married on Sunday, June 7, 1942, Mildred Maginnis (better known as "Billy") of Lakeland, Florida. The ceremony was performed at St. Matthew's Episcopal church, in Dallas, Texas. They now have a little daughter, Carolyn, born in Taft, California, on September 12, 1943.

bz.—Alice Amelia Robert was born in Duluth, Minnesota, on December 11, 1886. She has never married and now resides in New Orleans. It was from her that much of the data on this branch of the Robert family was obtained. She is a dear, sweet woman and is much loved by all the family, even the distant collateral cousins.

cz.—George Romeo Robert (he denies that he is a *Romeo*) was born in Duluth, Minnesota, on April 8, 1888. He is a civil engineer by profession and for many years has been prominent in road and bridge construction in Louisiana. He has been forced by the condition of his health to give up his professional career and is now engaged in breeding and raising fine cattle. He resides in Baton Rouge, La., where he and his good wife have a legion of friends. He married Mary Catherine Charles (better known as Mayme) on August 4, 1923, daughter of John Banister Charles and Teresa Neal. She was born in Humbolt, Kansas, but spent most of her life in Oklahoma where her father was widely known in banking circles. They have no children.

dz.—Alonzo Raphael Robert was born in New Orleans, La., on October 6, 1893, and is living there at this time. He married Mary Elizabeth Phillips in Nashville, Tennessee, on December 28, 1918. They have one, son, Randolph Beaure-gard Robert, born in New Orleans on June 4, 1922, and now serving in the armed forces of the United States.

d.—Edward Robert, fourth child of Leonidas Alonzo Robert, Jr., and Eleanor Gurney, never married and died in Skagway, Alaska, about 1908.

e.—Carrie Mary Robert, fifth child of Leonidas Alonzo Robert, Jr., and Eleanor Gurney, died unmarried in 1932.

f.—Tuzette Robert, sixth child of Leonidas Alonzo Robert, Jr., and Eleanor Gurney, is the only one of her generation now living (1944). She was married in 1906 to Edward J. Hawarden and now lives at 1608 East Sixth Street, Superior, Wisconsin. She has no children.

ii.—Mary Eliza Robert, second child of Leonidas Alonzo Robert and his first wife, Tuzette Eliza Pearce, was born on Bayou Boeuf, Rapides parish, La., on December 19, 1830. She was married to her cousin, James Cook, only son of Wilson Cook and Providence Tuzette Tanner. They had two daughters:—

      a.—Sarah Tuzette Cook.
      b.—Catharine Madolyn Cook.

a.—Sarah Tuzette Cook was born in Rapides parish, La., about 1852, and was married on December 5, 1871, at the residence of her grandfather, Leonidas Alonzo Robert, on Bayou des Glaises, Avoyelles parish, La., by the Rev. Elihu Kilpatrick Branch, to Walter Prince Ford, son of William Prince Ford and his first wife, Martha Providence Tanner. She and her husband were cousins. The date of this marriage is verified by an item in THE LOUISIANA DEMOCRAT (an Alexandria paper) of Wednesday, January 10, 1872. It reads as follows:—

MARRIED:—On the 5th of December at the residence of L. A. Robert, Bayou des Glaises, Louisiana, by the Rev. E. K. Branch, Mr. Walter P. Ford to Miss S. Tuzette Cook.

Mr. Ford was born on Bayou Boeuf, near Cheneyville, Rapides parish, La., on February 24, 1848, and died at his home there on April 24, 1916. We have no record of his wife's death but think it preceded his. Four children were born of this marriage:—

      William Henry Ford.
      Mary Ford.
      Jennie Ford.
      Kate Ford.*

b.—Catharine Madolyn Cook, daughter of James Cook and Mary Eliza Robert, was born in Rapides parish, La., about 1854 and was married in 1873 to Joseph Bass. Shortly afterwards they left Rapides parish and moved to St. Louis, Missouri, and then to Peoria, Illinois. At the latter place their only child, James Bass died at the age of fifteen. Several years later Mr. Bass died and in 1917 his wife died at the age of sixty-three.

iii.—William Columbus Robert, third child of Leonidas Alonzo Robert and his first wife, Tuzette Eliza Pearce, was

*For further data on these children see pages 283-5.

born in Rapides parish, La., on September 18, 1832, and died April 8, 1834.

iv.—Samuel Henry Robert, fourth child of Leonidas Alonzo Robert and his first wife, Tuzette Eliza Pearce, was born in Rapides parish, La., on July 30, 1857. He died unmarried during the Civil War while in the service of the Confederate Army.

v.—Catharine Ann Robert, first child of Leonidas Alonzo Robert and his second wife, Sarah H. Coffeen, was born on Bayou des Glaises, Avoyelles parish, La., on July 22, 1842. She was married on November 11, 1858, to Merida S. Neal, son of Joel Neal and Melissa McNeely,* and died on August 22, 1865, in her 23rd year. The date of her death is verified by an item in THE LOUISIANA DEMOCRAT of Wednesday, September 13, 1865, as follows:—

DIED:—On the 22nd of August, in the 23rd year of her age, and after a painful illness of two months, Catharine Ann, wife of Merida S. Neal.

Three children were born of this marriage:—
        a.—Melissa Neal.
        b.—Sarah Catharine Neal.
        c.—Samuel Neal.

a.—Melissa Neal was born November 12, 1859. She was usually called "Lizzie" and never married.

b.—Sarah Catharine Neal was born May 1, 1861, and was married March 17, 1881, to Jesse Wright Stafford, son of General Leroy Augustus Stafford and Sarah Catharine Wright. Both are now dead. They had seven children and many of their descendants are now living in Louisiana and Texas. A full account of them will be found in the compiler's book "General Leroy Augustus Stafford, His Forebears and Descendants."

c.—Samuel Neal lived to adult life but never married.

vi.—Cornelia Tuzette Robert, second child of Leonidas Alonzo Robert and his second wife, Sarah H. Coffeen, was born on Bayou des Glaises, Avoyelles parish, La., on July 25, 1845. While visiting her half brother, Leonidas Alonzo Robert,

---

* Melissa McNeely was probably a daughter of Paul G. McNeely and Esther Sarah Providence Grimball. If this surmise is correct then she was a grand-daughter of John Grimball, Jr., and Mary Robert (a daughter of Capt. Peter Robert and Anne Grimball).

Jr., in St. Paul, Minnesota, she married a Mr. Smith. As far as we can learn there were no children.

vii.—William Henderson Robert, third child of Leonidas Alonzo Robert and his second wife, Sarah H. Coffeen, was born on Bayou des Glaises, Avoyelles parish, La., on November 13, 1849, and died at Cheneyville, Rapides parish, La., on April 26, 1912. He married on November 21, 1872, Clara Alice Bailey who was born at Cheneyville, La., on December 2, 1850, and died there on January 16, 1905. She was a daughter of Walter Bailey and his wife, Margaret Gertrude Allen. Mr. Bailey was born at Bath, Somersetshire, England, on November 4, 1814, and died in Cheneyville, La., on Friday, November 23, 1860, at the age of forty-six. According to a notice of his death in THE LOUISIANA DEMOCRAT, an Alexandria newspaper, he had been a resident of Rapides parish for fourteen years prior to his death. His wife was born in Rapides parish, La., on January 10, 1822, and died in Cheneyville on June 3, 1900.* William Henderson Robert and his wife, Clara Alice Bailey, had eight children:—

a.—Alice Delight Robert, born September 2, 1873.
b.—Samuel Henry Robert, born November 6, 1875
c.—Walter Bailey Robert, born November 12, 1877.
d.—William Ford Robert, born October 28, 1879.
e.—Leonidas Alonzo Robert, III, born May 25, 1882.
f.—Frank Sill Robert, born November 11, 1884.
g.—Corwin A. Robert, born April 11, 1888.
h.—Joseph F. Robert, born November 13, 1892.

a.—Alice Delight Robert was married in Cheneyville, La., on September 28, 1892, to George Lewis Havard, son of Leroy Stafford Havard and Julia Caroline Wright, and grandson of John Havard and Joyce Calliham. Mr. Havard died at his home in Melville, La., on March 25, 1928. His wife is still living there at this date (1944). They had eight children:—

az.—Clara Havard.
bz.—Leroy Stafford Havard.
cz.—Julia Louise Havard.

* Margaret Gertrude Allen was probably a grand-daughter of William Allen and Dorcas Ogden (their sons were:—William O., Thomas, James, and Daniel G. Allen). Dorcas Ogden was a daughter of John Ogden and Martha Robert (daughter of Captain Peter Robert and Anne Grimball).

dz.—Douglas Alexander Havard.
ez.—Robert Edward Havard.
fz.—Katharine Wright Havard.
gz.—Page Augustus Havard.
hz.—Hazel Harriet Havard.

az.—Clara Havard was born at Walnut Bluff plantation, Big Cane, St. Landry parish, La., on February 24, 1894. She was married to John Boelens of Spring Lake, Michigan. They now reside in Opelousas, La., and have two sons:—John Havard Boelens, born in Marksville, La., on September 26, 1922, now an ensign in the U. S. Navy, and Leroy Havard Boelens, born in Baton Rouge, La., on June 22, 1927, now a student there at the State University. The elder, John Havard Boelens, was graduated from the High School at Marksville, La., on June 2, 1939, and attended Marion Institute at Marion, Alabama, for one year. He received from Congressman Leonard Allen of Louisiana an appointment to the U. S. Naval Academy at Annapolis, Maryland, and entered the Academy on June 14, 1940, graduating therefrom on June 7, 1944. He was married in the Church of the Epiphany (Episcopal) at Opelousas, La., by the Rev. H. Newton Griffith on June 14, 1944, to Gloria Elaine Gordon, daughter of the late Herbert Monteith Gordon and his wife, Anna Mary Dezauche. She was born in Baton Rouge, La., November 15, 1924, but spent most of her life in Opelousas, La. Her father, the late Herbert Monteith Gordon, was born November 6, 1881, died December 15, 1941, and married on January 26, 1905, Anna Mary Dezauche, daughter of John Sylvan Tabor Dezauche (born January 18, 1853, and died March 30, 1924) and Emma Aline Capps (born September 20, 1858, and died June 12, 1908). Mr. and Mrs. Dezauche were married November 23, 1880. Herbert Monteith Gordon was a son of James Huey Gordon (died November 14, 1884) and Hattie De Ford Monteith (born February 25, 1859, and died June 10, 1884) who were married May 1, 1879. Hattie De Ford Monteith was a daughter of Hiram R. Monteith and Malinda J. Penny who were married April 27, 1858.

Ensign John Havard Boelens and his bride are now at Jacksonville, Florida, where he will be stationed until August 9, 1944, when he will report at Norfolk, Virginia, for duty on the battleship Wisconsin.

bz.—Leroy Stafford Havard was born at Walnut Bluff plantation, Big Cane, St. Landry parish, La., on May 11, 1895. He served overseas in the First World War. He married in New Orleans on June 22, 1920, Bert Elise Richard, who was born September 21, 1899, and was a daughter of Mr. and Mrs. Gordy Richard of St. Landry parish, La. Leroy Stafford Havard lived in Marksville, La., where for many years he was prominent in the automobile business. He died at his home there on Saturday, April 12, 1941. Four children were born of this marriage:—

Leroy Stafford Havard, Jr., born October 13, 1921.
Frank Lampton Havard, born December 11, 1923.
Bernie Louise Havard, born March 21, 1925.
Eugene Wright Havard, born November 23, 1927.

The second of these children, Frank Lampton Havard, died in New Orleans at the age of fourteen on July 5, 1938. He was buried in the Cushman cemetery at Marksville, La. The other three are living at this date. The eldest, Leroy Stafford Havard, Jr., is in the U. S. parachute troops and when last heard of was stationed in Australia.

cz.—Julia Louise Havard was born May 13, 1901, and died in infancy.

dz.—Douglas Alexander Havard in spite of her name is a girl. She was born at Melville, La., on December 11, 1902, and was married on July 26, 1922, to McCleland Taylor of Jackson, Mississippi. They reside in that city at present and have one child, Alice Havard Taylor, born March 31, 1924.

ez.—Robert Edward Havard was born at Melville, La., on November 24, 1904, and is unmarried.

fz.—Katharine Wright Havard was born at Melville, La., on July 3, 1906, and was married on December 12, 1925, to Charles William Howard of Autaugaville, Alabama. They now reside in Baton Rouge, La., and have one child, Charles William Howard, Jr., born July 6, 1931.

gz.—Page Augustus Havard was born in Melville, La., on January 4, 1908, and died in infancy.

hz.—Hazel Harriet Havard was born in Melville, La., on December 22, 1911, and was married at Jackson, Miss., on Tuesday, November 24, 1936, to Edward Maxwell Yerger. They now reside at Mound, Madison parish, La., and have two children:—George Havard Yerger, born March 23, 1941, Edward Maxwell Yerger, Jr., January 7, 1944.

b.—Samuel Henry Robert, second child of William Henderson Robert and Clara Alice Bailey, was for many years a prominent business man in Cheneyville and Alexandria, La. He married on May 3, 1899, Mattie Wall, daughter of Wesley Winans Wall and Rebecca Currence Burr. She was born June 30, 1878. Mr. Robert died in Alexandria, La., about 1926, and his wife is yet living there. They had eight children:—

  az.—Samuel Wesley Robert, born March 17, 1900.
  bz.—Audrey Robert, born January 25, 1904.
  cz.—William Eugene Robert, born August 6, 1906.
  dz.—Marjorie Robert, born October 19, 1908.
  ez.—Edward Eldon Robert, born April 26, 1911.
  fz.—Mary Alice Robert, born October 21, 1915.
  gz.—Ruth Robert, born November 11, 1917.
  hz.—Frank Wall Robert, born July 19, 1920.

az.—Samuel Wesley Robert was born in Cheneyville, La., and educated at the Louisiana State University. He is a civil engineer by profession and now resides in Memphis, Tenn. He married on April 18, 1918, Blakely Beryl Calvit, daughter of William Tacitus Calvit and Susan Leckie Duke. They have no children.

bz.—Audrey Robert was born in Cheneyville, La., and was married to Paul Courregé of New Iberia, La., on May 3, 1927. They now reside at Reserve, La., where Mr. Courregé is Superintendent of Fabrication at the Godchaux Sugar Company. They have one child, Paul Robert Courrege.

cz.—William Eugene Robert was born in Alexandria, La., and married Floy Tugwell of Farmerville, La., in October, 1933. They have one daughter, Ossie Jean Robert.

dz.—Marjorie Robert was born in Alexandria, La., and was married to Uriah Jewell Westbrook of Union parish, La., on November 12, 1928. They have four children:—Elizabeth Jewell, Ruth, Robert Elgin, and Samuel Haile.

ez.—Edward Eldon Robert was born in Alexandria, La. He married Johnnie Mae Hardin of Camden, Arkansas, on December 13, 1938. They have no children as yet.

fz.—Mary Alice Robert was born in Alexandria, La. She was married to John Frederick Pickering, better known as

"Jack" Pickering, of Olothe, Kansas, on March 27, 1935. They have two children:—Frances Lorraine, and Robert McLaughlin.

gz.—Ruth Robert was born in Alexandria, La. She was married to Ralph Kilpatrick Stafford, son of Leroy Stafford and Priscilla Allen, on December 27, 1940. They have one son, Samuel Leroy Stafford, born in Bunkie, La., on Sunday, January 17, 1943.

hz.—Frank Wall Robert was born in Alexandria, La. He graduated from the Virginia Theological Seminary, near Alexandria, Va., in September, 1943, and was ordained to the ministry of the Episcopal Church by Right Reverend John L. Jackson, Bishop of Louisiana, at St. James Episcopal church in Alexandria, La., on Monday, October 18, 1943. He is now serving as minister-in-charge of Trinity Church and the Episcopal student center at Natchitoches, La., and at St. Paul's church at Winnfield, La. He is as yet unmarried.*

c.—Walter Bailey Robert, third child of William Henderson Robert and Clara Alice Bailey, was born at Cheneyville, La., on November 12, 1877. He was educated at the Louisiana State University, graduating from the school of engineering there in 1901. He was for many years connected with the Louisiana Highway Commission and with the U. S. Government in an engineering capacity. He has resided in Baton Rouge, La., for the past twenty-five years. On January 18, 1905, he married Mary Eleanor Clopton, better known as "Minnie," daughter of Dr. William Franklin Clopton and Julia Foote. She was born at Big Cane, St. Landry parish, La., March 1, 1879. Dr. Clopton came to Louisiana from Atlanta, Georgia, and practiced his profession for many years near Morrow, La. Mrs. Clopton was born at Lake Providence, La., her parents being William Foote and Sallie Parker. Walter Bailey Robert and his wife have two children:—

az.—Julia Alice Robert, born February 9, 1907.
bz.—Walter Bailey Robert, Jr., born October 7, 1910.

az.—Julia Alice Robert was born at Morrow, La., and was married to William Elliott Parker in 1925. They now reside in Greenwood, Miss., and have one son, William Elliott Parker,

* Note:—Rev. Mr. Robert is at present (1945) a chaplain in the U.S.N.R.

Jr., born December 9, 1925, who is now a student in the Louisiana State University.

bz.—Walter Bailey Robert, Jr., was born at Opelousas, La. He married on May 29, 1942, Margaret Elizabeth Gilcrease of Winnfield, La. They now reside in Baton Rouge, La., and have one daughter, Mary Almanda Robert, born February 15, 1944.

d.—William Ford Robert, fourth child of William Henderson Robert and Clara Alice Bailey, was born at Cheneyville, La., on October 28, 1879. He is married, lives at Oakdale, La., and has four children:— Daisy May, Clara, Corwin, and Samuel Robert.

e.—Leonidas Alonzo Robert, III, fifth child of William Henderson Robert and Clara Alice Bailey, was born at Cheneyville, La., on May 25, 1882. He has never married and lives at Melville, La. He is almost totally incapacitated by bad eye sight.

f.—Frank Sill Robert, sixth child of William Henderson Robert and Clara Alice Bailey, was born at Cheneyville, La., on November 11, 1884. He is a civil engineer and for many years lived at Lafayette, La. He married Wilda Meginley of Opelousas, La., daughter of Benjamin Meginley, who died April 21, 1932, at Lafayette, La. They had ten children:—Wilda, Iris, Frank Sill, Jr., Lucille, Clara Alice, Armand and John (twins), Samuel, Benjamin Meginley and William Henderson (twins). The first twins, Armand and John Robert, are now in the military service of their country. The second twins were named for their maternal and paternal grandparents respectively. Mr. Robert has recently married again and now lives in Cottonport, La. He is employed by the engineering department of the Louisiana Highway.

g.—Corwin Augustus Robert, seventh child of William Henderson Robert and Clara Alice Bailey, was born at Cheneyville, La., on April 11, 1888. He is a civil engineer and now lives in New Orleans. He married May Prushen and they have three children:—Corwin, William Warren, and Dorothy May Robert. The last of these children is now married.

h.—Joseph F. Robert, eighth child of William Henderson Robert and Clara Alice Bailey, died in infancy.

viii.—Ann Eliza Robert, youngest child of Leonidas Alonzo Robert and his second wife, Sarah H. Coffeen, and better known to her family and friends as "Nannie," was born on Waverly plantation, near Cheneyville, Louisiana, on January 20, 1854. She was married on April 26, 1870, by David May Calliham, Justice of the Peace, to Samuel Blum, and died in Cheneyville on March 28, 1896, at the age of forty-two. Eight children were born of this union:—

a.—Edward Loring Blum.
b.—Louis Robert Blum.
c.—Leonidas Alonzo Blum.
d.—Henry Simon Blum.
e.—Aubrey Becart Blum.
f.—Jeannette Adele Blum.
g.—Helen Sarah Blum.
h.—Samuel Price Blum.

a.—Edward Loring Blum married Sallie Wall, daughter of Wesley Winans Wall and Rebecca Currence Burr. They now reside in Cheneyville, La., and have no children.

b.—Louis Robert Blum married Ludie Smith, daughter of John Jordan Smith and Mary Ann Woods. They now reside in Cheneyville, La., and have no children.

c.—Leonidas Alonzo Blum married Agnes Hogan. They reside in Cheneyville, La., where Mr. Blum is a prominent merchant and planter. They have no children.

d.—Henry Simon Blum lived in Baton Rouge, La., for many years and died there in Setpember, 1941. He married and left four children:— Walter, Samuel, Edward, and Mary. Samuel is married and the daughter, Mary, is married to J. B. Efferson and has one child.

e.—Aubrey Becart Blum resides in New Orleans, is married and has three children, two boys and a girl.

f.—Jeannette Adele Blum has never married and has taught for many years in one of the public schools in Alexandria.

g.—Helen Sarah Blum was married to Jackson Smith Rawlins and now resides in Alexandria where Mr. Rawlins is a prominent business man. They have no children.

h.—Samuel Price Blum resides in Lafayette, La. He has never married.

4.—Rosella Ann Robert, fourth child of Joseph Robert
and Mary Hyrne Jaudon, was born in Wilkinson county, Mississippi, about 1807. She was married in Rapides parish, La.,
to her first cousin, Joseph Jerediah, son of Grimball Robert
and his first wife, Mary Sealey Cheney. For their descendants
see pages 73-75.

5.—Jane S. Robert, fifth child of Joseph Robert and Mary
Hyrne Jaudon, was born in Wilkinson county, Mississippi, about
1810. She was twice married, first to Joel (?) Coe, and second
to Francis Myers. The last record we have of Joel Coe was
on April 24, 1833, when he sold a slave to Joseph B. Robert.
In that transaction he is designated as being "of the Parish of
St. Landry." Jane S. Robert was probably a widow prior to
September 25, 1834, as on that date she purchases in her own
name property from Dr. Jesse D. Wright, and signs her name
as "Mrs. Jane S. Coe." Her brother Polhill Robert on January
21, 1836, sells "Jane S. Coe a lot of ground in the village of
Cheneyville." She was still the widow Coe on August 2, 1836,
when she sold "an equal and undivided half of two certain lots
in the village of Cheneyville to Ezra Bennett." By her first
marriage she had a daughter named Alma who married a
Bennet. In a letter to her step-father, Francis Myers, written
in 1854, she signs her name "A. C. Bennet"—probably Alma
Coe Bennet. She refers in it to her husband as "my dear
Curtis." Jane S. Robert married Francis Myers about 1840.
They had one son, Francis Myers, Jr., usually called Frank.
She died prior to 1849 as in that year Francis Myers went to
California with her brother, Thaddeus Sobieski Robert, in
search of gold. He was in San Jose, California, in 1857, and
as far as we can learn never returned to Louisiana.

5.—James Bordeaux Jaudon Robert, fifth child of Joseph
Robert and Mary Hyrne Jaudon, was born in Wilkinson county,
Mississippi, about 1814. He was brought to Louisiana by his
parents when quite young and spent the balance of his life
there on Bayou Boeuf, near Cheneyville, in Rapides parish. He
there married Martha Esther Pearce, daughter of Stephen
Pearce, and his first wife, Sally Goodwin Bray. She was born
on Bayou Boeuf, in Rapides parish, La., on August 11, 1820.
Both died at their home near Cheneyville but we have no record

of the dates of their deaths. Twelve children were born of this marriage:—

    i.—Charles Robert.
    ii.—Edward Robert.
    iii.—William Slaughter Robert.
    iv.—Thaddeus Robert.
    v.—Silas Robert.
    vi.—David M. Robert.
    vii.—John Pearce Robert.
    viii.—Amelia Robert.
    ix.—Eliza Jane Robert.
    x.—Elizabeth Robert.
    xi.—Werdner Robert.
    xii.—George Carlton Robert.

i.—Charles Robert died in infancy.

ii.—Edward Robert was one of the Cheneyville boys who volunteered for the Confederate Army during the Civil War. He was killed in battle at Appomattox, Virginia.

iii.—William Slaughter Robert, third son of James Bordeaux Jaudon Robert and Martha Esther Pearce, was born near Cheneyville, La., about 1840. He was better known to his friends as "Doc Robert." He was twice married. His first wife was Jane Taylor. They had two children:—

    a.—William Taylor Jaudon Robert.
    b.—Lena Robert.

Mr. Robert's second wife was Eunice Bailey, daughter of Walter Bailey and Margaret Gertrude Allen. Her sister, Clara Alice Bailey, was the wife of William Henderson Robert, a first cousin of William Slaughter Robert. Of this second marriage four children were born, all girls. They were:—

    c.—Ethel Robert.   )
    d.—Octavia Robert.) twins.
    e —Tuzette Robert.
    f.—Eunice Robert.

a.—William Taylor Jaudon Robert, son of William Slaughter Robert and his first wife, Jane Taylor, was born at Cheneyville, La., on October 24, 1872, and died at the home of his son, Frank Robert, in El Dorado, Arkansas, on July 8, 1941. He devoted his entire life to planting and was considered one of the best plantation managers on Bayou Boeuf. For many years he managed that portion of Greenwood plantation at

Cheneyville owned by the heirs of Mrs. Willie Campbell Scott. On February 13, 1895, he married Frances Elizabeth Warner, daughter of Stephen Ragan Warner and Nancy Paralee Pigg. She was born on January 25, 1879. Three children were born of this marriage:—

> az.—Edward Walter Robert.
> bz.—Frank Robert.
> cz.—Lessie Lucille Robert.

az.—Edward Walter Robert was born at Cheneyville, La., on January 21, 1897, and married on June 11, 1918, Tee Woods, daughter of Herbert Edgar Woods and Iler Watkins. She was born on February 8, 1897. They have one daughter, Nancy Claire Robert, born November 17, 1929.

bz.—Frank Robert was born at Cheneyville, La., on November 21, 1898, and now resides in El Dorado, Arkansas, where he is a conductor on the Missouri Pacific Railway. He married on April 3, 1924, Pauline Sprigg Gordon, who was born on July 30, 1904. She is the daughter of John Thomas Gordon (born May 6, 1862—died January 29, 1924) and Alice Ruth Percy (born February 9, 1867). They have one son, Frank Robert, Jr., born in New Orleans on April 13, 1927.

cz.—Lessie Lucille Robert, only daughter of William Taylor Jaudon Robert and Frances Elizabeth Warner, was born at Cheneyville, La., on September 11, 1900. She was married on July 29, 1919, to Douglas Mann Hueston, son of Willie Hueston and Bell Vienna. He was born on October 27, 1891, and is now Chief Dispatcher of the Missouri Pacific Lines. He and his wife reside in DeQuincy, La., and have no children.

b.—Lena Robert, daughter of William Slaughter Robert and his first wife, Jane Taylor, was married to George W. Stevens who is now dead. She has one son, George W. Stevens, Jr.

c.—Ethel Robert, eldest daughter of William Slaughter Robert and his second wife, Eunice Bailey, and the elder of the twins died young.

d.—Octavia Robert, younger of the twins of William Slaughter Robert and his second wife, Eunice Bailey, is living at this time but has never married.

e.—Tuzette Robert, third daughter of William Slaughter

Robert and his second wife, Eunice Bailey, was married to Louis Bartel. They have one daughter.

f.—Eunice Robert, fourth daughter of William Slaughter Robert and his second wife, Eunice Bailey, was married to Eric Coutard. We have no information as to any children.

iv.—Thaddeus Robert, fourth child of James Bordeaux Jaudon Robert and Martha Esther Pearce, was born near Cheneyville, La., about 1842. He probably bore the full name of his uncle *Thaddeus Sobieski Robert* but our record only shows his name as given above. He participated in the "Colfax Riot" in April, 1873, when the negroes attempted to take charge of affairs in Grant parish, and due to the menacing activity of the Federal Government against the participants he left Cheneyville and went to Texas, settling near Gatesville, in Coryell county, and there spent the remainder of his days, never returning to his native State. He married and left eight children. We regret our inability to obtain any information on them.

v.—Silas Robert, fifth child of James Bordeaux Jaudon Robert and Martha Esther Pearce, was born in Rapides parish, La., about 1845. He was probably named for his mother's brother, Silas Franklin Pearce. He died unmarried.

vi.—David M. Robert, sixth child of James Bordeaux Jaudon Robert and Martha Esther Pearce, was born near Cheneyville, La., about 1848. He married Providence Brewster and lived for many years in the vicinity of Forest Hill, Rapides parish, La. Every effort we have made to get information from the family has failed. The following death notice from the *Alexandria Town Talk* is the only data we have on his descendants :—

> DIED:—At the Pineville Charity Hospital, Monday, January 6, 1941, at 11:30 p. m., Wesley Robert, 68, of Woodworth, La. The deceased is survived by two brothers, W. L. Robert of Warren, Texas, and Henry Robert of Woodworth; two sisters, Mrs. Robert Ferguson of Ball and Mrs. A. A. Darby of Alexandria.

This Wesley Robert was a son of David M. Robert and Providence Brewster. His sister, Mrs. A. A. Darby, mentioned in the above notice, was Emma Robert. She was the second wife of Andre A. Darby who died in Alexandria on December

28, 1943. They had one daughter who married Leon Asscherick and has several children.

vii.—John Pearce Robert, seventh child of James Bordeaux Jaudon Robert and Martha Esther Pearce, was born near Cheneyville, Rapides parish, La., about 1850. He lived all of his life in the community where he was born and was principally engaged in farming. He married Mary Ann Sandifur and both have now been dead for many years. They had three children:—

a.—Mary Alice Robert.
b.—Simmon Geneva Robert.
c.—Willie Jaudon Robert.

a.—Mary Alice Robert was married to Stephen Rushing Jackson, son of Andrew Kendrick Jackson and Ella Pearce. Both are now dead. They had one son, Stephen Rushing Jackson, Jr., who is now postmaster at Cheneyville, La.

b.—Simmon Geneva Robert was married to James I. Hendrick of Shreveport, La. Both are now dead. They had one daughter, Ann Hendrick, who married William Henry Jordan.

c.—Willie Jaudon Robert was born at Cheneyville, La., on June 6, 1890, and still resides there. He married on December 29, 1914, Clara Augusta Heirtzler of Lecompte, La., where she was born August 12, 1896. They have two sons:—

James Luckett Robert, born January 12, 1919.
John Lewis Robert, born August 5, 1921.

Both of these sons are now serving in the armed forces of the United States, James Luckett in the army and John Lewis in the navy. The latter enlisted in August, 1940, and was on a destroyer at Pearl Harbor when the Japs attacked it on December 7, 1941. A letter written by him two days later informed his parents of his safety. He married September 15, 1944, Marie Lolette Bond, daughter of Mr. and Mrs. Myatt Bond of Golden Meadow, La.

viii.—Amelia Robert, daughter of James Bordeaux Jaudon Robert and Martha Esther Pearce, was born near Cheneyville, La., about 1852. She was married to Benjamin Spencer but we have been unable to get any information as to any descendants.

ix.—Eliza Jane Robert, daughter of James Bordeaux Jaudon Robert and Martha Esther Pearce, was born near Cheney-

ville, Rapides parish, La., and was married there in 1858 to
John Dawson Johnson, son of Charles Lewellyn Johnson and
Martha Rachel Cureton. There seems to have been considera
ble intermarriage about a century ago between the Johnson
Dawson and Cureton families. The early Dawson genealogy is
rather confusing, due to the fact that there are to be found in
the North Carolina records three John Dawsons, all living about
the same period. In Dr. Joseph A. Groves' book, THE ALSTON
FAMILY, on page 518, we find the will of Col. John Dawson of
Northampton county, North Carolina, made in 1762. It is more
than probable that he was the forebear of the Tennessee and
Louisiana Dawsons. This Col. Dawson was twice married,
first to Mary Thomas and second to Charity Alston (daughter
of John Alston and Mary Clarke). By his first marriage he
had two children, Henry and Mary Dawson. By his second wife
he had three children, Charity, Elizabeth and John Dawson,
who were minors at the time of the signing of his will in 1762.
From Elrie Robinson's interesting book, EARLY FELICIANA POL-
ITICS, we learn considerable about the Dawson and Johnson
families. Mr. Robinson tells us that John Bennett Dawson was
born in 1800 near Nashville, Tennessee, that he was a son of
Col. John Dawson and Sarah Barrow. This Col. Dawson, born
about 1770, in North Carolina, married Sarah Barrow in 1798—
probably in North Carolina—who was born May 14, 1773, and
was a daughter of William Barrow, Sr. Their son, John Bennett Dawson, attended Centre College at Danville, Kentucky,
and later moved to Louisiana. His parents died before January 1, 1817, as a letter on that date was written by his uncle,
William Barrow, Jr., giving his consent to his nephew, then a
minor of seventeen, to marry Margaret Johnson, daughter of
John Hunter Johnson and Thenia Muson, and a sister of Judge
Isaac Johnson of West Feliciana parish, La., who later became
the first democratic governor of Louisiana. This Johnson
family takes us back to Rev. John Johnson, an Episcopal minister, and his wife, Margaret Hunter, both of Liverpool, England.
Their son, Isaac Johnson, emigrated to Natchez, Miss., from
England. He soon became prosperous and influential in his
new home and was appointed one of the first alcaldes, or
judges, by Don Carlos de Grand Pre, Spanish Governor of the
Natchez District. He married Mary Routh who came to Mis-

sissippi with her brothers, Job and Jeremiah Routh, from Virginia. Some time later Isaac Johnson moved with his family to West Feliciana in Louisiana. He and his wife had twelve children. One of their sons, John Hunter Johnson, married Thenia Muson. He took an active part in the stirring scenes of the rebellion in Feliciana against the Spanish rule, was a member of the first Constitutional Convention of Louisiana and was a member of the legislature in 1815 at the time of the battle of New Orleans. He lived on his famous "Troy Plantation" and died there in 1819. He was the father of Isaac Johnson (governor of La. 1846-50), Margaret Johnson (wife of John Bennett Dawson), and Charles Lewellyn Johnson who moved to Rapides parish and married Martha Rachel Cureton, daughter of William H. Cureton and Mary Boaz Dawson. Mrs. Johnson had a sister, Margaret Dawson Cureton, who married Capt. George Benoist Marshall. After the death of William H. Cureton his widow (Mary Boaz Dawson) married William Prince Ford as his second wife.

Charles Lewellyn Johnson and Martha Rachel Cureton had five sons:— William Hunter, Isaac Cureton, Frank Bynum, Charles Lewellyn, Jr., and John Dawson Johnson. All of these married and left descendants. William Hunter Johnson married Rosa Dawson, a daughter of James H. Dawson and his first wife, Louisa A. Bonner (daughter of James Bonner). They had an only son, John Dawson Johnson, who resided at Boyce, La., and for more than thirty years was prominently known in banking circles throughout the state. He married Pauline Newman, a native of Winn parish, and they had three children, Dawson Allen, Mildred, and Elinor Johnson. William Hunter Johnson died comparatively young and his widow married Waverley Emmett Taylor by whom she had one daughter, Fannie Fee Taylor, who married Taylor Sanford Hickman and died recently, leaving three children, two sons and a daughter.

Isaac Cureton Johnson lived in Avoyelles parish, La., where he was sheriff for several years. He married Alzine Marshall (daughter of James Horace Marshall and Eliza Eugenia Pearce) and had, among other children, a son, Isaac Cureton Johnson, Jr., who graduated from the U. S. Naval Academy at Annapolis, Maryland, and is now a retired rear-admiral.

Frank Bynum Johnson married Miss C. S. Pollard and left two children. Charles Lewellyn Johnson, Jr., married Miss Emma Hackett and left four children.

John Dawson Johnson and his wife, Eliza Jane Robert, lived on Bayou Boeuf near Cheneyville, Rapides parish, La., where some of their descendants are living today. Mr. Johnson was born January 6, 1836, and died August 23, 1877. His good wife survived him more than fifty years and died near the scene of her birth and childhood in 1932, having lived nearly a century. The following notice of her death appeared in an Alexandria newspaper at the time:—

> DIED:—Near Cheneyville, on Saturday, September 24, 1932, Mrs. Eliza Jane Johnson, aged 93 years, 10 months, and 2 days, widow of John Johnson. She is survived by three sons and two daughters:— Joe and Sam of Waco, Texas, Robert and Miss Mary Johnson of Cheneyville, and Mrs. Mattie Monin of Long Leaf, La.

According to the above data Mrs. Johnson was born on November 22, 1838. Such being the case, she was probably the second or third child of James Bordeaux Jaudon Robert and Martha Esther Pearce, and *not* the ninth in order of birth as we have placed her here. Seven children were born of this marriage:—

a.—Martha R. Johnson, born March 14, 1859.
b.—Charles Edward Johnson, born June 20, 1860.
c.—Joseph Eugene Johnson, born March 10, 1862.
d.—Mary Johnson, born August 14, 1869.
e.—William Hunter Johnson, born November 24, 1870.
f.—Thaddeus Robert Johnson, born November 19, 1872.
g.—Samuel Meeker Johnson, born January 5, 1876.

a.—Martha R. Johnson, better known as "Mattie," died May 30, 1943, at the age of eighty-four. She was twice married. Her first husband was William Lynn Brown (son of William Robert Brown and Elmira Toler) by whom she had three children, and her second was Frank Monin by whom she had three children. See page 2 4 ᧒

b.—Charles Edward Johnson died September 19, 1873, aged thirteen years.

c.—Joseph Eugene Johnson moved to Waco, Texas, where he died on August 13, 1941. He married Annie Baillio, daughter of Gervais Baillio, Jr., and Elizabeth Morgan, and granddaughter of Judge Gervais Baillio of Rapides parish. Their residence in Waco, Texas, is verified by an item in the *Alexandria Town Talk* of May 4, 1889, which tells of the marriage there of Mrs. Johnson's sister, Lillian Baillio, to Alfred Chambers Pickett of New Iberia, La. Mr. and Mrs. Johnson had three children:—Charles Eugene, Joseph Edwin, and Gladys Johnson. The eldest married but left no children. The second, Joseph Edwin, married Fern Fuller and lives in Waco. They have no children. The youngest, Gladys, married Andrew Turcotte and has a son, Andrew Turcotte, Jr., who married Denise Nix and has one daughter, Ruanne Turcotte. Andrew Turcotte, Sr., died in September, 1942, at his home in Kingsville, Texas.

d.—Mary Johnson now resides at the old homestead near Cheneyville, with her brother Thaddeus Robert Johnson. She has never married.

e.—William Hunter Johnson died November 12, 1872, at the age of two.

f.—Thaddeus Robert Johnson, better known to his friends as "Bob," is living at this time at the old homestead near Cheneyville. He married Roberta Hetherwick who died suddenly a few years afterwards, leaving no children.

g.—Samuel Meeker Johnson lived in Waco, Texas, for many years, where he died November 18, 1940. He married Minnie Baumon and they had two children, John Dawson and Jane Johnson. The elder is married and has a son, John Dawson Johnson, Jr., now six years old (1944). Jane Johnson is unmarried at this time.

x.—Elizabeth Robert, tenth child of James Bordeaux Jaudon Robert and Martha Esther Pearce, probably died young as we find no record of her other than her birth.

xi.—Werdner Robert, eleventh child, also died young.

xii.—George Carleton Robert, twelfth child of James Bordeaux Jaudon Robert and Martha Esther Pearce, lived at Newellton, La., many years before his death. He married Clara Grayson and they had five children. There were twins,

Gilmore and Clarence Robert, who died in January, 1894, at the age of 16 months and two weeks respectively. The other three children reached adult life and are yet living. They are Eunice Lee Robert, born January 7, 1888, and married to Daniel N. Kelley of Foules, La.; Edward Moore Robert, born March 10, 1889, and living at Newellton, unmarried; George Carleton Robert, born March 1, 1891, and now living at Cheneyville, La., who graduated from Louisiana State University, served in World War I, and is now teaching in the public schools of Louisiana. He has never married.

6.—Thaddeus Sobieski Robert, sixth child of Joseph Robert and Mary Hyrne Jaudon, was born near Cheneyville, Rapides parish, La., on February 1, 1819. He completed his education in Shreveport, La., at one of the early institutions of learning in that section of the state. In 1849 he left Cheneyville for the California gold fields, going by way of the Isthmus of Panama —the overland route being little known at that time and very hazardous on account of the Indians. Several friends went with him, among whom were the Stafford brothers (William Maner and David Theophilus), and his brother-in-law Francis Myers. The younger Stafford brother, David Theophilus, died on the Isthmus from cholera, but the other brother went on to California. Mr. Robert never returned to Louisiana. His daughter, living at this date (1944) in California, has recently presented the compiler of these notes with some of her father's old letters which throw much light on his life in the west. He first engaged in the mercantile business in addition to prospecting for gold. Later he was elected judge of the county where he resided, and in 1861 was a member of the legislature. She also sent a Monterey County Democratic ticket on which his name appeared as a candidate for county clerk. We are unable to say whether or not he was elected. He died on January 25, 1873, from typhoid fever. In July, 1860, he married Catherine Corey in San Francisco, who survived him many years, dying in 1904. She was born in Enniskillen, County Fermanagh, Ireland, on May 1, 1829, and came to America when quite young. She was educated in Boston, Mass. They had one child, Mary Corey Robert, born April 23, 1862, in Pajaro, Monterey county, California. She is now Mrs. Green and resides in Glendale, California. She has no children.

E.
PROVIDENCE ROBERT.

Providence Robert, fifth child of Captain Peter Robert and Anne Grimball, was born in Beaufort District, South Carolina, on August 30, 1774. She there married Robert Tanner and came via Woodville, Mississippi, to Rapides parish, La., where she spent the remainder of her days. She and her husband had fifteen children, twelve of whom lived to adult life, married and left descendants. For a full account of this wonderful old couple and their progeny see PART THREE of this book.

F.
ANNE GRIMBALL ROBERT.

Anne Grimball Robert was born in Beaufort District, South Carolina, in what was then known as St. Peter's Parish, about 1776. She was the sixth child of Captain Peter Robert and Anne Grimball, and was married at the home of her parents in South Carolina on November 3, 1791, to Moses Hadley, a Baptist minister who had emigrated there from his native state of New York. He was a son of William Hadley and Elizabeth Warner of Yonkers, Westchester county, New York. This William Hadley was the third son of Joseph Hadley and Rebecca Dyckman, and the grandson of Joseph Hadley and his second wife, Mehetable Tippett, who was the son of George Hadley of Ipswich, Massachusetts, a first settler who landed in America in 1628.

Soon after 1800 many members of the Robert, Grimball and allied families banded together for the purpose of emigrating to that section of the country bordering on the southern part of the Mississippi river and then known as West Florida. A little later it was known as the Mississippi Territory. One of the chief promoters of this expedition was Robert Tanner who was also a son-in-law of Capt. Peter Robert, and the spiritual head of the enterprise was the Rev. Moses Hadley. The pioneers stopped in the present state of Mississippi and founded the town of Woodville, in Wilkinson county. There Moses Hadley and his wife built their home and reared their family. We are told by Paxton in his History of the Louisiana Baptists that in 1812 Moses Hadley and Lawrence Scarborough

were sent by the Mississippi Baptist Association to the Opelousas country in Louisiana to ordain Joseph Willis who was the
first Baptist preacher west of the Mississippi river. At Bayou
Chicot, in the parish of St. Landry, they constituted a church
on November 13, 1812, and called it Calvary. It was the first
Baptist church in Louisiana. Of this church Joseph Willis became pastor. It would appear from the best information obtainable that Rev. Moses Hadley continued his labors at Woodville until his death and there it is believed he and his wife
were buried. The Randolph family Bible tells us that the
youngest daughter of Moses Hadley and Anne Grimball Robert,
who was born in 1810, was married in Pinckneyville, Miss., on
March 20, 1828, to William Randolph. Pinckneyville is in
Wilkinson county and not very far from Woodville, so it may
have been that the Hadleys were living there at the time.

Rev. Moses Hadley and Anne Grimball Robert had six
children:—Thomas Benjamin Jefferson, Ann, Rachel, Thirza,
William Peter Gershom, and Esther Sarah Jaudon Hadley
They left many descendants, a full account of whom will be
found in the present compiler's book on The Stafford family,
Chapter VI, pages 203-226.

G

PAUL JABEZ ROBERT.

The name of Paul Jabez Robert has been handed down to
us as the seventh of the children of Captain Peter Robert and
Anne Grimball. He was born in Beaufort District, South
Carolina, about 1777, and came to Woodville, Mississippi, with
his parents soon after 1800. He married Sarah Tanner, daughter of Joseph Tanner and his first wife, Elizabeth Lanier.
Whether they were married in South Carolina or Mississippi
we are unable to say, though it is not unlikely that the marriage
took place in South Carolina. We have very little recorded
data relative to Paul Jabez Robert and his wife. We know
that at one time they lived near Cheneyville, in Rapides parish,
La., where many of their kindred had settled. The records of
the Lodowick Tanner Bible, kindly put at our disposal by Mrs.
George Ripley White of Centreville, Mississippi, who before
marriage was Eugenia Tanner, tell us that Paul Jabez Robert
and Sarah Tanner had three children:—Sarah, Cornelia and

Mariam. The third of these died in childhood. The eldest, Sarah Robert, was married to her first cousin, Robert Daniel Eldred (born September 18, 1821), son of Randal Eldred, Jr., and Esther Susannah Robert. We have been unable to find a record of any descendants. The second daughter, Cornelia Robert, was married to Vestal Gould, a native of Newberry, South Carolina, who was born there on December 10, 1812. In a copy of *The Constitutional,* an Alexandria newspaper, dated March 23, 1861, we find the following notice of his death:—

> DIED:—At the residence of L. A. Stafford, Esq., on the 24th of February, 1861, Vestal Gould, a native of Newberry, South Carolina, aged 48 years, 2 months and 14 days.

We find the name of Vestal Gould on the roster of the Rapides Volunteers, a company organized in Rapides parish for the Mexican War and commanded by Captain George Mason Graham. This company was a part of the Third Regiment, Louisiana Volunteers, and saw service on the Mexican border. From the best information available we are inclined to believe that Cornelia Robert died young, leaving no children.

H.
SARAH CATHARINE ROBERT.

Sarah Catharine Robert, eighth child of Captain Peter Robert and Anne Grimball, was born in Beaufort District, South Carolina, in 1778. We find this date recorded in the family Bible of Mrs. Irene Ethel (Tanner) Johns, a great niece of this lady, which is now the property of Mrs. Blanchard Iles of Oakdale, La., who is the great niece of Mrs. Johns. The same good book tells us that Sarah Catharine Robert died at Cheneyville, La., on January 9, 1820, and that she was married in South Carolina on September 24, 1801, to David Bettison who was born there on May 30, 1757. This date of David Bettison's birth is further verified by the church register of St. Helena Parish, South Carolina, which was published in the South Carolina Historical and Genealogical Magazine, Vol. XXIII, page 19. The entry reads as follows:—"David Bettison, son of David and Elizabeth Bettison of St. Helena Parish, was born May 30, 1757."

Mrs. Evalyn Park Selby Johnson of Marion, South Carolina, has compiled a very interesting and valuable little book entitled, THE FAMILY OF WILKINS, in which we learn that the Bettisons were established early in St. Helena Parish of Beaufort District, South Carolina. The first of the name she has a record of is Jonathan Bettison who married Hannah ———— and had a son, David, born May 16, 1718, and died November 1, 1761. This son David married Elizabeth Humphries on November 24, 1746, daughter of Thomas and Margaret Humphries, who was born June 1, 1729, and died in November, 1798. Mrs. Johnson gives the names of only two children of David Bettison and Elizabeth Humphries. One was Elizabeth, her ancestress, and the other was David who married Sarah Catharine Robert. Mrs. Johnson's ancestress, Elizabeth Bettison, was born October 9, 1747, and died November 12, 1777. She married John Wilkins on October 9, 1766. The St. Helena Parish register, mentioned above, has helped us out with some additional data on the Bettison family. We learn that the name was spelled in several ways, such as Batison, Betterson, and Bettison, the last being the commonly accepted one. We learn from the church register of St. Helena Parish, which was adjoining St. Peter's from which came so many of the South Carolina emigrants to Louisiana and Mississippi, that among the children of the above mentioned Jonathan Bettison and his wife Hannah were two sons, David and Jonathan. The latter's wife was named Sarah and they had several children, two of whom, Ann and Mary, died when young; Ann was buried July 4, 1754, and Mary on August 27, 1754. This same couple had two other children, Hannah who was born May 23, 1754, and Jonathan born May 3, 1757.

David Bettison, the other son of Jonathan and Hannah Bettison, who married Elizabeth Humphries, had a number of children, among whom were the following:—

Elizabeth Bettison, born October 10, 1747.
Mary Bettison, born February 22, 1749.
William Bettison, born February 22, 1755.
David Bettison, born May 30, 1757.

From these St. Helena records we are able to state that the first Jonathan Bettison and his wife Hannah had besides their sons David and Jonathan also a daughter named Elizabeth who married John Field, Jr., son of John and Mary Field of Chehaw, and they had a daughter, Keziah Field, born June 8, 1741.

A great grand-daughter of David Bettison and Sarah Catharine Robert, Mrs. Jeannette (Robinson) Murphy, herself a genealogist of note, tells us that David Bettison was a soldier in General Francis Marion's brigade during the Revolution. We have been unable to verify such military service from the South Carolina records. However, as Revolutionary paper work of a military character was ever at a low ebb of efficiency, and since many such records as were kept have been lost or destroyed, our failure to find David Bettison recorded among Marion's men is by no means to be accepted as a final conclusion that he was not one of them.

It was in 1801 that David Bettison claimed his bride and a few years later they joined the emigration train of the Grimball and Robert families in their long journey to the south-west and went to what is now Woodville, Mississippi. David Bettison was about forty-four years old when he married Sarah Catharine Robert which would incline us to the belief that he had been previously married, but there is no record to show that he was. His first three children were born in South Carolina, the next three in Mississippi, and the youngest in Louisiana. It is said that some of his older children went to school to a brother of Jefferson Davis in the Woodville neighborhood. About 1818 the Bettison family moved once more, and crossing the Mississippi river they treked to the banks of Bayou Boeuf in Rapides parish, La., near the present town of Cheneyville where many of their relatives had already settled. There Mrs. Bettison died on January 9, 1820, and Mr. Bettison on July 19, 1823. Their graves were not marked and today we know not the exact spot where their ashes rest. After the deaths of these two good people Mrs. Bettison's sister, Providence Robert, who had married Robert Tanner, took their three youngest children (all girls) into her home and reared them as her own. They were married from her home and two of them married her sons. Seven children were born to Sarah Catharine Robert and David Bettison, six of whom reached adult life. They were:—

1.—Anne Eliza Bettison.
2.—Martha Sarah Bettison (i).

3.—Joseph Roderic Bettison.
4.—Thomas Grimball Bettison.
5.—Eunice Rebecca Bettison.
6.—Esther Providence Bettison.
7.—Martha Sarah Bettison (ii).

We know that David Bettison left a will but since all the public .records in Rapides parish were destroyed in 1864 we know nothing of its contents except it provided that his estate was to be divided into lots of approximately the same value and equal to the number of children he left, and they were to draw or choose one of the lots as they became of age or married. This we learn from a meeting of the appraisers on January 25, 1825, at which time his eldest daughter was married and claimed her share of the estate. The executor of his will was Robert Tanner who had married Providence Robert, a sister of Mrs. Bettison. We will here insert the whole of the proceedings which took place in the division of his estate, feeling that due to the importance of the data and the interest it may prove to the present and future generations the space will be well taken up.

STATE OF LOUISIANA
PARISH OF RAPIDES.

Distribution of the Estate of David Bettison, deceased, into six lots according to the number of the heirs of said deceased, made by the undersigned under oath by order of the executors, the 25th day of January, 1825.

Lot First.

One tract of land in Wilkinson county, State of Mississippi, on Thompson's Creek, containing five hundred acres more or less at	$2,000.00
Negro man Pompey	400.00
Negro woman Lucy	450.00
Negro man John	300.00
1 horse	100.00
1 bed & furniture	40.00
1 pr. pistols	5.00
1 steer	12.00
1 wheel	5.00
4 sheep	14.00
1 note of hand on Rushton	100.00
Horn & spoons	152.00
	$3,578.00

Lot Second.

160 arpents land on Bayou Boeuf, Parish of Rapides, at	$2,000.00
Negro man Dick, aged 45	300.00
Polly & child	500.00
Negro man Henry	200.00
1 lot of hogs	90.00
1 sorel horse	50.00
1 horse cart	5.00
Timber wheels	5.00
1 bay horse	40.00
1 doz. chairs	6.00
1 coffee mill	2.50
Hoof iron	2.00
Shoe maker tools	1.00
Wheel & cards	7.00
4 head of sheep	14.00
Proportion of notes	313.00
	$3,535.50

Lot Third.

160 arpents land on Bayou Boeuf, Parish of Rapides, at	$2,000.00
Negro man Pargo	400.00
Negro woman Clarinda	400.00
Negro man William	275.00
1 ox cart	25.00
1 brown bay horse	75.00
1 gray mare	25.00
3 oxen	45.00
1 steer	9.00
1 grind stone	1.50
1 wheel	5.00
4 sheep	14.00
Proportion of notes	313.00
	$3,587.50

Lot Fourth.

160 arpents land on Bayou Boeuf, Parish of Rapides, at	$2,000.00
Negro woman Molly	450.00
Negro man Reuben	450.00
Negro woman Charlotte	300.00
Bed, etc.	35.00
Hand mill	10.00

Looking glass	1.00
Carpenter's tools	10.00
5 sheep	17.50
Proportion of notes	313.00
	$3,586.50

Lot Fifth.

160 arpents land on Bayou Boeuf, Parish of Rapides, at	$2,000.00
Negro woman Roset & child	375.00
Negro woman Arabella	225.00
Negro woman Rachel	150.00
Negro man Alexander	275.00
Plantation tools	30.00
Bay mare	40.00
13 head cattle	78.00
Bed, etc.	25.00
Shot gun	2.00
Kitchen furniture	30.00
Bed, etc. in pine woods	15.00
Fire irons	4.00
4 jars	1.50
1 table	2.00
1 pr. physic scales	1.50
5 sheep	17.50
Proportion of notes	313.00
	$3,584.50

Lot Sixth.

160 arpents land on Bayou Boeuf, Parish of Rapides, at	$2,000.00
Negro man Hampton	100.00
Negro man Randal	500.00
Negro woman Jenny	275.00
Negro woman Mary	250.00
1 yoke oxen	60.00
1 press	15.00
1 colt	10.00
1 book	10.00
1 shot gun	10.00
Trunks	6.00
1 loom	10.00
Table furniture	10.00
5 sheep	17.50

Proportion of notes 313.00
1 clock reel 1.50

$3,588.00

Total of Estate...................................$21,460.00

We the undersigned appraisers appointed by Robert Tanner, acting executor of the estate of David Bettison, deceased, to appraise and divide said estate according to the will of said Bettison, have appraised and divided it into lots as it stands stated, and we do hereby certify that Hadley P. Robert and Eliza his wife, daughter of said Bettison, have chosen and set aside Lot First containing land, negroes, etc., amounting in all to three thousand five hundred and seventy-eight dollars as their dividend of said estate, and that Lots second, third, fourth, fifth and sixth are held jointly among the five minor heirs of said estate. Given under our hands this 6th day of August, 1825.

Lodowick Tanner
Wm. W. Chambers
Joseph Robert.
Admitted to record 10th August, 1825.
Silas Talbert, Notary Public.

Whenever the other heirs became of age or married the remaining lots were re-appraised and numbered and each was given the privilege of having his or her choice of those left. On May 28, 1830, we find a record where Joseph Roderic Bettison chose Lot Third which at that time was valued at $3,006.33¼. He was given the same and receipted to Robert Tanner, Executor, for it. The appraisers were the same except that Joseph H. Boone took the place of Lodowick Tanner.

On November 29, 1831, Eunice Rebecca Bettison, who had just married Peter Tanner, came in for her share of her father's estate. This time William H. Cureton took the place of Joseph H. Boone as one of the appraisers, and Eunice Rebecca Bettison and her husband Peter Tanner chose Lot Second, appraised at the time for $3,357.33 1/3. On July 30, 1832, Thomas Grimball Bettison appeared for his portion of the estate. The appraisers were the same as when his sister, Eunice Rebecca Bettison, received her share. He chose Lot Fourth, then appraised at $3,305.33 1/3. On August 18, 1833, Esther Providence Bettison, who had married Jabez Tanner, came forward and claimed her portion of the estate. She chose Lot Fifth then appraised at $4,293.28 1/3. It will be seen that her part of the estate had increased considerably in value since it was first appraised. On March 16, 1835, Martha Sarah Bettison, youngest child of David Bettison, who had married George W. Haygood, came forward and claimed her portion. The appraisers at the time were Montfort Wells, J. D. Wright and L. A. Robert. All that remained of the estate was allotted to her. It was appraised at the time for $6,683.40. This was almost double the amount of the first appraisement ten years before.

1.—Anne Eliza Bettison was born in Beaufort District, South Carolina, in 1802. She came to Woodville, Miss., with her parents when a young child and then to Rapides parish, Louisiana, where she married in Cheneyville on July 22, 1824, her first cousin, Hadley Peter Robert, son of James Robert and Elizabeth Naylor. They moved to Washington county, Texas, some years later, where they died leaving seven children. See pages 41-45.

2.—Martha Sarah Bettison (i) was born in Beaufort District, South Carolina, in 1806 and died in early childhood.

3.—Joseph Roderic Bettison was born in Beaufort District. South Carolina, on April 14, 1809, and died in Louisville, Kentucky, on January 13, 1875. He was reared in Woodville, Miss., and Cheneyville, La. After receiving a splendid preliminary education he took up the study of medicine at the University of Louisville in which profession he afterwards became very prominent in both Louisiana and Kentucky. The old Cheneyville records show him as a resident of Iberville parish, La., where he practiced his profession for some years He married on December 22, 1831, at Plaquemine, Iberville parish, La., Ann Eliza Cathcart, daughter of Joseph Cathcart and Margaret Mann (born 1797, married 1814, and died January 5, 1819) of that parish. Dr. Bettison must have lived for some time at Little Rock, Arkansas, as his second child was born there in 1838. Soon after that date he located in Louisville, Ky., where he spent the remainder of his days, dying there on the date given above. His wife's father was formerly of Rockhill, South Carolina, and she was born at the home of her maternal grandparents at Maysville, Ky., on April 22, 1815. She died in Louisville on April 29, 1896, at the home of her granddaughter, Mrs. John William Brown. She and her husband were both buried in Cave Hill cemetery at Louisville. It is said that Dr. and Mrs. Bettison had eleven children but we have a record of only nine. There may have been two others who died at birth. The nine were:—

> i.—Joanna Araminta Bettison.
> ii.—Ulric Bettison.
> iii.—Byron Bettison.
> iv.—Mattie Bettison.
> v.—Eunice Bettison.
> vi.—Cathcart Bettison.
> vii.—Leora Bettison.
> viii.—David Bettison.
> ix.—Kate Bettison.

i.—Joanna Araminta Bettison was born November 7, 1832, and died August 3, 1833. She is buried across the river from Plaquemine, La.

ii.—Ulric Bettison was born in Little Rock, Arkansas, on October 26, 1838, and died in Louisville, Ky., August 16, 1900. As a boy he lived in Jeffersonville, Indiana, across the Ohio river from Louisville. He was a very brilliant man and when a mere boy taught school in Louisville. He went to New Orleans to visit his mother's people and there met, fell in love with, and married his first cousin, Margaret Mann Cathcart. She lived on the "lower coast" about 55 miles below New Orleans where she was born April 9, 1850. They were married July 4, 1867. She died in New Orleans on July 16, 1925, and was buried in St. Louis cemetery No. 2, in that city. Mr. Bettison was very prominent in educational circles in Louisiana. For many years he was Superintendent of the public schools of New Orleans, and later a professor of mathematics in the Sophie Newcomb College there. He died while on a visit to relatives in Louisville, Ky., and was buried there in the Bettison lot in Cave Hill cemetery. Mr. and Mrs. Bettison had six children:—

> a.—Harriett Ann Bettison.
> b.—Agnes Sinclair Bettison.
> c.—Margaret Cathcart Bettison.
> d.—Edmund Goldman Bettison.
> e.—Ellen Rapp Bettison.
> f.—Leora Norman Bettison.

a.—Harriett Ann Bettison was born in New Orleans, La., on December 3, 1868, and died there on August 26, 1891. She was married May 13, 1890, to Robert Edward Lee Grigsby of Trenton, Tennessee. Mr. Grigsby was a druggist and was prominent in his profession. He was connected for many years with The Southern Drug Company of Houston, Texas. Mrs. Grigsby died at the birth of her only child and was buried in St. Louis cemetery No. 2, in the family tomb built by her grandfather Cathcart in 1840. Mr. Grigsby lived for many years after his wife's death and died in Beaumont, Texas, on April 11, 1942, at the age of 79 years. He was buried by the side of his wife in New Orleans. As mentioned above, there was only one child born of this marriage:—

az.—Hattie Lee Grigsby.

az.—Hattie Lee Grigsby, only child of Robert Edward Lee Grigsby and Harriett Ann Bettison, was born in New Orleans, La., on August 26, 1891. She was married in New Orleans at St. Paul's Episcopal church on March 20, 1916, to Samuel Cyrus Lipscomb who was born in Cameron, Texas, on December 12, 1890. They now reside at 2403 Liberty Avenue, Beaumont, Texas. Mr. Lipscomb is a prominent attorney-at-law in Beaumont, and is the senior member of the firm of Lipscomb and Lipscomb. Three children were born of this marriage:—

Margaret Bettison Lipscomb, born August 9, 1917.
Anna Arledge Lipscomb, born August 9, 1917.
Harry Shepherd Lipscomb, born April 12, 1926.

The elder of the twins, Margaret Bettison Lipscomb, was married in Beaumont, Texas, on September 1, 1938, to Ben Hicks Stone, Jr., born in Amarillo, Texas, on November 30, 1914. They live in Amarillo where Mr. Stone is engaged in the practice of law. He belongs to the law firm of Stone, Stone and Stone, consisting of father and two sons. They have one child, Harriet Ann Stone, born March 12, 1940.

The younger of the twins, Anna Arledge Lipscomb, was married in Beaumont, Texas, on February 25, 1939, to James William Hodges, born in Bent, Texas, October 20, 1913. He is a petroleum engineer with The Sun Company. They have two children:—Susan Lee Hodges, born in Beaumont, Texas, September 1, 1940, and James William Hodges, Jr., born January 7, 1943.

The only son, Harry Sheperd Lipscomb, was a student at the Sewanee Military Academy for several years and is now (1944) taking a pre-medical course at Tulane University in New Orleans.

b.—Agnes Sinclair Bettison, second child of Ulric Bettison and Margaret Mann Cathcart, was born February 23, 1871, and died of yellow fever on October 23, 1878.

c.—Margaret Cathcart Bettison, third child of Ulric Bettison and Margaret Mann Cathcart, was born May 13, 1873, and is now living at Belle Chasse, a few miles below New Orleans. She graduated from Newcomb College with honors at the age of nineteen and taught chemistry for a while. She was married on September 15, 1897, to her first cousin, David Cathcart Bettison, son of David Bettison and Louise Racine. They lived in Louisville and Glasgow, Kentucky, for many years where Mr. Bettison was a successful tobacco broker. During the latter years of his life he lived at Belle Chasse, where he died November 7, 1935, leaving no issue. The following notice of his death is copied from the New Orleans Times-Picayune:—

BETTISON:—On Thursday, November 7, 1935, at 11:25 o'clock a. m., at his residence, Belle Chasse, Louisiana, David Cathcart Bettison, a native of Louisville, Kentucky, husband of Margaret C. Bettison, brother of Mrs. L. B. Brown of Louisville, Ky.
The funeral will take place this (Friday) afternoon, November 8, 1935, at 2 o'clock from the House of Bultman, St. Charles avenue at Louisiana avenue.

d.—Edmund Goldman Bettison, fourth child of Ulric Bettison and Margaret Mann Cathcart, was born in New Orleans on August 24, 1875. He never married, was in the tobacco business for many years in Louisville, Ky., and died there on October 12, 1939. He was buried in Cave Hill cemetery in Louisville.

e.—Ellen Rapp Bettison, fifth child of Ulric Bettison and Margaret Mann Cathcart, was born July 4, 1878. She never married and died August 9, 1938. The following notice of her death appeared in the New Orleans Times-Picayune:—

BETTISON:—On Tuesday, August 9, 1938, at 4:25 o'clock a. m., at Southern Baptist Hospital, Ellen Rapp

Bettison, in her 61st year, late of Belle Chasse, Louisiana, sister of E. G. Bettison of Louisville, Kentucky, and Mrs. D. C. Bettison of Belle Chasse, La., daughter of the late Margaret Cathcart and Professor Ulric Bettison.

The funeral will take place Wednesday morning, August 10, 1938, at 11 o'clock from the House of Bultman, St. Charles avenue at Louisiana avenue. Interment in St. Louis cemetery No. 2, Esplanade avenue.

f.—Leora Norman Bettison, sixth child of Ulric Bettison and Margaret Mann Cathcart, was born January 13, 1881, and died April 21, 1882.

iii.—Byron Bettison, third child of Dr. Joseph Roderic Bettison and Ann Eliza Cathcart, was born in Louisville, Kentucky, about 1840. He lived in Bowling Green, Kentucky, where he was engaged in photography. He married Mary Reese and they had two children:—Ethel Bettison of Bowling Green, and Colonel Reese Bettison, U. S. A. retired, of Wayne, Pennsylvania.

iv.—Mattie Bettison, fourth child of Dr. Joseph Roderic Bettison and Ann Eliza Cathcart, was born in Louisville, Ky., about 1842. She was married to Dr. John Percival and they had four children. We regret that this is the extent of our data.

v.—Eunice Bettison, fifth child of Dr. Joseph Roderic Bettison and Ann Eliza Cathcart, was born in Louisville, Ky. She was married to Ed Welburn and they had one child.

vi.—Cathcart Bettison, sixth child of Dr. Joseph Roderic Bettison and Ann Eliza Cathcart, was born in Louisville, Ky. He was never married and died in the Confederate Army when a young man.

vii.—Leora Bettison, seventh child of Dr. Joseph Roderic Bettison and Ann Eliza Cathcart, was born in Louisville, Ky. She was married to Professor Norman Robinson about 1865, one of the outstanding chemists of his day and also noted in the field of education. Both are long since dead. Mrs. Robinson sleeps in the cemetery at Orlando, Florida. They had an only child, Jeannette Cathcart Robinson, born June 30, 1866. She was married to John Hugh Murphy who has now been dead many years. Mrs. Murphy now resides near Canton, North Carolina. She has been noted for many years throughout the country as an entertainer in recitals and folklore songs. She is also a poetess of renown and a well known religious worker. She has two children:—John Hugh Murphy, Jr., and Eunice Murphy.

viii.—David Bettison, eighth child of Dr. Joseph Roderic Bettison and Ann Eliza Cathcart, was born in Louisville, Ky., and for many years was a well known photographer of that city. He married Louise Racine and they had three children:—

    a.—David Cathcart Bettison.
    b.—Percy Bettison.
    c.—Leora Maude Bettison.

a.—David Cathcart Bettison was a prominent citizen and successful tobacco broker of Louisville, Kentucky. He married on September 15, 1897, his first cousin, Margaret Cathcart Bettison, daughter of Ulric Bettison and Margaret Mann Cathcart. He died at his residence at Belle Chasse, La., on November 7, 1935, leaving no issue.

b.—Percy Bettison married Georgia Meriwether on June 21, 1887. They had three children:—

    az.—Percy Bettison, Jr., born November 9, 1888.
    bz.—Thornton Bettison, born June 8, 1892.
    cz.—David Cathcart Bettison, born August 21, 1894.

az.—Percy Bettison, Jr., married Anna Rothwell Bairlein on April 5, 1917. They have no children.

bz.—Thornton Bettison married Allene Giltner on October 18, 1924. They have one child, Thornton Bettison, Jr., born August 11, 1927.

cz.—David Cathcart Bettison married on July 19, 1919, Hazel Kesterson who was born July 20, 1899. They have one son, Dick C. Bettison, born June 19, 1921. David Cathcart Bettison married second, Helen Wolcott, who was born March 12, 1896. No children by the second union. Dick C. Bettison, the son by the first marriage, married Mavis Elaine, born May 16, 1920. They have two children:—David James Bettison, born January 6, 1941, and Susan Lee Bettison, born January 27, 1942.

c.—Leora Maude Bettison, third child of David Bettison and Louise Racine, was born in Louisville, Ky., and was married September 20, 1887, to John William Brown. She bore the

nickname of "Dixie" and is living at this time. She had fou:
children:—

az.—Leora Bettison Brown, born July 15, 1888.
bz.—Harriet Louise Brown, born March 1, 1892.
cz.—John Welburn Brown, born March 31, 1899.
dz.—Everett Cathcart Brown, born November 12, 1900

az.—Leora Bettison Brown was married to Samuel Fore
Dennis on October 15, 1910. They have one child, Elizabetl
Foree Dennis, who was married to Benjamin Hudson Milner or
July 2, 1938, and they have one child, Humphrey Hudson, bor1
October 15, 1940.

bz.—Harriet Louise Brown was married to Dr. Stuar
Graves on December 11, 1915, Dean of the Medical Departmen
of the University of Alabama. They have three children.

Jean Cathcart Graves, born October 8, 1917.
Marion Stuart Graves, born October 27, 1921.
Stuart Graves, Jr., born August 31, 1925.

The second of these children, Marion Stuart Graves, wa
married on September 1, 1942, to Robert Pierce Arrington.

cz.—John Welburn Brown married Barbara Hewett or
October 17, 1928. They have four children:—

Barbara Hewett Brown, born June 11, 1930.
John Welburn Brown, Jr., born May 28, 1932.
Hewett Brown, born May 10, 1937.
Peter Cooper Brown, born May 28, 1942.

dz.—Everett Cathcart Brown married Maria Marshal
Martin on March 20, 1937. They have two children:—

David Cathcart Brown, born March 26, 1939.
Michael Hunt Brown, born September 21, 1942.

ix.—Kate Bettison, ninth child of Dr. Joseph Roderic Bet
tison and Ann Eliza Cathcart, was born in Louisville, Ky. She
was married to Lyman Coleman Reed, at one time a prominen1
member of the faculty of Tulane University in New Orleans
He has now been dead for many years. Mrs. Reed lived to be
more than eighty years of age. They had five children.

a.—Warren Bettison Reed.
b.—Lyman Coleman Reed, Jr.
c.—Evelyn Cathcart Reed.
d.—Katherine Reed.
e.—Edna Reed.

a.—Warren Bettison Reed was proprietor of the Reed Art Gallery on Royal Street, in New Orleans. He died in May, 1942. He married Grace Gardner and they had three children:—Warren Bettison Reed, Jr., who is married and has two children; Lyman Coleman Reed, III, who is married and has a son; Gardner Reed who is married but has no children.

b.—Lyman Coleman Reed, Jr., is living at this date. He married Lillian Espey and they have three children:—Sallie Reed who is unmarried and teaches at Sophie Newcomb College; Lucile Reed who is married but has no children; Espey Reed who is married but has no children.

c.—Evelyn Cathcart Reed has never married.

d.—Katherine Reed has never married.

e.—Edna Reed was married to Marcellus Whaley, Dean of the Law School of South Carolina University at Columbia. They have five children.

4.—Thomas Grimball Bettison, fourth child of David Bettison and Sarah Catharine Robert, was born near Woodville, Mississippi, on July 27, 1811, and came to Rapides parish, La., with his parents in 1818. He married in 1838 Elizabeth Susan Rutledge, fourth child of Joseph Rutledge and Elizabeth Susannah Robert, who was born in Wilkes county, Georgia, in 1821, and came to Rapides parish, La., with her parents about 1835, where she met and married her husband who was her second cousin. Thomas Grimball Bettison and his wife resided near Cheneyville, Rapides parish, La., until 1850, when they moved to Avoyelles parish and lived there on Bayou Chopegue until Mr. Bettison's death on January 7, 1873. Mrs. Bettison died in Texas on October 7, 1894, where she was living with one of her children. This couple is particularly noted for the unusual size of their family—they were the parents of sixteen children. Mrs. Bettison was nineteen years old when her first child was born and forty-seven when the sixteenth arrived. Their children were:—

a.—William Cole Bettison, born January 20, 1840.
b.—Arkelius Audiburn Bettison, born March 12, 1842.
c.—Sarah Catharine Bettison, born January 26, 1844.
d.—Martha Frances Bettison, born March 12, 1846.
e.—Thomas Gillison Bettison, born December 25, 1847.
f.—David Rutledge Bettison, born October 12, 1849.

g.—Joseph Warren Bettison, born July 27, 1851.
h.—Ella Bettison, born April 7, 1853.
i.—Rufus Blakewood Bettison, born June 12, 1854.
j.—Eunice Bettison, born September 30, 1855.
k.—Luton Spurgeon Bettison, born June 18, 1857.
l.—Alvan Bettison, born June 29, 1860.
m.—Harvey Bettison, born September 16, 1861.
n.—Isaac Newton Bettison, born November 29, 1862.
o.—Robert Edward Lee Bettison, born Dec. 16, 1864.
p.—Elizabeth Susan Bettison, born August 21, 1868.

The eldest of the above children, William Cole Bettison, died on January 28, 1852, and the second, Arkelius Audiburn Bettison, died on October 29, 1843. The other nine sons reached adult life and married. We regret that we have been able to obtain so little information about the individual members of this large family.

d.—Martha Frances Bettison, the fourth of the above mentioned Bettison children, was married to a Mr. Hebert and moved to Houston, Texas, with him. She died there in January, 1937. The most definite information we have on her branch of the family is gleaned from a letter she wrote from Galveston, Texas, on January 31, 1923. It was written to her cousin, Mrs. U. H. Johns of Cheneyville, La., and was evidently a reply to one she had recently received. Mrs. Johns was Irene Ethel Tanner, a daughter of Paul Jabez Tanner and Esther Providence Bettison, and therefore a first cousin of Martha Frances (Bettison) Hebert. We quote the following from her letter:—

Yes, my brother Thomas married. He had two sons. His widow is living in California. They have a nice home and are doing well. One of the boys is married. David's widow is in California too. The only sister I have is there also; she has ten children, all married and have families and doing well. Ma died the 7th October, 1894, and Pa died in his home in Louisiana in 1873, he was 63 years old Ma was 73, she died here and was buried in Louisiana by the side of Pa. Sister Ella died in 1893. My brothe Isaac lives in San Antonio and is doing well. Harvey is in Houston, Luton in Cleburn, Rufus in Houston. My eldes child is a widow, living in Houston, has four girls and on boy. She lost two children, a girl and a boy. The gi had been married 10 months and burned to death. M boy David lost his second wife. He has two children, boy and a girl. He lives in Georgetown, Texas. Ulric has one boy and three girls. He lives in Houston. I have two girls and two boys single. One boy and the two girls are with me, and the other one lost his mind and is away in Wichita Falls, Texas . . . .

(signed) M. F. Hebert.

f.—David Rutledge Bettison, sixth child of Thomas Grimball Bettison and Elizabeth Susan Rutledge, seems to have been the only one of this numerous family who remained in his native State. He was engaged in the feed and livery stable business in Evergreen, La., for several years, and in 1888 moved his business to Marksville, La., where he lived until the time of his death which occurred about 1920. He was a deputy sheriff of Avoyelles parish for many years and also parish jailer. He was well known throughout that section of the country and liked by all who knew him. He married Martha Ada Keller at Holmesville, La., in 1878. They had four children:—

az.—David Lemuel Bettison, born 1880.
bz.—Susan Bettison, born 1882.
cz.—Elizabeth Lorena Bettison, born 1886.
dz.—Clifton Overton Bettison, born 1891.

We have been able to obtain very little data about these children and none at all about the two daughters.

az.—David Lemuel Bettison was a prominent Eye, Ear, Nose and Throat specialist in Dallas, Texas. He was killed in an automobile accident in 1930, and his only son, David, was killed by lightning about 1923, on his birthday.

dz.—Clifton Overton Bettison was killed in an automobile accident after reaching adult life. As far as we know he never married.

i.—Rufus Blakewood Bettison, ninth child of Thomas Grimball Bettison and Elizabeth Susan Rutledge, was living in Houston, Texas, when we last heard of him about 1923. We are unable to state whether or not he was married.

j.—Eunice Bttison, tenth child of Thomas Grimball Bettison and Elizabeth Susan Rutledge, married a Mr. Cary and is now living in Los Angeles, California, with her son.

m.—Harvey Bettison, thirteenth child of Thomas Grimball Bettison and Elizabeth Susan Rutledge, moved to Houston, Texas. He was living in 1923.

n.—Isaac Newton Bettison, fourteenth child of Thomas Grimball Bettison and Elizabeth Susan Rutledge, lived for many years in San Antonio, Texas, where he died on Saturday, September 18, 1937, at the age of seventy-four. His wife was Annie C. Vinson and is yet living. She was born in 1863 and they were married in 1889. Three children were born of this marriage:—

az.—Alix Reba Bettison, born 1890.
bz.—Hillary Newton Bettison, born 1896.
cz.—Anna Bee Bettison, born 1899.

az.—Alix Reba Bettison was married in 1915 to Ralph Lincoln Colby who is now General Agent for the Franklin Life Insurance Co. in the State of Indiana. They reside in Zionville which is only a short distance north of Indianapolis. They have two children:— Alix Bettison Colby, better known as "Sunshine," who was born in 1916, and Ralph Lincoln Colby, Jr., who was born in 1918. "Sunshine" was married on September 21, 1937, to George Spahr Losey. They now have two children:—Linda, born November 7, 1938, and George Spahr, Jr., born June 30, 1942. Ralph Lincoln Colby, Jr., married Danah Lyle Hesser of New Rochelle, New York, in 1940, and they have two daughters:—Katherine Reeder, born in May, 1942, and Ann Bettison, born November 3, 1944.

bz.—Hillary Newton Bettison married Mayaree Le Laurin. When we last heard of them they had no children.

cz.—Anna Bee Bettison was married to Royden K. Fisher. They have two children:—Robert Lee Fisher, born in 1920, and Lanier Fisher, born in 1930. Mr. and Mrs. Fisher resided in Chula Vista, California, where Mrs. Fisher died Friday, March 9, 1945.

oz.—Robert Edward Lee Bettison, fifteenth child of Thomas Grimball Bettison and Elizabeth Susan Rutledge, married Gussie Hill. They had no children and both were killed in the great Galveston storm of 1909.

5.—Eunice Rebecca Bettison, fifth child of David Bettison and Sarah Catharine Robert, was born near Woodville, Miss., on December 18, 1813. She was married in Cheneyville, La., on July 7, 1831, to her first cousin, Peter Tanner, son of Robert Tanner and Providence Robert. They left many descendants. See page 306

6.—Esther Providence Bettison, sixth child of David Bettison and Sarah Catharine Robert, was born near Woodville, Miss., on September 30, 1815. She was married in Cheneyville, La., on June 6, 1833, to her first cousin, Paul Jabez Tanner, son of Robert Tanner and Providence Robert. They left many descendants. See page 2 9 1.

7.—Martha Sarah Bettison (ii), seventh child of David Bettison and Sarah Catharine Robert, was born near Cheneyville, La., on August 15, 1818. She was married at Cheneyville in the early part of 1835 to Captain George W. Haygood. They lived for a while in Iberville parish, La., and then moved to New Orleans where Captain Haygood was a prosperous commission merchant. Both died there. On March 16, 1835, it is recorded that they receipted to Robert Tanner for Mrs. Haygood's portion of her father's estate. The record of this reads as follows:—

Personally appeared before me, W. B. Pearce, Notary Public in and for the Parish of Rapides, Martha S. Bettison (alias Haygood) assisted by her husband George Haygood, who acknowledged to have received of Robert Tanner, Executor to the will of her father David Bettison, deceased, six thousand six hundred and Eighty-three dollars and forty cents, being the full amount falling to her as one of the heirs of the said David Bettison, deceased, hereby releasing the said Robert Tanenr from all claims against him as executor thereof.

In testimony whereof the said Martha Haygood and George Haygood have hereunto subscribed their names before me said notary and the undersigned witnesses, this 16th day of March, 1835.

Witness:—   Martha Sarah Haygood
    L. A. Robert   G. W. Haygood.
    Peter R. Eldred.
                        Done before me
                        W. B. Pearce, Notary Public.

On March 28, 1835, we find where "Martha Haygood and her husband George Haygood, inhabitants of the parish of Iberville," sell to Peter Tanner for $3,000.00 a tract of land on the left bank of Bayou Boeuf "containing 100 arpents more or less, being one fourth of a 400 arpent tract of land bought by David Bettison of John Compton."

On the same date there is a record where Peter Tanner sells to Martha and George Haygood "inhabitants of the parish of Iberville" a tract of land on the left bank of Bayou Boeuf for $3,000.00, being "one fourth of a 400 arpent tract of land bought by David Bettison of John Compton." This was probably the same land which Peter Tanner purchased a few years previously from Thomas Grimball Bettison, brother of Martha Haygood.

Captain George W. Haygood and his wife, Martha Sarah Bettison, had one son, George Louis Haygood, who was born in New Orleans on November 22, 1837. He married and left descendants. See page **3ᴶ8**

I.

ESTHER SUSANNAH ROBERT.

Esther Susannah Robert, ninth child of Captain Peter Robert and his wife, Anne Grimball, was born in Beaufort District, South Carolina, on March 29, 1783. She was married there in February, 1801, to Randal Eldred, Jr., who was born June 1, 1780. He was a son of Randal Eldred, Sr., and Ann Newnamaker, and had a sister, Freelove Eldred, who married William A. Patterson. Shortly after their marriage Randal Eldred and Esther Susannah Robert emigrated to Woodville, Miss., with other members of the Robert family, and a few years later they came to Rapides parish, La. She died February 7, 1847, and he on January 19, 1850. After her death he married her younger sister, Mary Robert, as her third husband. Randal Eldred, Jr., and Esther Susannah Robert had five children:—

1.—Ann Martha Eldred, born December 16, 1802.
2.—Peter Robert Eldred, born January 9, 1806.
3.—Sarah Providence Eldred, born August 21, 1815.
4.—Randal Bettison Eldred, born February 14, 1817.
5.—Robert Daniel Eldred, born September 18, 1821.

1.—Ann Martha Eldred was married October 11, 1819, to Lodowick Tanner, and died March 29, 1872. Her husband was a son of Joseph Tanner and his first wife, Elizabeth Lanier, and was born August 22, 1795, probably in South Carolina, and died at his home on "Tiger Bend Plantation" on Bayou Boeuf,

Rapides parish, La., on October 5, 1849. They had eight children:—

    i.—Esther Eliza Tanner, born June 14, 1823.
    ii.—Thirza Caroline Tanner, born August 14, 1825.
    iii.—Mary Desirée Tanner, born June 25, 1828.
    iv.—Randal Tanner, born August 27, 1830.
    v.—Lemuel Tanner, born August 8, 1833.
    vi.—Edward Livingston Tanner, born May 6, 1835.
    vii.—Ellen Tanner, born August 14, 1837.
    viii.—Sarah Evalina Tanner, born December 30, 1839.

i.—Esther Eliza Tanner was married April 7, 1842, to Peter Baillio Compton, a son of John Compton and Amelia Baillio, who was born April 17, 1818, and died in August, 1864. His mother, Amelia Baillio, was a daughter of Pierre Baillio, born in 1769 and died January 8, 1821, and his wife, Magdelaine Emelie Lacour, born November 27, 1774, and died September 13, 1838. The latter was a daughter of Jean Baptiste Lacour and Marianne Leonard. Peter Baillio Compton and Esther Eliza Tanner had six children:—

    a.—Louisiana Compton, born March 2, 1843.
    b.—John Lodowick Compton, born July 30, 1845.
    c.—Peter Baillio Compton, Jr., born December 26, 1847.
    d.—Esther Compton, born February 28, 1850.
    e.—Thomas Moore Compton, born July —, 1852.
    f.—Henry Machen Compton, born ———— 1854.

a.—Louisiana Compton died in September, 1854, at the age of eleven.

b.—John Lodowick Compton married Mary Margaret Marshall in February, 1869, daughter of Captain George Benoist Marshall and Margaret Dawson Cureton. He died September 26, 1872. His death was recorded in THE LOUISIANA DEMOCRAT, an Alexandria newspaper, of Wednesday, November 6, 1872, as follows:—

> DIED:—On the 26th of September, 1872 John Lodowick Compton, aged 27 years, 1 month, and 27 days.

John Lodowick Compton and Mary Margaret Marshall had two children:—George Marshall Compton, born in December, 1869, and John Lodowick Compton, Jr., born April 24, 1873. Both married but we have not been successful in getting any definite data on the subject. After the death of her husband

Mary Margaret Marshall married R. Layson Walker, son of Dr. William P. Walker and Frances C. Skillman, and grandson of Andrew Skillman and Ann Stirling. She had several children by her second marriage.

c.—Peter Baillio Compton, Jr., lovingly known to his many friends as "Teenie Compton," was engaged in planting all his life in his native parish of Rapides. He married Mary Virginia Cooke of St. Landry parish, a daughter of Dr. Thomas Alfred Cooke, member of a prominent Virginia family who emigrated to Louisiana. Dr. Cooke was one of the fifth generation in direct line of descent from Mordecai Cooke of "Mordecai's Mount" in Gloucester county, Virginia. In delving into the early history of Virginia we first find Mordecai Cooke in Elizabeth City county in 1645 when he appears as a witness in a suit. The next year we find him recorded in York county. In 1650 he settled permanently in Gloucester county and his home there, "Mordecai's Mount," was known far and wide. He died there before 1667. In 1648 Mordecai Cooke married and he and his wife had at least five children. His fourth son, Giles Cooke, married and was the father of Giles Cooke who was a Burgess from Gloucester county from 1722 to 1727. This latter Giles was of "Wareham" and married and had a son named John, born about 1720 and died in 1795. This John Cooke married October 9, 1742, Elizabeth Lee, born January 15, 1728, daughter of Richard and Mary Lee of Abingdon Parish. They had four children:—Giles, John, Mary, and Thomas. The last mentioned, Thomas Cooke, was born in 1754 and died in 1809. He was three times married, his third wife being Catherine Bird Didlake whom he married in 1806. She died November 19, 1840. They had two children:—John Henry Cooke who inherited "Wareham," and Thomas Alfred Cooke, a posthumous child, who was born in 1809 and died in 1886. This posthumous child, Thomas Alfred Cooke, became a prominent physician, graduating from the Jefferson Medical College in Philadelphia and the Hotel Dieu of Paris, France. He came to Louisiana and settled near Washington, in St. Landry parish. He married in 1836 Fannie Susan Pannill of Rapides parish. They had twelve children and the eleventh of these was Mary Virginia Cooke, born in 1857, who married Peter Baillio Compton, Jr. We have no record of the date of Mr. Compton's death but it was sometime before 1930. His wife died at the home of her daughter, Mrs. Henry Schaffer, in Glendale, California, on Saturday, May 10, 1941. Her body was brought to Alexandria and buried in the Rapides cemetery in Pineville, La. Three children were born of this marriage:—Alfred Cooke Compton who married and went to California; Esther Compton* who married Milton Clark, a prominent lumberman of Rapides parish who died in Florida in 1930 leaving five children; and Elizabeth Compton, better known to her family and friends as "Bessie" who married Henry A. Schaffer now proprietor of the Glendale Paper Company of Glendale, California.

d.—Esther Compton, fourth child of Peter Baillio Compton, Sr., and Esther Eliza Tanner, died in April, 1851, at the age of one year.

e.—Thomas Moore Compton, fifth child of Peter Baillio Compton, Sr., and Esther Eliza Tanner, married Mary Machen, daughter of Dr. Henry Machen and Eleanor Compton. The only descendant of this couple of whom we know is Machen Compton now living in Rapides parish, La., who is married and has several children.

f.—Henry Machen Compton, the youngest child of Peter Baillio Compton, Sr., and Esther Eliza Tanner, as far as we can learn, never married. His death is recorded in THE LOUISIANA DEMOCRAT of Wednesday, October 23, 1878, as follows:—

> DIED:—At Armant Plantation, St. James parish, Louisiana, on Monday, October 7, 1878, H. M. Compton, aged 21 years, a native of Rapides parish and a son of the late Peter B. and Esther Compton.

The age given in this notice is obviously incorrect—he was twenty-four years old at the time of his death.

ii.—Thirza Caroline Tanner, second child of Lodowick Tanner and Ann Martha Eldred, was married June 5, 1845, to William James Compton, son of Samuel Compton and Jane Williams. She was born August 14, 1825, and died January

---

* Esther (Compton) Clark was run over and killed by an automobile in front of her home at Carmel-by-the-Sea, California, on Friday, April 7, 1944.

1, 1870. A notice of her death may be found in the issue of THE LOUISIANA DEMOCRAT of Wednesday, January 5, 1870. It reads as follows:—

> DIED:—At her residence on Red river, on Saturday the 1st inst., at 4:30 o'clock a. m., in the 45th year of her age, Mrs. Caroline T. Compton, wife of William J. Compton and daughter of the late Lodowick Tanner.

William James Compton and Thirza Caroline Tanner had three children:—

> a.—Charles Tanner Compton, born March 11, 1846.
> b.—Esther Ann Compton, born December 8, 1847.
> c.—Ellen Jane Compton, born February 1, 1849.

a.—Charles Tanner Compton married Lolette ————— on June 12, 1869. They had two children:—William James Compton, born December 5, 1870, and an infant son, born April 19, 1872, and died on the 24th of the same month.

b.—Esther Ann Compton was married in May, 1871, to N. H. Egleston. We have no further information of them.

c.—Ellen Jane Compton died December 3, 1862, at the age of 12 years.

iii.—Mary Desirée Tanner, third child of Lodowick Tanner and Ann Martha Eldred, was married June 15, 1848, to John Hiram Audebert, born August 19, 1821, a son of John Audebert and Henrietta Polhill, and a grandson of John Audebert and Judith Robert. This Judith Robert was the 7th child of Jacques Robert and Sarah Jaudon and a sister of Captain Peter Robert who married Anne Grimball. Consequently Mary Desirée Tanner and her husband, John Hiram Audebert, were cousins. She died October 7, 1867. We have no record of his death. They had eight children:—

> a.—Ann Martha Audebert, born June 3, 1849.
> b.—John Lodowick Audebert, born March 5, 1851.
> c.—Hennie Cheney Audebert, born December 5, 1852.
> d.—Caroline Judith Audebert, born November 21, 1854.
> e.—Mary Louisiana Audebert, born September 1, 1856.
> f.—Sallie Tanner Audebert, born April 2, 1859.
> g.—Ada Belle Audebert, born May 30, 1861.
> h.—Henry Pearce Audebert, born February 18, 1863.

Most of the above mentioned Audebert children lived to adult life but none of them ever married. At this date (1944) only one is living, Mary Louisiana Audebert, whom we lovingly speak of as "Cousin Mamie."

iv.—Randal Tanner, fourth child of Lodowick Tanner and Ann Martha Eldred, married March 17, 1853, Sarah Martin, who died October 31, 1853. His second wife was Ada Posthulwait, born June 11, 1830. He died June 6, 1870, without issue by either marriage. His second wife then married Samuel L. Compton on April 4, 1872.

v.—Lemuel Tanner, fifth child of Lodowick Tanner and Ann Martha Eldred, died June 11, 1834, at the age of ten months.

vi.—Edward Livingston Tanner, sixth child of Lodowick Tanner and Ann Martha Eldred, married Alice Winifred Glaze on October 11, 1859, daughter of John Adams Glaze and Mary Cocke, and grand-daughter of Joseph Cocke and Winifred Alston. Her grandmother, Winifred Alston, was a daughter of Philip Alston and Winifred Whitmel (daughter of Thomas Whitmel and Elizabeth Hunter Bryan of Bertie county, North Carolina). Phillip Alston was the fourth son of Colonel John Alston (the emigrant) and his wife, Mary Clarke. Colonel Alston was born at Felmersham, Bedfordshire, England, in 1673, and died in Chowan county, North Carolina, in 1758. The Alexandria Gazette of February, 1830, contained the following notice:—

John A. Glaze was married to Mary Cocke by Judge Thomas C. Scott on Thursday evening, February 9, 1830.

Alice Winifred Glaze was born in Avoyelles parish, La., on March 1, 1839, and died there on May 3, 1904. Edward Livingston Tanner died October 6, 1871, leaving six children. His widow on February 14, 1876, married Mark Richards Marshall whose first wife was Ellen Tanner, a sister of his second wife's first husband. Three children were born of this second union: —Mark Richards Marshall, Jr., Stella Marshall, and Alston Heiskell Marshall. All are dead at this date (1944). The six children of Edward Livingston Tanner and Alice Winifred Glaze were:—

   a.—Ellen Mittie Tanner, born August 6, 1860.
   b.—Mary Glaze Tanner, born December 26, 1861.
   c.—Edward Randal Tanner, born June 16, 1864.
   d.—Harry Alston Tanner, born January 29, 1867.
   e.—Lodowick Branch Tanner, born December 10, 1869.
   f.—Randal Glaze Tanner, born June 23, 1871.

a.—Ellen Mittie Tanner is the only one of the above children living at this date (1944).* She has never married and resides in Bunkie, La., where she is much beloved by all who know her.

b.—Mary Glaze Tanner was married December 26, 1881, to John Thomas Johnson who for many years was a prominent merchant of Bunkie, La. He was born December 8, 1851, in Bedford county, Tennessee, a son of James Johnson and Sallie Davidson, both of that State. After the death of James Johnson in 1863 his widow married a Dr. Gannaway. Mary Glaze Tanner and John Thomas Johnson had five children:—

   az.—Edward Livingston Johnson, born December 24, 1882.
   bz.—Louis Hollingshed Johnson, born April 13, 1884.
   cz.—Harry Alston Johnson, born August 4, 1888.
   dz.—Roy Davidson Johnson, born March 14, 1890.
   ez.—John Thomas Johnson, born November 2, 1898.
   az.—Edward Livingston Johnson died in infancy.

bz.—Louis Hollingshed Johnson married Annie Pratt on January 29, 1908. They had three children:—Mary Pratt Johnson, born April 28, 1909, and died May 13, 1910; Sarah Pratt Johnson, born July 18, 1913; Jonnie Louise Johnson, born Friday, March 7, 1919. The second of these, Sarah Pratt Johnson, was married October 13, 1939, to J. J. Yarborough, Jr. The youngest, Jonnie Louise Johnson, was married September 11, 1937, to Carlton Ray, Jr., and they have a son, Charles Louis Ray, born October 11, 1940. Annie Pratt, wife of Louis Hollinshed Johnson, died November 8, 1938, and on November 20, 1941, he married Pearl Marshall Sharp, daughter of James Horace Marshall, Jr., and Annie Clara Rush.

* Ellen Mittie Tanner died Wednesday, September 20, 1944, at the age of 84.

cz.—Harry Alston Johnson married Leila Havard Irion on November 10, 1914. She was a daughter of Dr. Clifford Hill Irion and his first wife, Kate Keary Stafford, and a granddaughter of General Leroy Augustus Stafford and Sarah Catharine Wright. Harry Alston Johnson died of traumatic pneumonia on September 20, 1923, at his home in Bunkie, La. His widow yet survives him. They had two children:—Kate Stafford Johnson, born July 15, 1917, and Harry Alston Johnson, Jr., born October 24, 1918. The former was married December 20, 1941, to Lieutenant Gilbert Watson Palmer, Jr., United States Army, recently promoted to the rank of major. They now have a son, Gilbert Watson Palmer, III, born August 29, 1943. Harry Alston Johnson, Jr., is now a Captain in the United States Army. He married January 31, 1942, Grace Ellen Slattery, daughter of the late Mr. and Mrs. Robert Ambrose Slattery of Shreveport, La. They now have a daughter, Grace Ellen Johnson, born May 4, 1943.

dz.—Roy Davidson Johnson married Annie Miles on January 7, 1913, daughter of Herman Winston Miles and Sarah Vance, and grand-daughter of Lemuel Miles and Susan Jackson. Mrs. Johnson's grandmother, Susan Jackson, was the only daughter of Stephen Jackson and Nancy Tanner. This Nancy Tanner was a sister of Lodowick Tanner and a daughter of Joseph Tanner and his first wife, Elizabeth Lanier. Thus it will be seen that Mr. Johnson and his wife are distantly related. They had four children:—Roy Davidson Johnson, Jr., born December 9, 1913, who married Alpha Lee Henderson on February 12, 1938, and now has two daughters, Marcy Ann Johnson, born July 6, 1939, and Alpha Lee Johnson, born March 11, 1943; Randal Vance Johnson, born Monday, January 20, 1919, who married Elaine Ventress on April 26, 1942; Bernard Audebert Johnson, born September 22, 1921, and died February 24, 1926; Donald Miles Johnson, born March 14, 1924, now serving as a radio-gunner on a B-26 medium bomber in France and holding the rank of sergeant.

ez.—John Thomas Johnson married Minnie L. Biles on February 27, 1918. She was born in New Iberia, La., on January 12, 1899, and was a daughter of William Alexander Biles and Sallie Ann Palmer, both natives of Trenton Tennessee. Mr. and Mrs. Johnson have two children:—John Thomas Johnson, Jr., born Monday, April 28, 1919; Alice Winifred Johnson, born July 14, 1923, and married to Walter Ross Peek on October 4, 1941.

c.—Edward Randal Tanner married his first cousin, Mary Henrietta Glaze, on May 20, 1891. She was born in Avoyelles parish, La., on September 10, 1868, and died May 9, 1942, and was a daughter of Middleton Glaze and Clarissa Eugenia Eldred. Middleton Glaze was the 4th child of John Adams Glaze and Mary Cocke, and was born in Avoyelles parish, La., on November 7, 1836. From the Glaze family Bible now in possession of Mrs. George Ripley White of Centreville, Miss., we learn that he married Clarissa Eugenia Eldred on April 4, 1860, and that he died November 14, 1913. She was a daughter of Peter Robert Eldred and Evolina Macelia Griffin. (See page 162.)

Edward Randal Tanner died March 6, 1893. Two children were born of his marriage to Mary Henrietta Glaze. They are:—

az.—Edward Livingston Tanner, born April 2, 1892.

bz.—Alice Eugenia Tanner, born October 31, 1893.

az.—Edward Livingston Tanner was born in Avoyelles parish, La., and was educated at Texas A. & M. College from which he graduated in 1914. He married Mary Florence Waggener who was born in Jefferson county, Missouri, in 1898. She was a daughter of Edward Waggener and Mary Florence Donnell, both natives of Jefferson county where Mr. Waggener was born in 1849, and his wife in 1856. Mr. and Mrs. Tanner now reside in Woodlake, Texas. They have no children.

bz.—Alice Eugenia Tanner was born in Avoyelles parish, La., and from the data given it will be seen that she was a posthumous child. She was married July 5, 1916, to George Ripley White who was born in Wilkinson county, Miss., on June 12, 1894. He was a son of Francis Eugene White, born in Wilkinson county on March 24, 1857, and died October 5, 1936, and Sarah Agnes Cason, born in Avoyelles parish, La., August 9, 1862, and died May 30, 1927. Mr. and Mrs. White now reside in Centreville, Wilkinson county, Miss. Mrs. White is greatly interested in genealogy and it was through her kindness that much of this data on the descendants of Esther Susannah Robert was obtained. They have two children:—

George Ripley White, Jr., born June 12, 1917.
Mary Adelaide White, born May 30, 1919.

The elder of these, George Ripley White, Jr., married Katherine Perkins Steger on September 14, 1940, a daughter of Edward Henry Steger, born in Tuscumbia, Alabama, and Ethlyn Perkins, born in West Feliciana parish, La. They have no children at this date.

Mary Adelaide White graduated from the University of Alabama in 1941 and was married to Henry Frith Hynson who was born in Bunkie, La., on November 15, 1918, son of William Ringgold Hynson and Virginia Lucile Williams, both of Bunkie, La. They have one child, Kathryn Ann Hynson, born August 29, 1942.

d.—Harry Alston Tanner, fourth child of Edward Livingston Tanner and Alice Winifred Glaze, was a very promising young man. He won by competitive examination an appointment to the U. S. Military Academy at West Point, N. Y., and after spending a year there was forced by ill health to resign. He returned home and died April 10, 1894. He never married.

e.—Lodowick Branch Tanner died January 17, 1879, at the age of ten years.

f.—Randal Glaze Tanner was employed as an accountant in the Custom House at New Orleans. He came home for the Easter holidays and suffered a cerebral hemorrhage from which he died on Easter Sunday, March 29, 1902. He never married.

vii.—Ellen Tanner, seventh child of Lodowick Tanner and Ann Martha Eldred, was married December 26, 1867, to Mark Richards Marshall, a native of Fredericksburg, Va., and a son of Horace Marshall and Elizabeth Heiskell. He was a first cousin of James Horace Marshall who married Eliza Eugenia Pearce (see page   in this book). Ellen Tanner died February 26, 1872, leaving one child, Alice Marshall, born December 30, 1868, and died March 30, 1894, unmarried. After his wife's death Mr. Marshall married Alice Winifred Glaze, widow of Edward Livingston Tanner, brother of his first wife.

viii.—Sarah Evolina Tanner, eighth child of Lodowick Tanner and Ann Martha Eldred, was married October 28, 1858, to Austin Willis Burges, son of Lovatt Samuel Burges, Sr., and Frances Cocke. She died on January 21, 1859, without issue, and in 1860 her husband married Mrs. Mary Dunwoody (McCoy) Rhodes by whom he had three children, two of whom died young.

2.—Peter Robert Eldred, second child of Randal Eldred, Jr., and Esther Susannah Robert, was born near Woodville, Wilkinson county, Miss., on January 9, 1806. His parents had moved there in 1804 from Beaufort District, South Carolina. A few years later they went to Louisiana where they established themselves on Bayou Boeuf, in Rapides parish, near the present town of Cheneyville. There Peter Robert Eldred grew to manhood. He married Evolina Macelia Griffin on April 15, 1830. The following notarial act further identifies her for us :—

STATE OF LOUISIANA
PARISH OF RAPIDES
     Before me W. B. Pearce, Notary Public in and for the State and Parish aforesaid, and the undersigned witnesses, personally came Evolina Griffin alias Eldred, who by and with the advice and consent of her husband Peter R. Eldred hath bargained, sold, transferred and delivered unto Joseph B. Robert of said State and Parish, all her right title and interest as one of the heirs of the late James and Elizabeth Griffin, dec'd., in and to three slaves named Jenny a woman, Bob a man, and a boy aged 7 or 8 years whose name is not remembered, being part of the undivided succession of the late Richard Miller, dec'd., of Adams county, in the state of Mississippi . . . . This sale is made for and in consideration of the sum of one hundred and twenty dollars which has been paid in hand by the said Joseph B. Robert to the said Evolina and Peter Eldred, the receipt of which is hereby acknowledged.
     This 28th day of November, 1832.

Witnesses :—   Joseph B. Robert.
     Joshua Pearce   Evolina Eldred
     John G. Pearce.   Peter R. Eldred
          Done before me,
               W. B. Pearce, Notary Public.

Peter Robert Eldred's wife was undoubtedly a daughter of James and Elizabeth Griffin, and Mrs. Griffin was probably a daughter of Richard Miller of Adams county, Miss. Sometime after the above date Mr. Eldred settled permanently in Avoyelles parish. His home was on Bayou des Glaises, one of the most fertile sections of Louisiana. He died there on March 3, 1846, and it is thought he was buried in Cheneyville where his parents were afterwards laid to rest. However, we have no authentic data on this. Four children were born of this marriage:—

        i.—Randal R. Eldred.
        ii.—Jefferson Eldred.
        iii.—Clara Eugenia Eldred.
        iv.—Mary Henrietta Eldred.

After the death of Peter Robert Eldred his widow married William Clopton who was born July 4, 1791, and died in October, 1871. Mr. Clopton is said to have moved to Louisiana from Atlanta, Georgia. His forebears undoubtedly settled in Virginia where the name is to be found in the earliest records of that colony. His wife died in 1872. There was one child from this marriage, William Franklin Clopton, who for many years was a prominent physician in central Louisiana (see page 118).

i.—Randal R. Eldred, eldest child of Peter Robert Eldred and Evolina Macelia Griffin, was born in Avoyelles parish, La., in 1832. He never married and died in 1884.

ii.—Jefferson Eldred, second child of Peter Robert Eldred and Evolina Macelia Griffin, was born in Avoyelles parish, La., in 1834, and is said to have married and moved out west. We have no worth-while record of him after this. The compiler of this data has been told recently that some of his descendants are living in Oakdale, Louisiana.

iii.—Clara Eugenia Eldred, third child of Peter Robert Eldred and Evolina Macelia Griffin, was born in Avoyelles parish, La., about 1836. She was married April 4, 1860, to Middleton Glaze, son of John Adams Glaze and Mary Cocke. He was born in Avoyelles parish, La., November 7, 1836, and died there November 14, 1913. His wife died January 28, 1891, having been the mother of ten children. They were:—

        a.—John Adams Glaze.
        b.—Evolina Glaze.
        c.—Clara Middleton Glaze.
        d.—Middleton Glaze, Jr.

e.—Mary Henrietta Glaze.
f.—Alice Winifred Glaze.
g.—Bettison Blakewood Glaze.
h.—William Clopton Glaze.
i.—Bessie Murdock Glaze.
j.—Winnie Irene Glaze.

a.—John Adams Glaze was born March 12, 1861, and died September 3, 1863, when two and a half years old.

b.—Evolina Glaze was born March 27, 1862, and died in 1936. She never married.

c.—Clara Middleton Glaze was born October 15, 1863, and died ——————————. She was married December 30, 1891, to George Chambers Pearce, son of James Lemuel Pearce and Sarah Goodwin Chambers (daughter of William Woodson Chambers and Sarah Ann Pearce). They had three children, all of whom are living at this date (1944). See page

d.—Middleton Glaze, Jr., was born October 4, 1865, and died December 23, 1906. He married December 31, 1891, Frances Alice Burges, daughter of John Mortimer Burges and Bettie Desirée Tanner (daughter of Branch Tanner and Desirée Wells). They had several children but all of our efforts to get in communication with any of them have failed.

e.—Mary Henrietta Glaze was born September 10, 1868, and married Edward Randal Tanner. (See page 160.)

f.—Alice Winifred Glaze was born December 27, 1869, and died October 7, 1874, at the age of five years.

g.—Bettison Blakewood Glaze was born July 20, 1872. For several years he managed a newspaper in Bunkie, La., known as the Bunkie Blade. In 1898 he enlisted in Company L, Second United States Volunteer Infantry and served in Cuba with his command. The compiler of these notes can give first hand testimony to this fact as he was acting as a recruiting officer for Company L at that time. In 1900 he left home and none of the family have heard of him since.

h.—William Clopton Glaze was born November 22, 1874. He enlisted in the army with his brother in 1898. While in the service he suffered a severe attack of typhoid fever and was never well afterwards.

i.—Bessie Murdock Glaze was born October 11, 1876, and is living at this date. She was married June 30, 1897, to Frank

Lampton Cason who died in November, 1913. They had six children:—

> Clopton Lampton Cason, born February 19, 1898
> Augusta Marguerite Cason, born July 6, 1900.
> Mary Blanche Cason, born March 24, 1902.
> James Henry Glaze Cason, born December 12, 1906.
> Frank Malcolm Cason, born September 22, 1908.
> Frank Lampton Cason, Jr., born July 5, 1911.

The second of these children died December 7, 1903, and the sixth in November, 1912. The third child, Mary Blanche Cason, was married in 1920 to Charles William Kelly of Monroe, La. They have four children:—Charles William Kelly, Jr., born February 22, 1921; John Henry Kelly, born June 6, 1923; Betty Blanche Kelly, born August 14, 1925; Kyle Ann Kelly, born September 2, 1939.

j.—Winnie Irene Glaze was born May 27, 1879, and is now living in Pomona, California. She has never married.

iv.—Mary Henrietta Eldred, fourth child of Peter Robert Eldred and Evolina Macelia Griffin, was born in Avoyelles parish, La., about 1838. She was married about 1855 to Dr. Bettison William Blakewood, a gentleman of culture and education who had recently settled in Avoyelles parish, coming there from South Carolina where he was born. His son, Mr. Eldred Griffin Blakewood, of Kleinwood, Avoyelles parish, La., gave us the following account of his paternal antecedents:—

> My grandfather Blakewood is my first ancestor that came to this country of whom I know anything about. He came to a place on the Savannah river fifteen miles up from Savannah, Georgia, in Beaufort District, South Carolina, from England in about the year 1800. His wife's name was Hannah Ritter, and she came from Holland, having married my grandfather in England. They were married probably ten or twelve years before they sailed for South Carolina, and had no children until after they came over here. I am told that my grandfather Blakewood was a member of the English Parliament until he left England. He had a brother who came with him but this brother never lived down South but immediately went on to the State of Maine. After coming over here my grandparents had four children—three girls and a boy. The eldest, Winifred, first married Edward Ricker, a railroad man and very wealthy. He died and she then married the Mayor of Savannah, Ga. The latter was much

older than my aunt and died in about the year 1855. She lived in Savannah from her first marriage until she died in 1896. There were no children. Sarah, the second daughter, married Edward Strobert of Savannah. They had one girl, Ellen. Margarette (called Maggie), the third daughter, married Edward Kieffer. They had two children, Edward Ricker and Ellen. All lived, died and were buried in Savannah.

Bettison William Blakewood, the son (my father), was born in the year 1808, reared at the above mentioned place, educated at Harvard University, where he also finished law, and practiced the same in Maine in 1830 to 1832, when he gave this up, returned to South Carolina and then concluded to study medicine. When he received his M.D. degree he married Mary Eleanor Tolbert near Charleston. He settled down at his old home and began his new profession. His first wife lived only about a year and died when their child, Mary Eleanor (always called Minnie), was born. Sister Minnie was married twice, first to Richard I. Rush of Kleinwood, La. This was a very unhappy marriage and the result was separation within a year. She then in the year 1876 married David S. Butler* from Big Cane, La., where they lived until 1885 and then moved to Osteen, Florida. There Mr. Butler died in 1898. Sister Minnie remained in the old homestead in Osteen until she died in 1920. Both are buried there. She never had any children. My father, Dr. Blakewood, shortly after the death of his first wife, moved to Louisiana and about 1855 married my mother, Mary Henrietta Eldred, daughter of Peter Robert Eldred and Evolina Macelia Griffin. They were married here where they lived until 1899. In that year they moved to Osteen, Florida, where my father died in 1900 and was buried there. My mother returned to Louisiana and lived here until she died in 1918. She was buried here in the Bayou des Glaises Baptist cemetery. My parents had seven children:—a.—Winifred, b.—Clara Eugenia, c.—Edward Ricker, d.—Florence Augusta, e. — Evolina Macelia, f.—Bettison William, Jr., g.—Eldred Griffin.

We are also indebted to Mr. Eldred Griffin Blakewood for the data given below relative to his sisters, brothers and himself.

---

* This was David Samuel Butler, son of Thomas Norris Butler and Mary Jane Calliham (daughter of John Young Calliham and Mary Jaudon Grimball.)

a.—Winifred Blakewood was born in 1856 and died in 1869. b.—Clara Eugenia Blakewood was born in 1858 and died in 1866.

c.—Edward Ricker Blakewood was born in 1860. He was educated at Keatchie College (La.), the Louisiana State University, and Tulane University, graduating in medicine from the last mentioned. He practiced his profession in Savannah, Georgia, and Osteen, Florida. In 1920 he returned to Louisiana and died soon afterwards. He never married.

d.—Florence Augusta Blakewood was born in Avoyelles parish, La., and was married there April 13, 1887, to Joseph Alexander Gray, son of Abram Marshall Gray and his second wife, Virginia Margaret Nutt. He was born on Bayou des Glaises, Avoyelles parish, La., on January 21, 1858, and died at his home near Marksville, La., on February 12, 1941. He was a great nephew of Abram Marshall Scott, one of the early governors of Mississippi. His wife is living at this date (1944). They had eight children:—

> az.—Helen Marion Gray.
> bz.—Abram Marshall Gray.
> cz.—Edward Blakewood Gray.
> dz.—Lee Scott Gray.
> ez.—Joseph Alexander Gray, Jr.
> fz.—Virginia Ellen Gray.
> gz.—John Albin Gray.
> hz.—Clifford Dalzell Gray.

az.—Helen Marion Gray, born March 12, 1888, married Esteen J. Rabalais, son of Ferrier Rabalais and Blanche Gauthier. They had seven children:—Marion Esteen Rabalais, born April 30, 1911, married October 6, 1935, Della Lemoine, daughter of Jules Lemoine and Eva Mayeux, one child Leonard Edward Rabalais, born July 10, 1936; Harold Lee Rabalais, born September 16, 1913; Joseph Alexander Rabalais, born January 7, 1915; Laurence Edward Rabalais, born October 18, 1918; Florence Virginia Rabalais, born September 19, 1920; Clifford Leslie Rabalais, born April 30, 1923; Ella Gene Rabalais, born March 16, 1926.

bz.—Abram Marshall Gray, born August 24, 1890, married Addie Curry, daughter of T. H. Curry of Ferriday, La. They have two children:—Abram Marshall Gray, III, born

April 17, 1914, and married April 6, 1935, Cecile Roy, daughter of Ulysses Roy and Ida Morrow—one child, Blakewood Morrow Gray; Juliette Gray, born Oct. 15, 1915, married May 12, 1936, William Woods of Greensville, Miss. Abram Marshall Gray and Addie Curry were divorced and he later married Lucy Diamond, daughter of James Diamond and Hattie Mayo of Century, Florida. There is one child by this second union, Eleanor Lee Gray, born February 11, 1925.

cz.—Edward Blakewood Gray, born January 2, 1893, died December 13, 1932. He married Lillie Tarpley, daughter of F. Tarpley of Mississippi, and had three children:—Billie Melba Gray, born February 18, 1918; Edward Blakewood Gray, Jr., born November 20, 1925; James Oliver Gray, born August 20, 1927.

dz.—Lee Scott Gray, born March 12, 1895, married Mary Elizabeth Jones, daughter of W. J. Jones of Laurel, Miss., who died July 31, 1933. He then married Ila Ruth McBride, daughter of O. J. McBride and Leila Simpson of Laurel, Miss. No issue by either marriage.

ez.—Joseph Alexander Gray, Jr., born April 5, 1897, married Nannie Tarpley, daughter of F. Tarpley of Mississippi. They have three children:—Jacquelin Gray, born April 9, 1924; Joseph Alexander Gray, III, born April 6, 1927; Mary Frances Gray, born October 2, 1933.

fz.—Virginia Ellen Gray, born April 21, 1900, married Alfred M. Moncla, son of Ernest Moncla and Alexandrine Cayer. They have four children:—Gloria Ellen Moncla, born November 23, 1924; Eldred Ernest Moncla, born May 30, 1926; Mary Carmen Moncla, born October 22, 1928; Virginia Carol Moncla, born July 28, 1936.

gz.—John Albin Gray, born August 27, 1903, married Sylvia Lafargue, daughter of Bijou Lafargue and Desdamona Joffrion, and had one child and was later divorced. He then married Josie Powers, daughter of Louis E. Powers and Augusta Lamkin.

hz.—Clifford Dalzell Gray, born September 7, 1906, married Marion Wolfe of Greenville, South Carolina.

e.—Evolina Macelia Blakewood was born in Avoyelles parish, La., in 1864, and is now living in Los Angeles, California. She married Alexander Anderson Whitlock from Marthaville,

La. They lived in Marthaville until 1896 and then moved to California where Mr. Whitlock died. They had two children: —Blakewood Whitlock, born in 1888, unmarried and now living with his mother; Claude Whitlock, born 1890, married and now living in California.

f.—Bettison William Blakewood, Jr., was born in Avoyelles parish, La., in 1867, and now living in Haynesville, La. His first wife was Ann Eliza George, daughter of John George and Mary Cheney of Big Bend, La., whom he married in 1895. They had one child, Alton Bettison Blakewood. This wife died in 1898 and he married in 1900 Irene Eliza Havard, daughter of James Monroe Havard and Irene Griffin, and grand-daughter of Henry Monroe Havard and Laura Robinson. Three children were born of this second marriage:—Ruby, William Havard, and Evolina. Alton Bettison Blakewood, son of the first marriage, was born in 1896. He now resides in Bunkie, La., and married Ophelia Rae of Boyce, La. They have one son, Alton Rae Blakewood, now in the U. S. Army. Ruby Blakewood, eldest child by the second marriage, was born in 1901 and married B. W. Cason who is now dead. They had three children:—Jeanne, Bettison Ward, and Janelle Cason, all now living in Haynesville, La. William Havard Blakewood, second child of the second marriage, was born in 1903 and is now living in Oxford, La., in the service of the Standard Oil Company. Evolina Blakewood, third child of the second marriage, was born in 1904, and married a Mr. Meredith. They live in Texas and have no children.

g.—Eldred Griffin Blakewood, seventh and youngest child of Dr. Bettison William Blakewood and his second wife, Mary Henrietta Eldred, was born November 1, 1871, at Kleinwood, Avoyelles parish, La. He received his education at Keatchie College, La., and the East Florida Seminary, now the University of Florida. His life work has been that of a farmer, cotton ginner, saw mill operator, merchant (owner of all), and in fact "everything that goes with country life and happiness, as well as sorrows and misfortunes." The quotation is from one of Mr. Blakewood's letters to the compiler of these notes. He married on April 15, 1896, Laura Lillian Bond, daughter of James Knox Polk Bond and Mary Anna Havard (eldest daughter of Henry Monroe Havard and Laura M. Robinson). They had seven children*.—az.—Madgie, bz.—Eldred Griffin, Jr., cz.—Lillian Bond, dz.—Mary Eleanor, ez.—Lewis Junius, fz.—Laurie Bettison, gz.—Violet Julia.

az.—Madgie Blakewood, born March 19, 1897, now resides in Port Arthur, Texas, but is temporarily at Houston in government service. She was married to Henry J. Ducote in 1920 and they have five children:—Flora Madge, born January 19, 1921, married in 1939 Ezra Whitney Fitch, now lives in Falfurious, Texas, and has one son, born in 1940; Henry J., Jr., born September 3, 1924, and now in the U. S. Navy, at sea; Carroll, born December 26, 1926; Blakewood, born December 8, 1928; Edith Claire, born July 26, 1931.

bz.—Eldred Griffin Blakewood, Jr., born January 7, 1898, was reared at Kleinwood, La., educated as a civil engineer at the Louisiana State University, served in the U. S. Marines one and a half years in World War I, worked as a highway engineer for many years, and then served for several years as City Engineer of Baton Rouge, La., where he now resides. He married Julia Gertrude Huffman of DeRidder, La., in 1925. They have four children:—Julia Gertrude, born July 12, 1926; Eldred Griffin, III, born August 14, 1927; Charles Huffman, born July 6, 1929; Blake Warren, born July 29, 1932.

cz.—Lillian Bond Blakewood, born January 7, 1901, married Thomas Wiley Jackson of Lecompte, La., in 1924, who died in September, 1935. She still resides in Lecompte and has one son, Thomas Wiley, Jr., born September 11, 1934.

dz.—Mary Eleanor Blakewood, born September 16, 1903, married William Samuel Marshall of Louisville, Ky. Their home is in New Orleans but Mr. Marshall is at present in the U. S. Marines and stationed in Washington, D. C. They were married in 1929 and have no children.

ez.—Lewis Junius Blakewood, born October 16, 1913, married Vivian Gremillion of Baton Rouge, La. They have no children. Mr. Blakewood was educated at the Louisiana State University as an electrical engineer. He is now in the U. S. Army Signal Corps, Air Ground Division, and is at present stationed at Red Bank, New Jersey.

fz.—Laurie Bettison Blakewood, born November 22, 1917, died June 4, 1933.

gz.—Violet Julia Blakewood, born August 17, 1924, is now a junior in the Louisiana State University.

3.—Sarah Providence Eldred, third child of Randal Eldręd, Jr., and Esther Susannah Robert, was born in Rapides parish, La., on August 21, 1815, and died December 16, 1868. She was married at the home of her parents on Bayou Boeuf, in Rapides parish, on November 6, 1834, to Ezra Bennett who had emigrated to Louisiana from Scipio, New York, where he was born September 13, 1808. Mr. Bennett taught school for several years in his adopted State and then engaged in planting, becoming one of the prominent plantation and slave owners on Bayou Boeuf, below Cheneyville. After the death of his wife he remarried and we find the following notice of his second wife's death in THE LOUISIANA DEMOCRAT of Wednesday, October 25, 1871:—

DIED:—At the residence of A. F. Currie, in East Feliciana parish, on Tuesday, September 22, 1871, Mrs. Minerva E. V. Bennett, wife of Ezra Bennett of this parish.

We are told by members of his family that Mr. Bennett was married a third time, but we have been unable to obtain the name of this lady. He died January 26, 1875. He only had children by his first marriage. They were:—i.—Frank M., ii.—David Maunsel, iii.—Mary Ellen, iv.—Charles Eldred, v.—Heber, vi.—Esther Ann, vii.—Melville, viii.—George W., ix.—Ida Augusta.

i.—Frank ·M. Bennett, born August 29, 1835, in Rapides parish, La., died December 26, 1874, married Columbia M. Phelps in Scipio, New York, on July 22, 1857. There were three sons born of this marriage:—Robert L. Bennett, born July 2, 1858, married Edith Brigden of Fleming, New York, and both died a few years ago in New York; Zilton Austin Bennett died on the road to Texas from Louisiana, May 11, 1863, when about 4 years old; Ernest Ezra Bennett, born July 1, 1863, married Josephine Wride of Auburn, New York, on October 29, 1884, and was killed March 15, 1925, in an automobile accident in Los Angeles, California.

ii.—David Maunsel Bennett, born September 24, 1837, died June 13, 1884. He entered the Confederate Army at the beginning of the Civil War and served through the entire course of it, holding a captain's commission at the end of hostilities. On August 17, 1859, he married Sarah Ophelia Pearce, daughter of Alanson Green Pearce and Sidney Elizabeth Kay.*

iii.—Mary Ellen Bennett, born in 1839, married in 1854 Stephen Samuel Pearce, son of Stephen Pearce, and his second wife, Anne Grimball (Tanner) Brown.†

iv.—Charles Eldred Bennett, born March 17, 1842, died September 20, 1843.

v.—Heber Bennett, born November 11, 1844, never married. He was killed May 17, 1865, near Alexandria, La., by the explosion of a cannon at the close of the Civil War.

vi.—Esther Ann Bennett, born October 27, 1846, died June 24, 1849.

vii.—Melville Bennett, born February 8, 1849, died October 20, 1876, married Mary Eliza Jackson. They had one child, Alice Levinia Bennett, born September 16, 1870, and died in 1925.

viii.—George W. Bennett, born February 22, 1851, died December, 1905. He was a prominent and prosperous business man in the Cheneyville neighborhood of Rapides parish, La. He married on July 14, 1875, Theoda Tower of Crystal Springs, Miss. They had six children:—Annie May, born March 26, 1877, never married; Lena Mary, born July 22, 1878, married Dr. Bickerstaff of Pensacola, Florida; Emma Providence, born August 28, 1880, married Percy Irion and had one daughter, Gladys, who married Felix Monschan and had a daughter, Nevers, born November 11, 1921; Myrtle Theoda, born June 14, 1882, married Clarence Pope and had three daughters and a son (George Bennett Pope); Fred Wadsworth, born August 1, 1883, never married; Maude Virginia, born March 23, 1885.

ix.—Ida Augusta Bennett, born December 1, 1853, died January 22, 1859.

4.—Randal Bettison Eldred, fourth child of Randal Eldred, Jr., and Esther Susannah Robert, was born February 14, 1817, in Rapides parish, La. He married a Miss O'Neal and died in September, 1867. We have no record of any descendants.

---

* A full account of their descendants will be found on page 352.
† See Page 359.

5.—Robert Daniel Eldred, youngest child of Randal Eldred, Jr., and Esther Susannah Robert, was born September 18, 1821, in Rapides parish, La. The family record says he married Sarah Robert, but just who she was we have been unable to determine. We have no record of any descendants.

J.
DANIEL ROBERT.

Daniel Robert, tenth child of Captain Peter Robert and Anne Grimball, was born in St. Peter's Parish, Beaufort District, South Carolina, about 1785. About the time he reached maturity his parents, in company with a large concourse of friends and relatives, emigrated to Mississippi and for several years lived in the vicinity of Woodville, in Wilkinson county. There on March 9, 1809, Daniel married Sarah Griffin and soon afterwards moved to Rapides parish, La. It seems quite likely that his wife was a sister of James Griffin whose daughter Evolina married Peter Robert Eldred, his (Daniel's) nephew. Daniel Robert probably stopped for a while on Bayou Boeuf where most of his people permanently settled, but in a short while he went to the upper end of the parish and "pitched his tent" on Bayou Rapides, near its source, in the vicinity of the present "Hot Wells." His property adjoined that of James Griffin, which was probably the inducement alluring him to that section of the parish. We believe he established his home there before 1815 and that later, in 1827, due to financial difficulties he transferred his property to his sister's husband, Randal Eldred, Jr., but continued to live there until he again acquired the title to it in 1829. The following deed passed before Silas Talbert, Notary Public, and witnessed by C. D. Brashear and John G. Pearce, on March 23, 1829, throws some light on the subject:—

STATE OF LOUISIANA, PARISH OF RAPIDES. Before me Silas Talbert, Notary Public in and for the parish aforesaid and the undersigned witnesses, came Randal Eldred of the parish aforesaid who acknowledges that for the consideration herein after expressed he hath bargained sold transferred and delivered unto Daniel Robert of the parish aforesaid the following property to wit, a certain tract or parcel of land situate lying and being in the parish of Rapides on the left bank of Bayou Rapides in descending, and adjoining land of James Griffin above and

Cuny below, and containing the quantity of four hundred superficial arpents, it being *the present residence* of the said Daniel Robert and it being that which I acquired of the said Daniel Robert on the 7th of May, 1827, which is now on record in the parish Judge's office of the parish of Rapides, and also the following slaves, etc. . . . This sale is made for and in consideration of the sum of $30,000.00 which the said Daniel Robert paid in hand to the said Eldred, the receipt of which is hereby acknowledged . . . .

Daniel Robert named his place "Oakland" and there he lived practically all of his long life. He became a prosperous planter and a prominent citizen. His wife, Sarah Griffin, died at her home on Bayou Rapides on January 14, 1835, in the 40th year of her age. This is verified by the inscription on her tombstone. She was buried in the family graveyard a short distance from the home. About 1837 Daniel Robert married his second wife, Emily Jane Collier, a native of Kentucky. She outlived him twenty years, dying April 3, 1886. Daniel Robert reached the advanced age of eighty-one and died at his home on July 2, 1866. He and his two wives rest in the family graveyard overlooking the bayou just above the site of the home. Eighteen children were born of these two marriages, ten of the first and eight of the second. They were:—

1st marriage.
1.—Cuthbert A. Robert.
2.—William Adonis Robert.
3.—Caroline Ann Robert.
4.—James Lawrence Robert.
5.—Rudolph Alanson Robert.
6.—Henry Augustus Robert.
7.—Duval Alanson Robert.
8.—Daniel Robert, Jr.
9.—Sophronia Emily Robert.
10.—Theodore Rousby Robert.

2nd marraige.
11.—Ann Robert.
12.—Sarah Jane Robert.
13.—Isaac Carlton Robert.
14.—Joseph Eldred Robert.
15.—Daniel Boone Robert.
16.—John Willis Robert.
17.—Benjamin Robert.
18.—Alice Adelaide Robert.

Many of these children died in early life or unmarried. 1.—Cuthbert A. Robert died in 1813. 4.—James Lawrence Robert lived to maturity but died unmarried. 5.—Rudolph Alanson Robert died in 1820 at the age of four years. 6.— Henry Augustus Robert died in 1828. 7.—Duval Alanson Robert died in 1829. Daniel Robert, Jr., died in 1829. 11— Ann Robert died in early childhood. 12.—Sarah Jane Robert died in infancy. 17.—Benjamin Robert died in infancy.

2.—William Adonis Robert, second child of Daniel Robert and his first wife, Sarah Griffin, was born in Rapides parish, La., in 1811. He never married. He was an enthusiastic and devout member of the Baptist church and was one of the noted evangelists of his day. Paxton, in his History of the Baptists of Louisiana, has the following to say about him:—

> Elder William A. Robert, son of Daniel Robert, was a native of Rapides parish. He was converted while attending college at Georgetown, Kentucky, and was licensed to preach. His greatest work was at Bayou des Glaises (Louisiana) where he founded one of the most efficient churches in the Association. After the close of his pastorate he retired to his plantation on Bayou Cotile, preaching in the surrounding country. When the Federal army invaded this part of the State he refugeed with his slaves to Texas, where he died in 1863. He never married.

3.—Caroline Ann Robert, third child of Daniel Robert and his first wife, Sarah Griffin, was born on "Oakland" plantation, the home of her parents on Bayou Rapides, on February 4, 1812. She was married by the Rev. O. D. Nash on January 20, 1831, to Daniel Thweate Haworth. His mother may have been a Thweate—a very prominent old family in Virginia in the early days. Mr. Haworth's plantation was known as "Hardscrabble" and was beautifully situated in a bend of Bayou Rapides on the right descending bank of that stream, about a mile below Lamothe's Bridge. There they resided until Mr. Haworth's death, May 7, 1853, in the 53rd year of his age, which date is verified by the inscription on his tomb in the old Robert graveyard on upper Bayou Rapides. His death was due to accidental drowning.

The Haworth family is said to be of Welsh origin. Just when the first of the name came to America we have no information. They were in Virginia at an early date and thence emigrated to Kentucky. From the family we learn that three Haworth brothers came to Louisiana from Kentucky sometime in the second decade of 1800. They were Harvey, Absolom Burnett, and Daniel Thweate Haworth. We first meet the youngest of these in Baton Rouge, La., where he married and was associated in business with Abraham Lobdell. They were proprietors of THE UNION HOTEL, and conducted a livery stable in connection with it. In an old copy of the BATON ROUGE GAZETTE of October 20, 1827, we read the following:—

> Departed this life on the morning of the 11th inst., at 3 o'clock, Mrs. Louisa Haworth, consort of Mr. D. T. Haworth of this place, aged 21 years and 11 months. He is now left alone with an infant son, only two years of age.

On November 12, 1827, we find the following item in the same paper:—

> Notice:—There is a dissolution of partnership of the firm of HAWORTH and LOBDELL.
>
> (signed) Dan T. Haworth.
Abraham Lobdell.

In the same issue of the Gazette the following advertisement may be seen:—

> THE UNION HOTEL will be conducted hereafter by Abraham Lobdell. He offers a good table and choice liquors from his bar. His stables are well accommodated.

After the death of his wife in Baton Rouge, as recorded above, Daniel Thweate Haworth evidently became dissatisfied with conditions there, and selling out his business in that city he moved to Rapides parish in the central part of the State. It appears likely, from information now at hand, that his two brothers had already settled there. The two-year-old child referred to in the above obituary was Enoch Haworth, who died in Rapides parish when about twelve years of age. According to the family Bible Daniel Thweate Haworth was born May 18, 1800. A short time after moving to Rapides parish he married Caroline Ann Robert, as has been recorded above.

Harvey Haworth seems to have been the eldest of the three brothers who emigrated from Kentucky to Louisiana.

He married in Rapides parish the widow of Benjamin Grubb, who was Sarah Sproul before her first marriage, a native of Madison county, Alabama. Nicholas Grubb, sometimes spelled *Grubbs,* probably the father of Benjamin, patented land in Rapides parish (then Spanish territory) as early as 1796. He came from Georgia where the family seem to have been very prominent. There was a Grubb District named for one of the early settlers of that name. Benjamin Grubb and Sarah Sproul, as far as we can learn, had two sons, Hartwell and Ira Grubb. The latter went to Texas and married there. He never returned to Louisiana. Hartwell Grubb was born, married and died in Rapides parish (the compiler of these notes can well remember him). He left three children, a son and two daughters. The son was named Web Taylor Grubb and died when a young man. The daughters, Irene and Sarah Grubb, went to Texas after the death of their father (probably at the request of their uncle, Ira Grubb) and married there. Harvey Haworth and Sarah (Sproul) Grubb had one daughter, Caroline C. Haworth, who first married James McKinney and then Theodore Rousby Robert—the latter was a brother of Caroline Ann (Robert) Haworth. There will be further reference to her later on.

Absolom Burnett Haworth, as far as our records show, never married. His tombstone may be seen today in the old McNutt Hill graveyard in western Rapides parish. The inscription on it reads as follows:—

ABSOLOM BURNETT HAWORTH

Born April 22, 1797, and
Died September 17, 1830.

The widow of Harvey Haworth—Sarah (Sproul) Grubb—married as her third husband, George Mai Taylor, a native of Huntsville, Alabama. At the time of this marriage he was an old man. He was born August 16, 1801, and married his first wife, Nancy Johnson McCartney, August 29, 1828. She was born in Talladega county, Alabama, January 9, 1812, and died in Madison county, Alabama, July 20, 1860. They had about ten children, all born in Alabama. Six of their sons served in the Confederate Army. After the death of his first wife Mr.

Taylor moved to Louisiana.   An Alexandria newspaper records
Mr. Taylor's death as follows:—

> DIED:—At Huntsville, Alabama, on July 5, 1886, George
> Mai Taylor, in the 85th year of his age. The deceased
> was long a resident of this parish where he had many
> friends. There are now residing here of his family two
> sons and two daughters.

The two sons referred to were Waverly Emmett Taylor
(better known as Web) and Percy Taylor. The latter recently
died when more than eighty years old. The two daughters
were Mrs. Clinton Robert Haworth and Mrs. Pleasant Waverly
Davidson, both of whom left many descendants.

After the death of her husband, Daniel Thweate Haworth
in 1853, Caroline Ann (Robert) Haworth married about 1858
Major James W. Sims, a native of Missouri but for some years
previous to his settling in Louisiana he was a resident of Red
River county, Texas. He died in Rapides parish on February
8, 1878, in the 73rd year of his age, and his wife died on June
8, 1888—the compiler has very distinct recollections of this
good old lady. She and her second husband were buried in the
old Robert graveyard on Bayou Rapides. The following item
is from a copy of the Alexandria Town Talk of June, 1888:—

> DIED:—At her residence on Bayou Rapides, on Friday,
> June 8, 1888, at 8 o'clock, Mrs. Caroline A. Sims, born
> Robert, aged 76 years. She was born on February 4, 1812,
> within 5 miles of where her spirit passed to its Maker.
> She was twice married, her first husband being Daniel
> Thweate Haworth, by whom she had several children, two
> of whom are living on Bayou Rapides—C. R. and L. B.
> Haworth. The funeral took place at 4 o'clock Saturday,
> the 9th, interment being made in the family burying
> ground.

Caroline Ann Robert and her first husband, Daniel
Thweate Haworth, had four children:—

> i.—Clinton Robert Haworth.
> ii.—Leander Bernard Haworth.
> iii.—Oscar Haworth.
> iv.—Daniel Thweate Haworth, Jr.

i.—Clinton Robert Haworth was born on "Hardscrabble"
plantation, on Bayou Rapides, in Rapides parish, La., on May

3, 1835, and died on July 20, 1909. He was riding home on horseback from Alexandria when he was seized with a fatal illness (probably coronary thrombosis) near the home of his good friend Dr. Smith Gordon, where he died within a short while. When his State seceded from the Union in 1861 he immediately enlisted in "The Stafford Guards" which became Company B, Ninth Louisiana Infantry. The original company roster shows him as a corporal. He served the entire period of that bloody conflict in Virginia and then returned to Louisiana and devoted himself to planting. He took an active part in all public affairs of his section of the country during the trying times of the so-called "Reconstruction." He was a highly respected, upright and honorable citizen—a real old-time Southern gentleman. He was elected and served as assessor of Rapides parish for several years. On February 15, 1866, he married Mary Sophronia Taylor, the Rev. B. F. White of the Methodist church performing the ceremony. She was a daughter of George Mai Taylor and Nancy Johnson McCartney, and was born in Jackson county, Alabama, on December 6, 1843. "Miss Molly," as we always called her, was one of those exuberant, attractive lovable characters who leaves an indelible impression behind them—one that always remains with you and is easily and pleasantly recalled. She outlived her husband many years (she always spoke of him or called him *husband*) and died on April 19, 1928, having reached the advanced age of eighty-five. Ten children were born of this marriage:—

      a.—Oscar Taylor Haworth, born October 17, 1867.
      b.—Caroline Haworth, born January 12, 1869.
      c.—Lucy Waverly Haworth, born December 18, 1870.
      d.—Archie Gordon Haworth, born December 27, 1872.
      e.—Un-named infant son, born December 27, 1874.
      f.—Percy Taylor Haworth, born February 24, 1876.
      g.—Oscar Stuart Haworth, born March 10, 1878.
      h.—Smith Gordon Haworth, born January 15, 1880.
      i.—Mary Margaret Haworth, born May 20, 1882.
      j.—Rosa Lillian Haworth, born August 17, 1884.

      a.—Oscar Taylor Haworth died October 25, 1867, when one week old.

      b.—Caroline Haworth died on September 15, 1873, in her 5th year.

c.—Lucy Waverly Haworth is living at this date (1944) and has never married. She resides in Alexandria, La., where for many years she has been in the employ of the Daily Town Talk.

d.—Archie Gordon Haworth was for many years prominent in the mercantile business in Louisiana—first in Boyce and later in Alexandria. At a still later period he moved to Los Angeles, California, where he died April 13, 1929. His body was brought back to Louisiana and buried in the Rapides cemetery in Pineville where his father and mother were buried. He married in Alexandria on October 17, 1900, Josephine Hoy, only child of Joseph Hoy and his second wife, Lelia Georgiana Wilkinson. They had five children:—

az.—Mary Lelia Haworth, born December 8, 1901.
bz.—Clinton Hoy Haworth, born February 6, 1904.
cz.—Douglas Gordon Haworth, born December 18, 1905.
dz.—Waverly Emmett Haworth, born September 4, 1907.
ez.—Archie Gordon Haworth, Jr., born March 25, 1910.

az.—Mary Lelia Haworth was born in Boyce, Rapides parish, La., and was married in Los Angeles, California, to Paul Dewey Miller. They have two children:—Barbara Ruth and David Lee Miller. The former was married September 18, 1943, to Charles Mortimer Kilpatrick. David Lee Miller is at this time (1944) a student at Texas A. & M. College.

bz.—Clinton Hoy Haworth was born in Boyce, Rapides parish, La., and married in California in August, 1925, Elizabeth Alexandria Strastny. He died suddenly in Los Angeles on February 11, 1937, leaving no issue.

cz.—Douglas Gordon Haworth was born in Alexandria, La., and married Doris Davis in Los Angeles, California. They have one daughter, Patricia Lee Haworth.

dz.—Waverly Emmett Haworth was born in Alexandria, La., and now lives in Seattle, Washington, where he married Marion Williams. They have three children:—Edward Emmett, born in May, 1938, Keith Dennis, born February 18, 1940, and Gale Ann, born November 27, 1943.

ez.—Archie Gordon Haworth, Jr., was born in Alexandria, La., and now lives in Los Angeles, California, where he married Irene Weirich. They have four children:—Carol Ann Haworth, born January 29, 1938, Archie Gordon Haworth, III, born January 29, 1940, Robert Allen Haworth, born August 14, 1941, and William Lawrence Haworth, born December 8, 1943.

e.—The fourth child of Clinton Robert Haworth and Mary Sophronia Taylor was a boy and died at birth unnamed.

f.—Percy Taylor Haworth was born at "Sunshine," his father's plantation on Bayou Rapides, in Rapides parish, La. For a quarter of a century he was engaged in farming and the mercantile business near the place where he was born. He now resides in Alexandria and holds the position of Registrar of Voters for Rapides parish. He married on September 14, 1912, Alice M. Earnest, who was born on November 29, 1894, on the old Keary plantation below Cheneyville, in Rapides parish, La. Her father, Benjamin Periece Earnest, was born near Monroe, La., on April 6, 1858, and died in Hot Springs, Arkansas, on March 28, 1903. He was a son of Samuel Earnest, born in east Georgia on January 5, 1812, and died on January 5, 1894, and who married on October 25, 1840, Lettie Barnes Rodgers of Vicksburg, Miss. Mrs. Haworth's parents were married on November 27, 1879. Her mother was Susannah Louisa Dixon, and was born near Jonesboro, Jackson parish, La., on March 23, 1862, and died on January 22, 1924, her parents being John Abernathy Dixon, born in Georgia on August 20, 1830, and died on February 4, 1901, and Martha Effejane Hogan, born in south Alabama on April 24, 1830, and died on February 26, 1917. They were married on March 24, 1853. Benjamin Periece Earnest after marrying came to Rapides parish and in 1885 purchased a portion of the plantation on Bayou Boeuf, just below Cheneyville, which at one time belonged to Captain Patrick Foley Keary whose wife was a niece of Jefferson Davis, President of the Confederacy. Mr. and Mrs. Percy Taylor Haworth have three children:—

az.—Mabel Haworth, born July 30, 1913.
bz.—Myrtle Jewell Haworth, born August 10, 1914.
cz.—Doris Marguerite Haworth, born Sept. 19, 1918

az.—Mabel Haworth was born at Cottonport, Avoyelles parish, La. She is as yet unmarried.

bz.—Myrtle Jewell Haworth was born at Perry, Taylor county, Florida, on August 10, 1914. She was married on

March 21, 1933, to Joseph Samuel Marler who was born in Rapides parish, La., on May 2, 1906. They have two children: —Joseph Samuel Marler, Jr., born at the Baptist Hospital, Alexandria, La., September 11, 1934; Alice Haworth Marler, born at the Texada Clinic, Alexandria, La., on Thursday, July 10, 1941.

cz.—Doris Marguerite Haworth was born September 19, 1918, on "Sunshine" plantation, Bayou Rapides, Rapides parish, La., the birth place of her father and the home of her grandfather. She was married on September 14, 1937, to Archie Cortez Perkins, son of John E. Perkins and the late Mrs. Perkins of Dallas, Texas. The ceremony was performed in Christ Church Chapel of St. James Episcopal church in Alexandria at six o'clock in the evening, by the Rev. H. N. Griffith, rector of the church of the Epiphany in Opelousas, La. They resided for a time in Arizona where Mr. Perkins was associated with his father who was superintendent of a construction work in that State. They have now returned to Louisiana and are living in Alexandria.

g.—Oscar Stuart Haworth lived for many years in Florida where he was engaged in the lumber business. He now resides in Natchitoches, La., where he is connected with a cotton oil company. He married on October 6, 1906, Blanche Elizabeth Texada who was born in Rapides parish, La., on March 29, 1884. She was a daughter of Lewis Manuel Texada and Blanche Preot, both of whom are now dead. Two children were born of this marriage:—

az.—Oscar Stuart Haworth, Jr., born June 7, 1908.
bz.—Marjorie Anita Haworth, born June 11, 1912.

az.—Oscar Stuart Haworth, usually called Stuart, is not married at this date (1944) and is in the U. S. Army.

bz.—Marjorie Anita Haworth was married on May 23, 1937, to Lawrence Elbert Hubley. They have one daughter, Judith Elaine Hubley, born November 29, 1938.

h.—Smith Gordon Haworth was engaged most of his life in the cotton oil business and at the time of his death was manager of the Broussard Cotton Oil Company at Broussard, La. He was shot and killed in his office there by Samuel Erwin, engineer of the mill, on January 1, 1929, being at the time 49 years old. His friends and family have never thought the homicide was justifable, despite the fact that his slayer was acquitt-ed by a jury. Be that as it may, Doc Haworth (as he was familiarly known to his friends) was an honest and upright man, a real Southern gentleman, and the compiler, who knew him intimately from early childhood, will never believe that he knowingly injured or attempted to injure any man. He married Katie Walker on July 3, 1924, and they had three children: —Mary Josephine Haworth, born July 23, 1925; Margaret Waverly Haworth, born February 7, 1927; Katherine Gordon Haworth, born October 1, 1928. All were born at Broussard, Lafayette parish, La., and are now living in Alexandria, La., with their mother.

i.—Mary Margaret Haworth, better known as "Dolly," was married on October 14, 1904, to Arnaud Preot Texada, son of John Augustin Texada and Annie Preot. They now reside in New Orleans where Mr. Texada holds a responsible position with one of the large wholesale hardware companies and have one son, Arnaud Preot Texada, Jr., born June 13, 1913, in New Orleans. This son completed his education in the school of engineering at Tulane University and located at Alton, Illinois. He married on June 18, 1940, Mildred Ernestine Rotureau of New Orleans. The following account of the wedding appeared in the New Orleans Daily States of June 19, 1940:—

> Christ Church Cathedral on St. Charles Avenue saw two weddings yesterday. At 9 a. m. Dean William H. Nes officiated, assisted by the Rev. Harry Tisdale, at the wedding of Mildred Ernestine Rotureau and Arnaud Preot Texada, Jr., son of Mr. and Mrs. Texada of New Orleans. A vested choir sang during part of the Eucharistic ceremony. Easter lillies, gladioli, peonies and candles decorated the altar and chancel. Given in marriage by her father, the bride wore a white silk marquisette dress trimmed with chantilly lace, a long tulle veil caught with orange blossoms, an antique diamond and pearl brooch and pearls, and carried lillies of the valley and white roses.
> Jacqueline Texada of Gainesville, Florida, was bridesmaid and only attendant and wore a mirror-blue silk marquisette dress banded in chantilly lace, a wide leghorn hat with amethyst velvet streamers on it and carried a bouquet of blue cornflowers and golden daisies. Charles M. Waters of Alexandria, La., was best man; John W. Waters of Alexandria, J. A. Texada, Jr., of Gainesville, Florida,

Ned Ferry and Carleton Buell were groomsmen and ushers.

The bridal couple left by motor for the East and for Canada and will live in Alton, Ill. The bride attended Newcomb College. The bridegroom was graduated from the Tulane engineering school.

j.—Rosa Lillian Haworth was married on March 27, 1912, to John Augustin Texada, Jr., son of John Augustin Texada and Annie Preot. The groom is better known to his friends as "Jack Texada." They reside in Gainesville, Florida, where Mr. Texada is engaged in the lumber business. He is a grandson of Lewis Emanuel Texada and Mary Hunter, a great grandson of Capt. John Augustin Texada and Lucy Welsh, and a great great grandson of Don Manuel Garcia de Texada (or Tejada), a native of Castile, Spain, and his wife, Mahala Trevillion of Tennessee. Before coming to Rapides parish, La., the Texadas lived in Natchez, Miss. Mr. and Mrs. "Jack" Texada have one child, Jacqueline Texada, born September 25, 1916, at "Castile," the old Texada homestead in Rapides parish, La. She was married on Saturday, October 26, 1940, at Holy Trinity Episcopal church, Gainesville, Florida, to William Augustus McGriff, Jr., son of Mr. and Mrs. William Augustus McGriff. They reside at Miami Beach, Florida. They have a son who was born at Gainesville, Florida, on March 10, 1944.

ii.—Leander Bernard Haworth, second son of Daniel Thweate Haworth and his second wife, Caroline Ann Robert, was born at "Hardscrabble," the plantation home of his parents on Bayou Rapides, in Rapides parish, La., about 1838. He was a gallant Confederate soldier and served throughout the period of the Civil War with the army in Virginia, remaining there the entire four years without once coming home on a furlough. After the war he settled down on "Hardscrabble" and devoted his energies to farming, remaining there until his death on January 22, 1903. He was buried in the old Robert graveyard on upper Bayou Rapides. Soon after returning home from Virginia he married Clara Mason, a native of Catahoula parish, La., born in 1850 and a sister of Leonard Mason who at one time was Secretary of State for Louisiana. The marriage probably took place in 1867 or there-abouts. Clara (Mason) Haworth died at her home on Bayou Rapides on February 11,

1891. This date is recorded in the Daniel Robert family Bible and also in the Alexandria Town Talk of February 14, 1891. There were ten children from this marriage, all of whom were born at "Hardscrabble." Many of them were the compiler's playmates in his boyhood days and many happy hours did he spend with them and their cousins, the children of Clinton Robert Haworth, in the thickly shaded yard at "Hardscrabble." Those ten children were:—

        a.—Daniel Mason Haworth.
        b.—Leander Bernard Haworth, Jr.
        c.—Mabel Haworth.
        d.—Clinton Robert Haworth.
        e.—Willie Mason Haworth.
        f.—Edgar Haworth.
        g.—Caroline Haworth.
        h.—Philip Haworth.
        i.—Leonard Haworth.
        j.—Clara Haworth.

    a.—Daniel Mason Haworth was born on "Hardscrabble" plantation, in Rapides parish, La., on October 15, 1869, and died on March 25, 1925. He married Susan Amelia Iles, daughter of Jesse Iles and Emma Crosby, on December 27, 1905. His wife is living at this date (1944). They had three children:—

        az.—Jesse Earl Haworth, born March 23, 1907.
        bz.—Clara Lillian Haworth, born February 7, 1909.
        cz.—Percy Taylor Haworth, born December 31, 1910.

    az.—Jesse Earl Haworth was born in Rapides parish, La., and by his energy, initiative and admirable traits of character has succeeded in the world and made friends for himself. He was for a number of years in the employ of the Guaranty Bank and Trust Company of Alexandria. He recently resigned his position there to take charge of the credit and accounting department of WELLAN'S, the largest department store in Alexandria. He married Eva Julia Sutherland on October 17, 1931. They have two children at this time:—David Earl Haworth, born in Alexandria, La., on Sunday, December 8, 1940, and Dan Patterson Haworth, born in Alexandria, La., on May 29, 1945.

    bz.—Clara Lillian Haworth, only daughter of Daniel Mason Haworth and Susan Amelia Iles, was married on October 9, 1925, to Andrew Dunnam Joyner, Jr., son of Andrew Dunnam

Joyner of Boyce, La. They have two children:—Shirley Ann Joyner, born November 11, 1937, and Minnie Diane Joyner, born Tuesday, November 30, 1943.

cz.—Percy Taylor Haworth married Stella Ashley on December 28, 1932. They have two children:—Jerry Ann Haworth, born at the Baptist Hospital in Alexandria, La., on Saturday, October 14, 1939, and Frederic Michael Haworth, born at the Baptist Hospital in Alexandria, La., on Tuesday, February 13, 1945.

b.—Leander Bernard Haworth, Jr., better known to his family and friends as "Tusie," was one of those big-hearted, good natured individuals who was always laughing and whom every one loved. He was born on "Hardscrabble," his father's plantation home in Rapides parish, La., about 1872, and married Alice Belgard, member of an old Rapides family. He and his wife have long since gone to another world. They left one child, Agalice Haworth, who was married to J. D. Harris and now has a daughter of her own, born at the Baptist Hospital in Alexandria, La., on Monday, August 11, 1937, at 11:15 p. m.

c.—Mabel Haworth, better known as "May," third child of Leander Bernard Haworth and Clara Mason, was born at her parents' home on Bayou Rapides, Rapides parish, La. The compiler remembers her as an industrious, hardworking girl who was always helping her mother care for the younger members of a large family. She was born about 1874, never married, and as far as we know is living at this time.

d.—Clinton Robert Haworth, fourth child of Leander Bernard Haworth and Clara Mason, was born at his parents' plantation home on Bayou Rapides, in Rapides parish, La., in 1876. He and the compiler are of the same age and were boyhood playmates. At this time he is a prominent planter and merchant on Bayou Rapides at Lamothe's bridge where he has lived for many years. He married on June 11, 1902, Mary Spencer who was born in Catahoula parish, La., on April 22, 1876. It is our impression that Mr. Haworth and his wife are cousins through the Mason family. Three children were born of this marriage:—

az.—Laurie Spencer Haworth.
bz.—Eloise Haworth.
cz.—Miriam Haworth.

az.—Laurie Spencer Haworth was born in Rapides parish, La., on August 4, 1903, and was married on January 23, 1929, to George Wallet Smith who was born in Chicago, Illinois, on January 26, 1906. They have no children.

bz.—Eloise Haworth was born in Rapides parish, La., on September 27, 1914, and was married in Shreveport, La., on August 8, 1932, to Stafford Ashley Cooper, son of Mr. and Mrs. T. B. Cooper. He was born in St. Louis, Missouri, on December 21, 1910, and reared in Shreveport. He is now an officer in the U. S. Army. We learn from an item in the Shreveport Times (1942) the following news of him:—

> Mrs. T. B. Cooper, of 2616 Lillian street, Shreveport, has received word that her son Stafford Ashley Cooper has been promoted from first lieutenant to captain in the army. Captain Cooper recently completed a special training course at Fort Monroe, Virginia, and now is on active duty with the 204th Coast Artillery. His wife is the former Eloise Haworth of Alexandria and they have a seven-year-old son, Spencer Cooper.

One child was born of this marriage, Stafford Spencer Cooper, in Alexandria, La., on September 15, 1934.

cz.—Miriam Haworth was born on Bayou Rapides, in Rapides parish, La., on March 23, 1918, and is as yet unmarried.

e.—Willie Mason Haworth never married and has for many years been an invalid from the results of an injury.

f.—Edgar Haworth married a Miss Walding in Rapides parish, La., and moved to Hollywood, California, where he has lived for many years. He has children but we have been unable to obtain any definite information of them. The following item from an Alexandria newspaper of June 14, 1941, refers to two of his sons:—

> Messrs. Woodie and Leon Haworth and Leonard Walding of Hollywood, California, are visiting their relatives, Mrs. Myrtle Walding and Miss Myrtle Lea Walding, 725 Scott street.

h.—Philip Haworth married Lola Walding and is now living near Alexandria, La. They have a number of children but we have been unable to get a correct record of them. We only know that one of their sons, Philip Buell Haworth, was honorably discharged from the army in 1944. He now lives in Alexandria, La., and married Mary Alice Jordan. They have a little daughter, Marilyn Janella, born at the Baptist Hospital in Alexandria on March 2, 1945.

i.—Leonard Haworth is married and living in Dallas, Texas, but we have been unable to get any definite data on him.

j.—Clara Haworth was born on January 30, 1891, two weeks before her mother's death. She was married to L. A. Mynatt and now lives in Dallas, Texas. They have no children as far as we know. Mr. Mynatt is now a civil service employee with the U. S. Army Air Corps.

iii.—Oscar Haworth, third son of Daniel Thweate Haworth and his second wife, Caroline Ann Robert, was born on "Hardscrabble" plantation, Rapides parish, La., about 1840. He died just before the outbreak of the Civil War of yellow fever.

iv.—Daniel Thweate Haworth, Jr., fourth son of Daniel Thweate Haworth and his second wife, Caroline Ann Robert, was born on "Hardscrabble" plantation, Rapides parish, La., about 1845. He married Sarah Mason of Catahoula parish, La., a relative of his brother Leander's wife, either a sister or cousin. At the time of this marriage she was the widow of Samuel C. Cuny of Sicily Island, in Catahoula parish. No issue. Mr. Haworth died in Alexandria, La., on March 27, 1872, from meningitis which he is said to have contracted on a steamboat while returning from New Orleans. THE LOUISIANA DEMOCRAT of Wednesday, April 3, 1872, makes the following mention of his death:—

DIED:—In Alexandria on Wednesday, March 27, 1872, Daniel T. Haworth, aged 27 years.

9.—Sophronia Emily Robert, ninth child of Daniel Robert and his first wife, Sarah Griffin, was born at "Oakland," her father's plantation home on upper Bayou Rapides, in Rapides parish, La., in 1825. She was married on January 6, 1853, to William White Whittington, Sr., who was born at Snow Hill, Worcester county, Maryland, in 1812, and was a son of Judge William Whittington and his wife, Sallie White. Judge Whittington and his wife were born in Maryland in 1770 and both died there, she in 1819 and he in 1826. William White Whittington, Sr., emigrated to Louisiana in 1836 and engaged in planting on Bayou Rapides, in Rapides parish, where he spent the remainder of his days. He married in 1838 Ann C. Holt, daughter of William Holt and widow of Henry Manadue. This wife died in 1849 leaving four children:—William White, Jr., Robert Holt, Sallie Gertrude (wife of Thomas Spence Smith), and Anna C. (wife of Lawrence C. Sanford). It was four years later that he married his second wife, Sophronia Emily Robert, and they had five children:—

         i.—John Rousby Whittington.
        ii.—Eugenia C. Whittington.
      iii.—Emma Sophronia Whittington.
      iv.—Clinton Robert Whittington.
       v.—Maude Whittington.

William White Whittington, Sr., died on January 16, 1891, and was buried in the Robert graveyard on Bayou Rapides. We have no record of the date of death of his second wife. According to the inscription on his tombstone he was born July 27, 1812.

i.—John Rousby Whittington and iv.—Clinton Robert Whittington both lived to be middle aged men but never married. The compiler has very distinct recollections of them. The former was a great hunter and spent most of his time in the woods. At that period deer were plentiful and camp hunts in the vast pine covered hills of Rapides and Vernon parishes, sometimes lasting a week or more, furnished the chief source of sport for the men. John Whittington was frequently one of the leading figures of these gatherings.

ii.—Eugenia C. Whittington, second child of William White Whittington, Sr., and his second wife, Sophronia Emily Robert, was born on Bayou Rapides, in Rapides parish, La., on June 26, 1859, and died at her home there on December 3, 1896. She was married on October 9, 1878, to Monroe Stewart Trimble, a native of Clarksville, Red River county, Texas, where he was born on November 14, 1853. He was a son of Judge William Trimble of that place. It would appear from information at hand that the Trimbles emigrated to Texas from Tennessee. Monroe Stewart Trimble was a nephew of Major James W. Sims, the second husband of Caroline Ann (Robert) Haworth, and it is likely that he came to Louisiana with his uncle. Mr. Trimble died at his home in Rapides parish, La., on December 26, 1900. He and his wife had ten children:—

> a.—Julia Sophronia Trimble, born September 26, 1879.
> b.—Emma Eugenia Trimble, born April 16, 1881.
> c.—William Stewart Trimble, born January 5, 1883.
> d.—David Sims Trimble, born March 5, 1885.
> e.—Margeritte Ellener Trimble, born March 17, 1888.
> f.—William White Whittington Trimble, born November 27, 1890.
> g.—Monroe Stewart Trimble, Jr., born November 27, 1890.
> h.—Eugene Neal Trimble, born November 25, 1892.
> i.—Iva Hortense Trimble, born September 21, 1894.
> j.—Eugenia Ruth Trimble, born December 3, 1896.

a.—Julia Sophronia Trimble was born on upper Bayou Rapides, in Rapides parish, La. The compiler of these notes still retains most pleasant recollections of her as a young girl. She was very animated and attractive and the memory of her has come down through the more than forty years which have elapsed since he last saw her, still fresh and vivid. She was married in Boyce, Rapides parish, La., on July 27, 1898, to John Louis Redden. They now live in Hendersonville, North Carolina, where they have been for many years, and have four children:—

> az.—Harriett Eugenia Redden, born February 16, 1900.
> bz.—Monroe Minor Redden, born September 24, 1901.
> cz.—Ethel Mabel Redden, born February 9, 1905.
> dz.—Arthur J. Louis Redden, born February 2, 1907.

az.—Harriett Eugenia Redden was married in Hendersonville, North Carolina, on February 5, 1920, to John Earl Bishop. As far as we know they have no children.

bz.—Monroe Minor Redden married Mary Belle Boyd in Raleigh, North Carolina, on October 28, 1923. They have two children:—Monroe Minor Redden, Jr., born June 1, 1926, and Robert McDuffie Redden, born November 19, 1930.

cz.—Ethel Mabel Redden was married in Hendersonville, North Carolina, in 1923, to Henry Siminton Brookshire, and they have two sons:—Henry Siminton Brookshire, Jr., born July 20, 1924, and Arthur James Brookshire, born June 14,

26. On October 25, 1936, Ethel Mabel Redden was married
e second time to Andrew Vincent Kelly in Elkton, Maryland.

dz.—Arthur J. Louis Redden married in Hendersonville,
rth Carolina, on June 29, 1929, Lena Ruth Page. They have
ree children:—Betty Page Redden, born July 2, 1930; Marian
lia Redden, born October 17, 1931; Arthur J. Louis Redden,
., born July 12, 1935.

b.—Emma Eugenia Trimble died on September 9, 1887.
e find a notice of her death in the Alexandria Town Talk of
at period which reads as follows:

> DIED:—At the family residence on Bayou Rapides,
> Friday night, September 9, 1887, at 11:30 o'clock,
> Emma Eugenia, 2nd daughter of M. S. Trimble and
> Eugenia C. Whittington, aged 7 years.

This child's death occurred two days prior to that of a
tle brother, and both events were part of a tragedy which
ocked the entire neighborhood at the time. In those days
rphine was dispensed in small bottles of a shape and size
nilar to those containing quinine and unless the label was
refully read one could easily be mistaken for the other. There
s no legal restriction on the sale of the drug—it could be
rchased by anyone at any country store. There were few
odynes known at that period and in every household you
uld always find a bottle of morphine. It was in a crystaline
wdered form and exceedingly bitter—similar in every re-
ect to quinine except in its effect. Several of the Trimble
ildren were sick with malaria and the mother in administer-
g them quinine mistook the bottles and gave them morphine
stead. A little later it was discovered what had happened
d doctors were hastily summoned. Everything humanly pos-
le was done to counteract the effect of the poisoning but in
ite of all efforts two of the children died, Emma Eugenia
d David Sims.

c.—William Stewart Trimble was born on upper Bayou
pides, in Rapides parish, La., and now lives in Alexandria.
was twice married, first to Jennie Kohler in 1904, and
ond to Ethel McDougal Jones in 1913. The first wife was
rn at Norman, La., in 1885, and died July 12, 1911. The
ond wife was born in Pensacola, Florida, December 24,

1875, and is living at this time. There were no children by the second marriage but by the first there were four:—

az.—Iva Angelice Trimble, born November 3, 1905.
bz.—William Sims Trimble, born November 26, 1906.
cz.—Monroe Edwin Trimble, born May —, 1909.
dz.—William Kohler Trimble, born March 13, 1911.

az.—Iva Angelice Trimble was born at Belldeau, La., and was married in Alexandria, La., on August 20, 1926, to Sherman V. Melder, born December 18, 1903, at Melder, Rapides parish, La. They have three sons:— Sherman V. Melder, Jr., born December 23, 1929; Richard Arlen Melder, born November 9, 1932; Jack Owen Melder, born November 18, 1934. The eldest was born at Glenmora, La., and the two younger ones at Alexandria.

bz.—William Sims Trimble, usually called *Sims*, married Bertha Whatley on October 4, 1930, in Alexandria, La. She was born in Pineville, La., on November 25, 1909. Mr. Trimble is an industrious and patriotic young man and is now in the service of his country, being a Machinist's Mate in the U. S. Navy Seabees. He and his wife have two children:— Simmy Jane Trimble, born in Alexandria, La., on October 9, 1932, and Terry Stafford Trimble, born in Alexandria, La., February 2, 1944.

cz.—Monroe Edwin Trimble, as far as we know, is unmarried.

dz.—William Kohler Trimble married Mary Louise Gredell at Poplarville, Mississippi, on June 20, 1936, where they now reside. His wife was born in Montrose, Miss., on July 9, 1912, and is a daughter of George Clemence Gredell and Lee Brame. They have one son, William Kohler Trimble, Jr., born at Hotel Dieu, New Orleans, La., on April 3, 1929.

d.—David Sims Trimble died on Sunday, September 11, 1887, as a result of the tragedy already mentioned. He was two years and six months of age at the time.

e.—Margeritte Ellener Trimble died August 1, 1895, at the age of seven years.

f.—William White Whittington Trimble, one of the twins, and usually called "Whit," was born on Bayou Rapides, in Rapides parish, La., and married Eula Madrist who was born

December 12, 1895. He died on November 10, 1935. Four children were born of this marriage:—

Billy Trimble, born November 26, 1917.
Jack Trimble, born February 17, 1921.
Joe Trimble, born December 23, 1926.
Dan Trimble, born November 5, 1928.

Dan, the fourth of these children, died June 13, 1929. We regret our inability to get their full names and more definite information about them.

g.—Monroe Stewart Trimble, Jr., the second of the twins, was born on Bayou Rapides, in Rapides parish, La. He married in Monroe, La., on April 5, 1913, Nora Carr, who was born there on March 26, 1894. They have two children:—

az.—Selena Ruth Trimble, born November 21, 1915.
bz.—Monroe Stewart Trimble, III, born December 21, 1916.

az.—Selena Ruth Trimble was married on December 26, 1930, to Albert Clay Erwin who was born in Natchez, Mississippi, on December 23, 1909.

bz.—Monroe Stewart Trimble, III, was born in Monroe, La., and married on May 31, 1937, at Ruston, La., Mildred Crawford who was born on October 19, 1918, at Plain Dealing, La. They have one son:—Richard Stewart Trimble, born at Plain Dealing, La., on March 12, 1938.

h.—Eugene Neal Trimble died on August 1, 1895, in the third year of his age.

i.—Iva Hortense Trimble was born on Bayou Rapides, in Rapides parish, La., and was married in Hendersonville, North Carolina, on May 5, 1912, by Rev. C. M. Cole, to Noah Cleveland Anders of that place who was born May 13, 1881. They now live in Jacksonville, Florida, where Mr. Anders is engaged in the building and contracting business. It is said he has been very prosperous in his endeavors. They have three daughters:

az.—Geneva Dell Anders, born February 23, 1913.
bz.—Cora Belle Anders, born May 3, 1915.
cz.—Flonnie Maye Anders, born September 3, 1921.

az.—Geneva Dell Anders was married to Leo Aswell of Norfolk, Virginia, on November 9, 1929. They had one daughter, Deloris Dell, born September 1, 1932. They were later divorced and on February 23, 1940, she was married to Frank Carlton Beckly of Jacksonville, Florida, a grandson of the late Napoleon Bonapart Broward, former governor of Florida.

bz.—Cora Belle Anders was married to Lee Roy Liles of Brunswick, Georgia, on November 11, 1939.

cz.—Flonnie Maye Anders is as yet unmarried.

j.—Eugenia Ruth Trimble, youngest of the ten children of Monroe Stewart Trimble and Eugenia C. Whittington, was born on Bayou Rapides, in Rapides parish, La., and was married on March 3, 1912, to A. D. Ellis. They now live at Henrietta, Texas, where three children were born to them:—

> Ovid James Ellis, born December 23, 1916.
> Helen Katherine Ellis, born April 16, 1922.
> Margaret Ellis, born October 23, 1927.

The eldest of these children died on April 5, 1927, in the 11th year of his age.

iii.—Emma Sophronia Whittington was born on Bayou Rapides, in Rapides parish, La., on September 27, 1860, and died in Alexandria, La., on July 25, 1925. She was married at the home of her parents on upper Bayou Rapides on June 4, 1884, to John William Hamilton who was born in 1841 in Virginia and died in Alexandria, La., on November 26, 1913. At the time of his marriage he was living in Austin, Texas. The ALEXANDRIA TOWN TALK records this marriage as follows:—

> MARRIED:—On Wednesday evening, June 4, 1884, at 8 o'clock, by the Rev. H. C. Duncan, Miss Emma S. Whittington to Mr. John W. Hamilton, at the residence of the bride's father, Mr. W. W. Whittington, Sr., on Bayou Rapides, this parish.

The compiler of these notes though but a child of eight years can vividly remember the occasion of this wedding. The bride's half brother, Robert Holt Whittington, resided on Bayou Rapides and was a near neighbor of the compiler's parents. After the ceremony the wedding party and their friends repaired to this brother's home where a reception and dance were held. My father was absent in Alexandria at the time attending to his duties in the assessor's office, but the

Whittington home was so close by that my mother decided it was her neighborly duty to attend the festival. Being the eldest of the six children then comprising our family it was delegated to me to take care of my little sisters and brothers while mother participated in the wedding feast. I well remember her returning home at a late hour and telling of the wonderful time everybody had, and how well Mr. Hamilton (the groom) played on the violin, and that she had danced with him and what a splendid dancer he was. More than half a century of time has passed since that eventful night but the remembrance of that occasion is yet vivid in my mind's eye. The bride and groom have long since answered the inevitable summons which comes to us all and there are few if any of the participants in that bridal feast now alive.

John William Hamilton and Emma Sophronia Whittington had five children, all of whom are living at this date (1944). They are:—

a.—Luckett White Hamilton, born February 20, 1886.
b.—Elizabeth Sophronia Hamilton, born November 6, 1888.
c.—John William Hamilton, Jr., born October 20, 1890.
d.—Arthur Storye Hamilton, born July 13, 1892.
e.—Maudrie Whittington Hamilton, born November 26, 1896.

a.—Luckett White Hamilton was born in Austin, Texas. He married in Alexandria, La., on April 26, 1909, Beatrice Baillio who was born in Alexandria on July 15, 1890. They have one child, Alice Burnice Hamilton, born in Alexandria on September 19, 1911, and was married on November 14, 1933, to J. Clyde Taylor who was born in New Orleans on November 22, 1900. They have one child, Shirley Jean Taylor, born in Alexandria on August 9, 1934.

b.—Elizabeth Sophronia Hamilton was born in Austin, Texas. She was married in Alexandria, La., on November 22, 1907, to Charles Herbert Wilder, son of ——————. He was born in Monroe, La., on March 30, 1878, and died in Alexandria, La., on September 23, 1934. Six children were born of this union:—

az.—Herbert Lawrence Wilder, born October 17, 1908.
bz.—Myrtle Elizabeth Wilder, born September 25, 1911.

cz.—Charles Hamilton Wilder, born April 12, 1914.
dz.—James Macklin Wilder, born August 19, 1916.
ez.—Marjorie Wilder, born June 29, 1919.
fg.—Margaret Wilder, born June 29, 1919.

az.—Herbert Lawrence Wilder was born in Alexandria, La., where he now resides and is well known as a prominent young business man. He married in Colfax, La., on August 31, 1935, Mrs. Evelyn Marie (Buckner) Nunnally who was born there on January 11, 1915, and who had one child by her first marriage, Betty Ruth Nunnally, born in Alexandria on December 20, 1933. Mr. and Mrs. Wilder have had four children, all of whom were born in Alexandria, as follows:—Herbert Lawrence Wilder, Jr., born June 16, 1936, and died August 9, 1937; Charles Herbert Wilder, II, born January 8, 1938; Evelyn Marie Wilder, born February 16, 1942; Mary Jacqueline Wilder, born July 23, 1943.

bz.—Myrtle Elizabeth Wilder was born in Alexandria, La., where she was reared and educated. She was married in Little Rock, Arkansas, on Monday, April 5, 1943, to Richard L. Copas, son of Mrs. L. L. Copas and the late Mr. Copas of Little Rock. They now reside in Little Rock where Mr. Copas is prominent in business circles.

cz.—Charles Hamilton Wilder was born in Alexandria, La., where he now resides and is prominent in business. He married on April 20, 1940, Ada Alice Moore. As yet they have no children.

dz.—James Macklin Wilder, better known as "Max," was born in Alexandria, La. He is now a staff sergeant in the U. S. Army. He married Bessie Karns on Tuesday, March 7, 1944, at Panama City, Florida. She is a daughter of Mr. and Mrs. Paul Karns of Dodge City, Kansas.

ez.—and fz.—Marjorie Wilder and Margaret Wilder, the twins, are as yet unmarried. We have heard rumors of a brave soldier boy now overseas who hopes to claim one of them when Hitler and Hirohito have been licked.

c.—John William Hamilton, Jr., was born in Austin, Texas, and married in Alexandria, La., on July 13, 1918, Virgie

Lacombe who was born at Echo, Rapides parish, La., on November 10, 1893. They have two children:—

John William Hamilton, III, born December 10, 1923.
Mary Nell Hamilton, born November 12, 1933.

d.—Arthur Storye Hamilton was born in Austin, Texas, and married at Colfax, La., on March 22, 1917, Virginia Pierce, who was born at Caruthersville, Missouri, on February 15, 1894. Six children were born of this marriage:—

Ralph William Hamilton, born November 13, 1921.
Marilynn Hamilton, born October 4, 1922.
Jack Pierce Hamilton, born August 19, 1924.
Robert Arthur Hamilton, born September 29, 1929.
Mary Virginia Hamilton, born August 31, 1931.
David Fielding Hamilton, born January 16, 1933.

The second and third of these children died in early childhood: Marilynn on May 15, 1928, and Jack Pierce on May 15, 1929.

e.—Maudrie Whittington Hamilton was born in Austin, Texas, and was married in Alexandria, La., on November 1, 1916, to Albert Finley McMain who was born at Woodworth, Rapides parish, La., on August 24, 1896. They now reside in Alexandria, La., and have one son, Albert Hamilton McMain, born in Alexandria on September 13, 1917. The compiler well remembers officiating as physician at his birth. He was graduated from the Louisiana State University and is now in the armed forces of his country. He married Ruth Soubiraa at Christ Church Cathedral (Episcopal), New Orleans, La., on March 4, 1945.

v.—Maude W. Whittington, youngest child of William White Whittington, Sr., and his second wife, Sophronia Emily Robert, was born on upper Bayou Rapides, in Rapides parish, La., on February 20, 1866, and is living in Alexandria at this date (1944). She was married about 1888 to Welsh Texada, son of Thomas Jefferson Texada and Martha Jane Gordon, who was born on Bayou Rapides, in Rapides parish, La., in 1868. They lived for many years in Lake Charles, La., and then moved to Alexandria where Mr. Texada died on Sunday,

December 24, 1939. They had many children but only three reached adult life and are living at this date. They are:—

> a.—Frank Neal Texada.
> b.—James Parker Texada.
> c.—Earnest Eugene Texada.

a.—Frank Neal Texada was born in Lake Charles, La., on September 11, 1901, and married on June 1, 1925, Mary Allen Southerland who was born in Pinebur, Mississippi, on October 11, 1905. They have five children:—

> Frank Neal Texada, Jr., born April 23, 1926.
> Lula Lorraine Texada, born May 17, 1928.
> Thomas Richard Texada, born November 21, 1929.
> Donald Edward Texada, born April 11, 1932.
> John Cary Texada, born March 15, 1940.

b.—James Parker Texada was born in Lake Charles, La., and married on December 23, 1924, Mildred Webb. They have three children: —

> James Louis Texada, born October 19, 1925.
> Dorothy Rae Texada, born December 21, 1929.
> Patricia Ann Texada, born February 28, 1932.

c.—Earnest Eugene Texada was born in Lake Charles, La., on March 4, 1910, and is unmarried at this time.

10.—Theodore Rousby Robert, tenth child of Daniel Robert and his first wife, Sarah Griffin, was born on "Oakland," his father's plantation home on upper Bayou Rapides, in Rapides parish, La., in 1828. He was twice married, 1st to Martha D. Rice of Marksville, La., on June 12, 1862, and 2nd to Caroline C. Haworth, only daughter of Harvey Haworth and Sarah (Sproul) Grubb. His second wife at the time of their marriage was the widow of James W. McKinney by whom she had two children, Iva Maggie and Kinchen McKinney. Her first marriage was recorded in THE LOUISIANA DEMOCRAT (an Alexandria newspaper) as follows:—

> MARRIED:—On Monday evening, the 7th inst., at the Methodist Episcopal church, by the Rev. A. J. Ivy, Mr. James W. McKinney to Miss Caroline Haworth, both of this parish.

Theodore Rousby Robert's first wife (Martha Rice) died on September 10, 1864, in the 18th year of her age, leaving one child:—

    i.—Lilly J. Robert.

At the time of his wife's death Mr. Robert was away from home in the Confederate Army. Of his second marriage there was one child born:—

    ii.—Adelaide Robert.

Theodore Rousby Robert lived to an advanced age, being over 80 at the time of his death. The compiler has very distinct recollections of him, having frequently visited in his home on Bayou Rapides when a young man. We find the death of his second wife recorded in the Alexandria Town Talk in the issue of Saturday, September 25, 1886, as follows:—

> DIED:—At her residence on Bayou Rapides, Wednesday, September 22, 1886, at 11:35 a. m., Caroline C. Robert, wife of T. R. Robert, aged 42 years. The cause of death was malarial fever. The funeral took place Thursday morning at 11 o'clock. The interment was made at the family burying ground near the residence on Bayou Rapides.

    i.—Lilly J. Robert, only child of Theodore Rousby Robert and his first wife, Martha D. Rice, was born on Bayou Rapides, in Rapides parish, La., in 1864. She was married to Randall Blackman Gormly of New Orleans. The *Alexandria Town Talk* of Saturday, December 29, 1888, contained the following item on this subject:—

> MARRIED:—At the residence of the bride's father, T. R. Robert, on Bayou Rapides, in this parish, on the evening of Wednesday, December 26, 1888, Mr. Randall B. Gormly to Miss Lillie J. Robert.

Mr. and Mrs. Gormly lived in Rapides parish for some years after their marriage—first on Bayou Rapides and then in Alexandria. On December 8, 1906, they left Alexandria and moved to Lake Charles, La., where they resided for the remainder of their days. Mr. Gormly died in Lake Charles on November 25, 1921, and his wife (Lilly Josephine Robert) died

there on January 14, 1928.   Both were buried in Graceland
cemetery in Lake Charles.   They had seven children:—

a.—Mattie Hortense Gormly, born October 19, 1889.
b.—Randall Adolph Gormly, born January 2, 1891.
c.—Theodore Robert Gormly, born February 3, 1893.
d.—Henry Austin Gormly, born January 24, 1896.
e.—Adelaide Carrie Gormly, born November 17, 1898.
f.—Fanny Elizabeth Gormly, born September 3, 1902.
g.—Alice Elizabeth Gormly, born July 6, 1906.

b.—Randall Adolph Gormly, second child of Randall Black-
man Gormly and Lilly Josephine Robert, was born in Rapides
parish, La.   He married Eunice Ola Stranghan in Lake Charles,
La., on June 27, 1916.   They are residing there at this time.
Two children were born of this marriage:— Theo Levin
Gormly, born March 5, 1917, at Lake Charles, La., and Jewell
Mae Gormly, born on November 18, 1924, also in Lake Charles.
The latter died on August 18, 1926.   The elder, Theo Levin
Gormly, married Jacqueline Brown of New Orleans on Decem-
ber 7, 1938.   They have one child at this time, Jacqueline Jean
Gormly, born in Lake Charles on October 13, 1940.

c.—Theodore Robert Gormly, third child of Randall Blackman Gormly and Lilly Josephine Robert, was born in Rapides
parish, La.   He married Ella Mae Hulin in Lake Charles on
May 14, 1919.   They have no children.

d.—Henry Austin Gormly, fourth child of Randall Blackman Gormly and Lilly Josephine Robert, was born in Rapides
parish, La.   He married Joel Elizabeth Rose in Lake Charles
on July 15, 1929.   They have two children:—Lillie Gormly,
born August 4, 1930, and Henry Austin Gormly, Jr., born
August 4, 1931.   Both were born in Lake Charles.

e.—Adelaide Carrie Gormly, fifth child of Randall Blackman Gormly and Lilly Josephine Robert, was born in Rapides
parish, La.   She was married to Forrest M. Wise in New Orleans on November 2, 1925.   They have no children.

f.—Fanny Elizabeth Gormly, sixth child of Randall Blackman Gormly and Lilly Josephine Robert, was born in Rapides
parish, La.   She was married to John H. Berger in New Orleans on November 2, 1920.   They have two children:—John
H. Berger, Jr., born August 24, 1921, and Katherine Elizabeth

Berger, born July 27, 1929. The former was born in Lake Charles, La., and the latter in Memphis, Tennessee.

g.—Alice Elizabeth Gormly, seventh child of Randall Blackman Gormly and Lilly Josephine Robert, was born in Rapides parish, La. She was married to Jeff C. Morris in Longview, Texas, on August 4, 1937. They have no children as yet.

ii.—Adelaide Robert, only child of Theodore Rousby Robert and his second wife, Caroline (Haworth) McKinney, was born on Bayou Rapides, in Rapides parish, La., about 1875. She was a lovely and charming girl, and it was the compiler's privilege and pleasure to know her well in his younger days when he frequently visited her home and spent many happy hours with her and her pretty cousin, Julia Trimble. She never married and died of yellow fever in early adult life.

13.—Isaac Carlton Robert, third child of Daniel Robert and his second wife, Emily Jane Collier, was born at "Oakland," his father's plantation home on Bayou Rapides, in Rapides parish, La., about 1842. He never married and died at the old homestead at an advanced age.

14.—Joseph Eldred Robert, fourth child of Daniel Robert and his second wife, Emily Jane Collier, was born at "Oakland," his father's plantation home on Bayou Rapides,, in Rapides parish, La., on January 9, 1844. He never married and died there on January 23, 1924. The Alexandria Daily Town Talk of that period reported his death as follows:—

ROBERT:—At the family residence, Oakland Plantation, Bayou Rapides, Rapides parish, La., at 4 o'clock p. m., on Wednesday, January 23, 1924, Joseph E. Robert, aged 80 years and 14 days. Deceased had been a lifelong resident of Rapides parish. He is survived by one brother, D. B. Robert, and one sister, Mrs. Alice Trimble, both of Rapides parish. His funeral took place at 3:30 o'clock this afternoon, from the family residence, where services were conducted. Interment was made in the Robert cemetery on Oakland plantation.

An article appearing in one of the local newspapers of that period and signed "Mrs. Robert Brown, Morgan City," gives something more definite about his life. We quote the following from it:—

> Joseph E. Robert, born January 9, 1844, passed away while sitting by the fireside in the home of his birth, with his sister, who had tenderly nursed him during his declining years. When seventeen he joined the Second Louisiana Cavalry and was honorably discharged at the close of the war. He attended school several years at Mt. Lebanon College. Shortly after the war he lost his father, Daniel Robert, one of the pioneers of Rapides parish. On his young shoulders fell the responsibility of caring for his mother, sister, and younger brothers, and he remained faithful until the mother died and the children were grown. After ten years of teaching he joined his sister, Mrs. Alice A. Trimble, and his brother, Daniel B. Robert, and lived at Oakland Plantation, the old family home, the remainder of his life.

15.—Daniel Boone Robert, fifth child of Daniel Robert and his second wife, Emily Jane Collier, was born at "Oakland," his father's plantation home on Bayou Rapides, in Rapides parish, La., in 1846. He married on January 13, 1876, Maggie McKinney, daughter of James W. McKinney and Caroline C. Haworth. They had two children:—Daniel Sproul Robert, born November 29, 1878, and died September 15, 1888, and Carrie C. Robert who died September 3, 1883, when an infant. The wife of Daniel Boone Robert died September 6, 1883. He lived more than forty years after that date but never re-married. His death occurred about 1926 at the age of eighty.

16.—John Willis Robert, sixth child of Daniel Robert and his second wife, Emily Jane Collier, was born at "Oakland," his father's plantation home on Bayou Rapides, in Rapides parish, La., on March 16, 1849, and died near the site of his birth on April 8, 1900. He married in 1875 Elizabeth Lucy Texada, born in Rapides parish, La., in 1856, eldest child of Thomas Jefferson Texada and Martha Jane Gordon. Her paternal grandparents were Captain John Augustin Texada and Lucy Welsh, and the great grandparents were Manuel Garcia de Texada and Mahalah Tervillion. Her maternal grandparents were Smith Waddell Gordon and Elizabeth Malissa Wells. The Gordons were an old Virginia family of Scotch origin, and the Wells were among the first settlers of Louisiana, dating back to Samuel Levi Wells, born at Manchac, La., in 1764. John Willis Robert and Elizabeth Lucy Texada had thirteen children:—

 i.—John Willis Robert, Jr., born May 13, 1876.
 ii.—Martha Gordon Robert, born February 14, 1878.
 iii.—Ethel Robert, born January 8, 1880.
 iv.—Virginia Robert, born March 9, 1881.
 v.—Lucy Texada Robert, born February 11, 1883.
 vi.—Edwin Hunter Robert, born September 3, 1884.
 vii.—Bertha Robert, born December 13, 1885.
 viii.—Alwin Texada Robert, born April 6, 1887.
 ix.—Kate Margaret Texada, born August 31, 1889.
 x.—Elizabeth Robert, born January 22, 1892.
 xi.—Alice Robert, born January 3, 1894.
 xii.—Frank Neal Robert, born February 7, 1898.
 xiii.—Margaret Ker Robert, born February 7, 1898.

Five of these children died in infancy or early childhood, viz.: Ethel, Virginia, Bertha, Alice, and Margaret Ker.

i.—John Willis Robert, Jr., married Annie Dustman of New Orleans. He is in the employ of the Texas and Pacific Railway and now resides at Addis, La. He and his wife have no children.

ii.—Martha Gordon Robert, better known as "Mattie," has been twice married. Her first husband was a Mr. Griffin by whom she had a daughter, Mattie Griffin. Her second husband was a Mr. Seymour from Minnesota, and her daughter by her first marriage was married to this gentleman's son by a former marriage. Mr. and Mrs. Seymour now live in Oklahoma City.

v.—Lucy Texada Robert was married in June, 1902, in the Methodist Rectory at Boyce, La., to Dr. Andrew Jackson Robinson James, son of William Calvit James and Ella Elizabeth Robinson. Dr. James died in 1907 from injuries received from a boiler explosion in a saw mill. They had two children:—

 a.—Martha Neal James, born February 29, 1904.
 b.—William Calvit James, Jr., born August 17, 1906.

a.—Martha Neal James was married to Flem J. Jordan, Jr., of Boyce, La. They have no children at this time.

b.—William Calvit James, Jr., is unmarried and is now serving in the U. S. Army.

Lucy Texada (Robert) James was married the second time at Mansfield, La., on September 12, 1915, to Benjamin Harri-

son Baker, son of John Edward Baker and his wife, Margaret
Donohoe. He was born in Alexandria, La., on August 13, 1887,
and now holds a responsible position as an engineer with the
Standard Oil Company of Louisiana. They have two children:

    c.—John Gordon Baker, born April 20, 1916.
    d.—Benjamin Harrison Baker, Jr., born August 10, 1917.

Both of these sons, as far as we can learn, are unmarried
at this time and are serving in the armed forces of their country in the great world struggle for liberty now going on.

vi.—Edwin Hunter Robert married Gussie Baillio, member
of an old and highly respected Rapides family. He died at the
Baptist Hospital in Alexandria, La., on Saturday, May 29,
1937, and was buried in Greenwood Memorial Park in Pineville, La. Beside his wife he left three children:—

    a.—Marguerite Robert.
    b.—Helen Beatrice Robert.
    c.—John Willis Robert, III.

a.—Marguerite Robert was married in 1939 to Glenn
Terrell of Boyce, La. They have a daughter, Glennda Elizabeth Terrell, born Friday, January 26, 1940.

b.—Helen Beatrice Robert was married in 1937 to Charles
M. Bollar. They have a son, Charles M. Bollar, Jr., born Saturday, July 29, 1939.

c.—John Willis Robert, III, married his cousin, Margaret
Davidson Andrews, in 1936. She is a daughter of Thomas
Smithwick Andrews and Elizabeth Texada. They now reside
in Boyce, La., and have a son, Thomas Edwin Robert, born
Friday, July 23, 1937.

viii.—Alwin Texada Robert resides in Boyce, La. He
married a Miss Sayes and they have children but we have been
unable to obtain any definite information about them.

ix.—Kate Margaret Robert was married to D. C. Fuller
and now lives in New Mexico. Our attempts to contact her
have proven futile.

x.—Elizabeth Robert was married to A. S. Gresham and
now resides in Shreveport, La. We have been unable to get
any further information.

xii.—Frank Neal Robert married a Miss Murphy and we are informed that they now live in Shreveport, La.

18.—Alice Adelaide Robert, eighth and youngest child of Daniel Robert and his second wife, Emily Jane Collier, was born at "Oakland," her father's plantation home on Bayou Rapides, in Rapides parish, La., in 1853. She was married on February 10, 1876, to Edmond A. Miller who died the following year. THE LOUISIANA DEMOCRAT (an Alexandria newspaper) in its issue of Wednesday, May 9, 1877, contained the following notice of his death:—

> DIED:—At his residence on Cotile in this parish, on the 25th of April, 1877, Edmond A. Miller, aged 31 years. He was born in Coburg, Saxony, in 1846, and left there to make America his home when he was 17 years old. He was a resident of this parish for the past 5 years, and was married to Miss Alice Robert, a lady belonging to one of our oldest and most respected families. He leaves his wife and one daughter to mourn his loss.

We have always understood that Mr. Miller took his own life. The one child born of this marriage was Emily Jane Miller, better known to her family and friends as "Janie." She was born in Rapides parish, La., on Friday, December 1, 1876. She was a very pretty and promising young girl and died at the age of nineteen. She contracted typhoid fever while attending school at the Normal College at Natchitoches, La., and died on July 23, 1895. She was buried in the family graveyard on Bayou Rapides.

In June, 1897, twenty years after the death of Mr. Miller, Alice Adelaide (Robert) Miller was married to Monroe Stewart Trimble who was the widower of her niece, Eugenia C. Whittington. Mr. Trimble had just lost his wife and was left with six little children (see page 190). This good lady whose heart was yet bleeding from the loss of her only child found solace in caring for and rearing all those great nephews and nieces. She was a true mother to them. She had no children of her own by this second marriage. Mr. Trimble died December 26, 1900, and for many years afterwards this good woman was employed as a public school teacher on Bayou Rapides. In this capacity she endeared herself to all the children of the community—no teacher was ever more beloved. She died in 1935 at the age of eighty-two and was laid to rest beside her people in the old family burying ground on Bayou Rapides within sight of the spot where she was born.

K.
MARTHA ROBERT

Martha Robert, daughter of Captain Peter Robert and Anne Grimball, was born in St. Peter's Parish, Beaufort District, South Carolina. We are not at all certain as to her place in the order of birth among the twelve children of her parents. She may have been among the first of the twelve or she may have been the eleventh, as we have placed her here. In the latter case she would have been born about 1788, but we are inclined to believe that her advent into the world was somewhat earlier. We are led to this conclusion after considering the probable age of the children of William Allen, as will be shown later. It is not improbable that these Allen children were her grandchildren. Martha Robert came to Woodville, Mississippi, when many members of her family emigrated there soon after 1800. She was married to John Ogden, very probably in South Carolina. They appear to have lived most of their lives in or near Woodville, Miss., but they undoubtedly resided for a while in Rapides parish, La. The records show that John Ogden bought 800 arpents of land on Bayou Boeuf, in Rapides parish, La., from John Compton on November 6, 1816. He subsequently returned to Mississippi, and we find a record where he sold this same land to Hadley P. Robert (his wife's nephew) on September 30, 1833, for $10,000.00. In the deed he is designated as "John Ogden of the State of Mississippi, Wilkinson County." We know from this he was living as late as that date, but we have no information as to whether his wife was living at that time. It is probable that she was not, as her name does not appear in the deed. We find no further mention of him in Rapides parish. But we do find a Dorcas Ogden* mentioned in the business transactions of the

---

* State of Louisiana, Parish of Rapides.—Before me W. B. Pearce, Notary Public in and·for the Parish and State aforesaid, and the undersigned witnesses, came *Dorcas Ogden* late widow of William Allen, deceased, and present wife of Starky Barfield . . . . This 2nd day of April, 1831. (From W. B. Pearce's notarial book, p. 165.)

Cheneyville neighborhood at that period. It is our belief that she was a daughter of John Ogden and Martha Robert. On April 2, 1831, in a deed passed before W. B. Pearce, a Notary Public for Rapides parish, we read the following:—"Came Dorcas Allen, late widow of William Allen, deceased, at present wife of Starky Barfield." The first official record of this lady appears on December 17, 1828, when as "Dorcas Allen" she purchases property, and Thomas Allen signs as a witness. The fact that her husband was not mentioned in the transaction shows she was then a widow. Her next appearance on the official records is on March 11, 1830, when she purchases a slave from William O. Allen. At that time she signs as "Dorcas Allen," which shows she was still a widow. Then on March 26, 1831, she sells land on Bayou Boeuf, "the same on which Thomas Allen and James Allen now reside." This was evidently a partition sale. At that time she signs as "Dorcas Barfield with the advice and consent of her husband Starky Barfield." Those signing the deed with her were "Anna O'Quin assisted by her husband John O'Quin, Thomas Allen, William O. Allen, James Allen, Daniel G. Allen, the heirs and legal representatives of William Allen, deceased, late of the said Parish and State." It would certainly appear from this transaction that these Allen heirs were the children of Dorcas (Ogden-Allen) Barfield. There are other transactions which substantiate this. On April 26, 1832, we find one of a similar nature. It was transacted before W. B. Pearce, Notary Public, on April 26, 1832, and is as follows:—"Personally appeared Dorcas Barfield by and with the advice and consent of her husband Starky Barfield, Anna O'Quin by and with the advice and consent of her husband John O'Quin, Thomas Allen, James Allen, and Daniel Allen, heirs of the succession of William Allen, deceased, who acknowledge to have received of William O. Allen payment in full for the following negroes which the said William O. Allen purchased at the sale of the property of said succession on the 25th day of March, 1831." If our surmise is correct, and it certainly seems fully corroborated by legal evidence, then these Allen heirs mentioned above are the children of Dorcas (Ogden-Allen) Barfield and therefore the grandchildren of Martha Robert and her husband, John Ogden. Such being the case the descendants of the Allen brothers mentioned above and of their sister Anna Allen who married Rev. John O'Quin, are all descendants of Captain Peter Robert and his wife, Anne Grimball.

L.
MARY ROBERT.

Mary Robert, daughter of Captain Peter Robert and Anne Grimball, was born in St. Peter's Parish, Beaufort District, South Carolina, about 1790, and it seems quite probable from available data that she was the youngest of their twelve children. She came to Woodville, Miss., soon after 1800 with her parents and is particularly noted in the family annals for her matrimonial proclivities, having been three times married. She outlived all of her husbands. Her first choice was her double first cousin, John Grimball, Jr., son of John Grimball, Sr., and Elizabeth Robert. His mother was *her* father's sister, and her mother was *his* father's sister. John Grimball, Jr., and Mary Robert were married in Woodville, Miss., by Rev. Moses Hadley (brother-in-law of Mary Robert), and came to Rapides parish, La., where they spent the remainder of their lives. They owned property in both Avoyelles and Rapides parishes, and had five children:—i.—Peter Robert Grimball, ii.—Paul Jabez Grimball, iii.—Sarah J. Grimball, iv.—Esther Grimball, v.—Elizabeth Grimball.

The second husband of Mary Robert was John R. Simmons. The only mention we find of him in the early records of Rapides parish is on December 5, 1827, when he and his wife sell 130 acres of land on Bayou Boeuf to Rev. George Anderson Irion. They had no children. As her third husband Mary Robert took Randal Eldred, Jr., who was the widower of her sister, Esther Susannah Robert. He died January 19, 1850. They had no children. She was still living in 1853 as is shown by a notarial record of that year in which she is mentioned as "Mrs. Mary Robert, widow of the late John Grimball and Randal Eldred, deceased."

We regret that our data on the children of Mary Robert and her first husband, John Grimball, Jr., is not as complete as we would like it to be.

i.—Peter Robert Grimball, the eldest of the five children, married Mary Tercy and moved to St. Mary's parish in the southern part of Louisiana where two of his first cousins, sons of Grimball Robert, had settled. The only information we have of him after this is to be found in a notarial record in Rapides parish of February 25, 1828, a part of which reads as follows:—

> Know all men by these presents that I, Peter R. Grimball, at present residing in the parish of St. Mary's in the State of Louisiana, and formerly of the parish of Rapides, have made, named, constituted, appointed and ordained my friend Dr. J D. Wright of the parish of Rapides my lawful attorney, etc., to represent me in the settlement and division of the estate of my father, John Grimball, deceased, etc. And further to make use of all lawful ways and means to procure a separation and divorce between me and my wife Mary Grimball, formerly Mary Tercy.

ii.—Paul Jabez Grimball, the second son, married but we have been unable to obtain the name of his wife. They had at least one son, 1.—John Paul Grimball. It would appear from the official records that Paul Jabez Grimball moved to Avoyelles parish, La., and we find him there as late as January 10, 1860, when he sold 43 acres of land to Ebenezer Dibblee, "being land which the said vendor acquired from the State of Louisiana." In this deed he is designated as "Paul Jabez Grimball, a resident of the parish of Avoyelles."

1.—John Paul Grimball, son of Paul Jabez Grimball, lived in Cheneyville, Rapides parish, La., where he was engaged in the mercantile and hotel business in partnership with E. Stapleton under the name of "Stapleton and Grimball." He married Julia Matthews, daughter of Peyton and Adeline Matthews. Peyton Matthews was a son of John Matthews of South Carolina and Polly Bretheth of Richmond, Virginia. After the death of John Paul Grimball, which occurred prior to May 15, 1866, Julia Matthews married Franklin Agrippa Robert, a son of Joseph B. Robert and a grandson of Joseph Robert and Mary Hyrne Jaudon. The following transaction from an old notarial book of the Cheneyville neighborhood is of interest:—

STATE OF LOUISIANA
PARISH OF RAPIDES

Be it remembered on this 15th day of May, A. D. 1866, I, George B. Marshall, a Notary Public in and for the Parish of Rapides and State aforesaid, duly appointed, commissioned and sworn, in obedience to a commission issued from the 9th Judicial District Court in and for the Parish and State aforesaid, at the instance of Mrs. Julia Grimball of the Parish and State aforesaid, and to me Notary directed, bearing date the 5th day of May, A. D. 1866, to take an inventory and make due appraisement of all property, rights and credits belonging to the estate of the late John Paul Grimball, deceased, formerly of this Parish and State, did repair to the late residence of the said decedent, situated in the said Parish (in the village of Cheneyville), and having appointed Messrs. Robert Hart and Linn Tanner as appraisers, residents of said Parish and State, and they being by me first duly sworn as such we proceeded to make the following inventory and appraisement, to-wit:—

Inventory and appraisement of STAPLETON and GRIMBALL'S co-partnership in store and hotel as follows:—

Accounts due Stapleton & Grimball:

Kendrick Jackson, due Dec. 28, 1866	$ 54.50
L. Drake, due Apr. 19, 1866	26.51
John Unsworth, due Jan. 24, 1866	32.90
Andrew Jackson, due Jan. 26, 1866	44.80
John H. Dawson, due Jan. 24, 1866	27.60
Henry Murphy, due Jan. 26, 1866	3.05
Abraham Andrews, due Jan. 1, 1866	135.00
Dr. Johnson, due Dec. 24, 1866	96.50
Total	$420.86

Amount of stock of groceries in store:—
An itemized list is given amounting to................$387.51
Amount of John P. Grimball's discount individual interest in the hands of his merchants, Bellog Noblam and Co., New Orleans............$1,153.96
Three cows and calves @ $10.00 each................ 30.00

Total amt. of his interest................$1,183.96

Recapitulation:—

Accounts due Stapleton & Grimball	$ 420.86
Amt. of stock in store of Stapleton & Grimball	387.51
Amt. of J. P. Grimball's individual interest	1,183.96
Total	$1,992.33

And we the said Notary and Appraisers having inventoried and appraised to the best of our several abilities all the property, rights and credits that were exhibited to us by the said Mrs. Julia Grimball and E. Stapleton, Jr., as the property of the said estate, we have closed this inventory and appraisement amounting in the aggregate to the sum of $1,992.33. In testimony whereof we have hereunto subscribed our names on the day and date above mentioned.

Robert Hart
Linn Tanner
Appraisers.

Witnesses:—W. H. Pollard
                    W. T. Pollard.
          Done before me, George B. Marshall, Notary Pub.

John Paul Grimball and Julia Matthews had two sons:— a.—Charles Grimball and b.—Luther Grimball.

a.—Charles Grimball, born January 7, 1862, is now living in Evergreen, Avoyelles parish, La., at the age of eighty-two. He married Elizabeth Mary Barron, daughter of Hypolite Barron and Celeste Moreau. They had six children:—

> az.—Lula Grimball.
> bz.—Joseph Grimball.
> cz.—Lela Grimball.
> dz.—Eva Grimball.
> ez.—Annie Grimball.
> fz.—Alice Grimball.

az.—Lula Grimball, born October 7, 1887, married her 1st cousin, Foster Grimball, on June 9, 1914. They have one child, Donald W. Grimball, born May 28, 1915, and married to Katie Mae Ford. This son entered the military service of his country and was recently reported "missing in action." The Alexandria Town Talk of June 28, 1944, carried the following item relative to him:—

> Sergeant Donald W. Grimball, 29, son of Mr. and Mrs. Foster Grimball, formerly of Evergreen, La., and now of New Orleans, was reported missing in action June 14th over France. Sgt. Grimball, who worked several months in Alexandria before entering service, was an aerial gunner on a Flying Fortress. His wife, Mrs. Katie Mae Grimball, lives in DeRidder, La. He entered service March, 1943, and for a while was stationed at the Alexandria Army Air Field.

bz.—Joseph Grimball died in infancy.

cz.—Lela Grimball, born May 20, 1892, married Alcide Dozat. They had one child, born July 17, 1913, who married Euris Turner and had one child. Lela (Grimball) Dozat married 2nd Mitchell Broussard and their children are:—Elson, Hilda, Nolan, Miller, and a daughter whose name we were unable to learn.

dz.—Eva Grimball, born May 4, 1894, married J. J. Riche. Their children are:—Jimmie Lee, Sadie, Annie Mae, and Therese Nell.

ez.—Annie Grimball, born November 28, 1896, died January 18, 1922, married Dewey Moreau. Their children are:— R. A., and Charles who died in infancy.

fz.—Alice Grimball, born November 27, 1903, married Charles Robbins. Their children are:—Charles, Barbara Marie, and Alonzo.

b.—Luther Grimball, born August 3, 1867, died October 31, 1929. He married December 24, 1885, Julia Anne Langlais, daughter of Leandre Langlais and Elmira LeMoine. They had ten children:—

> az.—Clifton Grimball.
> bz.—John Tilden Grimball.
> cz.—Eddie Grimball.
> dz.—Foster Grimball.
> ez.—Lessie Elmira Grimball.
> fz.—Mattie Julia Grimball.
> gz.—Lillie Adell Grimball.
> hz.—Leroy Grimball.
> iz.—Alva Grimball.
> jz.—Willie Grimball.

az.—Clifton Grimball, born September 24, 1886, married Adell Ringling on April 30, 1914. They had two children:— Cecil and Luther.

bz.—John Tilden Grimball, born January 1, 1889, married Alma ————————. They have no children.

cz.—Eddie Grimball, born June 19, 1891. He has never married.

dz.—Foster Grimball, born March 4, 1893, married his 1st cousin, Lulu Grimball. See preceding page.

ez.—Lessie Elmira Grimball, born June 19, 1895, married Marion Chambers on August 18, 1912. They have two children:—Myrtle, born February 9, 1915, and Charles, born February 12, 1917.

fz.—Mattie Julia Grimball, born September 25, 1898, married George Neyland on December 15, 1921. They have two children:—Margie, born October 22, 1922, and Carol Madge, born September 20, 1927.

gz.—Lillie Adell Grimball, born in 1900, died young.

hz.—Leroy Grimball, born August 24, 1902, has never married.

iz.—Alva Grimball, born September 19, 1906, has never married.

jz.—Willie Grimball, born May 31, 1910, has never married.

iii.—Sarah J. Grimball, daughter of John Grimball, Jr., and Mary Robert, was married to George Keller, but we can find no record that they ever had any children. The document given below substantiates the statement that George Keller was her husband and that she was a daughter of Mary (Robert) Grimball:—

Parish of Rapides, November 3, 1824.—Received of Mary Grimball, widow of the late John Grimball, deceased, of the parish above mentioned and of the State of Louisiana, the sum of four hundred and eighty-one dollars in full of all demands against the estate of the said John Grimball, and all right, title or claim we or either of us may in any way now have or may hereafter have against the estate of the said Mary Grimball after her death, excepting one share in her part of the tract of land whereon the said Mary now plants.

$481.00   George Keller
            Sarah J. Keller

Witnesses:—
  Jacob Keller
  Joseph Robert.

Admitted to record April 25, 1825.
Silas Talbert, Notary Public.

STATE OF LOUISIANA
PARISH OF RAPIDES

Personally appeared before me one of the Justices of the Peace in and for the State and Parish above written, Joseph Robert, who being duly sworn saith that he saw George Keller and Sarah Keller, his wife, sign the within receipt and he further saith that Jacob Keller signed with himself as witness. Sworn and subscribed to before me this 14th day of February, 1825.

Joseph Robert.

J. D. Wright, Justice of Peace.

The Kellers came to central Louisiana from South Carolina about the dawn of the nineteenth century. There were George, Jacob, John, and William. It is not improbable that they were brothers and were the sons of Jacob Keller of Orangeburgh District, South Carolina, whom the census of 1790 shows as living there at that time. His family consisted of one white male over 16 years of age (who was himself), four white males under sixteen years of age (his four sons), and seven white females—one of whom was his wife and the others his daughters. We do not know whether Jacob Keller ever came to Louisiana. On the 10th of February, 1825, a Jacob Keller who signs his name as *Jacob Keller, Jr.,* gives certain property to his children:—"For the consideration, good will and affection he bears for his children, to-wit, Robert H. Keller and Amanda J. Keller." This would indicate he was a son of *Jacob Keller, Sr.,* who was probably the Jacob Keller of Orangeburgh District mentioned above. The Kellers first came to America with the German settlers of Orangeburgh, South Carolina, in 1735. Mathias Keller was the first of the name we find recorded amongst them when in 1740 he married Maria Handsley.

iv.—Esther Grimball, the second daughter of John Grimball, Jr., and Mary Robert, probably died young or unmarried as we find no later record of her.

v.—Elizabeth Grimball, the third daughter of John Grimball, Jr., and Mary Robert, is also an uncertain quantity in our record. The Lodowick Tanner family Bible tells us that Joseph Tanner, father of Lodowick, married as his third wife Eliza Grimball. She may have been this Elizabeth Grimball.

This concludes our story of the twelve children of Captain Peter Robert and his good wife, Anne Grimball.

BIBLIOGRAPHY:—

Records found in Court House at Woodville, Mississippi.

Notarial Records kept by Silas Talbert and William Bray Pearce, Notaries for Rapides parish, Louisiana.

Stub Entries to Indents for Revolutionary Claims in South Carolina, by A. S. Salley, Jr.—Books U-W, page 149.

Probate Court Records of Rapides parish, Louisiana.

Old letters and papers of the Robert family placed at the disposal of the Compiler by various members of the family.

Robert and Brewer Records compiled and now in the possession of Mrs. Evelyn (Brewer) Gray of Lecompte, La.

Data on the descendants of Joanna Lawton Rutledge furnished by Mrs. John W. Keller of Avoyelles parish, La.

Data on the descendants of Joseph Sadler Rutledge furnished by Mrs. Joseph Sadler Rutledge, Jr., of Walker, La.

Wilkinson County, Mississippi, record Book I, pages 168, 169, 170.

Data on Joseph Robert and his descendants furnished by his great grand-daughter, Mrs. Alice (Robert) Havard of Mellville, La., and Miss Alice Amelia Robert of New Orleans.

Data on James Bordeaux Jaudon Robert and his descendants furnished by his grandchildren, George Carleton Robert, Jr., and Miss Mary Johnson, of Cheneyville, La.

Paxton's History of the Baptist Church of Louisiana, pages 121-41-44-46-56, 216, 386, 503-17.

Data on Daniel Robert and his descendants furnished by his daughter, Mrs. Alice Adelaide (Robert) Trimble(now dead), from her father's family Bible.

Records of the Haworth family Bible now in possession of Mr. P. T. Haworth of Alexandria, La.

Tombstone inscriptions in the Daniel Robert graveyard on Bayou Rapides, in Rapides parish, La.

Data on descendants of Sophronia Emily Robert, compiled by Mrs. Maudrie (Hamilton) McMain of Alexandria, La.

Death and marriage notices found in Alexandria papers:— THE LOUISIANA DEMOCRAT and THE ALEXANDRIA TOWN TALK.

Descendants of John Willis Robert furnished by his daughter, Mrs. Benjamin Harrison Baker of Alexandria, Louisiana.

Data from old Cheneyville notarial records now the property of Mrs. Herman Duncan of Alexandria, La.

Tombstone inscriptions in the Christian cemetery and the Cheney graveyard at Cheneyville, La.

Family of Wilkins, by Evelyn Selby Johnson, pages 17, 25.

Descendants of Esther Susannah Robert from the Lodowick Tanner family Bible, now property of Mrs. George Ripley White of Centreville, Mississippi.

Bettison data furnished by Mrs. Ralph Lincoln Colby of Zionsville, Indiana, and by Mrs. D. C. Bettison of Belle Chasse, La., and by Mrs. Stuart Graves of Tuscaloosa, Alabama.

Bettison Bible records furnished by Mrs. Samuel C. Lipscomb of Beaumont, Texas.

South Carolina Historical and Genealogical Magazine, Vol. XXIII, page 19.

Pearce Data furnished by Mrs. R. L. Bailey, Jr., of Opelousas, La.

Proctor data furnished by Mrs. Julia (Proctor) Pendleton, of Tyler, Texas.

Brashear data furnished by Mrs. Bert Joseph Jackson of Beaumont, Texas, who before marriage was Celima Agnes Brashear.

Pearce data furnished by Mrs. Robert Bolling Miles of Alexandria, La.

Alanson Green Pearce data furnished by Mrs. Anna Caroline Morris of Bunkie, La.

Grimball Robert data furnished by Mr. C. A. Riddle of Marksville, La.

Peter William Robert records furnished by Miss Effie A. Hargrove of Oakdale, La.

Franklin Agrippa Robert records furnished by Mr. Louis Davis Robert of Sunset, La.

Lucy Frances Robert data furnished by Mrs. Robert M. Guillot of Marksville, La.

Riddle data furnished by Mrs. Charles Addison Riddle of Marksville, La.

PART THREE.

THE TANNER FAMILY.

PREFACE.

THE TANNER HERITAGE.

What shall the Tanners of my generation leave as a heritage for those to follow? Let's visit with the Tanners of several generations back and see what they left.

A loud knock on the door brings out great great grandfather Robert. He is a civil engineer and has surveyed almost all of central Louisiana. He has assembled quite a fortune in land. Great great grandmother asks us to have a seat on the cool and spacious porch. Life seems so calm and peaceful. We see slaves everywhere. They do all the work. Great great grandmother and the children soon join us. She tells us that she has fifteen children and three adopted ones. A little bright eyed boy claims our attention and we notice that he won't let anyone tease one of the little adopted girls. His name is Peter.

Years pass on and we next visit great grandfather Peter and his wife the little adopted girl. This time we sit in the parlor and watch the great logs burn in the huge fire place. Great grandfather and great grandmother seem very happy together and we learn they have ten children. Robert, the eldest, is a big handsome boy.

Time marches on and our next stop is with grandfather Robert. There's hustle and bustle in the air because the Civil War is just over. Grandmother feels that her world is tumbling down. She doesn't know how she will manage without the slaves. They gave to the world eleven children. What heritage did they leave? They left the priceless jewels of courage and character. The Golden Rule and all it implies was practiced by them.

Now, after all these years, we the Tanners of today find that courage and character plus the Golden Rule are the important things of life. The material things are good, but like the rose, are soon gone. So to you Tanners who are to come, we hand down the same old heritage, with the hope that when you write your part of the Family Tree you will leave to your posterity courage, character and the Golden Rule.

> This preface was written by Miss Mamye K. Tanner of Evergreen, Louisiana, the great great granddaughter of the first Robert Tanner.

THE TANNER FAMILY.

The Tanners in whom we are interested came from England and appeared in the American colonies in the earliest days of their settlement. J. C. Hotten in his valuable work, "LIST OF EMIGRANTS TO AMERICA," records the presence in Virginia of Daniel and Josias Tanner in 1618 and 1624. On page 184 he tells us that Daniel Tanner was among "The living in Virginia" on February 16, 1623. He was then at "Bass's Choise" of which Captain Nathaniel Bass was the head. Then on page 243 we find this same Daniel Tanner recorded in the "Muster of Lieutenant Thomas Purfruy" in 1624. We are there told that he was forty years old and came over in the SAMPSON in 1618. On page 228 we meet Josias Tanner, aged twenty-four, who is there listed in "The Muster of the Inhabitants of James Cittie" on January 24, 1624. He appears at that time to have been living at "James Island." These two early pioneers were undoubtedly the first Tanners to land on the American continent. We have no further trace of them but it is not improbable they were the progenitors of the later generations of the Tanners whom we find in Henrico county, Virginia, and in whom we are interested.

In the New England Historical and Genealogical Register, Vol. 47, page 354, we meet another Daniel Tanner who was in Lower Norfolk county, Virginia, in 1640, and we learn from the same source that his wife's name was Charity, and that he married her on November 24, 1614, at St. Paul's Church, Canterbury, England, and that they had a son, John, baptized October 14, 1627. This Daniel Tanner made his will November 17, 1653, and left his property to Lemuel Mason and his wife. This would convey the idea that his own wife and his son had died previously and that he had no other heirs. There was a creek in the vicinity of the present city of Norfolk which bore his name and we frequently find mention of it in the old Norfolk records.

James Savage, in his "Genealogical Dictionary of New England," records a Nicholas Tanner as being in Swansea, Massachusetts, in 1663. Later (in 1666) he was town clerk in Rehoboth in that colony, and then we find no further record of him or any one bearing the name of Tanner. He appears to have been the only one of that name in New England.

Brumbaugh, in his great work "Revolutionary War Records of Virginia," tells us that there were four Tanners in the Revolutionary service from that colony. They were John, Paul, Peter and William Tanner.

In the Virginia Historical Magazine, Vol. 13, pages 176, 179, 181, in a "List of Tithables of the Parish of King William" for the years 1736, 1737, and 1738, we find the names of Edward Tanner and Edward Tanner, Jr. Their names appear in the midst of those of the Huguenot settlement at Manakintown in that Parish, but whether or not they themselves were Huguenots we are unable to say. Some of our Louisiana Tanners claim that their forebears were originally French, so the Tanner name on this Huguenot list may be more than a coincidence. This claim is further strengthened by Mrs. Emma Rouse Lloyd in her interesting book, "Clasping Hands with Generations Past," in which she tells us something of a Tanner family related to herself. On page 61 she says, "Robert Tanner came from Alsace with the 1717 colony and settled in what is now Madison county, Virginia, and patented 350 acres of land there in 1728. He brought with him his wife, Maria, and children." She further tells us that there were five of these children, the eldest of whom was Christopher who married Elizabeth Aylor and whose will, dated May 12, 1781, Madison county, Virginia, mentions his seven children. According to Mrs. Lloyd this first Robert Tanner was an attorney and practiced law in Madison county. She also makes the assertion that the names of *Tanner* and *Turner* are synonymous. We are willing to admit that spelling in those far off days did some curious things but we can not believe it ever made *Tanner* out of *Turner* or vice versa. Her Tanners were evidently Huguenots but they were definitely not of the same people as the Tanners in whom we are interested.

Landon C. Bell, in his great work "CUMBERLAND PARISH, LUNENBURG COUNTY, VIRGINIA," which has been such a great help to genealogists, tells us of other Tanners living in that section. In his list of Tithables for that Parish during the years 1759 and 1760 he gives us the names of Lucius, Matthew and Thomas Tanner.

Mr. W. Mac. Jones, Director of the Genealogical Bureau of Virginia, furnishes us with the following list of Tanners who served in the American Revolution from Virginia:—

Abraham Tanner, Madison County.
Christopher Tanner, Culpeper County.
David Tanner, served in the Illinois Regiment.
Frederick Tanner, in Kentucky County militia.
George Tanner, in Grayson's Regiment in 1777.
Jacob Tanner.
John Tanner, in 1st Virginia Regiment.
Michael Tanner, later of Buncombe County, N. C.
Nathan Tanner, in 3rd, 4th and 7th Continental Line and 1st Light Dragons.
Peter Tanner.
Seth Tanner, in 5th Continental Line.
William Tanner, served in several regiments.

The same authority furnishes us with the following list of Tanners from the Virginia Index of Wills:—

Mary Tanner, Albemarle, will 1760.
Thomas Tanner, Amelia, will 1765.
Edward Tanner, Amelia, will 1770.
Lodowick Tanner, Amelia, will 1773.
Branch Tanner, Amelia, will 1793.
Branch Tanner, Jr., Amelia, will 1794.
Field Tanner, Amelia, inventory 1799.
Michael Tanner, Bedford, will 1777.
Nathaniel Tanner, Bedford, will 1781.
Joseph Tanner, Chesterfield, will 1757.
Edward Tanner, Harrison County, inventory 17—.
Joseph Tanner, Henrico County, inventory 1698.
Thomas Tanner, Isle of Wight, inventory 1666.
Christopher Tanner, Madison County, inventory 1797.
Lewis Tanner, Mecklenburg County, inventory 1766.
Daniel Tanner, Norfolk County, will 1653.
Paul Tanner, Northampton County, will 1709.
Anne Tanner, Pittsylvania County, inventory 1784.
Floyd Tanner, Pittsylvania County, will 1799.
Edward Tanner, Surry County, will 1685.
Thomas Tanner, Westmoreland County, will 1708.
Martha Tanner, Westmoreland County, will 1733.

The following Tanner marriages are recorded in Amelia County, Virginia:—

Leonard Claiborne and Fanny Tanner, November 13, 1788.
John Drake and Polly Tanner, November, 1809.
William Grant and Sally Tanner, January 18, 1793.
Anthony Lumpkin and Lucy Tanner (widow), June 17, 1829.
Peter Wilson and Patsey Tanner, May, 1796.
Lodowick Tanner and Ann Johnson (widow), May 4, 1764.
Branch Tanner and Mary Page Finney, January 2, 1764.
William Tanner and Betsy Powell, February, 1810.
Edward Tanner and Martha Powell, June, 1810.
Elam Tanner and Mary Claiborne (daughter of Leonard C.), May, 1804.
Field Tanner and Lucy Hastings, May, 1813.
Grief B. Hawkins and Martha Tanner, September 4, 1820.
Thomas Huddleston and Milly Tanner, April 12, 1774.
Thomas Huddleston and Patsey Tanner, August, 1798.
Henry H. Southall and Nancy Tanner, August, 1795.
Branch Tanner was security at marriage of Edward Hastings and Martha Finney.

The older generations of our Louisiana Tanners always claimed that their progenitors were among the early settlers of Virginia. This was undoubtedly true. When emigration below the James river ascended that stream and went above the falls to settle Henrico county there were Tanners among those hardy pioneers. Sometime before the American Revolution several of the name followed the southern tide of home-seekers and settled in South Carolina. After the census of 1790 one of the South Carolina branch, Robert Tanner, moved with his family to Wilkinson county, in the Mississippi Territory, and later to central Louisiana where the name has become prominent as well as plentiful in Rapides and Avoyelles parishes. This branch is usually referred to by our old timers as the ROBERT TANNERS, to distinguish them from the descendants of Joseph Tanner who came to the same section of Louisiana at the same period. There is no doubt that the two were related but we are unable to ascertain the exact degree of kinship. We are more particularly interested in the scope of this work with the ROBERT TANNERS but before giving them further attention we will devote a few pages to their kinsmen, the JOSEPH TANNERS.

We know nothing definite of Joseph Tanner prior to his coming to Louisiana, but the family names which have been handed down through his progeny are so identical with those of the Tanners of Henrico, Amelia and Chesterfield counties, Virginia, as to constitute more than a mere coincidence. We have been unable to authenticate the connection but will insert here such data as we have accumulated, hoping that in the future some one will use it as a key for unraveling this genealogical tangle. Our conviction is that Joseph Tanner of Louisiana is a descendant of the Joseph Tanner whom we find in the annals of Henrico county, Virginia, in 1662. This pioneer's son, Joseph Tanner, Jr., had by his first wife, Ann Floyd, two sons, Joseph III and Thomas, and it is not improbable that our Louisiana Joseph was a great grandson of one of these sons.

Some years ago Rev. Clayton Torrence, now editor of the Virginia Magazine of History and Biography, published an article on the Tanner family in William and Mary Quarterly, 1st Series, Vol. XXV, pp. 87-95, and 198-205. We will insert here an extensive quotation from that article:—

JOSEPH TANNER appears first in the Henrico county, Virginia, records. He had a patent of land there as early as March, 1662. The old Tanner home was located in that section of Henrico county lying south of the James river (now in Chesterfield Co.) in Bermuda Hundred. Joseph Tanner died prior to 1677. He married Mary, surname unknown, who was born in 1639 and died in 1700. She married second Gilbert Platt of Henrico county. Her will was dated March 18, 1699. Joseph Tanner and his wife, Mary, had the following issue:—
1.—Joseph Tanner, Jr., 2.—Edward Tanner, 3.—Mary Tanner, 4.—Martha Tanner.

1.—Joseph Tanner, Jr., was born about 1662 and died prior to February, 1698. He lived in Henrico county and was twice married. He married first in 1682 Ann Floyd, and second in 1689 Sarah Hatcher, widow of Matthew Turpin and daughter of Edward Hatcher of Henrico. His second wife married as her third husband Samuel Oulton. There were two sons by the first marriage, (i) Joseph Tanner, III, and (ii) Thomas Tanner. By the second marriage there were two sons, (iii) Lodowick Tanner, and (iv) Lewis Tanner.

2.—Edward Tanner, second child of Joseph Tanner, Sr., and his wife, Mary, was born in Henrico county about

1664 and died in 1719. He married Mary (probably daughter of Henry Hatcher and Ann Lound). His will is dated August 13, 1719. In it he mentions sons:—Edward, John, Joseph, and daughters Ann, Martha, Mary and Elizabeth. One of his daughters, Martha, married Edward Stewart. On October 8, 1745, Mary Tanner and Joseph Tanner of Goochland county convey to Henry Hatcher of Henrico county 160 acres of land on south side of James river in Henrico county (these were probably the children of Edward).

The will of Edward Tanner of Raleigh Parish, Amelia county, was dated December 12, 1769. He mentions his wife (name not given), daughter Elizabeth Coleman, son Robert Tanner, daughter Ann Clay, and son Field Tanner. Besides we find the following in it:—"The 208 acres which I own in Mecklenburg county to be sold and the money equally divided between Jeremiah and Edward Tanner. Residue to be sold and money equally divided (after payment of my debts) between Jeremiah Tanner, Edward Tanner, Field Tanner, Milley Tanner and Martha Tanner." Executors of the will were, sons Jeremiah Tanner and Robert Tanner. This Edward Tanner was probably a grandson of Edward son of Joseph, Sr.

3.—Mary Tanner, daughter of Joseph Tanner, Sr., and his wife, Mary, married William Ligon (sometimes given as Liggon) of Henrico county. William Ligon's will was dated January 21, 1688. He mentions his sons, Thomas, William, John and Joseph, and daughter Mary; also Thomas Farrar, Jr., who was probably a grandson.

4.—Martha Tanner, daughter of Joseph Tanner, Sr., and his wife, Mary, married Thomas Jones of Henrico county, and second Edward Haskins of Henrico. The will of Thomas Jones was dated January, 1688. He names his son Thomas Jones, his daughter Lucretia, and his wife, Martha. Thomas Jones, Jr., moved to Surrey county and from him descends a numerous family in Brunswick and Lunenburg counties. Descendants of Edward and Martha (Tanner-Jones) Haskins are numerous in Southside Virginia, principally in Chesterfield and Brunswick counties.

(i) Joseph Tanner, III, son of Joseph Tanner, Jr., and Ann Floyd, was born about 1684. His father was dead in 1698 and we find him under the guardianship of Peter Field in April, 1699. He was of age in 1708 and was a magistrate in Henrico county.

(ii) Thomas Tanner, second son of Joseph Tanner, Jr., and his first wife, Ann Floyd, was born about 1686. In a deed of June 30, 1708, he is referred to as Thomas Tanner of Bristol Parish, Prince George county. It is not improbable that Thomas Tanner of Amelia county, whose will was dated March 6, 1763, was *this* Thomas Tanner. He mentions his daughter Martha Brown, son Nathaniel Tanner, son Joseph Tanner, grandson Archelaus Tanner, grand-daughter Elizabeth Johns, daughter Judith Johns and son Joel Tanner. On October 4, 1799, Joel Tanner, Sr., of Nottoway county deeds to Sally Tanner widow of Floyd Tanner, and Floyd Tanner son of Thomas Tanner.

Joel Tanner of Nottoway county, will dated July 31, 1802, mentions grandson Joel Tanner, son of Thomas Tanner; wife Lucy; daughter Martha; grand-daughters Lucy Ann Grissett and Elizabeth Coleman Green; daughter Martha and her husband Jesse D. Green; son David Tanner; son Joseph Tanner.

(iii) Lodowick Tanner, son of Joseph Tanner, Jr., and his second wife, Sarah (Hatcher) Turpin, was born in 1692 and died in Amelia county in 177—. He moved to Amelia county acquiring much land and amassing a comfortable estate. He married 1st Frances Branch, daughter of Thomas Branch and Elizabeth Archer, of Henrico county. His second wife was Ann Johnson (widow). There was no issue by the second union. His first marriage took place before December 4, 1727. His children were:—Elizabeth who married William Osborne (many descendants); Sarah who married Peter Jones; Branch who married Mary Page Finney (many descendants). The will of Lodowick Tanner of Amelia county is dated August 10, 1773. He mentions his son Branch, grand-daughter Frances Tanner, grandson Branch Tanner, daughter Sarah Jones, Branch Osborne, and daughter Elizabeth's five children.

(iv) Lewis Tanner, son of Joseph Tanner, Jr., and his wife, Sarah (Hatcher) Turpin, was living as late as August, 1773.

It will always be a matter of much regret to all of us who e interested that Rev. Clayton Torrence did not extend his search through two more generations. However, we will ways be grateful to him for what he has done. He shows us at the Tanners were allied with many of the pioneer families of the Old Dominion, such as the Cockes, Finneys, Lygons, Branches and Archers.

Briefly expressed the Cocke connection is as follows:—

1.—Richard Cocke, 1600-1665, Lt. Col. and Burgess.
2.—Thomas Cocke, 1638-1697.
3.—Thomas Cocke, 1662-1707.
4.—Mary Cocke, married Rev. Wm. Finney and died in 1727.
5.—William Finney, Amelia Co., married Mary ——?
6.—Mary Page Finney married Branch Tanner, January 2, 1764.

Branch Connection:—

1.—Christopher Branch (son of Lionel and Valentia Branch) born in England 1602, died in Virginia 1681, married 1619 Mary Addie, daughter of Francis Addie. Came to Virginia on the "London Merchant" March 1619-20. Was living at "ye college lands," Henrico, 1623-24, with son Thomas, aged 9 months. He later patented land at or near Arrowhattocks, Chesterfield county. Was member of House of Burgesses for Henrico in 1639. Justice of Peace for Henrico in 1656. Will probated in Henrico county February 20, 1681-2. Children were:—Thomas, William and Christopher.

2.—Thomas Branch of "Kingsland," Henrico county, married Elizabeth ————? Children:—Thomas, Matthew, James, Elizabeth and Martha. Elizabeth married Melchizedeck Richardson, and Martha married Richard Ward.

3.—Thomas Branch (Thomas 2. Christopher 1), born 1658, died 1728, married Elizabeth, daughter of George Archer. Children:—Thomas, William, James, Tabitha, Agnes, Elizabeth, Frances (married Lodowick Tanner), Mary, Amy, Margery.

William Branch, second son of the first Christopher, married Jane ————? and their daughter, Mary Branch, married 1st Thomas Jefferson and 2nd Joseph Mattox.

Our Joseph Tanner came to Louisiana about 1815. We are inclined to believe that his first wife died prior to or very soon after this move. We are also inclined to believe that he came via South Carolina and there probably met up with his kinsman Robert Tanner, who was about to move farther south, and

ime along with him to Wilkinson county, Mississippi, and still
ter to Rapides. parish, Louisiana. Whenever we learn the
ame of this Joseph Tanner's father we feel assured of being
ole to trace his lineage back to the early Tanners of Henrico
ounty. We have reason to believe that his mother's name was
liza. (See pages 48, 49, 50.)

Fortunately for us the family Bible records of Lodowick
anner (son of this Joseph) have been preserved and from
lem we learn much about the family after arriving in Louis-
ina. According to this good book Joseph Tanner was four
mes married. His wives in succession being, Elizabeth
anier, Betsey Pearce, Eliza Grimball, and Joyce (Thomas)
Tilliams. The first wife was the mother of his eight children
nd she probably died before he came to Louisiana—either in
outh Carolina or Wilkinson county, Mississippi. There were
o children by the second or third marriages. His second wife,
letsey Pearce, may have been the widow of William Pearce
rho died in 1813, being also that gentleman's second wife.
Ier maiden name is unknown to us. The third wife, Eliza
rimball, is also a matter of speculation with us. She may
ave been the daughter of Thomas Grimball and Ann Audebert
rho first married Dr. David McRae, or it is possible that she
lay have been the daughter of John Grimball, Jr., and Mary
.obert. After carefully looking up all the Grimballs who came
o Mississippi and Louisiana the compiler is satisfied that those
wo ladies mentioned above are the only two of that name who
rere eligible as Joseph Tanner's third wife. We have been
ortunate in obtaining more definite data on his fourth wife,
oyce (Thomas) Williams. She was a daughter of Captain
ames Thomas and Elizabeth Calliham of Edgefield county,
outh Carolina. Her mother was a daughter of David Calli-
am, Sr., who emigrated from Lunenburg county, Virginia,
bout 1770 to Edgefield District, South Carolina, and after the
.evolution to Washington county, Georgia, where he died
ometime prior to 1790. Her elder brother, John Calliham,
.ied in Rapides parish, Louisiana, just prior to 1825, and
nother brother, David Calliham, Jr., died near Woodville,
Mississippi, on May 5, 1833. Joyce Thomas father died in
outh Carolina about 1803 and his children then moved to
Mississippi and Louisiana. Joyce Thomas married Thomas

Williams in South Carolina and came to Mississippi with him. They had three daughters and after his death his wife moved to Rapides parish, Louisiana, where other members of her family had gone. The daughters were:—Matilda, Eliza, and Carolina Williams. In the notarial record books of Silas Talbert and William Bray Pearce, Notary Publics for Cheneyville, Louisiana, in those early days we find recorded several transactions which tell us something of Joyce Williams and her three children. The first item we find relating to them is dated October 14, 1825, and is in the form of a power of attorney given by "Joyce Williams, now Joyce Tanner, of Rapides parish, to William Brunson of South Carolina, to look after any interests she may have in South Carolina." This William Brunson was her brother-in-law, being the husband of her sister, Sarah Thomas. Of date a few days later, we find the following in these same notarial records:—

> At a family meeting of the relatives and friends of Joyce Williams, alias Joyce Tanner, they mutually agree and advise that she be appointed tutoress to her minor children to-wit:—Matilda, Eliza, and Caroline Williams.
>
> Cheneyville, October 31, 1825.
>
> R. H. Marshall—Leroy Stafford
> D. M. Calliham—William Hoggatt
> J. C. Thomas.
>
> Witnesses:—
> Branch Tanner
> R. B. Marshall.

About seven years later we find in these valuable old records the following item:—

> Personally appeared Joyce Tanner, her husband Joseph Tanner, Carolina Tanner, her husband Asa R. Tanner, and Eliza Williams, who do by these presents release and relinquish all their rights, title and interest unto Matilda Glover, to the following slaves * * * * *
>
> This 5th day of January, 1832.
>
> Witnesses:—   Joyce Tanner
>   Lodowick Tanner   Joseph Tanner
>   Branch Tanner   Caroline Tanner
>   Jacob Huff.   Asa Tanner
>   Eliza Williams
>   Matilda Glover
>   Martin Glover.

Soon after this record of transfer we find the following item in the same book:—

Before me, W. B. Pearce, notary public of Rapides, personally appeared Matilda Glover by and with the advice and consent of her husband, Martin Glover; Carolina Tanner by and with the advice and consent of her husband, Asa Tanner; and Eliza Williams, who do by these presents relinquish and release all their rights, title and interest in and unto the following slaves, to their mother, Joyce Tanner, * * * * * * *

The "five relatives and friends of Joyce Williams" mentioned in the family meeting above were all members of her family. R. H. Marshall was the third husband of her sister, Elizabeth Thomas; D. M. Calliham was her first cousin; J. C. Thomas was her brother; Leroy Stafford was the husband of her first cousin, Elizabeth Susan Calliham; William Hoggatt was the husband of her first cousin, Lucy Calliham.

Matilda Williams, the eldest of the daughters of Thomas Williams and Joyce Thomas, married Martin Glover who was probably a son of David Glover and Elizabeth Thomas, sister of Joyce. If this assumption is correct then Martin Glover and his wife were first cousins. David Glover and Elizabeth Thomas had a daughter, Mary Glover.

Caroline Williams, the youngest child, was married to Asa R. Tanner, a son of Joseph Tanner and his first wife, Elizabeth Lanier. So Joseph Tanner was her step-father and her father-in-law. (See page 230).

As far as we can learn Eliza Williams, the second daughter, was never married. We are certain she was single as late as 1832.

The Lodowick Tanner family Bible records tell us that Joseph Tanner and his fourth wife, Joyce (Thomas) Williams, had two children, a son who was killed and a daughter named Robe Ann Tanner. This daughter was twice married, first to Fujeance Ory and second to August Gautier. By the first marriage she had two daughters, Esther and Agnes, neither of whom ever married. By the second marriage she also had two children, Effie and Joseph Tanner Gautier. The son never married but the daughter, Effie, was twice married. Her first husband was Fernando Francesco De Frandez de Lava, and her second was Frank J. Lebrano. We have no record of any children by either union.

Joseph Tanner and his first wife, Elizabeth Lanier, had eight children:—

1.—Lemuel Tanner married Celeste Thibadoux and their children were:—Joseph, Esther, Elizabeth, Lemuel, Mary, Rozilla, Robert, Washington, Wayne, Bridget, Louise. We regret our inability to locate any descendants of these children.

2.—Nancy Tanner married Stephen Jackson and their children were:—Susan, Reuben, Joseph, Andrew. Susan Jackson married Lemuel Miles; Reuben Jackson married Emily Sutton; Joseph Jackson married Caroline Carson; Andrew Jackson married Eliza Chambers, daughter of William Woodson Chambers and Sarah Ann Pearce. (See Part Four).

3.—Rhoda Tanner married James Pearce and their children were:—Avenel, Joseph, Amanda, James Lemuel. The first three died in childhood. The last, James Lemuel Pearce, married the widow of his first cousin, Joseph Willing Tanner, who was Sarah Goodwin Chambers, daughter of William Woodson Chambers and Sarah Ann Pearce. (See Part Four).

4.—Sarah Tanner married Paul Jabez Robert, son of Captain Peter Robert and Anne Grimball. Their children were:—Sarah, Cornelia, Mariam. Sarah Robert married her first cousin, Robert Daniel Eldred, son of Randal Eldred, Jr., and Esther Susannah Robert. They had no children as far as we can ascertain. Cornelia Robert married Vestal Gould and left no issue. Mariam died in childhood.

5.—Lodowick Tanner married Ann Martha Eldred, daughter of Randal Eldred, Jr., and Esther Susannah Robert. Their children were:—Esther Eliza, Thirza Carolina, Mary Desirée, Randal, Lemuel, Edward Livingston, Ellen, Sarah Evolina. (See page 152).

6.—Esther Tanner married Joshua Pearce. Their children were:— Eliza, Alzine, William, Joseph, Esther, Mordella. (See Part Four).

7.—Branch Tanner married Desirée Wells, daughter of Willing Wells and Rosalie Meuillon. Their children were:—Joseph Willing, Jane Wells, Rose, Branch, Jr.,

Bettie Desirée, Mary Esther. See the compiler's book, "The Wells Family of Louisiana," pages 165-6-7-8-9.

8.—Asa Tanner married twice; 1st Caroline Williams, 2nd Ellen Woodson. Children by the first marriage were: —Janetta, May, Frances, Theophilus. Of these, May and Theophilus died young. Janetta married William Woodson, no issue. Frances, better known as "Fannie", married Silas Franklin Pearce, son of Stephen Samuel Pearce and Sally Goodwin Bray. (See Part Four). No issue by second marriage.

This brings to an end our story of Joseph Tanner and his descendants. It is greatly to be regretted that we have so little to record of this early pioneer and his progeny, but it is our fond hope that some day some one will find the hidden data necessary to connect him up with his forebears in Virginia.

We will now focus our attention on ROBERT TANNER, the patriarch of that extensive family which for more than a century has been prominent on Bayou Boeuf, near Cheneyville, in Rapides parish, Louisiana. Recently in looking over a very interesting book entitled, "Biographical and Historical Memoirs of Mississippi," we found the following item:—

The Tanner settlement of 1804 was made four miles southwest of Woodville. Robert Tanner set out from Beaufort District, South Carolina, with a pioneer company of 97 persons, arrived on the banks of the Tennessee they built rude boats and sailed down the rivers to Fort Adams.

We had always known that Robert Tanner took an important part in this expedition but the above item would indicate that he was the leader of it, so much so that the place where these emigrants established themselves in Mississippi was officially known as "The Tanner settlement." He was always a dominant character and at that time was just 35 years of age, so we are not surprised to learn that he outshone his father-in-law, Captain Peter Robert, who was supposed to be the head of this great family expedition.

We are told that prior to the American Revolution many of the Virginia Tanners emigrated to other colonies, particularly South Carolina. The census of 1790 shows the following of that name in South Carolina:—William, John, Benjamin,

Catherine, Ned, Noah, and Robert. The last mentioned lived in St. Peter's Parish, Beaufort District, and we do not hesitate to claim him as the father of the Robert Tanner who married Providence Robert and went to Mississippi and then to Louisiana. This claim is further strengthened by the fact that our Robert Tanner is frequently mentioned in the records as "Robert Tanner, Jr." And we have recently found another item to fortify the above statement. In the South Carolina Historical and Genealogical Magazine, Vol. XLV, page 43, under the heading of "Abstracts From Records Of Court Of Ordinary," we find the following:—

> Dedimus issued to Robert Tanner to qualify Samuel Jones administrator of the estate and effects of Thomas Jones, late of St. Peter's Parish, as nearest of kin.
>
> July 10, 1771.

This would indicate that our Robert Tanner's father was established in St. Peter's Parish, South Carolina, as early as 1771, and the fact that a *dedimus* was issued to him proclaims him to be a man of standing in his community. He was evidently not a stranger in the land at the time and therefore it would be safe to say he was well established there. His son, Robert, in whom we are particularly interested, was born in 1769 and it is likely that he himself was a man in his early manhood in 1771, probably less than thirty years old. A careful study of Rev. Clayton Torrence's article quoted in preceding pages would lead us to believe that this Robert Tanner of St. Peter's Parish, Beaufort District, descended from Joseph Tanner, Sr., of Henrico county, Virginia, through the latter's son Edward Tanner, being a son of Edward Tanner of "Raleigh Parish," Amelia county, who was a grandson of Edward, son of Joseph, Sr. This conclusion seems to us to be sufficiently reasonable to be acceptible as a probable fact. Any way, it is the most definite statement we can make relative to Robert Tanner's forebears at this time. The family Bible of Mrs. Irene Tanner Johns of Cheneyville, Louisiana, a granddaughter of Robert Tanner and Providence Robert, tells us that Robert Tanner was born in Beaufort District, South Carolina, on February 14, 1769, and that he married there on February 14, 1793, Providence Robert, fifth child of Captain Peter Robert and Anne Grimball. The good book further relates that Providence Robert was born near Robertville, Beaufort District, South Carolina, on August 30, 1774. The place of her nativity is close to the line now separating the present counties of Jasper and Hampton, both of which were at that time a part of Beaufort District.

Robert Tanner was a civil engineer and followed that profession most of his life. A few years after his marriage he left South Carolina and with a large concourse of the Robert and Grimball families, (his wife's people) emigrated to the Mississippi Territory, then better known as West Florida. This body of related homeseekers settled near the present site of Woodville, in Wilkinson county, and there Robert Tanner was much occupied in surveying the wild lands of that locality. He was also engaged to lay off the town of Woodville. After spending several years there he decided to move again and in 1813 in company with other members of his wife's family crossed the Mississippi river and went into Louisiana which had just the year before been received into the Union as another state. They settled permanently on Bayou Boeuf, in Rapides parish, near the present town of Cheneyville. Linn Tanner, whom the compiler of these notes can well remember, states in a letter to his cousin, Mrs. Leora Robinson, of Louisville, Kentucky, that his grandfather, Robert Tanner, was employed for $40.00 to survey and lay out the streets of Woodville. This apparently small sum was quite a large amount of money in those days and his grandson says it was a great help to him in pursuing his journey to Rapides parish. According to this same letter his pioneer grandfather first settled on a quarter section of land in Rapides which he bought from the government. He was then employed as a government surveyor and for a time was kept very busy as new settlers were swarming into this section of the state. He invested his money in lands and at the time of his death left a plantation to each of his children. Mr. Linn Tanner further states in his letter to Mrs. Robinson that in 1860 he borrowed from Dr. Robert Kilpatrick (a relative) a record of the family which was complete back to the time of Louis XIV, at which period the famly were living in France. We are inclined to believe that Mr. Tanner is here referring to the Robert family and not the Tanners. About this time the Civil War began and Mr. Tanner entered the

Confederate Army. During one of the raids of the Federal Army under General Banks his home was pillaged and his copy of the family record as well as the original book were either destroyed or stolen.

Rev. W. E. Paxton in his "History of Louisiana Baptists" on page 143, in writing of Rev. Joseph Willis, has the following to say:—

> He extended his labors to Cheneyville, on Bayou Boeuf, in the Parish of Rapides, some fifty or sixty miles higher up the country, where many of his Mississippi acquaintances had settled, among whom were some of the members of the church on Bayou Chicot. Among these settlers on the Bayou Boeuf, twenty-five or thirty miles below Alexandria, were Robert Tanner, and his son, Robert Linn Tanner, the Elder Robert with his two sons, Baynard C. and Peter W. Robert, also some of the Cheneys and Jacksons, all of whom were related. In 1816 a church was constituted here and called Beulah.

Robert Tanner soon became one of the outstanding men in the vicinity of his Louisiana home, and wielded much influence in religious and social matters. He acquired large tracts of fertile land on Bayou Boeuf in the Cheneyville neighborhood, soon owned many slaves and reached a high degree of affluence in that community. His home was on the right descending bank of the bayou, about one and a half miles above the town of Cheneyville, and near the site of it may be seen today his tombstone and that of his wife. An avenue of spreading evergreen oaks leads to the old home-site, and there today (but in a different house) lives Mrs. Joseph Eugene Munson, a lineal descendant. Robert Tanner died there on September 28, 1839, from an attack of yellow fever. His wife, Providence Robert, survived him about sixteen years and died on January 14, 1856. She was a truly good and noble woman, affectionately known as "Aunt Provie" to all of her many nieces and nephews. Though the mother of fifteen children she adopted and reared three nieces, daughters of her dead sister, Sarah Catharine Robert, who had married David Bettison. Twelve of her fifteen children reached adult life, were married and left descendants. The fifteen children were:—

A.—Anne Tanner, born November 19, 1793.
B.—Frances Tanner, born January 11, 1795.

C.—Anne Grimball Tanner, born October 16, 1796.

D.—Robert Linn Tanner, born January 18, 1798.

E.—Sarah Adeline Tanner, born September 27, 1799.

F.—Peter Tanner (i), born January 17, 1801.

G.—Esther Elvira Tanner, born May 6, 1802.

H.—Jane Sophronia Tanner, born January 14, 1804.

I.—Providence Tuzette Tanner, born December 27, 1805.

J.—Henry Tanner, born January 23, 1807.

K.—Martha Providence Tanner, born November 10, 1808.

L.—Paul Jabez Tanner, born April 22, 1810.

M.—Peter Tanner (ii), born November 3, 1811.

N.—Rosalind Harley Tanner, born April 7, 1813.

O.—Mary Matilda Tanner, born October 11, 1815.

Three of the above children died young, viz: Anne, Peter (i), and Henry.

B.

FRANCES TANNER.

Frances Tanner, second child of Robert Tanner and Providence Robert, was born in Beaufort District, South Carolina, and came to Rapides parish with her husband about 1813. Her parents first resided in Woodville, Mississippi, after they left South Carolina, and it was there in 1812 that she met and married William Pearce, Jr., son of William Pearce, Sr. He and his young bride came to Cheneyville, in Rapides parish, Louisiana, and it was there that their three children were born:— Eliza, Sarah Providence and Alanson Green Pearce. Mrs. Pearce died at her home near Cheneyville on April 13, 1821. Her husband survived her for several years. We know that he was living as late as January 23, 1830, since on that date we find a record where he sold land on Bayou Boeuf to Robert Tanner. A full account of their descendants will be found in Part Four of this book.

C.

ANNE GRIMBALL TANNER.

Anne Grimball Tanner, third child of Robert Tanner and Providence Robert, was born in Beaufort District, South Carolina, and came to Louisiana with her parents when about six-

teen years of age. She was twice married: first to William
Brown, and second to Stephen Pearce. Her second husband
was a brother of William Pearce, Jr., who married her sister
Frances. We find a record of the death of her first husband
in THE ALEXANDRIA GAZETTE, one of the early newspapers of
Rapides parish. The item in it reads as follows:—

> William Brown, a highly respected planter, died Friday,
> November 6, 1829.

Anne Grimball Tanner was married to William Brown
about 1815. He was a prominent citizen and planter of the
Bayou Boeuf country near Cheneyville. There was a Hugh
Brown living in that vicinity about the same time whom we
find signing as a witness to the will of Samuel Levi Wells in
1815, and in 1818 there is a record of his purchasing the property of Willis Wells on Bayou Boeuf. It is not unlikely that
he was a brother of the William Brown we have under consideration. It appears very likely from such data as we have that
our William Brown was a native of Martin county, North
Carolina. We find an official record in which Martha Keller
of Rapides parish, Louisiana, wife of Jacob Keller, on December 7, 1825, acknowledges receipt of a draft given her by
Reuben Carnal for $500.00 on Wilkins and Linton of New Or-
leans, which was for money paid the said Carnal (attorney-in-
fact for Martha Keller) by William R. Brown of Martin county, North Carolina, executor of the estate of Abner Brown, deceased, of said state and county, and willed to Martha Keller
by the said Abner Brown. This transaction was witnessed by
Anne G. (Tanner) Brown which indicates that these were her
husband's people. We know that William Brown and Anne
Grimball Tanner had one son and that he was named William
Robert Brown. It is our belief that he was named for his paternal grandfather who was undoubtedly the "William R.
Brown, executor of the estate of Abner Brown." It is our conclusion that Abner Brown was the father of Mrs. Martha
Keller and the grandfather of our William Brown. The fact
that William Brown named his plantation on Bayou Boeuf
"Williamsburg" is strongly significant. The county-seat of his
native county, Martin, was "Williamston" which is synonymous
with "Williamsburg."

William Brown died comparatively young, leaving an only son, as far as we can ascertain, William Robert Brown, born about 1818. Within less than a year after the death of her first husband, Anne Grimball (Tanner) Brown was married to Stephen Pearce, whose first wife (Sally Goodwin Bray) died about the same time as Mr. Brown, having been the mother of eleven children. This second marriage took place on September 30, 1830, and Mr. Pearce died October 18, 1833. Anne Grimball (Tanner-Brown) Pearce died July 27, 1852. An only son, Stephen Samuel Pearce, was born of this second union on the day of his father's death. There is a very numerous progeny from this son of the second marriage. See Part Four.

William Robert Brown, only son of Anne Grimball Tanner and her first husband, William Brown, was born on Bayou Boeuf, Rapides parish, La., about 1818. He married about 1840 Elmira Toler, daughter of Joel Toler. Mr. Brown like his father was a prominent citizen and planter on Bayou Boeuf, and died at his home there sometime before July 31, 1866. On that date George B. Marshall and John O. Pickens were appointed to "appraise the estate of the late William R. Brown, deceased." Their appraisement showed his estate was worth $65,862.00, which at that period indicated he was a man of considerable wealth. His landed property, in those proceedings, was designated as "Williamsburg Plantation," and described as bounded on the north by Bayou Boeuf, on the east by Loyd's plantation, and west and south by lands of John O. Pickens. It was also stated that this property was acquired "before marriage" which probably meant that he inherited it.

On September 13, 1866, "Elmira Toler, widow of William R. Brown, deceased," appoints Thomas J. Toler of said State and Parish, her attorney-in-fact. This was probably her brother. Mrs. Elmira (Toler) Brown died August 29, 1869. We find the following notice of her death in THE LOUISIANA DEMOCRAT of Wednesday, September 8, 1869:—

> DIED:—At her residence on Bayou Boeuf on the morning of the 29th ult., Mrs. Elmira Brown, wife of the late William R. Brown, and daughter of the late Joel Toler, in the 45th year of her age. She had been a resident of Rapides more than 25 years.

William Robert Brown and Elmira Toler had nine children :—

    1.—Allison Brown.
    2.—Ellen Brown.
    3.—Henry Jackson Brown.
    4.—Sarah Brown.
    5.—William Lynn Brown.
    6.—Tanney Brown.
    7.—Rosa Brown.
    8.—Silas Brown.
    9.—Talton Edwin Brown.

1.—Allison Brown, eldest of the above children, was born about 1841 and died unmarried at the age of twenty-five.

2. Ellen Brown was born in Rapides parish, Louisiana, about 1843. She was twice married. Her first husband was William Sneed who was said to have been a very fine man and owner of a steamboat line on the Mississippi river. He died a few years after their marriage and sometime later she was married to a man named Fontaine who became Master of one of her boats known as the "General Hodges." They lived on this boat and it was there that she died. She had no children by either marriage.

3.—Henry Jackson Brown, third child of William Robert Brown and Elmira Toler, was born on Bayou Boeuf, near Cheneyville, in Rapides parish, Louisiana, on August 6, 1847, and died at his home there when well past middle life. He married on June 21, 1870, Martha Esther Bailey, better known to her family and friends as "Hettie." She was a daughter of Walter Bailey, native of Bath, Somersetshire, England, and his wife, Margaret Gertrude Allen. She was born in Rapides parish, Louisiana, on January 12, 1849, and died there on September 20, 1932. This marriage was announced in the LOUISIANA DEMOCRAT, an old Alexandria newspaper, in the issue of Wednesday, July 13, 1870, as follows :—

> MARRIED :—On June 21, 1870, at Beulah Baptist Church, Cheneyville, Louisiana, by the Rev. Thomas Lansdell, Miss Hettie Bailey to Mr. Henry J. Brown.

Mr. and Mrs. Brown had nine children. They were:—

    a.—William Robert Brown.
    b.—Walter Frith Brown.

c.—Allison Brown.
d.—Frank Silas Brown.
e.—Ellen Esther Brown.
f.—Alice Ryan Brown.
g.—Mary Brown.
h.—Edward Jouett Brown.
i.—Robert Anatole Brown.

a.—William Robert Brown married Amelia Pike of Memphis, Tennessee. Both are now dead. They had six children, three daughters and three sons.

b.—Walter Frith Brown was born about 1873 in Rapides parish, Louisiana. He married Mattie Armstrong. Both are now dead. They had two children:—Mildred Brown who married William Ponder and has one child, Ellen Ponder, George Bowie Brown who married but has no children.

c.—Allison Brown was born in Rapides parish, Louisiana, about 1875. He married Fannie Furlough and both are now dead. They had one daughter, Allie, who died young.

d.—Frank Silas Brown was born in Rapides parish, Louisiana, about 1877, and has been twice married. His first wife was Sallie Nunnally of New Orleans, by whom he had two children. His second wife was Robena Jeannette (Duvall) Griffin, widow of Ed Griffin and daughter of Charles Winchester Duvall and Nellie Jackson, and grand-daughter of William H. Duvall and Delia Melvina Pearce. They had two children:—Audrey and Frank Silas Brown, Jr.

e.—Ellen Esther Brown, fifth child of Henry Jackson Brown and Martha Esther Bailey, was born in Rapides parish, Louisiana, on March 12, 1879. She was married on February 25, 1898, to Heber Livingston Pearce, son of Stephen Samuel Pearce, and Mary Ellen Bennett. He was born near Evergreen, Avoyelles parish, Louisiana, on January 25, 1874. Mr. and Mrs. Pearce stem from the same ancestry. He is a grandson of Anne Grimball Tanner whose second husband was Stephen Pearce, and she is a great grand-daughter of the same lady whose first husband was William Brown. They now live at Denham Springs, Louisiana, and have six children:—

az.—Mary Ellen Pearce, born December 23, 1898.
bz.—Heber Livingston Pearce, Jr., born August 13, 1900.
cz.—Martha Aline Pearce, born April 2, 1904.

> dz.—Alice Marr Pearce, born February 15, 1906.
> ez.—Edward Joseph Pearce, born July 11, 1910.
> fz.—Claud Bennett Pearce, born December 19, 1914.

az.—Mary Ellen Pearce was married September 2, 1922, to Frank John Ricard who was born in France on August 27, 1897, and was brought to this country when three years old. His parents are Frank Ricard and Theresa Artigues who settled in Natchitoches parish, Louisiana, where they are yet living. Mr. and Mrs. Ricard now reside in Denham Springs, Louisiana, and have four children:—

> Mary Elizabeth Ricard, born September 25, 1923.
> Catherine Pearce Ricard, born January 29, 1926.
> Marguerite Agnes Ricard, born February 26, 1928.
> Frank John Ricard, Jr., born November 3, 1931.

bz.—Heber Livingston Pearce, Jr., resides in Denham Springs, Louisiana, and is supervisor of public schools for Livingston parish. He married Clyde Josie Lawler who was born January 29, 1898. They have one child, Caroline Adele Pearce, born August 15, 1927.

cz.—Martha Aline Pearce was married to Otto Adams of Sparta, Kentucky, where they now reside. They have no children.

dz.—Alice Marr Pearce was married on July 13, 1935, to John Odom Sullivan of Denham Springs, where they now reside. They have one child, Marilyn Sullivan, born December 17, 1937. Mr. Sullivan holds a responsible position with the Louisiana National Bank of Baton Rouge, Louisiana.

ez.—Edward Joseph Pearce married Myra Osgood and they have one child, Rose Marie Pearce, born April 23, 1940.

fz.—Claud Bennett Pearce is unmarried at this time and is now serving in the United States Army.

f.—Alice Ryan Brown, sixth child of Henry Jackson Brown and Martha Esther Bailey, was born in Rapides parish, Louisiana, about 1881. She was married to Thomas Worthy of Jackson, Louisiana. They have one son, Thomas Marion Worthy, who married Hazel Edwards and has a daughter named June.

g.—Mary Brown, seventh child of Henry Jackson Brown and Martha Esther Bailey, was married to Edward Randall who for sometime has been sheriff of Franklin parish, Louisiana. They have one son, Anatole Randall.

h.—Edward Jouett Brown, eighth child of Henry Jackson Brown and Martha Esther Bailey, was born in Rapides parish, Louisiana, about 1885. He is now a professor at the North-East Center (an extension of Louisiana State University), at Monroe, Louisiana. He married Louise Marston and they have four children:—Louise, Mary Esther, Virginia, and Edward Jouett Brown, Jr.

i.—Robert Anatole Brown, youngest child of Henry Jackson Brown and Martha Esther Bailey, was born in Rapides parish, Louisiana, about 1887. He is usually called "Tole." He married Blanche Brooks from Winnsboro, Louisiana. They have no children.

4.—Sarah Brown, fourth child of William Robert Brown and Elmira Toler, and better known to her family as "Mittie," was born in Rapides parish, Louisiana, about 1847, and was married to Lawrence Bushnell. They had eleven children:—

> a.—Lawrence Robert Bushnell.
> b.—Winona Bushnell.
> c.—Elma Allison Bushnell.
> d.—Ethel Bushnell.
> e.—Rosa Bushnell.
> f.—Vera Bushnell.
> g.—Ellen Aurelia Bushnell.
> h.—Meredith Arden Bushnell.
> i.—Douglas Franklin Bushnell.
> j.—Reginald Sneed Bushnell.
> k.—Aubrey Bushnell.

a.—Lawrence Robert Bushnell married Mary T. Taylor on June 4, 1899. They had two children:—

> az.—Mary Alice Bushnell, born May 2, 1900.
> bz.—Robert Taylor Bushnell, born June 1, 1902.

b.—Winona Bushnell was married to William Clarence Grayson on January 23, 1889. They had six children:—

> az.—Ina Clyde Grayson, born June 20, 1891.
> bz.—Vivian Viola Grayson, born July 2, 1893.
> cz.—Lorainne Grayson, born August 8, 1895.
> dz.—Lawrence Grayson, born February 11, 1897.
> ez.—Mary Edelene Grayson, born February 2, 1900.
> fz.—William Carl Grayson, born April 13, 1902.

c.—Elma Allison Bushnell married Ella Lambert. They had five children:—

az.—Reginald Bushnell.
bz.—Roderick Bushnell.
cz.—Clayton Bushnell.
dz.—Donovan Bushnell.
ez.—Elric Bushnell.

d.—Ethel Bushnell was married to Charles R. Elliott on December 25, 1898. They had nine children:—

az.—Winona Elliott.
bz.—Maxwell Elliott.
cz.—Mary Eltie Elliott.
dz.—Claudia Elliott.
ez.—Florence Elliott.
fz.—Ima Elliott.
gz.—Marjory Elliott.
hz.—Charles R. Elliott, Jr.
iz.—Evelyn Elliott.

e.—Rosa Bushnell was married to George G. Stubblefield They have one son, George G. Stubblefield, Jr.

f.—Vera Bushnell was married to Fred Williams in September, 1904. They had three children:—

az.—Janice Williams.
bz.—Sarah Williams.
cz.—Annie Rose Williams.

g.—Ellen Bushnell died when quite young.

h.—Meredith Arden Bushnell married but we have been unable to get the name of his wife. They have one child whose name is also unknown to us.

i.—Douglas Franklin Bushnell married but we have been unable to ascertain the name of his wife. They have two children:—

az.—Betty Ruth Bushnell.
bz.—Horace Bushnell.

j.—Reginald Sneed Bushnell married Alma Woods in 1916 They have one child, Lois Bushnell.

k.—Aubrey Bushnell died in infancy.

5.—William Lynn Brown, fifth child of William Robert Brown and Elmira Toler, was born in Rapides parish, Louisiana, about 1849, and married Martha R. Johnson (better known as "Mattie"), daughter of John Dawson Johnson and Eliza Jane Robert. They had three children:—

> a.—Samuel Meeker Brown.
> b.—Rosa Proctor Brown.
> c.—Jennie May Brown.

a.—Samuel Meeker Brown was never married. He went over-seas with the United States Army in World War I, and nothing further has ever been heard of him.

b.—Rosa Proctor Brown was married to Simon Levy and has no children.

c.—Jennie May Brown was married to Gordon Ogé, son of John Ogé of St. Landry parish, and has four children:—Dorothy Ellen, George Gordon, Robert Johnson, and Rosemary.

William Lynn Brown died in middle life and his widow (Mattie Johnson) then married Frank Monin of Long Leaf, Louisiana, and had three children:— Ella, Joe and Ben. Ella married a Mr. Gunn and now lives at Glenmora, Louisiana. Mr. and Mrs. Monin are both dead at this time. She died in Lake Charles, Louisiana, at the home of her son Ben on Sunday, May 30, 1943, and was buried in the Butter graveyard near Forest Hill, in Rapides parish, Louisiana.

6.—Tanney Brown, sixth child of William Robert Brown and Elmira Toler, was born about 1850 and died the same day.

7.—Rosa Brown, seventh child of William Robert Brown and Elmira Toler, was born about 1851 and died at the age of ten.

8.—Silas Brown, eighth child of William Robert Brown and Elmira Toler, was born about 1853 and died when young, of yellow fever.

9.—Talton Edwin Brown, youngest child of William Robert Brown and Elmira Toler, was born on Bayou Boeuf, in Rapides parish, Louisiana, on June 9, 1855, and died at his home near Lloyd's Bridge, Rapides parish, Louisiana, on November 27, 1897. He married on February 12, 1886, in Rapides parish, Louisiana, Mary Catherine Harper, daughter of William Houston Harper of Hazlehurst, Mississippi, and Mar-

tha Rosa Ross of Ringgold, Louisiana. She was born at Winnfield, Louisiana, on June 23, 1868, and is living at this date
(1944) in Lecompte, Louisiana. Mr. and Mrs. Brown had five
children:—

> a.—Elmyra Brown, born December 26, 1886.
> b.—William Lynn Brown, Jr., born December 21, 1888.
> c.—Bertha Olevia Brown, born November 14, 1890.
> d.—Dorothy Mae Brown, born November 20, 1892.
> e.—Esther Pearce Brown, born December 7, 1894.

a.—Elmyra Brown was born in Rapides parish, Louisiana,
and was married on July 19, 1904, to Wade Hampton Jones of
Lecompte, Louisiana. Mr. Jones has been prominent in his
community for many years as a banker and planter. He assisted in the organization of the Bank of Lecompte of which
he is now president. He has always taken a great interest in
civic affairs, especially in public education, and for more than
a quarter of a century has been a member of the Rapides Parish School Board of which he is now president. Two children
were born of this marriage:—

> az.—Margaret Jones, born August 5, 1905.
> bz.—Wade Hampton Jones, Jr., born February 14, 1911.

az.—Margaret Jones was married on February 28, 1922,
to Dr. Samuel Davis Gore, a prominent orthodontist of New
Orleans. They have one child, Samuel Davis Gore, Jr., born
March 5, 1927.

bz.—Wade Hampton Jones, Jr., is the efficient cashier of
the Bank of Lecompte. He married Elizabeth Margaret Ma-
gruder on August 24, 1933. They have one child, Wade Hampton Jones, III, born August 14, 1937.

b.—William Lynn Brown, Jr., is a prominent planter on
Bayou Boeuf, near Lecompte, Louisiana, in the vicinity of
where he was born. He married Lilha St. Paul Bordelon on
December 12, 1917, a daughter of Ferdinand M. Bordelon and
Emily Kilpatrick Branch, and a grand-daughter of Rev. Elihu
Kilpatrick Branch and Elizabeth H. Brunson. They have two
children:—

> az.—Katherine Branch Brown, born March 2, 1919.
> bz.—William Lynn Brown, III, born October 17, 1922.

The elder of these was married to Robert Clayton Wright of Lecompte, La.

c.—Bertha Olevia Brown was twice married, first to Arthur Behrens on September 1, 1912, and second to Charles Henry McFarland on August 29, 1929. There is one child by the first marriage, Arthur Behrens, Jr., born November 19, 1919.

d.—Dorothy Mae Brown was married to Dr. Victor Kirkpatrick Allen on December 17, 1919. He is a prominent physician in Tulsa, Oklahoma, where they now reside. They have one child, Dorothy Ann Allen, born March 17, 1924.

e.—Esther Pearce Brown was married on December 17, 1919, to Robert Carl Elder. She and her sister Dorothy Mae had a double wedding. Mr. Elder was born in Hancock county, Illinois, on December 13, 1892, and was a son of Frank H. Elder and Josie Hurst of Pennsylvania. He was a civil engineer by profession and died at Jacksonville, Illinois, in the hospital at that place, following an operation for ruptured appendix. One child was born of this marriage, Robert Carl Elder, Jr., born February 6, 1924.

D.

ROBERT LINN TANNER.

Robert Linn Tanner was the fourth child and eldest son of Robert Tanner and Providence Robert, and was born in Beaufort District, South Carolina, on January 18, 1798. He was brought to Wilkinson county, Mississippi, by his parents when about six years old, and when fifteen he came with them to Rapides parish, Louisiana, and there spent the remainder of his days, becoming one of the most prosperous and outstanding men in his community. In Paxton's History of Louisiana Baptists, on page 495, we find the following mention of him:—

> Deacon Robert Lynn Tanner, a prominent layman, who long lived at Cheneyville, in Rapides parish, was born in Beaufort District, S. C., in 1793[1], and removed with his father, Robert Tanner, also a Baptist, to Rapides parish in 1813. He was baptized in 1826, and soon after united with Beulah Church at Cheneyville, and was made a dea-

[1] The correct date of his birth is 1798.

con of that church. He was a man of large means, and contributed liberally to the service of God. For many years he bore almost alone the salary of his pastor. He frequently acted as Clerk and for many years presided as Moderator of the Louisiana Association, and on several occasions acted as Vice-President of the Baptist Convention. He died in 1870.[2]

The spelling of his middle name is given at different times as *Linn* and *Lynn*. We are inclined to accept the former as correct, especially as Mr. Linn Tanner of a later generation, and nephew of the subject of this sketch, always signed his name in that manner. He was a highly educated gentleman and well versed on the history of his family and we feel that we can make no mistake in accepting his authority on the subject.

Robert Linn Tanner married in August, 1826, Marion Hervery Irion, a daughter of Rev. George Anderson Irion and his wife, Rebecca Hunt. There seems to have existed some confusion as to this lady's correct name, but that stated above was given us by her son, Walter Lodowick Tanner. In many of the legal transactions in which she took part her name is sometimes given as "Mary Ann Irion." In one instance we find the following:—"Then came to these presents Madam Mary Ann H. Irion, wife of R. L. Tanner, and by him authorized, who intervened and became a party to this act." She here signs the document with her husband as "Mary A. H. Irion." The name of Irion is said to have originally been Von Erion, which would indicate that the family were people of prominence in the old country. The Irion family for more than a century and a quarter has been outstanding in Louisiana. (See Part Four).

Robert Linn Tanner died at his home near Cheneyville, Louisiana, on August 29, 1869. The date of his death is verified by THE LOUISIANA DEMOCRAT (an Alexandria newspaper) of Wednesday, September 15, 1869. The item in it reads as follows:—

> DIED:—On the 29th of August, at his home on Bayou Boeuf, Robert Lynn Tanner, in the 71st year of his age.

---

[2] This should be 1869.

We have no record of the date of his wife's death but feel fairly certain it occurred prior to his own.

Robert Linn Tanner and Marion Hervery Irion had nine children, four of whom died in infancy. The five who reached maturity were:—

1.—Ellen Aurelia Tanner.
2.—Robert Linn Tanner, Jr.
3.—Octavia Tanner.
4.—Emma Augusta Tanner.
5.—Walter Lodowick Tanner.

1.—Ellen Aurelia Tanner was born on her father's plantation near Cheneyville, Rapides parish, Louisiana, on May 20, 1829, and died in Cheneyville on October 29, 1907. She was married at the home of her parents on December 16, 1847, to George Childs Smith. He was a native of Waterbury, Connecticut, where he was born February 26, 1824, and died in Cheneyville on February 14, 1896. Mr. and Mrs. Smith lived for many years on their plantation on Red river, a few miles above the Avoyelles parish line, where Mr. Smith was one of the "well-to-do" planters in those halcyon days of peace and plenty. In 1862 their already large holdings were increased by the addition of more land donated by Mr. Tanner, as we learn from a deed executed by him on December 5, 1862. It is there stated that "Robert Linn Tanner gives his daughter Ellen Aurelia Smith 480 acres of land on the right bank of Red river, bounded above by lands owned and belonging to Levi Wilson, and below by lands belonging to William Pearce." In this deed he also gives her twenty-six negro slaves. Then on July 17, 1867 (due to results of the Civil War), he executes a document before Mark R. Marshall, Notary Public, in which he "recalls that part of the foregoing deed referring to the twenty-six slaves released from slavery by the Proclamation of Abraham Lincoln, President of the United States, but that he does by these presents bequeath and donate to his aforesaid daughter, Madam Ellen Aurelia Smith, wife of George C. Smith, the lands described in the foregoing deed of gift." The Smith plantation was named "Echo", and on a portion of the same land today there is a town bearing that name. It is said that the name was suggested by the loud echo so distinctly heard when any one on the north bank of the river hallooed to some one on the south bank. George Childs Smith and Ellen Aurelia Tanner had three children:—

       i.—Mary Cornelia Smith.
      ii.—Annie Lynn Smith.
    iii.—Harvey Tanner Smith.

    i.—Mary Cornelia Smith, better known to her family as "Nina," was born on Echo plantation, Rapides parish, Louisiana, on September 25, 1848, and died at Lafayette, Louisiana, on September 18, 1929. She was married to T. Jay Lacy. They had no children.

    ii.—Annie Lynn Smith was born on Echo plantation, Rapides parish, Louisiana, on December 10, 1849, and died at Bay St. Louis, Mississippi, on August 30, 1902. She was married on October 25, 1871, to John Collins Grimes, son of William Bryan Grimes and Sarah Marina (Ellis) Lanier, who was born on his father's plantation in Rapides parish, Louisiana, in 1841, and died at Bay St. Louis, Mississippi, on January 9, 1906.

    William Bryan Grimes, father of John Collins, was born October 4, 1811, at Williamston, Martin county, North Carolina, and married in 1838 Sarah Marina Ellis of Pitt county, North Carolina, who at the time was the widow Lanier with one child, Laulette Lanier. This daughter afterwards married Pascal Hickman of Rapides parish, La., and had one son, Preston Pascal Hickman, better known to his friends as "Pack Hickman," who married Daisy Rogers and had several children. Mr. Grimes' real name, so it is said, was *Greams*, his father being descended from the Clan of Greams in Scotland. However, he had so much trouble in getting his mail, from his name being incorrectly spelled, that he changed it to *Grimes*. William Bryan Grimes came to Louisiana about two decades prior to the Civil War. He was a successful cotton broker and an extensive cotton planter. He was always called the "Old Gentleman" (even when comparatively a young man) by every one from North Louisiana to New Orleans. His plantations were on both sides of Red river about twenty miles below Alexandria, being a large land owner in both Rapides and Avoyelles parishes. There is a location on the north side of the river still known as "Grimes' Bluff," so called on account of the steep banks of the river formed by the pine hills which at that point reach to the edge of the water. It is a very picturesque spot when viewed from the south bank of the river and it was near there that Mr. Grimes built his home. We have no record of the death of William Bryan Grimes but it must have occurred before 1885. The ALEXANDRIA TOWN TALK contained the following notice of his wife's death:—

> DIED:—At the family residence on Red river, on July 24, 1887, Mrs. Sarah M. Grimes, in the 81st year of her age. She was a native of Pitt county, North Carolina, and a resident of Louisiana since 1826.

We would judge from the above notice that Mr. Grimes married his wife in Louisiana instead of North Carolina. He was born in 1811 and was surely not married to her before 1826. They had three children:—John Collins Grimes who married Annie Lynn Smith; Tillman Lanier Grimes who married Jennie Palmer and left four children, Jennie, Palmer (wife of Dr. E. de Nux), Benjamin, and Eloise; Judith Watts Grimes who married Dr. Samuel Gilbert Compton and had seven children, Fannie, Leonard, Ellis, Laulette, Samuel Gilbert, Grimes, and Eleanor.

John Collins Grimes, eldest child of William Bryan Grimes and Sarah Marina (Ellis) Lanier, was one of the first students to matriculate at the Louisiana State Seminary of Learning and Military Academy—now the Louisiana State University. It was then under the superintendency of William Tecumseh Sherman, afterwards so prominent in the Civil War. When that great conflict broke out John Collins Grimes was among the first to enlist in defense of his country. He became a lieutenant in Company A, Eighth Louisiana Cavalry, and served until paroled at the termination of the war. Of the marriage between himself and Annie Lynn Smith five children were born:—

> a.—Mary Cornelia Grimes.
> b.—William Bryan Grimes.
> c.—Marion Irion Grimes.
> d.—Annie Laurie Grimes.
> e.—Marie Louise Grimes.

a.—Mary Cornelia Grimes, eldest child of John Collins Grimes and Annie Lynn Smith, was born on Ingleside plantation, Avoyelles parish, Louisiana, in 1872. This plantation was on the north side of Red river almost opposite the present village of Echo in Rapides parish. Mary Cornelia is better known to her family as "Nina." She was married to Charles F. Jordan and now resides at Ukiah, California. They have no children.

b.—William Bryan Grimes, only son of John Collins Grimes and Annie Lynn Smith, was born on Ingleside plantation, Avoyelles parish, Louisiana, on June 27, 1874, and died in Oregon, where he was living, in 1934. He was married and left three daughters.

c.—Marion Irion Grimes, third child of John Collins Grimes and Annie Lynn Smith, was born on Ingleside plantation, Avoyelles parish, Louisiana, in 1876. She was twice married: —first to John Leland Henderson, and second to Martin Ruhberg. She now resides in Prineville, Oregon. She has two sons by her first marriage:—Robert Lynn Henderson and Elliot Henderson.

d.—Annie Laurie Grimes, fourth child of John Collins Grimes and Annie Lynn Smith, was born on Ingleside plantation, Avoyelles parish, Louisiana, on August 18, 1878. She lived for several years on the Mississippi coast where her parents had gone on account of their health and was married there at Trinity Church, Pass Christian, on March 8, 1904, to Thomas Hewes Hewes who was born July 30, 1868, at Pleasant View plantation, Oscar Postoffice, Pointe Coupee parish, Louisiana, where they now reside. They have had four children:—

az.—Elliot Henderson Hewes, born May 30, 1906.
bz.—Thomas Hewes Hewes, Jr., born April 11, 1908.
cz.—Marie Louise Hewes, born March 14, 1910.
dz.—Annie Laurie Grimes Hewes, born November 15, 1919.

az.—Elliot Henderson Hewes is unmarried at this time. He is a construction engineer in government employ and is at present stationed in New Orleans.

bz.—Thomas Hewes Hewes, Jr., died June 19, 1909, when one year of age.

cz.—Marie Louise Hewes was married on October 18, 1933, to David Miller Mims of Minden, Louisiana. At present they are residing in Baton Rouge, Louisiana, and have one child, Thomas Hewes Dougald Mims, born August 26, 1934.

dz.—Annie Laurie Grimes Hewes has decided to "live alone" a while longer and seek "a career." She is at present employed by the Standard Oil Company at Baton Rouge as a laboratory technician.

e.—Marie Louise Grimes, youngest child of John Collins Grimes and Annie Lynn Smith, was born on Ingleside plantation, Avoyelles parish, Louisiana, on June 7, 1884. She was married at the residence of Mr. Elliot Henderson at Pass Christian, Mississippi, on January 25, 1910, to John Grover Delesdernier, son of John Grover Delesdernier and Sarah Ann Evans, who was born in New Orleans, Louisiana, on January 2, 1867. His father was born at Michias Port, Maine, on June 26, 1818, and died in New Orleans in 1894, and his mother was born in New Orleans on August 1, 1837, and died there in May, 1906. They were married in New Orleans on December 11, 1858. Mr. and Mrs. Delesdernier now reside in San Antonio, Texas, and have no children.

iii.—Harvey Tanner Smith, only son of George Childs Smith and Ellen Aurelia Tanner, married Ellen DeBerry who was born at Aransas Pass, Texas, in 1869, and died December 31, 1932, leaving no issue. Mr. Smith was born July 1, 1857, and died October 14, 1934.

2.—Robert Linn Tanner, Jr., second child of Robert Linn Tanner and Marion Hervery Irion, was born near Cheneyville, Rapides parish, Louisiana, in 1843, and died at his home there on Thursday, February 23, 1888. THE ALEXANDRIA TOWN TALK of February, 1888, records his death as follows:—

> DIED:—At the family residence near Cheneyville, Louisiana, on Thursday, February 23, 1888, R. L. Tanner, in the 46th year of his age.

Robert Linn Tanner, Jr., married Matilda Sannie Calloway on December 31, 1868. She was born about 1853 and died October 22, 1893. We find this date of her death confirmed by an item appearing in THE ALEXANDRIA TOWN TALK of Saturday, October 28, 1893. It reads as follows:—

> DIED:—At the family residence near Cheneyville, Louisiana, on Saturday night, October 22, 1893, San-

ny Colloway, wife of the late Robert Linn Tanner, Jr., aged about 40 years.

Mr. and Mrs. Tanner had six children. They were as follows:—

    i.—Walter Irion Tanner.
    ii.—Hampton Paxton Tanner.
    iii.—Mary Cornelia Tanner.
    iv.—Hervery Tanner.
    v.—Everard Hamilton Tanner.
    vi.—Benjamin Hartwell Tanner.

i.—Walter Irion Tanner was born near Cheneyville, Rapides parish, Louisiana, on October 18, 1869, and is living at this date (1944). He married his cousin, Mary Katherine Hetherwick, on August 30, 1893, who was a daughter of Clarence Hetherwick and Mary N. Rusk, and was born December 20, 1875. They reside in Cheneyville at this time and have three children:—

    a.—Robert Clarence Tanner.
    b.—Mary Cornelia Tanner.
    c.—Charles Hetherwick Tanner.

a.—Robert Clarence Tanner was born in Cheneyville, Louisiana, on February 10, 1895. He entered the United States Army during World War I and served over-seas. After returning home he married Amy Jackson from Oak Ridge, Louisiana. They have no children.

b.—Mary Cornelia Tanner was born in Cheneyville, Louisiana, on June 12, 1897, and was married on December 24, 1919, to Lucien Quitman Campbell of New Orleans. They now reside in Abeline, Texas, and have one daughter, Mary Anna Campbell, born October 11, 1920.

c.—Charles Hetherwick Tanner was born in Cheneyville, Louisiana, on September 4, 1900. He married Ethel Settoone of Springfield, Louisiana. They have no children.

ii.—Hampton Paxton Tanner, second child of Robert Linn Tanner, Jr., and Matilda Sannie Calloway, was born near Cheneyville, Louisiana, on January 27, 1871, and died February 13, 1872.

iii.—Mary Cornelia Tanner, only daughter of Robert Linn Tanner, Jr., and Matilda Sannie Calloway, was born near

Cheneyville, Louisiana, on August 20, 1873, and died at her home there on October 12, 1914. She was married at Cheneyville, Louisiana, on Tuesday, September 27, 1892, to James Buchanan Slay who was a prominent citizen and planter in that community. Mr. Slay was born in Jasper county, Mississippi, on August 24, 1857, and died at his home near Cheneyville, on February 9, 1927. He was a son of William Slay and Laura Ann Hargroves, and had the following sisters and brothers:—William Alfred, R. O., Ben Hilburn, Althea, and Alice Slay. Mr. Slay's paternal grandfather was Nathan Slay whose children were:—Alfred, Carney, William, Nathan, and Martha (Patsy). James Buchanan Slay and Mary Cornelia Tanner had five children:—

a.—Arthur Clyde Slay, born July 17, 1893.
b.—James Lea Slay, born November 22, 1895.
c.—Laura May Slay, born July 30, 1904.
d.—Ruby Cornelia Slay, born March 1, 1907.
e.—Katie Belle Slay, born May 18, 1911.

a.—Arthur Clyde Slay married Juett Belle Jones on August 17, 1920, at Shreveport, Louisiana. He died at Cheneyville, Louisiana, on September 10, 1927, leaving two children:— James Robert Slay, born September 8, 1921, and Margaret (Peggy) Slay, born November 2, 1924.

b.—James Lea Slay was born near Cheneyville, Rapides parish, Louisiana, and now resides in Alexandria where he is a valuable employee in the large furniture establishment of the Hemenway-Johnson Company. He married Frances Ocheltree on January 14, 1922, and they have one son, James Richard Slay, born July 26, 1923. This son attended the Louisiana State University and then entered the United States Army. He is now an Aviation Cadet at Maxwell Field, Alabama.

c.—Laura May Slay was born near Cheneyville, Rapides parish, Louisiana, and was married on June 27, 1942, to Albert Victor Saucier, son of Victor Saucier and Noami Broullette.

d.—Ruby Cornelia Slay was born near Cheneyville, Louisiana, and was married on May 6, 1938, to Otto Smith Newman, son of James Irvin Newman and Ora Smith. They have no children.

e.—Katie Belle Slay was born near Cheneyville, Louisiana, and is yet unmarried. She is a teacher in one of the Alexandria public schools.

iv.—Hervery Tanner, fourth child of Robert Linn Tanner, Jr., and Matilda Sannie Calloway, was born September 4, 1874, and died December 4, 1874.

v.—Everard Hamilton Tanner, fifth child of Robert Linn Tanner, Jr., and Matilda Sannie Calloway, was born near Cheneyville, Louisiana, on March 27, 1877, and died on Sunday, May 18, 1941. He served his country in the Spanish-American War and was on duty for several years in the Philippine Islands. He married Frances Meadeariss Calton, daughter of James Calton and Sally Pearce, and grand-daughter of William Lodowick Pearce and Martha Frances Meadeariss, and great grand-daughter of Joshua Pearce and Esther Tanner. They resided in Alexandria for many years and had three children: —Edward Kennedy, Arthur Bryan, and Melonoise Tanner. Mrs. Tanner is yet living.

vi.—Benjamin Hartwell Tanner, sixth child of Robert Linn Tanner, Jr., and Matilda Sannie Calloway, was born near Cheneyville, Louisiana, on December 15, 1878. He has never married and is living at this time in Cheneyville.

3.—Octavia Tanner, third child of Robert Linn Tanner and Marion Hervery Irion, was born near Cheneyville, Louisiana, about 1845. She was twice married, first to H. A. Parton, and second to John Lewis Campbell. There was one child by the second marriage, Edward Campbell, who now lives at Rayne, Louisiana, is married and has children.

4.—Emma Augusta Tanner, fourth child of Robert Linn Tanner and Marion Hervery Irion, was born near Cheneyville, Louisiana, about 1849. She was married to William James Sylvester Johnson. Both are long since dead. They had two children:—

i.—William James Johnson.
ii.—Augusta Johnson.

i.—William James Johnson was born near Cheneyville, Louisiana, and is yet living near the place of his nativity. He is better known among his family and friends as "Jimmy

Johnson." He married Elizabeth Lea of Clinton, Louisiana, and they have had four children:—

a.—Augusta Johnson.
b.—Pryor Lea Johnson.
c.—Sylvester Johnson.
d.—Gordon R. Johnson.

a.—Augusta Johnson was married to Thomas Clanton Foote, son of Dr. Charles A. Foote and Margaret Gambrell. They now reside in Cheneyville, Louisiana, and have one son, James Clanton Foote, born August 29, 1920, and now in the military service of his country.

b.—Pryor Lea Johnson was born near Cheneyville, Louisiana, where he now resides and is the genial proprietor of a restaurant and filling station. He is well and favorably known to all the traveling public. Besides his business he devotes much of his energies to the cultivation of rare and beautiful flowers, and a generous portion of it to sporting with the "finny tribe." He married on December 8, 1939, Georgie Elizabeth Grayson, daughter of Mr. and Mrs. Wiley Grayson. A son, Pryor Lea Johnson, Jr., was born on Friday, February 21, 1941, and died August 1, 1941, and a daughter, Elizabeth Ann Johnson, was born August 3, 1944.

c.—Sylvester Johnson was born near Cheneyville, Louisiana. He married Blanche Jewell. They have no children.

d.—Gordon R. Johnson was born near Cheneyville, Louisiana, and was a prominent member of the dental profession, living in Bunkie, Louisiana. He married Bessie May Adams and they had one son, Gordon R. Johnson, Jr., born in 1937. Dr. Johnson died May 16, 1938, at Atlanta, Georgia, and was buried in Cheneyville, Louisiana. His death was a very sad, tragic affair. He was a first lieutenant in the dental reserve corps and was on his way to a training camp in Georgia. He had stopped over night in Atlanta and put up at a hotel near the depot so as to get an early start the next morning. During the night a terrible fire broke out in the hotel and he was cut off from escape. Rather than remain in his room and be burned alive he leaped from a window and was killed.

ii.—Augusta Johnson, only daughter of William James Sylvester Johnson and Emma Augusta Tanner, was born near Cheneyville, Louisiana, and was married to John Healey of

Opelousas, Louisiana. Mr. Healey died in New Orleans on Thursday, November 23, 1939, and was buried in Opelousas. Four children were born of this marriage:—William James Healey, a prominent dentist in New Orleans who married a Miss Fux and has one son, Charles Johnson, also a dentist who is married and has a daughter named Dorothy; Emma Healey who married a Fontenot and has a daughter, Thelma; Thelma Healey who married a Johnson; Bessie Healey who married a Black.

5.—Walter Lodowick Tanner, youngest child of Robert Linn Tanner and Marion Hervery Irion, once well and familiarly known to every one in central Louisiana as "Lod Tanner," was born near Cheneyville, Rapides parish, Louisiana, on the banks of Bayou Boeuf, on February 16, 1854, and died at his home in Alexandria, Louisiana, on Friday, November 1, 1929. He died poor in worldly goods but rich (fabulously so) in the love and esteem of his friends. No man ever knew him who did not like him. He possessed two qualities which were outstanding and made him one of the most interesting and entertaining individuals it was ever the present writer's good fortune to know—an infallible memory and an inimitable manner in telling things. He grew up in those trying days of "reconstruction" following the Civil War, and was one of a band of young men who went from Cheneyville to help their white friends in quelling the Negro insurrection, now famous as the "Colfax Riot," which occurred on Easter Sunday morning, 1873, at Colfax, Louisiana. He was uncompromising in his political convictions and did much towards freeing his country from "carpet-bag" rule.

On January 29, 1874, "Lod Tanner" married Ella McConnell Jouett. She was born in Rapides parish, Louisiana, on July 18, 1853, and died at her home in Alexandria on Sunday, October 18, 1942, being 89 years old. Seven children were born of this marriage:—

       i.—Mary Theresa Tanner—died in infancy.
      ii.—Marion Augusta Tanner.
     iii.—William Lodowick Tanner.
     iv.—Edward Charles Tanner.
      v.—McArinah Octavia Tanner.
     vi.—Ida Haas Tanner.
    vii.—David Jefferson Tanner.

ii.—Marion Augusta Tanner was married to Charles Edward Carnes who for many years has been prominent in the public school system of Louisiana. They had no children. Mr. and Mrs. Carnes were living in Crowley, Louisiana, when Mrs. Carnes died in 1943.

iii.—William Lodowick Tanner was born near Cheneyville, Louisiana, on October 9, 1879. He has lived in Alexandria, Louisiana, for many years, and there married on May 4, 1904, Georgie Anderson, daughter of Dr. J. C. Anderson. She died there on June 12, 1915, leaving three children:—

        a.—William Lodowick Tanner, Jr.
        b.—Calvin George Tanner.
        c.—Betty May Tanner.

a.—William Lodowick Tanner, Jr., was born in Alexandria, Louisiana, on September 16, 1907. He was an electric welder in the employ of the government at one of the large army camps near Alexandria after being discharged from the Marine Corps in February, 1944. He died Monday, May 1, 1944.

b.—Calvin George Tanner was born in Alexandria, Louisiana, on November 26, 1910. He is unmarried at this time and is serving in the U. S. Army.

c.—Betty May Tanner was born in Alexandria, Louisiana, on July 14, 1914. She was married to Martin Broussard and has two children, both girls.

iv.—Edward Charles Tanner was born near Cheneyville, Louisiana, on May 28, 1881. He now resides in Opelousas, Louisiana. On November 6, 1912, he married Pearle Rogers who was born October 1, 1890. She was a daughter of Andrew Jackson Rogers, born August 13, 1851, and Mary Isabella Owens, born April 26, 1855. They have three children:—

        a.—Edward Charles Tanner, Jr.
        b.—Gordon Rogers Tanner.
        c.—Barbara Ann Tanner.

a.—Edward Charles Tanner, Jr., was born in Alexandria, Louisiana, on November 13, 1913. He lives in San Antonio, Texas, and is employed by the Coco Cola Company there. In 1941 he married Thedo Frances Henderson who was born

August 28, 1921. One child, Nancy Diane, was born June 26, 1944.

   b.—Gordon Rogers Tanner* was born in Pineville, Louisiana, on September 1, 1917. He is unmarried at this time and is a staff sergeant in the U. S. Coast Artillery. At present he is stationed at San Diego, California.

   c.—Barbara Ann Tanner was born in Shreveport, Louisiana, on December 9, 1934.

   v.—McArinah Octavia Tanner was married to Dr. Albert Sidney Wilson. They resided in Morgan City, Louisiana, where Dr. Wilson died in August, 1942. They had three children:—

> a.—Maurinne Wilson.
> b.—David Cannon Wilson.
> c.—Albert Jouett Wilson.

The eldest of these is married at this time.

   vi.—Ida Haas Tanner never married. She lived with her sister in Crowley, Louisiana, where she died Friday, June 23, 1944.

   vii.—David Jefferson Tanner never married. He resided in Alexandria, Louisiana, for many years where he was well known and liked by all who knew him. He provided for his father in his old age and when he had passed away he continued to care for his mother and sister until his own death which took place in Alexandria on July 3, 1941. He was a good man; may he rest in peace.

E.

SARAH ADELINE TANNER.

   Sarah Adeline Tanner, fifth child of Robert Tanner and Providence Robert, was born in Beaufort District, South Carolina, on September 27, 1799, and died near Cheneyville, Rapides parish, Louisiana, on November 25, 1820, being just twenty-one years of age. She came with her parents to Wilkinson

---

* Gordon Rogers Tanner was commissioned 2nd Lieutenant July 20, 1942, at Camp Davis, North Carolina. He was commissioned 1st Lieutenant November 17, 1942, and in July, 1943, he was promoted to Captain. He was killed in an airplane accident in California on October 10, 1944, and buried in Greenwood Memorial Park in Pineville, La., on October 18, 1944.

county, Mississippi, when scarcely four years of age, and then a few years later they brought her to Louisiana. She was married at the home of her parents, near Cheneyville, Louisiana, on February 2, 1816, to James Hall Tanner Kilpatrick, a native of Georgia who had moved to Louisiana with his twin brother, Andrew Conger Kilpatrick, who later married a sister of Sarah Adeline Tanner. They were sons of Andrew Kilpatrick and Jane Nichols of Iredell county, North Carolina, and it is not unlikely that these brothers were born there, but if so they went to Georgia when quite young. Mrs. Julian C. Lane of Statesboro, Georgia, gives us some valuable information on the Kilpatrick family in her book, "Key and Allied Families," page 357. She tells us that three Scotchmen named *Kirkpatrick* participated in the Scotch Rebellion of 1745 and after the defeat of their forces at Culloden fled to Ireland and changed their name to *Kilpatrick*. They emigrated to America, one settling in New Jersey, one in North Carolina, and one in South Carolina. She also tells us that the "Yankee" cavalry leader, General Kilpatrick, was of the New Jersey branch; the Kilpatricks of Alabama and Mississippi are of the South Carolina branch; those of Georgia and Louisiana are of the North Carolina branch. Andrew Kilpatrick was a school teacher for a Scotch-Irish colony on the Yadkin river in Iredell county, North Carolina, where it is said he remained for twenty-two years. He married Jane Nichols and they had the following children:—Euphemia born 1773, Mary born 1775, Parmelia born 1777, Joseph N. born 1779, Joshua W. born April 7, 1782, William born 1784, Jane born 1786, James Hall and Andrew Conger (twins) born July 24, 1788, Alexander M. (son by a second marriage) born 1790. Joseph N., Joshua W., and Andrew Conger Kilpatrick were Methodist preachers, and James Hall Tanner was a Baptist preacher. Joseph N. was so opposed to slavery that he went to Indiana and settled. Andrew Conger at an early date settled on Bayou Boeuf, in Rapides parish, Louisiana.

James Hall Kilpatrick who was born in Iredell county, North Carolina, July 24, 1788, came to Louisiana when nineteen years of age and taught school for several years. While there he participated in the battle of New Orleans in 1815. He married in 1816 (as has already been stated) Sarah Adeline Tanner and they had two sons, one of whom died in infancy. The other, Robert Tanner Kilpatrick, was a prominent physician in Navasota county, Texas. James Hall Kilpatrick, after the death of his wife in 1820, added "Tanner" to his name in accordance with some Louisiana inheritance law (so it is said), and this accounts for the "Tanner" in his name. He returned to Georgia* soon after his wife's death and there on June 22, 1822, married Harriett Eliza, daughter of Batt Jones and a grand-daughter of Abraham Jones. They had five children:— Washington L., James H., Elizabeth, Mary, and Sarah. The two sons of this marriage were prominent Baptist preachers in Georgia.

G.

ESTHER ELVIRA TANNER.

Esther Elvira Tanner, 7th child of Robert Tanner and Providence Robert, was born in Beaufort District, South Carolina, on May 6, 1802, and died in Rapides parish, Louisiana, on April 21, 1865. She was married at the home of her parents near Cheneyville, Louisiana, on May 17, 1821, to Henry Jackson, son of Reuben Jackson and Susannah Richardson (See Part Four).

Mr. Jackson was born in South Carolina on March 5, 1797, and died at his home near Cheneyville, Louisiana, on February 26, 1856. He and his wife were buried in the family graveyard on his plantation about three miles above Cheneyville. Mr. Jackson was an extensive planter, a very prominent citizen, and took a lively interest in civic and religious affairs. He was "a pillar" of the Beulah Baptist Church in Cheneyville for many years, and we find his name recorded as secretary or clerk of that first church in 1845. He remained steadfast to Beulah Church when the great schism came in 1845 and almost

---

* James H. T. Kilpatrick returned to Louisiana for a short time in 1825 as is shown by a deed passed on July 27, 1825, before Silas Talbert, Notary Public, in which he sells a tract of land on Bayou Boeuf. The deed states that he purchased the land from John Ogden on November 6, 1816, also that he is now a resident of Burke county, Georgia. He died in 1869. The John Ogden mentioned in the deed was the husband of Martha Robert, 11th child of Captain Peter Robert and Anne Grimball, and an aunt of Mr. Kilpatrick's first wife.

wrecked the religious unity of the Robert and Tanner families
Brothers and sisters took opposite views and fought for their
convictions, and out of the smoke came the Cheneyville Christian or Campbellite Church. Mr. Jackson's brother-in-law
Paul Jabez Tanner, and two of his wife's brothers-in-law
William Prince Ford and William Hetherwick, were among the
leaders in this break from the Baptist creed.

Henry Jackson and his wife, Esther Elvira Tanner, had
five children:—

        1.—Robert Henry Jackson.
        2.—Josiah Augustus Jackson.
        3.—Sarah Jane Jackson.
        4.—Matilda Ann Jackson.
        5.—Stephen Tanner Jackson.

1.—Robert Henry Jackson, eldest child of Henry Jackson
and Esther Elvira Tanner, was born on his father's plantation
near Cheneyville, Rapides parish, Louisiana, on August 2, 1822,
and died there on September 11, 1863. He was twice married;
his first wife being Mary Melvina Jackson (no relation, as far
as we know) whom he married on February 8, 1844. She was
a daughter of Elzaphan Jackson and Mary Stokes and was
born on August 4, 1826, and died on March 3, 1859. Two
children were born of this marriage:—

        i.—William Franklin Jackson.
        ii.—Mary Ella Jackson.

Robert Henry Jackson married his second wife, Sarah
Maria Baillio, on June 3, 1862. She was born in Rapides parish, Louisiana, on May 25, 1840, and died in May, 1867. She
was a daughter of Sosthene A. Baillio and Sarah Maria Crain,
and a grand-daughter of Pierre Baillio and Magdelaine Emelie
Lacour. Pierre Baillio is said to have been a colonel of dra-
goons in Napoleon Bonaparte's army and came to Louisiana
directly from France with a large grant of land from the
French government. Some of his family had his passport a
few years ago but it appears to have been lost or misplaced.
Pierre Baillio was in Natchitoches parish for a while after
reaching this country and later settled permanently in Rapides
parish. His tomb and that of his wife may be seen today in

the Rapides cemetery in Pineville. The inscriptions on them read as follows:—

PIERRE BAILLIO
who died January 8th, 1821, aged 52 years, 6 months, and 11 days.

MAGDELAINE EMELIE LACOUR
daughter of Jean Baptiste Lacour and Marlanne Leonard, and wife of Pierre Baillio, who was born November 27, 1774, and died September 13, 1838, aged 63 years, 9 months and 16 days.

Sarah Maria Baillio's mother was a daughter of James I. Crain from either Fauquier or Loudon counties, Virginia, and probably a brother or relative of Colonel Robert Alexander Crain who played a prominent part in early Rapides history and was a participant in the famous Sand Bar duel in 1827. It appears from the tomb stone inscriptions in the Rapides cemetery that she was the second wife of Sosthene A. Baillio whose first wife was Louise Evelena Heno, a daughter of John Baptiste and Emelie Heno and died August 18, 1830.

Robert Henry Jackson and his second wife, Sarah Maria Baillio, had one child:—

iii.—Robert Henry Jackson, Jr.

i.—William Franklin Jackson, son of Robert Henry Jackson and his first wife, Mary Melvina Jackson, was born near Cheneyville, Louisiana, and never married. He was a popular young man and came to a very untimely and unfortunate end. He was shot and killed in Cheneyville on November 30, 1880, by Edward Cullom Marshall as the result of a family feud. Jackson had killed James Horace Marshall some time previously who was a brother of his slayer.

ii.—Mary Ella Jackson, daughter of Robert Henry Jackson and his first wife, Mary Melvina Jackson, was born near Cheneyville, Louisiana, on March 8, 1856, and died there on October 8, 1883. She was married on April 21, 1875, to William Flynn Hays who was born on August 12, 1847 and died on February 25, 1916. Two children were born of this marriage:—

a.—Lillian Lansdell Hays.
b.—Mary Ella Hays.

After the death of his wife, Mary Ella Jackson, Mr. Hays married again and had five children, two sons and three daughters, by this second union. His second wife was Miss Pet Gayle of Clinton, Louisiana.

a.—Lillian Lansdell Hays was born near Cheneyville, Louisiana, in 1878, and died there at the home of her sister, Mrs. Mary E. Munson, on Sunday, May 7, 1939, at 7 p. m. She never married.

b.—Mary Ella Hays was born near Cheneyville, Rapides parish, Louisiana, in 1880. She was married to Joseph Eugene Munson who died about 1924, leaving her with four children. She was Mr. Munson's second wife and at this date (1944) resides near Cheneyville on the original home-site of her great great grandfather, Robert Tanner. Her children are:—Mary Dennett Munson who married Warren N. Christopher, professor of bacteriology at the Louisiana State University and at present an officer in the United States Army; Dorothy Munson who married Laurence Lovell and now lives at Woodriver, Illinois; Lillian Hays Munson who married Washington T. Wallace and now resides in Monroe, Louisiana; Robert Jackson Munson who married Orelle Boone and now lives at Cheneyville, Louisiana.

iii.—Robert Henry Jackson, Jr., only child of Robert Henry Jackson and his second wife, Sarah Maria Baillio, was born near Cheneyville, Rapides parish, Louisiana. on July 16, 1863. He became a prominent planter and business man in his community, was the first president of the Bank of Cheneyville, and served as a member of the Rapides parish Police Jury for several years. He married on April 14, 1896, Medora Mathews, daughter of Joel Mathews and Annie Chase. She died in Cheneyville on March 19, 1919, leaving four children. Mr. Jackson lived many years after his wife's death, reaching the age of 78. He died at his home near Lecompte, Louisiana, on Monday, March 9, 1942, and was buried in the Rapides cemetery in Pineville, Louisiana. His four children were:—

a.—Joel Early Mathews Jackson.
b.—Elizabeth Carter Marshall Jackson.
c.—Robert Davenport Slaughter Jackson.
d.—Ann Paul Chase Mathews Jackson.

a.—Joel Early Mathews Jackson now resides near Lecompte, Louisiana, where he is engaged in planting. He married on March 7, 1926, Corinne Kendall of Ruston, Louisiana. They have two children:—Joel Early Mathews Jackson, Jr., born January 17, 1927, and Jeanne Marie Jackson, born December 22, 1929.

b.—Elizabeth Carter Marshall Jackson was married to James Allen Madison Skelton on August 27, 1929. They have one son, James Allen Madison Skelton, Jr., born August 26, 1930, and better known to his family as "Tito."

c.—Robert Davenport Slaughter Jackson was never married. He joined the United States Marines some years prior to World War II and died in service. It is our impression that he was drowned.

d.—Ann Paul Chase Mathews Jackson was married to Gilbert Wayne Daniels on Saturday, August 30, 1941. They now reside in Guatemala City, Guatemala, at Mansion San Francisco.

2.—Josias Augustus Jackson, second child of Henry Jackson and Esther Elvira Tanner, was born on January 19, 1824, and died in infancy.

3.—Sarah Jane Jackson, third child of Henry Jackson and Esther Elvira Jackson, was born near Cheneyville, Rapides parish, Louisiana, on August 13, 1827, and died there on August 15, 1897. She was first married on October 5, 1843, to Edwin Charles Herbert who was born in Norfolk, Virginia, on November 25, 1815, and emigrated to Louisiana when a young man. He died in Rapides parish, Louisiana, on February 23, 1846, leaving two children:—

        i.—Cornelia Herbert.
        ii.—Edwin Charles Herbert, Jr.

About 1855 Sarah Jane Jackson married as her second husband, Henry Brown Ferguson, who was born on January 8, 1825, in Brunswick county, Virginia, and emigrated to Louisiana in January, 1852. He died near Cheneyville, Louisiana, on December 14, 1867. THE LOUISIANA DEMOCRAT of Wednesday, December 25, 1867, verifies the time of his death with the following item:—

> DIED:—Suddenly on the 14th inst., at his residence in this parish, H. B. Ferguson, in the 43rd year of his age. He was born and reared in Brunswick county, Virginia, but had resided in Louisiana since January, 1852.

Five children were born of this second marriage:—

iii.—Esther Rebecca Ferguson, born December 13, 1856.
iv.—Jarrett Josiah Ferguson, born August 4, 1858.
v.—Henry Lockhart Ferguson, born November 10, 1859.
vi.—Rosa Ferguson, born October 16, 1861.
vii.—Henry Herbert Ferguson, born March 2, 1865.

All of the above children by the second marriage died in early childhood except the youngest, Henry Herbert Ferguson, who married Estelle Lea of Jackson, Louisiana. He died on August 13, 1928, leaving no issue. His widow is living at this date (1944).

i.—Cornelia Herbert, daughter of Sarah Jane Jackson and her first husband, Edwin Charles Herbert, was born near Cheneyville, Rapides parish, Louisiana, on December 25, 1844. She was married on September 18, 1866, to Joel Newsom Murphey who was born November 15, 1838, and died February 17, 1882. THE LOUISIANA DEMOCRAT of Wednesday, September 26, 1866, contained the following notice of this marriage:—

> MARRIED:—On the 18th inst., at the residence of H. B. Ferguson, on Bayou Boeuf, by the Rev. Thomas Lansdell, J. N. Murphey of Bienville parish, to Miss Cornelia Herbert of this parish.

Cornelia (Herbert) Murphey died on August 26, 1882, leaving six children:—

a.—James Herbert Murphey.
b.—Edwin Charles Murphey.
c.—Rosa Murphey.
d.—Ida Murphey.
e.—Joel Newsom Murphey, Jr.
f.—Lena Murphey.

a.—James Herbert Murphey, eldest of the above children, was born July 10, 1867, and died on March 23, 1914. He married Lilla McDowell and they had seven children:—Joel, Rozier, James, Thomas, Edwin Burges, William Baillio, and Lillian Murphey. The second of these children, Rozier, is now a prominent dentist in Shreveport, Louisiana. He is married and has two children, a son and a daughter. The fifth, Edwin Burges, married Kate Tanner Stafford, daughter of Leroy Stafford and Priscilla Allen. They live in Ann Arbor, Michigan, and have a son, Edwin Stafford Murphey, born March 22, 1941, and a daughter, Catherine Allen Murphey, born May 25, 1944.

b.—Edwin Charles Murphey was born in Rapides parish, Louisiana, on February 15, 1869, and died in a hospital at Bunkie, Louisiana, on Monday, February 23, 1944, aged 78. He devoted most of his life to farming. For several years he lived in St. Landry parish, Louisiana, and later returned to Rapides where for many years he managed most successfully one of the large plantations of the Weil Company near Cheneyville. On January 13, 1897, at Opelousas, Louisiana, he married Minnie Vester Malone. She was born at Arizona, Louisiana, on February 28, 1876, and died at Ruston, Louisiana, on July 19, 1910. She was a daughter of William Adam Malone and Sallie Scarf Nicholson. Six children were born of this marriage:—

> az.—Lucille Murphey.
> bz.—Rosalie Murphey.
> cz.—Lascom Edwin Murphey.
> dz.—Minnie Malone Murphey.
> ez.—William Bertrand Murphey.
> fz.—Sallie Gladys Murphey.

az.—Lucille Murphey was born at Opelousas, Louisiana, on April 14, 1898, and died on July 9, 1899.

bz.—Rosalie Murphey was born at Opelousas, Louisiana, on December 8, 1899, and was accidentally drowned on July 28, 1913.

cz.—Lascom Edwin Murphey was born in Alexandria, Rapides parish, Louisiana, on September 5, 1901. He married Madelon Rachal on November 12, 1927. Like his father he has devoted his energies to farming and for some years was manager of a large plantation near Franklin, Louisiana. While there the present World War began and he entered the United States Army. He now holds the rank of a captain and is stationed at this writing at Berkeley, California. He and his wife have two children:—

Lascom Edwin Murphey, Jr., born September 15, 1928.
Paul Bertrand Murphey, born January 9, 1933.

The first of these children was born in Natchitoches and the second in Franklin, Louisiana.

dz.—Minnie Malone Murphey was born in Alexandria, Rapides parish, Louisiana, on September 23, 1903. She was married on July 23, 1927, to Allen Richard Fontane. They reside in Hessmer, Avoyelles parish, Louisiana, and have four children:—

Marguerite Denise Fontane, born April 18, 1929.
Patricia Ann Fontane, born February 18, 1931.
Edwin Richard Fontane, born August 7, 1932.
Minnie Murphey Fontane, born January 27, 1935.

The first three of the above children were born in Hessmer and the fourth in Lecompte, Louisiana. The third child died on January 7, 1933.

ez.— William Bertrand Murphey was born in Alexandria, Rapides parish, Louisiana, on November 17, 1905. He married in East Baton Rouge parish, Louisiana, on June 22, 1940, Helen Morgan Stuart, better known to her family and friends as "Peggy." She was a daughter of Walter Bynum Stuart and Mary Alice Morgan. The ceremony took place at the country home of her brother, Walter Bynum Stuart, Jr., a few miles north of the city of Baton Rouge. His father acted as his "best man." William Bertrand Murphey followed in the footsteps of his father and was for some years manager of one of the largest plantations near Franklin, in St. Mary's parish, Louisiana. Though a young man his reputation was already outstanding in his chosen work when the present war came on to disturb the peace and threaten the safety of civilization. He immediately entered the military service of his country and is now a lieutenant in the Naval Reserve. He is presently stationed at Tampa, Florida.

fz.—Sallie Gladys Murphey was born in Ruston, Louisiana, on January 28, 1908. She was married on November 27, 1931, to Louis Earl Rutledge, son of Joseph Morrison Rutledge and Lura Tanner. Mr. and Mrs. Rutledge are both descendants of Robert Tanner, the pioneer to Rapides parish, he being a twice great grandson and she a thrice great grand-daughter. They now reside in Cheneyville, Louisiana, where Mr. Rutledge has the agency for the Sinclair Oil Company. They have one lovely little daughter, Sallie Ann Rutledge, born November 28, 1939.

　　c.—Rosa Murphey, daughter of Joel Newsom Murphey and Cornelia Herbert, was born on September 6, 1870. She married Dodge Rougeou and they had one daughter named Cornelia.

　　d.—Ida E. Murphey, daughter of Joel Newsom Murphey and Cornelia Herbert, was born on August 19, 1873, and was married to her cousin, Colbert Murphey, who was a son of Captain James Pollard Murphey of the Confederate States Army, a native of Talledega, Alabama, and his wife, Mary Colbert of Mount Lebanon, Louisiana. Ida E. Murphey died in Alexandria, Louisiana, on March 19, 1932, and her husband, Colbert Murphey, died there on December 29, 1934. Six children were born of this marriage:—

> az.—Thelma Georgia Murphey.
> bz.—Joel Newsom Murphey, III.
> cz.—James Colbert Murphey.
> dz.—Mord Roberts Murphey.
> ez.—Jack H. Murphey.
> fz.—Mabel Glenn Murphey.

　　az.—Thelma Georgia Murphey was born on July 20, 1899, at Donaldsonville, Louisiana, and was married on April 14, 1919, to W. Jennings Davis. They now live at Ewing, Texas, and have three children:—Juanda Violet, Nancy Elizabeth, and Donald Rand Davis.

　　bz.—Joel Newsom Murphey, III, was born at Ruston, Louisiana, on July 30, 1901. He now resides in Alexandria where he holds an important position on the staff of the ALEXANDRIA DAILY TOWN TALK. He first married Etha Bennett in 1924 and they had one child, Gene Murphey, born in June, 1925. On April 12, 1930, he married Lucille Higdon and they have two children:—

> Colbert Warren Murphey (Pat), born February 16, 1932.
> Joeleene Vera Murphey, born June 12, 1934.

cz.—James Colbert Murphey was born at Ruston, Louisiana, on August 28, 1902, and died at the age of 21 at Haslam, Texas, on August 1, 1923.

dz.—Mord Roberts Murphey was born at Ruston, Louisiana, on March 20, 1904, and died at the age of fourteen.

ez.—Jack H. Murphey was born at Minden, Louisiana, on September 20, 1909, and married Joy Nugent on May 15, 1930. He died June 11, 1942, at Las Vegas, Nevada.

fz.—Mabel Glenn Murphey was born in Shreveport, Louisiana, on April 23, 1911, and married John L. McCutcheon on October 17, 1933. They have no children at this time.

e.—Joel Newsom Murphey, Jr., son of Joel Newson Murphey and Cornelia Herbert, was born in Rapides parish, Louisiana, on July 5, 1876. Whether he is living or not at this time we can not say with any degree of certainty as nothing has been heard of him for many years. After reaching adult life he left Louisiana and we have no further record of him.

f.—Lena Murphey was born on July 14, 1878. As far as we are able to learn she has never married.

ii.—Edwin Charles Herbert, Jr., second child of Edwin Charles Herbert and Sarah Jane Jackson, was born near Cheneyville, Rapides parish, Louisiana, on July 8, 1846, and died at his home in Alexandria, Louisiana, on September 15, 1914. He served with distinction in the Confederate Army during the whole period of the Civil War, and on November 18, 1873, married Cornelia Knox Stafford, fifth child of General Leroy Augustus Stafford and Sarah Catharine Wright. His wife died in Los Angeles, California, on October 17, 1926. Both were buried in the Rapides cemetery in Pineville, Louisiana. They had nine children:—

> Cornelia Knox Herbert.
> Edwin Charles Herbert, III.
> Sarah Catharine Herbert.
> Leroy Augustus Stafford Herbert.
> Eloise Stafford Herbert.
> Augusta May Herbert.
> Joseph Meeker Herbert.
> Arthur Wright Herbert.
> Esther Wright Herbert.

For a full account of these children and their descendants
see page 127 in the writer's work, GENERAL LEROY
AUGUSTUS STAFFORD, His Forebears and Descendants.

4.—Mathilda Ann Jackson, fourth child of Henry Jackson
and Esther Elvira Tanner, was born October 7, 1829, and died
in infancy.

5.—Stephen Tanner Jackson, fifth child of Henry Jackson
and his wife, Esther Elvira Tanner, was born June 29, 1832.
He is said to have been a most promising young boy but unfortunately was killed by lightning when fifteen years old.

H.

JANE SOPHRONIA TANNER

Jane Sophronia Tanner, eighth child of Robert Tanner
and his wife, Providence Robert, was born in St. Peter's
Parish, Beaufort District, South Carolina, on January 14, 1804.
She was brought by her parents when but a few months old to
Wilkinson county, Mississippi, and later to Rapides parish,
Louisiana, where she died on March 26, 1851. She was married at the home of her parents near Cheneyville, Rapides
parish, Louisiana, in 1821, to Andrew Conger Kilpatrick, a
Methodist minister, who was born probably in Georgia on July
24, 1788, and emigrated to Rapides parish, Louisiana, with his
twin brother, James Hall Tanner Kilpatrick, in the first quarter of the nineteenth century, where he died on December 31,
1849. He and his brother were sons of Andrew Kilpatrick
and Jane Nichols of Iredell county, North Carolina, whence
they emigrated to Georgia. These twin brothers married two
Tanner sisters.

Andrew Conger Kilpatrick and Jane Sophronia Tanner had
six children:—

1.—Robert Mortimer Kilpatrick, born August 20, 1822.
2.—James Bingley Kilpatrick, born August 28, 1824.
3.—Andrew Milton Kilpatrick, born July 16, 1829.
4.—Joshua Young Kilpatrick, born June 4, 1831.
5.—Martha Adeline Kilpatrick, born July 27, 1836.
6.—Edwin Lawrence Kilpatrick, born October 9, 1841.

Two of these children, James Bingley and Martha Adeline,
died in infancy. The fourth child, Joshua Young, as soon as

he was grown, went to Texas and located in Henderson county. He was living there as late as December 9, 1854, but whether he married and left children we are unable to say. The youngest child, Edwin Lawrence, was living on December 9, 1854, at which time he was thirteen years old. We are unable to learn anything further of him and it is likely that he died young.

Andrew Conger Kilpatrick appears to have been much occupied in the performance of his ministerial duties and we find frequent references to him as officiating at baptisms, marriages and funerals on Bayou Boeuf, but he evidently had time for other affairs and seems to have been a good business man as he left a large estate to his children. On December 9, 1854, his eldest son, Robert Mortimer Kilpatrick, sells his plantation and home to Jabez Tanner, his brother-in-law. It is described as consisting of nine hundred and eighty-five arpents of land "on the left bank of Bayou Beouf in descending, about three miles below the town of Cheneyville, bounded above by lands belonging to Jabez Tanner and below by lands belonging to Peter Tanner." There were two sales recorded in this transaction. One in which Robert Mortimer Kilpatrick, acting for himself, and as "attorney-in-fact for his absent brother, Joshua Young Kilpatrick, now a resident of Henderson county, in the State of Texas," sells their undivided three fourths interest in the property—"the same being their portion which they acquired from the estate of their deceased parents, and by purchase from Andrew Milton Kilpatrick of his undivided fourth in said estate." In the second sale Robert Mortimer Kilpatrick, as Tutor for his minor brother, Edwin Lawrence Kilpatrick, sells the latter's "undivided fourth interest in the estate of his parents."

1.—Robert Mortimer Kilpatrick died on March 11, 1875, at the age of fifty-three. He was twice married. In 1856 he married Charlotte Ann Wood who was born August 2, 1840, and died September 13, 1858. They had one son, Milton Kilpatrick, born September 2, 1858, and died the following year. The proximity of her son's birth to her death would indicate that Mrs. Kilpatrick died as a result of that birth. The second wife was Louisiana E. Wood, a sister of his first wife, whom he married in 1862. She died on May 2, 1887. By the second marriage there were six children:—

    a.—Mortimer Kilpatrick, born January 27, 1863.
    b.—Louisa Jane Kilpatrick, born July 21, 1864.
    c.—Oscar Kilpatrick, born June 28, 1866.
    d.—Lottie Kilpatrick, born April 5, 1868.
    e.—Louella Kilpatrick, born June —, 1870.
    f.—Henry Wood Kilpatrick, born November 10, 1872.

The second and sixth of these children died in infancy.

    a.—Mortimer Kilpatrick lived to middle life, residing in Alexandria, Louisiana, where he was well known and liked. As far as we know he never married.

    c.—Oscar Kilpatrick lived in Jennings, Louisiana, for many years. He was married and left two children. The following notice of his death appeared in the Alexandria Daily Town Talk of July 11, 1938:—

DIED.

    "KILPATRICK—At the family residence, Jennings, Louisiana, Monday, July 11, 1938, Mr. Oscar Kilpatrick, 72. The deceased is survived by his widow, two children, Mortie Kilpatrick, and Mrs. William Stinson, both of Lafayette. Two sisters, Misses Lottie and Luella Kilpatrick, both of Alexandria.

    d.—Lottie Kilpatrick never married and lived in Alexandria, Louisiana, all of her life. She died at the Mid-State Hospital, Pineville, Louisiana, on Wednesday, December 27, 1939. She was buried in the Mount Olivet cemetery in Pineville. We quote the following from her obituary in the Alexandria Daily Town Talk of December 27, 1939:—

    "Miss Kilpatrick was a member of one of the oldest Rapides parish families, being a daughter of the late Robert Mortimer Kilpatrick and Louisiana Woods Kilpatrick. She is survived by one sister, Miss Luella Kilpatrick of this city, and two nephews, Ray Kilpatrick of Texarkana, and Charles M. Kilpatrick of Roanoke, Louisiana.

We can not place the nephew "Ray Kilpatrick." The nephew "Charles M. Kilpatrick of Roanoke" is probably the son "Mortie Kilpatrick" mentioned in the obituary of her brother Oscar Kilpatrick.

3.—Andrew Milton Kilpatrick, third son of Jane Sophronia Tanner and Andrew Conger Kilpatrick, was born in Rapides parish, Louisiana, on July 16, 1829, and died at his home in August, 1895. He married in 1859 Margery Eliza Cushman who was born on February 11, 1836, and died on July 29, 1868. They had four children:—

  i.—Charles Mortimer Kilpatrick, born June 7, 1860.
  ii.—Ralph Kilpatrick, born December 21, 1861.
  iii.—Herbert Kilpatrick, born November 7, 1863.
  iv.—Ellen Kilpatrick, died in infancy.

  i.—Charles Mortimer Kilpatrick was born in Avoyelles parish, Louisiana, near the present site of Eola, and died at his home near Washington, Louisiana, on May 28, 1920. He was buried in the Rapides cemetery in Pineville, Louisiana. Mr. Kilpatrick was prominent in Louisiana politics and successively held the offices of Clerk of Court and Sheriff of Rapides parish for a number of terms. He married in 1885 Lizzie Tarlton Caffery. She died on October 7, 1897, leaving three children:—

  a.—Anna Margery Kilpatrick.
  b.—Jeanie Cushman Kilpatrick.
  c.—Alix Kilpatrick.

Mr. Kilpatrick married his second wife on July 7, 1898. She was Cornelia Knox Herbert, daughter of Edwin Charles Herbert, Jr., and Cornelia Knox Stafford. They had six children, three of whom died in infancy. The three reaching adult life are:—

  d.—Elizabeth Kilpatrick.
  e.—Charles Mortimer Kilpatrick, Jr.
  f.—John Thornton Kilpatrick.

  a.—Anna Margery Kilpatrick was married in 1913 to John Samuel Wheadon, son of Thomas Carey Wheadon and Floretta Butler. They now reside in Alexandria, Louisiana, and have one child:

  az.—Mary Virginia Wheadon.

az.—Mary Virginia Wheadon was born in Alexandria, Louisiana, on December 14, 1915, and was married in 1936 to Charles Camille de Gravelles, Jr., son of Dr. Charles Camille de Gravelles and Mary Nations of Morgan City, Louisiana. This young couple now reside in Lake Charles, Louisiana, and have three daughters, Alix de Gravelles, born Thursday, February 24, 1938, at 6 p. m., Elizabeth Claire de Gravelles, born August 12, 1942, and Virginia de Gravelles, born June 23, 1944.

b.—Jeanie Cushman Kilpatrick was married in 1914 to Lamar Herbert. They have had two children:—Charles Kilpatrick Herbert, born June 30, 1915, and died October 10, 1920; Margery Earle Herbert, born April 9, 1921.

c.—Alix Kilpatrick was married to Raphael Bloch in 1914. They now reside in Ringgold, Louisiana, and have two sons:—

az.—Samuel Wheadon Bloch, born December 24, 1917.
bz.—Raphael Bloch, Jr., born January 30, 1919.

az.—Samuel Wheadon Bloch is unmarried at this time and is in the U. S. Army where he holds the rank of a sergeant. He is presently stationed at Camp Beauregard, Louisiana.

bz.—Raphael Bloch, Jr., better known as "Tim," is at this time a Major in the U. S. Air Corps. He graduated from Kelly Field, Texas, in June, 1941, and was sent to Hickman Field, Honolulu. He was in the fight when Pearl Harbor was bombed on December 7, 1941, and later participated in the battle at Midway Island where his plane was shot down but fortunately not a member of his crew was lost, although they were adrift in the ocean for fourteen hours. He was afterwards promoted first lieutenant, then captain, and now major. He married Phyllis Barton after returning to the States, daughter of Mr. and Mrs. Roy B. Barton of Napoleonville, Louisiana. She is a graduate of the Louisiana State University. They now have a daughter, Ann Kilpatrick Bloch, born in Alexandria, Louisiana, on Sunday, January 30, 1944.

d.—Elizabeth Kilpatrick, daughter of Charles Mortimer Kilpatrick and his second wife, Cornelia Knox Herbert, was born in Alexandria, Louisiana, on January 18, 1908. She has lived in Los Angeles, California, for the past twenty years and was married there on Saturday, April 29, 1939, to Charles

Osgood Perpall. They have one daughter, Elise, born August 20, 1941.

 e.—Charles Mortimer Kilpatrick, Jr., was born in Alexandria, Louisiana, on June 17, 1909. He has lived in Los Angeles, California, for the past twenty years and is now an attorney there. He married at Ventura, California, on Saturday, September 18, 1943, Barbara Ruth Miller, daughter of Paul Dewey Miller and his wife, Mary Lelia Haworth. Both he and his wife are descendants of Captain Peter Robert and Anne Grimball.

 f.—John Thornton Kilpatrick was born in Alexandria, Louisiana, on September 30, 1910, and lived a great portion of his life in Los Angeles, California. He now resides in New Orleans where he is employed by a large ship building company. He married there on Saturday, July 3, 1943, Mary Worthington Hayward, daughter of Mr. and Mrs. Wilmer Hayward of that city.

 ii.—Ralph Kilpatrick was born near Eola, Avoyelles parish, Louisiana, on December 21, 1861, and graduated in medicine from Tulane University, New Orleans, Louisiana, in 1885. He practiced his profession for many years in Cheneyville and then moved to Alexandria where he continued to perform the duties of his calling until his death on Thursday, May 14, 1936, having devoted half a century of his life to the relief of human ills. He was a good man, a good doctor, and a high-toned Christian gentleman. *Requiescat in pace.*

Dr. Kilpatrick married on October 15, 1891, Alice Pierson, eldest daughter of Judge David Pierson of Natchitoches, Louisiana, and his wife, Sidney Amanda Pipes. Three children were born of this marriage, all of whom now reside in Alexandria. They are:—

   a.—Sydney Margery Kilpatrick.
   b.—David Pierson Kilpatrick.
   c.—Nainette Cushman Kilpatrick.

 a.—Sydney Margery Kilpatrick was born in Cheneyville, Rapides parish, Louisiana, on July 28, 1892. She has never married and for many years has held a prominent position on the teaching staff of the Bolton High School in Alexandria. Her subject is mathematics.

b.—David Pierson Kilpatrick is in the fire insuranc business in Alexandria. He married in 1927 Marion Wood o Syracuse, New York, and they had one child, Margaret Alic Kilpatrick, born May 4, 1928. Some years later Mr. Kilpatric and his wife were divorced, and on Wednesday, August 2₄ 1938, he married at Wills Point, Texas, Mary Ethel Spears daughter of Mr. and Mrs. Sam Spears of that place. They nov have one daughter, Mary Alice, born Saturday, October 1(1942.

c.—Nainette Cushman Kilpatrick was married in 1925 t John Worthie Cox of Baton Rouge, Louisiana. They have tw children:—Florence Alice Cox, born December 24, 1925, an Ralph Kilpatrick Cox, born August 26, 1927.

iii.—Herbert Kilpatrick, third son of Andrew Milton Kil patrick and Margery Eliza Cushman, was born near Eola Avoyelles parish, Louisiana, on November 7, 1863. He was ; prominent physician and practiced his profession for man; years in the country around Washington, St. Landry parish Louisiana. He married in 1891 Jennie Maud Pearce, daughte: of Stephen Samuel Pearce and Mary Ellen Bennett. She wa born near Evergreen, Avoyelles parish, Louisiana, on Februar; 24, 1869. Like her husband she also descended from Rober Tanner and Providence Robert. Dr. Kilpatrick died at hi home on October 30, 1930. His wife is yet living in Washing ton, Louisiana. Four children were born of this marriage:—

a.—Mary Margery Kilpatrick, born June 11, 1892.
b.—Stephen Milton Kilpatrick, born September 20, 1893.
c.—Lizzie Caffery Kilpatrick, born July 26,1898.
d.—Ralph Cushman Kilpatrick, born March 19, 1900.

a.—Mary Margery Kilpatrick was married to John Ferd inand Wartelle of St. Landry parish, Louisiana, on June 28 1924. They have no children.

b.—Stephen Milton Kilpatrick married Myrtle Pipes ii June, 1927. They have two children:—John Herbert Kil patrick, born March 3, 1930, and Catherine Kilpatrick, bori November 29, 1932.

c.—Lizzie Caffery Kilpatrick was twice married; first ii 1919 to Alcede J. Toulme, and second in December, 1924, t(Ross Watts. There are no children by either marriage.

d.—Ralph Cushman Kilpatrick married Sally Christina Rogueberg of Oslo, Norway, in June, 1928. He died on October 12, 1933, leaving no issue.

I.

PROVIDENCE TUZETTE TANNER.

Providence Tuzette Tanner, ninth child of Robert Tanner and Providence Robert, was born near Woodville, Wilkinson county, Mississippi, on December 27, 1805, and died near Cheneyville, Rapides parish, Louisiana, on December 10, 1824, at the age of nineteen. She was married in 1823 to Wilson Cook, a native of South Carolina who had emigrated to Louisiana. He died near Cheneyville on October 1, 1824. We have not been successful in ascertaining his father's name but it appears quite likely that he himself was a nephew of Eliza Tuzette Cook who was the second wife of Grimball Robert. If this surmise is correct then his grandparents were Wilson Cook and Judith O'Bannon of Beaufort District, South Carolina. Providence Tuzette Tanner and Wilson Cook had one son:—

1.—James Cook.

1.—James Cook, only child of Wilson Cook and Providence Tuzette Tanner, was born near Cheneyville, Louisiana, in 1824, and married about 1848 Mary Eliza Robert (his cousin), daughter of Leonidas Alonzo Robert and his first wife, Tuzette Eliza Pearce. She was born in Rapides parish, Louisiana, on December 19, 1830. We have no record of the death of either Mr. Cook or his wife. It is probable that they died young. They had two children:—

i.—Sarah Tuzette Cook.
ii.—Catherine Madolyn Cook.

i.—Sarah Tuzette Cook was married on December 5, 1872, to her cousin, Walter Prince Ford. They had four children. (See page 112).

ii.—Catherine Madolyn Cook was married to Joseph Bass in 1873. (See page 112).

K.

MARTHA P. TANNER.

Martha P. Tanner (her middle name was probably Provi dence) was the eleventh child of Robert Tanner and Providenc Robert, and was born near Woodville, Wilkinson county, Mis sissippi, on November 10, 1808. She came to Rapides parish Louisiana, with her parents when a mere child, and there, a their home near Cheneyville, she was married in 1828 to Wil liam Prince Ford, son of Jesse Ford and Dulla Barry Prince She died near Cheneyville on January 11, 1849.

William Prince Ford was born, according to the statemen of one of his grand-daughters, in Eminence, Kentucky, in 1803 His first American ancestor was John Ford who came t Massachusetts about 1679 from England. One of this John Ford's sons moved to the colony of Virginia and it was one o *his* descendants who followed the trail blazed by Daniel Boon and went into that beautiful country now known as Kentucky Just when he went there we are not certain, but it was ver soon after Boone made known the wonders of that hitherto un explored territory.

Jesse Ford, the father of William Prince Ford, came t Louisiana from Kentucky about 1816, and as far as we car ascertain brought with him his wife and four children. Hi wife was Dulla Barry Prince, daughter of William Prince whe was a native of Virginia where he was born on May 19, 1752 He (William Prince) emigrated to South Carolina and there served in the Revolutionary Army. His military record is substantiated by A. S. Salley, Jr., in his "Stub Entries to Indents for Revolutionary Claims," Book R, page 48. Soor after the Revolution William Prince with his wife Elizabeth and their children, and his brother Francis Prince, went to Kentucky and settled in Livingston county. That part of it where he lived was afterwards separated and called Caldwell county. He deeded land for the purpose of founding the town of Princeton, which was named for him. Since then a monu- ment has been erected there in his honor. His will was written June 7, 1808. Besides his wife Elizabeth, the following children are named in that instrument:—Enoch, Sally, Dulla Barry, Nancy, Elisha, Thomas, William, Francis and Elizabeth. There is considerable information on William Prince and his family in a History of Caldwell County, by Clausine R. Baker. On page 202 in that book we find the following item:—"Dulla Barry Prince's father was William Prince. She married Jesse Ford in about 1800. Their children were:—John, William, Ann, Eliza, Jesse, Franklin, Elvira, Edwin, Sarah Jane, Mary Louisa and Samuel." Some of these children may have remained in Kentucky but we are inclined to think that most of them died in infancy as we have been able to find a record of only four, viz: William Prince, Franklin, Eliza, and Sarah Jane.

Franklin Ford,* the second son mentioned, was a noted Presbyterian minister of Shreveport, Louisiana, who married and left three daughters:—Antoinette Ford who married Dr. John J. Scott of Shreveport and left issue; Mary Ford who married a Crane and left two children, one of whom married Will Foster of Caddo parish, and the other, Miss Lewis Crane, is yet living and unmarried; Margaret Ford who married a Greene and left no issue.

Eliza Ford, daughter of Jesse Ford and Dulla Barry Prince, married a Mr. Richardson and as far as we can learn left no descendants. She was born in Kentucky in 1807 and came to Louisiana with her parents when nine years old. The THE ALEXANDRIA TOWN TALK of Saturday, August 26, 1893, contained the following notice of her death:—

> DIED:—At the residence of her nephew, Mr. Edwin G. Hunter, near Alexandria, on Monday morning, August 21, 1893, Mrs. Eliza Richardson, a native of Rapides parish, aged 86 years.

> Mrs. Richardson's maiden name was Ford. She was a sister of the mother of Messrs. Robert P., Benjamin K., and Edwin G. Hunter, and Mrs. E. L. Brown. She was buried in Mount Olivet cemetery.

* It would seem Franklin Ford was engaged in other business besides the ministry. We read in "Twelve Years A Slave", by Northrup, page 105,the following:—"Wm. Ford unfortunately became embarrassed in his pecuniary affairs. A heavy judgment was rendered against him in consequence of his having become security for his brother, Franklin Ford, residing on Red River, above Alexandria, and who failed to meet his liabilities . . . . It therefore was necessary to dispose of eighteen slaves, myself among the number."

Sarah Jane Ford, daughter of Jesse Ford and Dulla Barr Prince, was married to Colonel Robert Alexander Hunter, a early pioneer of Rapides parish, a noted lawyer, at one tim State Senator, and a veteran of the Mexican War. She wa born in Kentucky on December 9, 1815, and died in Rapide parish, Louisiana, in October, 1852. She was married t Colonel Hunter on March 10, 1831, and left three sons and on daughter to reach adult life, several children dying in infanc

William Prince Ford, son of Jesse Ford and Dulla Barr Prince, came to Rapides parish, Louisiana, about 1816 when lad of thirteen years. His parents settled on Bayou Boeuf an there he grew to manhood and later became one of the pros perous citizens of that section of the parish. Near his hom lived that hardy pioneer, Robert Tanner, the sire of fiftee children. He became an intimate of the Tanner home and upo reaching the age of maturity married Martha, the eleventh o these numerous children, as has been previously stated. Thi lady died after twenty years of married life and William Princ Ford later married Mary Boaz Dawson, then the widow o William H. Cureton. There was no issue from this secon marriage. Mrs. Cureton had two grown daughters at the tim of her marriage to Mr. Ford:—Martha Rachel Cureton wh married Charles Lewellen Johnson, and Margaret Dawso Cureton who married Captain George Benoist Marshall.

William Prince Ford was probably more noted for his re ligious activities than anything else he did. After his marriag he lived on Spring Creek in Rapides parish and in addition t his farming and the operation of a saw mill, dedicated much o his time to the work of the Baptist church. He later objecte to some of its tenets and after withdrawing his membershi became one of the founders of the "Campbellite Church" i Cheneyville. From a "History of the Baptists of Louisiana,' by Rev. William E. Paxton, we learn the following of him:—

W. P. Ford was born in Henry county, Kentucky, Januar 5, 1803. He was a brother of the late Rev. J. Frankli Ford, formerly President of Minden Female College, a Presbyterian minister of distinction. Elder W. P. For is mentioned by Benedict in his History of the Baptists a one of the efficient ministers of the Louisiana Associaton He was baptized by Elder George A. Irion at Cotile, i

Rapides parish, in the year 1829. The year following he moved to the neighborhood of Cheneyville and became a member of the Baptist Church there. In 1835 he removed to the neighborhood of Spring Hill, and in 1841, in company with 14 others, was constituted into a church by that name. Here in 1844, at the request of the church he was ordained to the Gospel ministry by Elder B. C. Robert, Thomas Rand and A. J. Spencer.

About 1841 a difficulty grew up in the Cheneyville church in reference to the article of Faith, one of which was a declaration of belief in the eternal and unconditional election of a definite number of the human family to grace and glory, from which a number of the recently-added members dissented. They made several unsuccessful attempts to modify the article, but the older members, who, however, were in the majority, were unyielding. and required an assent as unconditional as the doctrine itself. Just at this juncture a preacher of the "Current Reformation", by the name of McCall, made his appearance in the place and commenced preaching. At length, in 1842, a large number of the Cheneyville church, finding the old members unyielding in their adhesion to the Articles of Faith, withdrew and constituted a Campbellite church. In 1845 Mr. Ford was charged: 1st, with having administered the Lord's Supper to the Campbellite church at Cheneyville; 2nd, with having ordained elders in said church; 3rd, with having thus given countenance to the schism in the Cheneyville Baptist Church. Upon the investigation of these charges he was expelled from the Springhill church, March 16, 1845. He then united with the Reformers, in which connection he continued until his death, which occurred August 23, 1866, though for many years he had ceased to preach. His son, B. J. Ford* in a letter to me dated May 10, 1869, says:—"My father was never reconciled to the Baptist Church, as a church; but during his last years there was a good feeling between him and the members of the Baptist churches in that section."

An item in the LOUISIANA DEMOCRAT (an Alexandria newspaper) of Wednesday, September 5, 1866, verifies the date of death of Mr. Ford as given by Rev. Paxton in the quotation above. It reads as follows:—

DIED:—At his residence on Bayou Boeuf, Rapides parish, Louisiana, on the 23rd of August, William P. Ford,

---

* This should be *J. R. Ford* instead of B. J. Ford.

in the 64th year of his age, and for the last 50 years a resident of this parish.

William Prince Ford and his first wife, Martha P. Tanner, had four children to reach maturity. They were:—

       1.—Jesse Robert Ford, Sr.
       2.—Samuel Ford.
       3.—Mary Louise Ford.
       4.—Walter Prince Ford.

1.—Jesse Robert Ford, Sr., was born near Cheneyville, Louisiana, in 1829, and died there in 1880. He married Lida Calaway (or Calloway) who was a native of Waycross, Georgia. They had two children:—

       i.—Margaret Ford.
       ii.—Jesse Robert Ford, Jr.

i.—Margaret Ford was living near Richmond, Virginia, a few years ago. We have been unable to obtain any very definite information about her.

ii.—Jesse Robert Ford, Jr., was born near Cheneyville, Louisiana, about 1856. He married Desirée Pearce, daughter of James Lemuel Pearce and Sarah Goodwin Chambers. Mr. Ford lived in Alexandria, Louisiana, for many years and died at his home there when past middle life from pneumonia. His wife and four children survived him. (See Part Four).

2.—Samuel Ford never married and died in Louisville, Kentucky, in 1870.

3.—Mary Louise Ford was born near Cheneyville, Louisiana, in 1839, and died in 1919. She was married to Milton M. Calaway (or Calloway), a brother of Lida Calaway who was the wife of her brother, Jesse Robert Ford, Sr. According to the best information obtainable they had many children. It is said that eleven of them died in early infancy and four reached maturity. Of the latter, two were killed in the great San Francisco earthquake. One son, Edwin H. Calaway, was living in Riverton, Wyoming, a few years ago, and another, Shivers Calaway, when last heard from was a resident of Roswell, New Mexico.

4.—Walter Prince Ford, youngest child of William Prince Ford and his first wife, Martha P. Tanner, was born near Cheneyville, Rapides parish, Louisiana, on February 24, 1848, and died at his home there on April 24, 1916. He was familiarly known to his family and friends as "Wat Ford." He married on December 5, 1872, Sarah Tuzette Cook, a daughter of James Cook and Mary Eliza Robert. Mr. Ford and his wife were second cousins. Her mother (Mary Eliza Robert)was a daughter of Leonidas Alonzo Robert and his first wife, Tuzette Eliza Pearce, and a grand-daughter of Joseph Robert and Mary Hyrne Jaudon. James Cook, her father, was an only son of Wilson Cook and Providence Tuzette Tanner. A recent letter from a member of the family refers to Sarah Tuzette Cook as being of St. Mary's parish, Louisiana.

It is not unlikely that her parents lived there at one time and that she was born there, but the compiler of these notes has the impression that her parents died when she was quite young and that she and her sister were reared in the home of their grandfather, Leonidas Alonzo Robert. It is quite certain that she married from her grandfather's home, as is verified by the following item from the LOUISIANA DEMOCRAT of Wednesday, January 10, 1872:—

MARRIED:—On the 5th of December at the residence of L. A. Robert, Bayou des Glaises, Louisiana, by the Rev. E. K. Branch, Mr. Walter P. Ford to Miss S. Tuzette Cook.

Four children were born of this marriage:—

  i.—William Henry Ford.
  ii.—Mary Ford.
  iii.—Jennie Ford.
  iv.—Kate Ford.

i.—William Henry Ford, better known to his friends as "Harry," was born near Cheneyville, Rapides parish, Louisiana, on October 19, 1873, and died April 12, 1920. "Harry" was prominent and well liked in his community and a successful farmer. He married at Washington, Louisiana, on December 15, 1898, Mary Crawford, daughter of James Willoughby Crawford and Adelaide Lavinia LaNoue. She was born at Cheneyville, Louisiana, on October 16, 1873, and is living there at this date (1944). They had six children, five of whom reached maturity as follows:

    a.—Walter Prince Ford, II.
    b.—Adele LaNoue Ford.
    c.—William Henry Ford, Jr.
    d.—Charles Crawford Ford.
    e.—Thomas Gibbes Morgan Ford.

a.—Walter Prince Ford, II, was born September 4, 1899, and died at Hotel Dieu in New Orleans on January 14, 1919.

b.—Adele LaNoue Ford was born August 17, 1902, and is married at this time. She resides in Baton Rouge, Louisiana, and holds a responsible position in the Fidelity Bank and Trust Company.

c.—William Henry Ford, Jr., was born November 17, 1904. He married Lottie Linda Ganson at Cheneyville, Louisiana, on November 30, 1926, and several years later they were divorced. They had no children. On October 8, 1939, he married Edith Victoria Reeves, daughter of John Reeves and Ida Mabel Singley. She was born at Long Leaf, Rapides parish, Louisiana, on May 19, 1922. They have two children:—William Henry Ford, III, born in Lecompte, Louisiana, on Saturday, September 7, 1940, and Rosa Mary Ford, born in Bunkie, Louisiana, on Tuesday, February 17, 1942.

d.—Charles Crawford Ford was born April 27, 1907, and married Annie Lois Bridwell at Cheneyville, Louisiana, on March 27, 1932. They have one child, Charles William Ford, born at Bunkie, Louisiana, on September 3, 1934.

e.—Thomas Gibbes Morgan Ford was born June 19, 1909, and married Mabel Claire Joyner at Boyce, Louisiana, on August 22, 1929. She was a daughter of Mr. and Mrs. Andrew Joyner of that place. Five children have been born of this marriage:—Morgan Dunnam Ford, born September 10, 1930; Walter Prince Ford, III, born September 24, 1933, and died November 2, 1937; William Marcus Ford, born May 6, 1937; Frances Elize Ford, born July 20, 1939; Mary Lynelle Ford, born Sunday, November 28, 1943.

ii.—Mary Ford was married to Ambrose Miller, son of Isaac C. Miller of Alexandria, Louisiana. They had one child, Bessie, who married a Mr. Thompson.

iii.—Jennie Ford has never married and for many years has been a teacher in the public schools of Louisiana.

iv.—Kate Ford was married to Charles Louis Crawford, son of James Willoughby Crawford and Adelaide Lavinia LaNoue. Mr. Crawford died on November 21, 1927, leaving a widow and four children:—

a.—Charles Louis Crawford, Jr.
b.—Kathleen LaNoue Crawford.
c.—Louise Ford Crawford.
d.—Walter James Crawford.

a.—Charles Louis Crawford, Jr., was born July 3, 1908, and married Mildred Coiron Avegno on June 2, 1937. They have one child, Charles Louis Crawford, III, born February 25, 1938.

b.—Kathleen LeNoue Crawford was born October 21, 1910, and was married on October 5, 1936, to Esmond A. Grosz. They have one child, Edmond A. Grosz, Jr., born June 29, 1937.

c.—Louise Ford Crawford was born November 5, 1911, and is unmarried at this time.

d.—Walter James Crawford was born March 29, 1914, and married Sarah Pipes in 1941.

L.

PAUL JABEZ TANNER

Paul Jabez Tanner, twelfth child of Robert Tanner and Providence Robert, was born near Woodville, Wilkinson county, Mississippi, on April 22, 1810, and died at his home on Bayou Boeuf, near Cheneyville, Rapides parish, Louisiana, on December 26, 1863. Mr. Tanner was one of the prominent and outstanding men of the Bayou Boeuf country in the early days of the development of that section of Rapides. Besides being very wealthy he is said to have been a very generous, kind and humane man, and his elegant brick mansion (yet standing) was the center of a widespread hospitality. He was possessed of strong religious convictions and was one of the charter members of the First Christian Church of Cheneyville. He was noted for his generous contributions toward the support of his church. He was a leading character in the great

schism which occurred in the Beulah Baptist Church at Cheneyville in the early forties, and which caused more commotion
in that community than was ever known there before or since.
Most of the members of Beulah Church consisted of Tanners,
Roberts, and their connections, and the disagreement which
arose, as in all family affairs, became very bitter, even lasting
through two generations. Mr. Tanner, in 1845, wrote and
published an article entitled, AN ACCOUNT OF THE RISE
AND PROGRESS OF THE STATE OF AFFAIRS IN THE
RELIGIOUS WORLD AT CHENEYVILLE. It was rather a
lengthy article but is of such importance that we will here
insert it in full:—

> My father (Robert Tanner) was one of the first set-
> lers on Bayou Boeuf in 1813. In 1816 there was a Baptist
> church formed at this place (Cheneyville) of a few mem-
> bers. Various was its state and condition to the year
> 1841. The church was formed on a creed or articles of
> faith which have ever been a source of contention and bad
> feelings.

> About the year 1828 there was a preacher employed
> to preach and take charge of the church, by name of
> George A. Irion, who contended against the creed, and it
> was after a hard struggle and much contention voted to
> "lie on the shelf," an expression meaning that it was to
> have no weight or authority in the church.

> Some years after this, said Irion moved away; the
> church dwindled to a name. In 1834 the Home Mission-
> ary Society sent out James B. Smith, who produced some
> excitement and a number were added to the church. He
> preached nearly two years, and left, and a man by the
> name of Seiz was employed by the *neighborhood* to preach,
> under whose labors the church began to decline. After a
> year or two he left, and there was no one to take charge
> of the flock, which numbered at this time about 60 mem-
> bers. The church was for three or four years from this
> time without any stated minister or preaching. The in-
> tervals between preaching were of long duration; for it
> is well known that among Baptists, unless there is a
> preacher, there is no meeting.

> We were supplied occasionally by our Methodist
> friends until the year 1841, when an elderly gentleman,
> P. W. Robert by name, was written for by a member of
> the Methodist church to come and baptize him; and when

he came the situation of the church (if church it could be called, for it had only name to live) was truly lamentable. It had dwindled to a name, and those who claimed to be members were entirely engrossed with the world. There was but one house in which famliy worship was maintained. Elder P. W. Robert was truly a man of God. He commenced lecturing publicly and privately in a manner that was entirely new to this place, for, in preaching, he held up Christ in front of himself. He read the Word of the Lord and caused the people to understand the meaning thereof. In a very short time there was a considerable stir amongst the people. Persons who had not been on friendly terms for years were induced to become reconciled. To be concise, he preached about a year, and baptized in this region about four hundred persons.

The first Lord's Day in August, 1841, there were forty-three persons baptized at Cheneyville, among whom was the writer of this. All things at thi time seemed to be going well. There was a call for the association to be revived (for it had failed to meet for several years). The meeting was held at Hickory Flat, on the third Friday in October, 1841. To this association were several young members sent as delegates from the church at Cheneyville. I was at the association, but not a delegate. On the morning of the meeting of the association, we, then and there for the first time, saw the articles of Faith; and oh! such a faith! Several were astonished when they heard them read!

I wish here to be somewhat particular, as I consider this the commencement of the present state of affairs. I was reading the articles to a company of some fifteen persons, when I read the Fourth Article, which reads: "We believe in the eternal unconditional election of a definite number of the human family to grace and glory." A young preacher by the name of A. J. Spencer stopped me and requested me to read it again. I did so, when he said: "If that be true I have no further use for the Bible"; to which remark several agreed. This is, in truth, the beginning of all the strife and discord that has ensued. The association went forward with the business. There were several new churches added. The Spring Hill church came near being rejected on account of its having received a member, who had been baptized by a Pedobaptist minister. The Bayou Rouge church was not readily received because it had not inserted in its creed the doctrines. The association over, we returned home; some of us with the determination to have the creed altered.

On our return to Cheneyville we there found a preacher named McCall. He was requested to preach. He did so to a large assembly. His subject was spiritual influence. Whilst he was preaching it appeared to me the whole congregation were delighted. I judged from the countenances of those I saw. P. W. Robert appeared to be much pleased. As soon as McCall had finished, Elder B. C. Robert arose and complained of being unwell. He then went on to say that if what he had just heard was the truth, he had been preaching error for twenty years, and sat down without appointing a time to teach us the right way. On which P. W. Robert arose and said what he had heard was the truth. He then went on and preached a severe sermon against the old way of doing business. Now the campaign may be said to be fairly opened. There were a number of persons present, who wished to be baptized, but the church was declared to be out of order, and they were not baptized. P. W. Robert and McCall were denounced as Campbellites, and that, too, by individuals who had previously compared the preaching of P. W. Robert to that of the Apostle Paul. Affairs were now in a very bad way. Parties began to arise in the church. At the next meeting of the church a call was made to read the articles of Faith, of the church, and here we can see the state in which the church had been; for it was forgotten that they had been laid on the shelf. The book however, was produced and the articles read. Many were astonished, saying the Baptists had no creed but the Bible. There were strong objections made to several parts of it. A move was made for amendment. The old members and their party put it off from time to time, for more than a year, the state of things, in the meantime, growing no better, each side denouncing the other. "Campbellites," "factionists," etc., were applied to one, and "Hardshells" to the other.

At this time I do not suppose there was an individual in the neighborhood who knew Mr. Campbell or the tenets he taught. For my part I did not, never having read a page of his writings in my life. I did not know in what century he lived, but being denounced as a Campbellite I inquired what Mr. Campbell taught, and was told that baptism was all he taught for salvation; for instance, catch a man, pull him into the water, duck him and he would be saved. I was induced to write for some periodicals in order to find out whether I was a Campbellite or not, and lo! such as they call Campbellites I am, for any one who has no creed but what is contained in the

Bible is a Campbellite. Well, be it so. But at this time I was for a creed. The party with which I acted was willing to have a moderate creed, one that was according to the Bible.

The next thing which widened the breach was the calling of A. J. Spencer to ordination. He was one who opposed the creed. The vote of the church stood 26 in favor and 7 opposed. Many did not vote, myself one. Spencer was told if he would sign the creed he would be ordained; if not, he could not. One law of the church is that the majority shall rule, in all cases except touching fellowship, when the vote shall be unanimous. This was not a case of fellowship, yet Spencer was not ordained. Sometime after he changed his doctrine. This materially added to the discontent, one party striving for liberty, the other opposing it.

Things went on this way until October, when the meeting of the association being at hand, each party desired to send delegates holding their views; and were taking measures to effect that object, when it was remarked by the preacher (Spencer) that it would be a stigma upon the church for them to send the young members as delegates to the Association. On hearing this I determined to use my influence with the young members not to offer their services nor to vote. I so far succeeded that none of them were elected. We now considered ourselves as having "no part in David." We clearly saw that unless peace was speedily restored there would be a division. I, at that time, determined to withdraw, but, by persuasion of W. P. Ford, was induced to hold on until after the association, thinking there might be something done during the meeting which would produce peace. But when the association convened the breach was widened, if possible, for instead of preaching Christ and Him crucified it was doctrine and doctrine and such like; and that handled so poorly that nothing was effected. The meeting continued six days. Seven preachers were present, and obtained one convert, who had been previously converted by P. W. Robert. Suffice it to say, the association over and no reconciliation, we determined to make one more effort for liberty of conscience and peace; for I can safely say that there was not an individual who wished to be separated from the Baptists. Our friends, our relations and our interest was with them. But we could not remain without liberty of conscience. The confession begins: "We who have been baptized upon a profession of faith and repentance, promise by divine assistance to believe, profess, stand by and defend the following doctrines or articles of faith." Now we could not believe them, therefore, we could not defend them. We believed they were contrary to the Bible. We had to lie to God or man, or withdraw. But before we would do it we appointed a meeting at my house, and several of the opposite side were invited to attend, one of which was the deacon Henry Jackson. He was requested to take the chair and open the meeting with prayer. He did so. After a discussion in which there was nothing affected, a proposition was made that one side should draw up a confession or articles of faith and the other to have the privilege of erasing what they disapproved. It was rejected.

We afterwards held another meeting, at which there was but one side represented, and drew up articles that were satisfactory to us; and pledged ourselves to use our influence to have them adopted at the next meeting in lieu of the old ones. Each was to see his respective friends in the meantime. Many said they would not oppose nor favor it. The opposers were the oldest members of the church. We came to the conclusion that if it was forced on them they would withdraw, and if any did withdraw it ought to be those who came into the church last. I spoke to them and told them they would be the cause of a division in the church; to which they replied they could not help it. I then said to one of them I was in hopes he would not, but did hope that all who could not believe the articles or confession of faith would leave, that they might have peace, which remark was made in the meeting of the church. I asked for a letter of dismission for myself and wife. J. B. Robert asked for one also. We were all refused letters, because it was known we would not join a Baptist church. The church was in a strait. They would not give us letters of dismission and they could not exclude us, for there was not and never had been any charge of immoral conduct, or holding heretical views, against us. I then observed to them that they had better erase our names, which they did. It is true there was much said which it would do no good to record.

After our withdrawal, we still continued to attend their meetings, there being no church in the neighborhood in which we were willing to take membership. This continued until the month of May following, when we were organized into a church of eight members, by G. W. H. Smith, an evangelist. Since which time we have done as well as we could, though bad enough. The church now numbers about eighty members, has one bishop, two deacons and an evangelist. Our manner of conducting our meeting is to assemble every Lord's Day for the purpose of prayer, praise, exhortation, breaking of bread and fellowship. Now, fellow citizens, you have a concise and fair statement of the rise and progress of the present state of things. If there has been aught dictated in malice I am not aware of it. If I have in writing shown any partiality, or made any false statement, I am not sensible of it. That there has been a great deal of personal defamation on both sides is to be deplored; but there is a time when forebearance ceases to be a virtue. That time is now. I have, therefore, given this short history, that all may read and judge for themselves. I pray God all may act in that manner that when we shall have to give our account at the bar of God we may do it with joy and not with grief.

JABEZ TANNER.

Paul Jabez Tanner married on June 6, 1833, his first cousin, Esther Providence Bettison, daughter of David Bettison and Sarah Catharine Robert. She was born near Woodville, Wilkinson county, Mississippi, on September 30, 1815, and died near Cheneyville, Rapides parish, Louisiana on March 7, 1871. THE LOUISIANA GAZETTE (of Alexandria, Louisiana) of June, 1833, verifies the date of the above marriage by the following item:—

> On the 6th inst., the following marriage ceremony was performed by the Rev. A. C. Kilpatrick: Mr Jabez Tanner of Bayou Boeuf to Miss Esther P. Bettison of the same place.

Mr. and Mrs. Tanner were buried in the old Christian graveyard at Cheneyville. They were the parents of thirteen children:—

1.—Un-named baby, born ————————, 1834.
2.—Fredonia Tanner, born May 23, 1835.
3.—Erskine Tanner, born ————————, 1837.
4.—Linn Tanner, born December 31, 1838.
5.—Henry Tanner, born February 6, 1842.
6.—Irene Ethel Tanner, born February 13, 1844.
7.—Albert Tanner, born April 12, 1846.
8.—Graham Tanner, born April 4, 1848.
9.—Sidney Tanner, born April 22, 1850.
10.—Milton Tanner, born September 13, 1852.

11.—Cecil Tanner, born October 24, 1854.
12.—Lorell Tanner, born November 26, 1856.
13.—Estelle Tanner, born February 11, 1859.

Four of these children died in infancy. The first at birth; Erskine, the third, during the same year he was born; Graham, the eighth, died September 15, 1850; Estelle, the thirteenth, died September 10, 1863, at the age of four years.

2.—Fredonia Tanner, second child of Paul Jabez Tanner and Esther Providence Bettison, was born near Cheneyville, Rapides parish, Louisiana, and was married there on September 29, 1858, to Robert Hart who was born on Spring Creek, near Elmer, in Rapides parish, Louisiana, on June 25, 1833. He was a son of Jesse Hart of Savannah, Georgia, and Nancy Holloway of Mississippi. He came to Cheneyville in 1856 and there met his wife. He was a Confederate soldier and served in Company I, Consolidated Crescent Regiment, under Captain William J. Calvit of Rapides parish. Mr. and Mrs. Hart lived near Rosa, in St. Landry parish, Louisiana, and both died there, he on Monday, September 12, 1910, and she on October 16, 1914. They had six children:—

i.—Henry Hart.
ii.—Calvit Hart.
iii.—Rena Jennie Hart.
iv.—Nettie Hart.
v.—Jesse R. Hart.
vi.—Edward S. Hart.

i.—Henry Hart and ii.—Calvit Hart both died in infancy.

iii.—Rena Jennie Hart was married to John Heath of St. Landry parish, Louisiana. They had two children, Bessie and Harry Heath. John Heath was shot and killed in a personal difficulty with Charlton Wright Havard of Big Cane, Louisiana. After his death Rena Jennie Hart married Rev. Joseph Cole, a Christian minister, and lived for many years in Baton Rouge. It is our impression that she had one son by her second marriage. Her daughter, Bessie Heath, was married to Levi Kelly and lives in Bunkie, Louisiana. She has two daughters, one of whom, Lilla Kelly, was married about 1936 to Crawford H. Ellis, President of the United Fruit Company. She was the second wife of Mr. Ellis. Their marriage has quite a bit of romance surrounding it. Miss Kelly was attending the Louisiana State University working on her master's degree and needed some material about tropical countries in the Caribbean area for her thesis. She interviewed Mr. Ellis for that purpose and it was then that their courtship began.

iv.—Nettie Hart was married to Thomas Clanton Foote of St. Landry parish, Louisiana. They have five children:— Carol, Vivian, William, Gordon, and Rena Foote. We regret that we have been able to get so little information about these children. We only know that Vivian Foote was married to Milton D. Bell and has two sons. The elder of these, Milton D. Bell, Jr., was educated at the Louisiana State University and is now in the U. S. Army.

v.—Jesse R. Hart married Eva DeJean of St. Landry parish. Mr. Hart died some years ago leaving one son.

vi.—Edward S. Hart married Lilly Dumartrait who was a half niece of Eva DeJaen. They lived at Eunice, Louisiana, where Mr. Hart died on Sunday, November 30, 1941, leaving two daughters.

4.—Linn Tanner, fourth child of Paul Jabez Tanner and Esther Providence Bettison, was born near Cheneyville, Rapides parish, Louisiana. He married Fannie P. Pollard on August 11, 1859, at Fayetteville, Arkansas. She was born January 30, 1840, and was a daughter of Dr. Wade Hampton Pollard and Emily Francis. Dr. Pollard was a native of Virginia where he was born September 13, 1812. He married Emily Francis and emigrated some time later to Arkansas, locating in Fayetteville where he died November 24, 1893. His wife was born November 15, 1815, and died January 22, 1889. Dr. Pollard was a son of William Pollard who was born in Fredericksburg, Virginia, in 1761, and Frances Hampton who was born in Winchester, Virginia.

Linn Tanner (whether or not he was named for his uncle, Robert Linn Tanner, we are uncertain—he always signed his name just *Linn Tanner*) was widely and favorably known throughout the South. He was a popular contributor to several well known farm and literary journals, and to the newspapers of Louisiana. Possessed of an unusually bright mind which had been cultivated by a splendid education, he was a most entertaining writer of both verse and prose. He served in the Confederate Army as a private soldier during the Civil War, and later took an active part in freeing his country from the evil of "Carpet-bag" rule during the trying period of so called "reconstruction." The following paragraph from a tribute to his memory by a friend which was published in one of the local papers will not be amiss here:—

> In all the relations of life he was a true and devoted Christian man, who never swerved from what he conceived to be the path of duty, nor neglected the calls of mercy. For many years, till age and disease prevented his attendance, his seat in the house of God was never vacant when he was able to fill it. His own house was the genial home of the visiting preacher, and his Christian hospitality was unsurpassed. He always had the firmness of his convictions of truth and duty, and no one was ever left in doubt as to where he stood on all social, religious and political questions.

Linn Tanner died at his home in Cheneyville, Louisiana, on July 21, 1910, and his good wife died there on July 14, 1916. They had eleven children, of whom the following three died in early childhood:—Jack Tanner died June 11, 1884; Archie Tanner died September 7, 1884; Blanche Tanner died July 14, 1891. The following eight children lived to maturity:—

> i.—Wade Hampton Tanner, born August 30, 1860.
> ii.—George Jabez Tanner, born November 25, 1862.
> iii.—Harley Linn Tanner, born November 27, 1863.
> iv.—Lura Tanner, born June 4, 1866.
> v.—Desdemona Tanner, born September 25, 1870.
> vi.—Percy Tanner, born October 14, 1872.
> vii.—Early Tanner, born November 24, 1874.
> viii.—Ora Tanner, born March 8, 1882.

i.—Wade Hampton Tanner, eldest child of Linn Tanner and Fannie P. Pollard, was born near Cheneyville, Rapides parish, Louisiana, and married on December 2, 1891, Frances Ida Cook of Chatham, Virginia, where she was born April 17, 1870. He must have left his native State when quite a young man as a letter written by his father in 1898 mentions him as being a merchant in Fort Worth, Texas, and there he continued to reside until his death on February 24, 1940. He married his wife in Fort Worth and she is yet living there. They had two children:—

        a.—Anna Mae Tanner.
        b.—Wade Hampton Tanner, Jr.

      a.—Anna Mae Tanner was born in Fort Worth, Texas, on October 30, 1893, and was married in San Antonio, Texas, on May 3, 1919, to Captain Claude LeRoy Drennon, who was born May 21, 1894. Captain Drennon was prominent in the Officers Reserve Corps and held the rank of Lieutenant Colonel in it at the outbreak of World War II. He was soon called into active service and was holding the rank of a full colonel when his untimely death occurred on Sunday, December 20, 1942, from an abscess of the brain. He left one daughter, Frances Loraine Drennon, born November 5, 1920. Mrs. Drennon is now residing at her home, 1725 Fifth Avenue, Fort Worth, Texas.

      b.—Wade Hampton Tanner, Jr., was born in Fort Worth, Texas, on April 19, 1896. He married Mrs. Ruby Robinson and they have one child, Eleanor Ann Tanner. They reside in Cleburne, Texas.

      ii.—George Jabez Tanner, second child of Linn Tanner and Fannie P. Pollard, was born near Cheneyville, Rapides parish, Louisiana, and died March 15, 1928. His death occurred suddenly at 7:40 p. m. in an automobile about thirty miles south of Shreveport, Louisiana, while en route home from a visit to his brother in Fort Worth, Texas. He was buried in the old Christian church cemetery at Cheneyville. On October 7, 1898, he married Ella Elizabeth Grayson, daughter of Overton Grayson and Georgia Eubanks—the latter a native of Georgia. Mrs. Tanner was born at Columbia, Caldwell parish, Louisiana, on March 26, 1865, and is living at this time (1944). Four children were born of this marriage:—

        a.—Charlotte Tanner, born October 5, 1891.
        b.—Clifford Clyde Tanner, born March 3, 1893.
        c.—Linno Tanner, born June 12, 1896.
        d.—George Ray Tanner, born May 11, 1900.

      a.—Charlotte Tanner, better known as "Lottie," was married in September, 1915, to P. E. Harper. They reside in Pine Bluff, Arkansas, and had one child, George Jabez Tanner Harper, who died at the age of two years.

b.—Clifford Clyde Tanner married Eva Rae Caldwell, a native of north Louisiana. They reside in Cheneyville and have two children : —

> az.—Mary Elizabeth Tanner.
> bz.—James Douglas Tanner.

az.—Mary Elizabeth Tanner is unmarried at this time and has a position with the State government at Baton Rouge.

bz.—James Douglas Tanner married Carmen Williamson, daughter of Mr. and Mrs. S. D. Williamson of Hineston, Rapides parish, Louisiana. The ceremony was performed by the Rev. N. I. Terrell at the home of the bride's parents at Hineston, on Saturday, September 28, 1940, at 9 p. m. They now have a son, James Clyde Tanner, born Friday, October 16, 1942.

c.—Linno Tanner married Eva Sloan. They have one daughter, Maurice Aurelia Tanner, born September 9, 1920. This daughter was married in the First Christian Church of Alexandria, Louisiana, on Thursday evening, December 24, 1942, to Private Henry Travis Kimball, eldest son of Mr. and Mrs. H. T. Kimball of Pineville, Louisiana. Private Kimball is in the mechanical division of the Army Air Corps and is now stationed at Lake Charles, Louisiana.

d.—George Ray Tanner married Delia Cole. They have six children:— Georgie Ray, aged 22; Lurline, age 20; George Jabez, age 18; Kenneth Milton, age 16; Jennie Sue, age 13; Cherrie D., age 10. These ages were computed in 1944.

iii.—Harley Linn Tanner, third child of Linn Tanner and Fannie P. Pollard, was born near Cheneyville, Rapides parish, Louisiana, and died there on September 24, 1898, at the age of thirty-four. He married Lillie Mason and they had four children :—

> a.—Florence Tanner.
> b.—Rollie Tanner.
> c.—Clifton Tanner.
> d.—Harley Linn Tanner, Jr.

a.—Florence Tanner was married to Allie Poole. Both are now dead. We have no record of any descendants.

b.—and d.—Rollie Tanner and Harley Linn Tanner, Jr., went to Texas some years ago and we have no further record of them.

c.—Clifton Tanner married Edna Ruby Cannon, daughter of Clifton Cannon* and Annie L. Joffrion. They have a son, Clifton Cannon Tanner, who enlisted in the U. S. Army Air Corps in 1942. He was married in Homestead, Florida, on July 1, 1943, to Janet Henderson O'Connor. The following account of this marriage appeared in a local newspaper:—

> Miss Janet Henderson O'Connor of New York City and Corporal Clifton Cannon Tanner of Cheneyville, Louisiana, flight engineer at Homestead Field, Florida, were married July 1st, in the Homestead church of the Nazarine. The ceremony was performed by the Rev. Earl P. Scott, pastor of the church. The bride, a daughter of Mrs. Margaret O'Connor of New York, is a student of Columbia University. The bridegroom, son of Mr. and Mrs. Clifton Tanner of Cheneyville, was a student at Louisiana Tech when he enlisted a year ago.

iv.—Lura Tanner, fourth child of Linn Tanner and his wife, Fannie P. Pollard, was born near Cheneyville, Rapides parish, Louisiana, on June 4, 1866, and died on October 30, 1935, in Oakdale, Louisiana, at the home of her eldest daughter, Mrs. Blanchard Iles. She was married on February 8, 1887, to Joseph Morrison Rutledge who was born in Rapides parish, Louisiana, on January 4, 1862, and died at the Baptist Hospital in New Orleans on Sunday morning, October 27, 1940, at 6:50. He was buried in the old Christian church cemetery at Cheneyville, Louisiana, beside his wife. Mr. Rutledge was a son of George Walter Rutledge (born 1805) and Annie Jane McBride (born 1828), both natives of Camden county, North Carolina. Mr. Rutledge had a brother (Henry Rutledge) and a sister (Laura Rutledge), neither of whom left descendants. The sister is yet living (1944). Mr. Rutledge resided all of his life on his plantation near Cheneyville where he was most highly

---

* Clifton Cannon, prominent in Avoyelles and Rapides parishes, was born in the former May 24, 1856. Was sheriff there in 1888. His father, Col. Fenelon Cannon, born Nov. 18, 1825, in Trigg Co., Ky., married Mary Elizabeth Boots, daughter of Major John Boots of Roanoke, Va., and came to Avoyelles parish, La., as a young man, and was on the 1st Board of Supervisors of the La. Seminary (now State University). Had 4 sons:—Lester, Clifton, Courtney, and Fenelon, Jr. Clifton married Annie L. Joffrion, daughter of State Senator E. J. Joffrion, on Dec. 23, 1875. 5 daughters.

regarded for his irreproachable character. He took an active part in civic affairs and was eminently successful as a planter. Nine children were born of this marriage:—

> a.—Jewel Rutledge, born 1891.
> b.—Linnie Rutledge, born 1893.
> c.—Curtis Elree Rutledge, born 1895.
> d.—Vera Tanner Rutledge, born 1897.
> e.—Joe Wheeler Rutledge, born 1899.
> f.—Leota Rutledge, born 1902.
> g.—Haddock Ewell Rutledge, born 1904.
> h.—Louis Earl Rutledge, born 1908.
> i.—Doris Rutledge, born 1910.

a.—Jewel Rutledge, the eldest of these children, died in infancy.

b.—Linnie Rutledge was born near Cheneyville, Rapides parish, Louisiana, on June 6, 1893, and was married there on December 23, 1916, to Dr. Blanchard Iles, born in Calcasieu parish, Louisiana, December 20, 1891. Dr. Iles was a son of Franklin Pierce Iles and Mollie Rollins, and a grandson of Demcy Iles, Jr., and Martha Perkins. His father was a grandson of Demcy Iles Sr., born in South Carolina on February 11, 1796 and he was a son of William Iles who, it is said, served in the Revolutionary Army for seven years. Demcy Iles, Sr., came to Calcasieu parish, Louisiana, when a young man and there married Sarah Cherry on July 26, 1821. Dr. Blanchard Iles is a prominent citizen in Oakdale and is considered one of the outstanding dentists of central Louisiana. He served as mayor of his town for several years. He is also outstanding in another particular and if the reader is curious to know what it is he or she has only to ask the fish in the streams and the quail in the woods. Dr. and Mrs. Iles have three daughters:—

> az.—Dorothy Lou Iles, born January 10, 1918.
> bz.—Mildred Lee Iles, born November 20, 1919.
> cz.—Blanche Iles, born May 26, 1922.

az.—Dorothy Lou Iles graduated from the Louisiana State University in 1939, and was married at Oakdale, Louisiana, on March 23, 1940, to E. Coates Stuckey, son of E. Coates Stuckey and Hattie Irene Kilpatrick. He was born in West Monroe, Louisiana, on May 1, 1917, and graduated from the School of

Commerce at the Louisiana State University. He is now connected with the Department of Internal Revenue of Louisiana. They are residing in Alexandria at this time, and have two children:—Linnie Lou Stuckey, born at Oakdale, Louisiana, on Tuesday, December 9, 1941, and Blanchard Iles Stuckey, born at Oakdale, Louisiana, on Saturday, February 12, 1944.

bz.—Mildred Lee Iles was educated at the South Western Institute at Lafayette, Louisiana, and at the State Normal College, Natchitoches, Louisiana, and graduated from the latter institution in 1941. She was married at Oakdale, Louisiana, on Monday, April 13, 1942, at 8:30 p. m., at the First Baptist Church, to Corry Winston Oakes, son of Mr. and Mrs. Walter Oakes of Atlanta, Georgia. They resided in Atlanta until Mr. Oakes entered the military service of his country. There have been born of this marriage:—Corry Winston Oakes, Jr., born June 29, 1943, at Atlanta, and Judith Ann Oakes, born June 30, 1944, at Atlanta.

cz.—Blanches Iles, better known as "Sunny," is unmarried at this date, but *apparently* not for long. She was educated at the University of Texas and at Centenary College at Shreveport, Louisiana, graduating from the latter institution in 1943.

c.—Curtis Elree Rutledge is a prominent dentist of Bunkie, Louisiana. He married in 1921 Prudence Hewitt, daughter of Mr. and Mrs. Zachary Taylor Hewett of Long Leaf, Louisiana. Mrs. Hewett was a daughter of Dr. Edmond Ellison Smart and his wife, Harriett Neal. Dr. Smart was for many years a physician of outstanding prominence and a leading political factor in Vernon parish, Louisiana, which parish he represented in the state senate. Curtis Elree Rutledge and Prudence Hewett have two children:—

      az.—Curtis Elree Rutledge, Jr., born 1922.
      bz.—Lura Hope Rutledge, born 1923.

az.—Curtis Elree Rutledge, Jr., married December 9, 1944, Annie Laurie Johnson from Atlanta, Ga.

d.—Vera Tanner Rutledge was married in 1927 in Jacksonville, Florida, to George M. Fencannon, where they now reside. They have no children.

e.—Joe Wheeler Rutledge lives at Cheneyville, Louisiana, where he was born, and besides being extensively interested in

planting he has charge of the local rural mail delivery. He
married in 1919 Bertie Kees, a daughter of Mr. and Mrs. J.
Lafayette Kees of Pineville, Louisiana. They have four children:—

> az.—Joe Edwin Rutledge, born 1920.
> bz.—Ethlyn Rutledge, born 1922.
> cz.—Evelyn Beryl Rutledge, born 1922.
> dz.—Joy Rutledge, born 1933.

az.—Joe Edwin Rutledge received his degree in dental
surgery at Loyola University, New Orleans, in September,
1943, and immediately entered the Dental Corps of the U. S.
Army with the rank of lieutenant. He is presently stationed
at Salt Lake City, Utah.

cz.—Evelyn Beryl Rutledge was married June 22, 1944, at
the First Christian Church in Cheneyville, La., to J. W. Williamson, son of Mr. and Mrs. R. L. Williamson of Pineville,
Louisiana.

f.—Leota Rutledge was married in 1924 to Millard Lipscomb who was a veteran of World War I. They had one child,
Millard, born in 1928, in New Mexico. Mr. Lipscomb died in
1929 and on April 4, 1942, Leota Rutledge married C. N. Neely.
They reside at this time in California.

g.—Haddock Ewell Rutledge is a prominent and successful dentist and now resides in Pineville, Louisiana, where he
practices his profession. He married Mabel Clark in 1928 and
they have two girls:—

> az.—Ann Rutledge, born 1930.
> bz.—Lynn Rutledge, born 1933.

Mr. and Mrs. Rutledge were divorced in 1939 and he then
married Gertrude Cartwright. At present they have one son:—

cz.—Haddock Ewell Rutledge, Jr., born November 4, 1940.

h.—Louis Earl Rutledge resides in Cheneyville, Louisiana,
where he has the agency for the Sinclair Oil Company. He
married November 27, 1931, Sallie Gladys Murphey, daughter
of Edwin Charles Murphey and Minnie Vester Malone. Mr.
and Mrs. Rutledge are both descendants of Robert Tanner and
Providence Robert. They have a little daughter, Sallie Ann
Rutledge, born November 28, 1939.

i.—Doris Rutledge was married in Baton Rouge, Louisiana, on September 11, 1937, to Walter C. Knotts of Wisner, Louisiana, son of Mr. and Mrs. W. S. Knotts. They now reside in Wisner, Franklin parish, Louisiana, where Mr. Knotts is extensively engaged in planting. They have two children:—

    az.—Doris Lynn Knotts, born August 21, 1939.
    bz.—Nancy Rutledge Knotts, born September 22, 1943.

v.—Desdemona Tanner, fifth child of Linn Tanner and Fannie P. Pollard, was born near Cheneyville, Rapides parish, Louisiana. In the family circle she was usually called "Dessie." She was married to Dr. W. Henry Wooldridge of Fairfield, Texas. They have five children:—

    a.—Lucy Wooldridge.
    b.—Tanner Wooldridge.
    c.—Lura May Wooldridge.
    d.—Linn Wooldridge.
    e.—Frances Wooldridge.

The youngest of these, Frances, died in infancy.

a.—Lucy Wooldridge was married to Albert Miles of Fairfield, Texas, and has two children:—Preston and Gloria Miles.

b.—Tanner Wooldridge married but we have been unable to obtain the name of his wife. It is our understanding that he has two children.

c.—Lura May Woolridge was married to Arthur Brubaker of Houston, Texas, and has a son and daughter.

d.—Linn Wooldridge married a Miss McElvane and has children.

vi.—Percy Tanner, sixth child of Linn Tanner and Fannie P. Polard, was born near Cheneyville, Rapides parish, Louisiana. On September 13, 1900, while in a theater at Fort Worth, Texas, he was killed by the shooting of a wooden cannon ball from the stage. It was shot towards the audience and he was the only person struck by it. He was unmarried.

vii.—Early Tanner, seventh child of Linn Tanner and Fannie P. Pollard, was born near Cheneyville, Rapides parish, Louisiana, married in April, 1908, Grace Miles of Bunkie,

Louisiana, and died at Cheneyville on Saturday, April 7, 1945. They had two daughters:—

    a.—Grace Elise Tanner.
    b.—Sarah Frances Tanner.

    a.—Grace Elise Tanner was married on Saturday, December 6, 1941, to Stephen Rushing Jackson, Jr., son of Stephen Rushing Jackson and Alice Robert. She is his second wife.

    b.—Sarah Frances Tanner was married November 19, 1938, to Cyrus B. Burley of Lake Charles, Louisiana. They are now residing in New Iberia, Louisiana, and have two daughters:— Helen Elise Burley, born in Houma, Louisiana, December 25, 1939, and Susan Adair Burley, born in New Iberia, Louisiana, October 8, 1942.

    viii.—Ora Tanner, youngest child of Linn Tanner and Fannie P. Pollard, was born near Cheneyville, Rapides parish, Louisiana. She was married August 22, 1907, at the home of her brother-in-law, Dr. W. Henry Wooldridge, in Fairfield, Texas, to Louis D. Martin. They resided for many years at Eola, Avoyelles parish, Louisiana, where Mr. Martin died on Saturday, March 19, 1938. He was born in Opelousas, Louisiana, on August 7, 1877. They had four children:—

    a.—Alice Ray Martin, born November 29, 1908.
    b.—Louise Martin, born January 15, 1910.
    c.—Louis D. Martin, Jr., born July 29, 1912.
    d.—Miller Lee Martin, born September 27, 1916.

    a.—Alice Ray Martin lived for many years in Riverdale, Maryland, where she taught in the high school. She was married August 26, 1942, to Nelson Forsyth Caldwell who was born in Alton, Illinois, on October 11, 1899. They now reside at 2640 Victory Parkway, Cincinnati, Ohio, and have a son, Michel Desmarais Caldwell, born in Washington, D. C., June 2, 1943.

    b.—Louise Martin was married in July, 1928, to Daniel Berton Townsend. They have two children:—Daniel Berton Townsend, Jr., born June 8, 1929, and Doris Ray Townsend, born October 3, 1935.

    c.—Louis D. Martin, Jr., is in the employ of the Shell Oil Company in Washington, D. C. He is unmarried.

d.—Miller Lee Martin married on September 27, 1937, Mary Gorman of Rockville, Maryland. He is in the employ of the government in Washington and attends night school at George Washington University in that city.

5.—Henry Tanner (sometimes recorded as *Henry E. Tanner*), fifth child of Paul Jabez Tanner and Esther Providence Bettison, was born near Cheneyville, Rapides parish, Louisiana, on February 6, 1842. He volunteered in Company B, Ninth Louisiana Infantry and served in Virginia throughout the Civil War in a most creditable and gallant manner. After the close of the war he returned home and lived for a while at Evergreen, Louisiana, where he married on December 22, 1868, Mary E. Johnson, widow of Henry Johns, who was born in 1841 and died in 1899. Later he returned to the Cheneyville neighborhood and acquired his father's old homestead where he resided until his death at an advanced age on September 14, 1927. He was the last surviving member of Company B, Ninth Louisiana Infantry. The beautiful old home, known as "Magnolia," is now owned by his niece, Mrs. Robert Harris. Mr. and Mrs. Tanner had four children, three of whom died when quite small. Only one reached maturity, Bennie Tanner, and he died at the age of twenty-one, unmarried. The following account of his death appeared in a local newspaper at the time:—

DIED:—At Jackson, Louisiana, May 15, 1891, Bennie E. Tanner, son of Mr. Henry E. Tanner and Mrs. Mary E. Tanner, of Cheneyville, Rapides parish, Louisiana. The deceased was born at Evergreen, Avoyelles parish, Louisiana, and has been for nearly two years finishing his education at the Centenary College at Jackson, where he was taken with typhoid malaria, which after a lingering illness of thirteen days caused his death, age twenty-one years, four months. His remains, in charge of his mother and father, were brought by rail to Cheneyville, May 16th, from which place they were escorted to the Christian Church cemetery by one of the largest processions we have ever witnessed at this place.

6.—Irene Ethel Tanner, sixth child of Paul Jabez Tanner and Esther Providence Bettison, was born near Cheneyville, Rapides parish, Louisiana, on February 13, 1844, and died there on May 13, 1928. She was married on March 7, 1871, to Uriah Haden Johns of Shelbyville, Kentucky, where he was born April 11, 1844. He moved to Rapides parish, Louisiana, and became an outstanding citizen and prominent planter in the Cheneyville neighborhood. He died there on Tuesday, January 22, 1918. They had no children. The family Bible of Mrs. Johns has been of great assistance in compiling this history of the Tanner family. This good lady was much interested in her people and had a record of them in her Bible for several generations. This valuable old book is now the property of her great niece, Mrs. Blanchard Iles of Oakdale, Louisiana, who kindly loaned it to the compiler.

7.—Albert Tanner, seventh child of Paul Jabez Tanner and Esther Providence Bettison, died on January 26, 1871, at the age of twenty-five. He was unmarried as far as we can ascertain.

9.—Sidney Tanner, ninth child of Paul Jabez Tanner and Esther Providence Bettison, was born near Cheneyville, Rapides parish, Louisiana, an April 22, 1850. He was a successful planter and one of the substantial citizens of the Bayou Boeuf country. He died at his home there on October 7, 1904. He married on December 17, 1878, Sarah Annie Pearce, born August 21, 1856, and died August 1, 1924. She was a daughter of Stephen Samuel Pearce, and Mary Ellen Bennett, and a grand-daughter of Stephen Samuel Pearce, and his second wife, Anne Grimball (Tanner) Brown. Her grandmother (Anne Grimball Tanner) and her husbad's father (Paul Jabez Taner) were sister and brother, therefore she and her husband were second cousins. They had seven children, three of whom died very young. Those reaching maturity were:—

> i.—Mary Esther Tanner.
> ii.—Sidney Otis Tanner.
> iii.—Annie Laurie Tanner.
> iv.—Pauline Tanner.

i.—Mary Esther Tanner was married to William Tillery on July 7, 1907. They now reside in Cheneyville and have one daughter:—

> a.—Gayle Tillery, born January 17, 1911.

a.—Gayle Tillery was married to Coleman Beasley on December 24, 1938. They have one daughter, Mary Linn Beasley, born June 15, 1940.

ii.—Sidney Otis Tanner, only son of Sidney Tanner and Sarah Annie Pearce, was born near Cheneyville, Rapides parish, Louisiana, on June 22, 1885. He still resides there and is engaged in planting. He married Lois Bazemore on July 27, 1907, who was born May 4, 1888, and was a daughter of Thomas Evans Bazemore and Nora Daniel. Two children were born of this marriage:—

a.—Tom Otis Tanner, born December 31, 1917
b.—Sidney Norman Tanner, born January 9, 1920.

a.—Tom Otis Tanner finished his technical education at the Hemphill Diesel Engineering School of Memphis, Tennessee, and is now employed by the Louisiana Ice and Electric Company in Bunkie, Louisiana. He married on April 19, 1942, Margaret Williamson of Fort Worth, Texas.

b.—Sidney Norman Tanner is unmarried at this time.

iii.—Annie Laurie Tanner was married to Robert Harris who is a native of one of the eastern States. Mr. Harris is a successful planter and is highly respected in his community. They reside below Cheneyville in the old Paul Jabez Tanner home on "Magnolia," which they own, one of the show places on Bayou Boeuf. They have no children.

iv.—Pauline Tanner was married to a Mr. Williams. They had no children and are now divorced.

10.—Milton Tanner, tenth child of Paul Jabez Tanner and Esther Providence Bettison, was born near Cheneyville, Rapides parish, Louisiana, on September 13, 1852, and died in New Orleans on June 30, 1915. He never married.

1.—Cecil Tanner, eleventh child of Paul Jabez Tanner and Esther Providence Bettison, was born near Cheneyville, Rapides parish, Louisiana, on October 24, 1854, and died there on May 8, 1906, unmarried.

12.—Lorell Tanner, twelfth child of Paul Jabez Tanner and Esther Providence Bettison, was born near Cheneyville, Rapides parish, Louisiana, on November 26, 1856, and died there on June 18, 1913. He married Dora Reynolds of New Orleans on October 6, 1880. They had two daughters:—

    i.—Maude Tanner.
    ii.—Sidney Tanner.

i.—Maude Tanner was married to Owen Heath of St Landry parish, La., and had two sons:—Eugene Heath who died when six months old, and Marion Day Heath who married Elizabeth Brown of Lake City, Florida. After the death of Owen Heath, Maude Tanner married Harry Livingston Rell of New Orleans. They have one child, Maude, who married John Sanders of Natchitoches, La. They live in Jackson, Miss., and have a son, John Sanders, Jr.

ii.—Sidney Tanner was married to Clarence Louis Dupre of New Orleans, where they now reside. They have a son, Clarence Louis, Jr., born in 1923, unmarried and now an ensign in the U. S. Coast Guard and serving over-seas at this date.

M.

PETER TANNER (ii).

Peter Tanner (ii), thirteenth child of Robert Tanner and Providence Robert, was born near Woodville, Wilkinson county, Mississippi, on November 3, 1811. He was brought to Louisiana as a small child by his parents when they emigrated to the Bayou Boeuf section of Rapides parish. Mr. Tanner became one of the prosperous and influential citizens of his community, took an active part in public affairs and represented his parish in the State Legislature prior to the Civil War. He lived on his plantation below Cheneyville on the left descending bank of Bayou Boeuf. This property consisted of 3,400 acres of land, bounded above by his brother, Paul Jabez, and below by property of Patrick F. Keary and brothers. On December 12, 1859, Mr. Tanner sold this large plantation to James Lemuel Pearce for $77,400.00, and moved to Evergreen, Avoyelles parish, Louisiana, where he died in June, 1864. He married on July 7, 1831, his first cousin, Eunice Rebecca Bettison, a sister of Esther Providence Bettison who married his elder brother, Paul Jabez Tanner. She was a daughter of David Bettison and Sarah Catharine Robert, emigrants from Beaufort District,

South Carolina, and was born near Woodville, Wilkinson county, Mississippi, on December 18, 1813. She lived thirty years after the death of her husband but never remarried, and died near Cheneyville, Louisiana, on May 5, 1894. The following notice of her death is taken from the ALEXANDRIA TOWN TALK of Saturday, May 19, 1894:—

> DIED:—On May 5, 1894, at the home of her son, Mr. Charles Tanner, who lives near Cheneyville, Louisiana, Mrs. Eunice Rebecca Tanner, nee Bettison. The deceased was born December 18, 1813, at Woodville, Mississippi, and was educated at Jackson, Louisiana. She was married to the late Mr. Peter Tanner, July 7, 1831. Mr. Tanner served in the legislature of this State and died in 1864.

Mr. and Mrs. Peter Tanner had ten children:—

1.—Robert Tanner.
2.—Virgil Tanner.
3.—Clara Tanner.
4.—Clifford Tanner.
5.—Stanley Tanner.
6.—Alice Tanner.
7.—Horace Tanner.
8.—Providence Tanner.
9.—David Tanner.
10.—Charles Tanner.

1.—Robert Tanner, eldest child of Peter Tanner and Eunice Rebecca Bettison, was born in Rapides parish, Louisiana, on April 6, 1832, and died at his home in Avoyelles parish, Louisiana, in June, 1911. He married in 1860 Anna Tanner (no relation), a daughter of William Tanner. She was born in Louisville, Kentucky, on January 22, 1840, and died in Avoyelles parish, Louisiana, in 1913. She spent a considerable part of her young life in Washington, D. C., where her father was employed in the construction department of the telegraph company. Robert Tanner and his wife spent their entire time after marriage at their plantation home on Bayou Rouge, near Evergreen, in Avoyelles parish, Louisiana, and it was there that their eleven children were born. They were:—

i.—Peter Tanner.
ii.—Sarah Metcalfe Tanner.
iii.—Marion Tanner.

iv.—William Tanner (i).
v.—Lyle Stanley Tanner.
vi.—William Tanner (ii).
vii—George Tanner.
viii.—Arthur Tanner.
ix.—Mable Tanner.
x.—Edward Ned Tanner.
xi.—Virgil G. Tanner.

Of these children, Peter, William (i), and Mabel died in childhood. The youngest, Virgil G. Tanner, died in early adult life, unmarried.

ii.—Sarah Metcalfe Tanner, better known as "Sallie," was born in Avoyelles parish, Louisiana, on June 11, 1864, and died there on December 2, 1939. She was married March 14, 1888, to John Burns Brunson, son of Daniel Brunson and Sarah Elizabeth Moss. He was born October 7, 1864, and died May 22, 1940. They had six children:—

a.—Daniel Brunson, born December 24, 1888.
b.—Kate Orme Brunson, born November 26, 1890.
c.—Hazel Burns Brunson, born August 27, 1892.
d.—John Thurman Brunson, born January 7, 1895.
e.—Sallie Roberta Brunson, born January 15, 1897.
f.—Platt Tanner Brunson, born October 5, 1899.

a.—Daniel Brunson married Katherine Everett on October 4, 1910. They had one son. John William Brunson, born October 25, 1911, and died September 24, 1928. Daniel Brunson's wife died soon after this and on August 3, 1939, he married Lou Ella Smith.

b.—Kate Orme Brunson was married October 2, 1912, to John Sidney Wright, son of Dr. Porter Bagley Wright and Sidney Jemima Kemper. His father was a native of Darien Center (near Alden), New York, where he was born July 30, 1849, and his mother was a native of Avoyelles parish, Louisiana, having been born there December 7, 1859, and was a daughter of Henry Clay Kemper and Virginia Ann Pearce (daughter of Alanson Green Pearce). John Sidney Wright and Kate Orme Brunson have had five sons:—

az.—John Brunson Wright, born July 16, 1915.
bz.—Henry Clay Wright, born April 9, 1917.

cz.—Robert Lynn Wright, born December 1, 1919.
dz.—Alanson Burns Wright, born January 8, 1922.
ez.—William Daniel Wright, born January 9, 1924.

az.—John Brunson Wright married Kathleen Bourland of Amory, Mississippi, on November 18, 1939. He is now in the military service of his country. (See Part Four).

bz.—Henry Clay Wright married Marjorie Escudé on December 23, 1939. They have a daughter, Martha Kay Wright, born September 9, 1941. (See Part Four).

cz.—Robert Lynn Wright is unmarried at this time and is in the military service of his country.

dz.—Alanson Burns Wright enlisted in the U. S. Marines at the outbreak of the present war and was killed in action in the Solomon Islands on October 21, 1942.

ez.—William Daniel Wright is in the military service of his country at present and is unmarried.

c.—Hazel Burns Brunson died April 21, 1910, unmarried.

d.—John Thurman Brunson married Vera Bazemore on November 4, 1918. He died July 12, 1940, and she on March 24, 1943. They had two children:—

az.—John Burns Brunson, II.
bz.—Barbara Marie Brunson.

az.—John Burns Brunson, II, was born March 19, 1921. He is unmarried as yet and is in the military service of his country.

bz.—Barbara Marie Brunson was born November 15, 1925, and is unmarried at this time.

e.—Sallie Roberta Brunson was married April 20, 1920, to William Henry Quirk. They have two sons:—

az.—William Boyd Quirk, born February 6, 1921.
bz.—Daniel Brunson Quirk, born June 2, 1928.

az.—William Boyd Quirk is unmarried and is in the military service of his country.

f.—Platt Tanner Brunson married Vivian Dorseman on January 31, 1931. They have no children.

iii.—Marion Tanner, third child of Robert and Anna Tanner, was born in Avoyelles parish, La., on July 24, 1866, and died there on January 14, 1918. She was married on December 18, 1895, to William Blacker Brunson, a first cousin of John Burns Brunson who married her sister, Sallie Tanner. Mr. Brunson was born October 8, 1857, and died June 18, 1896. One child was born of this marriage:—

    a.—Nancy Lois Brunson, born September 7, 1896.

    a.—Nancy Lois Brunson was married April 8, 1914, to Milton Cage Kelley, who was born April 8, 1880, and died May 8, 1938. His wife now resides in Bunkie, La. They had four children:—

    az.—Vivian Camilla Kelley, born October, 18, 1916.
    bz.—Gladys Belle Kelley, born June 30, 1920.
    cz.—Hazel Virginia Kelley, born July 5, 1926.
    dz.—Mitchel Brunson Kelley, born February 18, 1935.

    az.—Vivian Camilla Kelley was married on July 17, 1937, to Jesse Oliver Moore. They have a daughter, Martha Marion Moore, born April 21, 1939.

    bz.—Gladys Belle Kelley is unmarried at this time and is in the military service of her country.

    v.—Lyle Stanley Tanner, fifth child of Robert and Anna Tanner, was born in Avoyelles parish, La., on July 8, 1870, and died at his home there on January 17, 1943. He married Mary Elizabeth Barnes on March 23, 1892. She was born in England on April 8, 1871, and is living in Evergreen, La., at this date. She was a daughter of Edmund W. Barnes and Mary Elizabeth Tanner, the latter being a daughter of William Tanner and his second wife, Octavia Graham. Mary Elizabeth was therefore a half sister of Anna Tanner, the wife of Robert Tanner. Mr. Barnes was a native of England and began life in America as a messenger boy for the Western Union Telegraph in New Orleans. He continued with that concern the balance of his life and eventually became the manager of it. He and his wife made numerous trips to England and their daughter, Mary Elizabeth Barnes, was born in that country. During a yellow fever epidemic in New Orleans Mr. Barnes and several of his children died of it. The children of Lyle Stanley

Tanner and Mary Elizabeth Barnes and those of Arthur Tanner and Irene Barnes have a double relationship—two brothers married two sisters. It is an amusing problem to decipher the exact degree of kinship between the various members of these two branches of the family. Lyle Stanley Tanner and Mary Elizabeth Barnes had six children:—

a.—Robert Barnes Tanner, born February 18, 1893.
b.—Hortense Lyle Tanner, born July 7, 1896.
c.—Hattie Lee Tanner, born September —, 1898.
d.—Bertie Nena Tanner, born September 30, 1900.
e.—Mamye K. Tanner, born December 27, 1903.
f.—Virgil Genin Tanner, born September —, 1905.

a.—Robert Barnes Tanner served in the army during World War I. He married Louise Cromwell in May, 1928. They have two children:—

az.—Robert Cromwell Tanner, born June —, 1929.
bz.—Charles Rhea Tanner, born March —, 1931.

b.—Hortense Lyle Tanner was married October 12, 1920, to Thomas Roy Flournoy. They have two children:—

az.—Thomas Roy Flournoy, Jr., born December 26, 1921.
bz.—Mary Belle Flournoy, born November 18, 1927.

az.—Thomas Roy Flournoy, Jr., is unmarried and is in the U. S. Army at this time.

c.—Hattie Lee Tanner was married April 27, 1929, to Dr. R. E Henderson. They have no children.

d.—Bertie Nena Tanner was married in March, 1927, to Clarence Henry Flowers. They have two children:—

az.—Clarence Henry Flowers, Jr., born June 8, 1928.
bz.—Ronald Dale Flowers, born November 1, 1933.

e.—Mamye K. Tanner, the fifth of the children of Lyle Stanley Tanner and Mary Elizabeth Barnes, has never married and is now living in Evergreen, La. She has a distinct talent for writing and is indeed the "poet laureate" of the family. The compiler of this book can unhesitatingly add that she is "no mean favorite of the muse." She has obligingly supplied a preface for this section of our book and has generously permitted the additional use of one of her recent poems in this compilation, which we here insert below:—

PATTERNS ALL.

By

MAMYE K. TANNER

1943.

The needles go, to and fro,
Knitting a khaki sweater.
Weeks later, a comrade takes off this sweater
And gently places it under the head of a
    fallen buddy,
And his head makes a pattern
    on this sweater pillow.

The needles go, to and fro,
Now 'tis a shawl of bravest blue.
Afterwards, tired old eyes will see the
    emblem, "Am. Red Cross,"
And courageous lips will say,
    "God Bless Them,"
As the patterns of the shawl stoops to caress
    the bent old shoulders.

The needles go, to and fro,
This time I see the Christ.
He has a sad face
And a broken heart.
I listen as I hear Him say,
"The patterns of humanity
Are not those of Christianity."

The needles go, to and fro,
'Tis a little red suit.
Later, a tiny tot is zippered up
And on his way to an air-raid shelter.
And the pattern of this suit
Comforms to that of his warm little body.

The needles go, to and fro,
This time, the Germans, Japs,
United Nations and all
With bowed heads are asking
    God for forgiveness.

And in His tender mercy and
    loving kindness
God is helping each nation make
    a better pattern for living.

The needles go, to and fro,
And again I see the Christ.
As He lifts His head there's a smile of
    triump and joy as He says,
"The pattern of humanity now forms
    the pattern of Christianity."

f.—Virgil Genin Tanner, the sixth of the children of Lyle Stanley Tanner and Mary Elizabeth Barnes, married Sylvia Gagnard on June 12, 1931. They have three children:—

Virgil Genin Tanner, Jr., born June 25, 1932.
Mary Carolyne Tanner, born March 6, 1934.
Lyle Abel Tanner, born March 13, 1944.

vi.— William Tanner (ii) was born in Avoyelles parish, La., on March 29, 1872, and died there on November 23, 1943. He married on December 29, 1899, Flavilla Goudeau, born January 27, 1878, daughter of P. H. Goudeau and Sally Avery. Mrs. Tanner is yet living. They had five children, one of whom, Helen, died in infancy. Those living are:—

a.—Sallye Tanner, born November 18, 1900.
b.—Villa Tanner, born January 22, 1912.
c.—William Tanner, Jr., born October 24, 1914.
d.—Marvin Tanner, born August 16, 1917.

a.—Sallye Tanner was married on July 10, 1926, to Eugene A. Toinette. They have one child:—

Sallye Gene Toinette, born August 29, 1929.

b.—Villa Tanner was married on November 25, 1934, to Ray Mathieu and they had two children:—

Wilmer Ray Mathieu, born August 18, 1937.
Marvin Tanner Mathieu, born August 13, 1943.

The elder of these children died January 4, 1939.

c.—William Tanner, Jr., married Gloria Rabalais on April 11, 1942. He is now serving in the U. S. Army.

d.—Marvin Tanner is unmarried and is now serving in the U. S. Army.

vii.—George Tanner, son of Robert and Anna Tanner, was born in Avoyelles parish, La., on September 29, 1874. He married Julia Ann West on January 31, 1900. She was born August 7, 1877, and was a daughter of Rufus Clarence West and Annie Gill. They have four children:—

a.—Robert Harris Tanner, born November 23, 1900.
b.—Albert Newton Tanner, born February 27, 1908.
c.—Edna Tanner, born October 26, 1912.
d.—Rufus Clarence Tanner, born January 12, 1917.

a.—Robert Harris Tanner married Annie Mae Ducote on May 5, 1937. They have one child:—

Robert Harris Tanner, Jr., born July 13, 1938.

b.—Albert Newton Tanner married Beulah Belle Waddell on August 23, 1936. They have no children.

d.—Rufus Clarence Tanner married Oleta Mae Hawthorne on May 18, 1941. They have no children at present and he is serving in the U. S. Army.

viii.—Arthur Tanner, son of Robert and Anna Tanner, was born in Avoyelles parish, La., on December 18, 1876, and died at his home there on February 6, 1939. He married on February 6, 1907, Irene Barnes, born October 31, 1887, and died February 14, 1942. She was a daughter of Edmund W. Barnes and Mary Elizabeth Tanner, and was a sister of Mary Elizabeth Barnes who married Lyle Stanley Tanner, a brother of Arthur Tanner. Arthur Tanner's mother and his wife's mother were half sisters, so he and his wife were half first cousins. They had six children:—

a.—Anna Tanner, born January —, 1908.
b.—Arthur Genin Tanner, born August 22, 1909.
c.—William Peter Tanner, born December 4, 1912.
d.—Evelyn Marion Tanner, born February 14, 1915.
e.—Ralph St. Clair Tanner, born April —, 1920.
f.—Rodger Lloyd Tanner, born September 24, 1924.

a.—Anna Tanner was married to A. L. Gremillion on December 31, 1936. She died March 15, 1942, leaving one child:—

Patricia Ann Gremillion, born September —, 1937.

c.—William Peter Tanner married Ernestine Marcelle on November 26, 1939. They have one child:—

Jerry Stevens Tanner, born November 7, 1941.

d.—Evelyn Marion Tanner was married in March, 1937, to Hershel McDaniel, who is now serving in the U. S. Army. They have two children:—

Rodger Scott McDaniel, born May —, 1938.
Hershel William McDaniel, born March —. 1942.

e.—Ralph St. Clair Tanner is unmarried at this time and is in the U. S. Army, now stationed somewhere in the South Pacific.

f.—Rodger Lloyd Tanner is unmarried and is also in the U. S. Army, now stationed somewhere in the South Pacific. The brothers were in different units and neither knew where the other was stationed. Sometime recently they met in New Caledonia. As a relative expressed it, "They just looked up and saw one another."

x.—Edward Ned Tanner, usually known as "Ned Tanner," tenth child of Robert and Anna Tanner, was born in Avoyelles parish, La., on November 4, 1879. He married on July 16, 1908. Josephine Couvillion, born June 8, 1885, daughter of P. A. Couvillion and Luvenia Jeansonne. Four children were born of this marriage:—

a.—Ethel Cecil Tanner, born January 24, 1910.
b.—Lolly Lee Tanner, born October 4, 1912.
c.—Donald Vance Tanner, born May 4, 1918.
d.—Infant boy who died at birth, twin of Donald.

a.—Ethel Cecil Tanner was married January 21, 1933, to Robert Ducote, son of Horace Ducote and Eugenie Garrot. They had one child who died at birth.

b.—Lolly Lee Tanner was married December 24, 1933, to Clyde Ducote who is now serving in the U. S. Army. They have had three children, one of who died at birth. The two living are:—

Mary Joe Ducote, born January 31, 1938.
Evelyn Joy Ducote, born September 27, 1943.

c.—Donald Vance Tanner married Helen Rabalais on September 26, 1942. He is now a lieutenant in the U. S. Army. They have one son:—Donald Vance Tanner, Jr., born in Bunkie, La., on Sunday, March 5, 1944.

2.—Virgil Tanner, second child of Peter Tanner anu his wife, Eunice Rebecca Bettison, was born in 1834, and died young.

3.—Clara Tanner, third child of Peter Tanner and his wife, Eunice Rebecca Bettison, was born in 1836 and died young.

4.—Clifford Tanner, fourth child of Peter Tanner and his wife, Eunice Rebecca Bettison, was born in 1838 and died young.

5.—Stanley Tanner, fifth child of Peter Tanner and his wife, Eunice Rebecca Bettison, was born near Cheneyville, Rapides parish, La., on August 1, 1840. He lived most of his life in Avoyelles parish, near Evergreen, where he was engaged in farming. In his later years he returned to Rapides parish and resided in Cheneyville. In 1874 he married Ann Eliza Gibson of Mississippi. He died at Cheneyville, La., in 1909, and his wife some years previously. They had four children:—

> i.—Peter E. Tanner.
> ii.—Roger Irving Tanner.
> iii.—Guy Gibson Tanner.
> iv.—Eunice Tanner.

i.—Peter E. Tanner never married. He was born near Evergreen, La., in 1875, and was a prominent dentist in Shreveport, La., where he lived for more than thirty years. He died at his home there on December 27, 1938, quite suddenly of a heart attack. He was buried in the Baptist cemetery at Cheneyville, La.

ii.—Roger Irving Tanner was born near Evergreen, Avoyelles parish, La., on December 1, 1877. He married at Biloxi, Mississippi, on December 18, 1912, Mattie Guice, daughter of Stephen Lee Guice and Mattie Pipes. She was born at Natchez, Miss., on November 5, 1894. Mr. and Mrs. Tanner have lived for many years at Abbeville, La. They have two children:—

    a.—Anne Elizabeth Tanner, born January 30, 1914.
    b.—Sadie Guice Tanner, born October 26, 1916.

    a.—Anne Elizabeth Tanner was born at Biloxi, Miss., and was married February 2, 1936, at Las Vegas, Nevada to Allen Henry Klopfenstein who was born at Lansing, Michigan, on January 30, 1912. He is the son of Dr. Walter Allen Klopfenstein and Ruth Goodenough. They have three children:—
Kay Anne who was born April 16, 1939, at Pomona, California, Roger Allen who was born February 16, 1942, at Pomona, California, Walter William who was born June 7, 1944, at Pomona, California.

    b.—Sadie Guice Tanner was born at Abbeville, La., and was married on February 19, 1934, at Lake Charles, La., to Adolph Louis Brasseaux, who was born at Abbeville, La., February 19, 1912. He is a son of Adolph Louis Brasseaux, Sr., and Rita LeBlanc. They have two children:—Jeanne Anne, born at Abbeville, La., on January 12, 1936, Rita Camille, born at Beaumont, Texas, on January 28, 1943.

    iii.—Guy Gibson Tanner born near Evergreen, Avoyelles parish, La., on October 6, 1880, and now resides in Baton Rouge, La., where he has held for many years an important position in the parish school board office. Before coming to Baton Rouge Mr. Tanner taught school for some time at Cheneyville, La., and it was thus that he met his wife who was also teaching there. He married on July 3, 1918, Anna Whitaker of Baton Rouge, a daughter of Thomas Lilley Whitaker and Nellie Brown. She was born in Baton Rouge in 1892. They have one son:—

    a.—Guy Gibson Tanner, Jr.

    a.—Guy Gibson Tanner, Jr., was born November 5, 1919, in Baton Rouge, La. He graduated with honors from the school of mechanical engineering of the Louisiana State University in 1941. He now holds a very responsible position with the Standard Oil Company and is stationed at their plant in Baton Rouge. He married on Monday, October 12, 1942, Beth Edna Salathe, daughter of Mr. and Mrs. John Edward Salathe of New Orleans. They have two children:—Mary Elizabeth, born in Baton Rouge, La., September 18, 1943, and Thomas Gregory, born in Baton Rouge, La., June 9, 1945.

iv.—Eunice Tanner, only daughter of Stanley Tanner and Ann Eliza Gibson, was born near Evergreen, Avoyelles parish, La. She lived to maturity and died a few years ago, unmarried.

6.—Alice Maude Tanner, sixth child of Peter Tanner and Eunice Rebecca Bettison, was born near Cheneyville, Rapides parish, La., on December 6, 1843, and died in New Orleans on June 19, 1928. She was educated in the local schools at Cheneyville and later attended "Emma Holcomb Seminary," a finishing school for young ladies at Nashville, Tennessee, where she completed her education. She was married on November 1, 1866, in New Orleans, to George Louis Haygood of that city, a son of Captain George W. Haygood and Martha Sarah Bettison (daughter of David Bettison and Sarah Catharine Robert). He was born in New Orleans on November 22, 1837, and died there October 14, 1918. He and his wife were first cousins, their mothers being sisters. Mr. and Mrs. Haygood lived for many years in Cheneyville, La., and their eight children were born there. These children were:—

i.—Clifford Stanley Haygood, born August 3, 1867.
ii.—Ulric Linn Haygood, born June 23, 1870.
iii.—Albert Tanner Haygood, born March 4, 1872.
iv.—Sarah Cornelia Haygood, born February 15, 1874.
v.—George Bettison Haygood, born June 6, 1876.
vi.—Dessie Maude Haygood, born January 2, 1878.
vii.—Jesse Willard Haygood, born August 12, 1879.
viii.—Theoda Caroline Haygood, born March 3, 1881.

Five of these children died young and unmarried:—Clifford Stanley Haygood was drowned at Moss Point, Miss., September 23, 1887, at the age of twenty; Ulric Linn Haygood died October 14, 1871; Albert Tanner Haygood died August 28, 1881; Dessie Maude Haygood died August 24, 1878; Jesse Willard Haygood died October 22, 1881.

iv.—Sarah Cornelia Haygood, fourth child of George Louis Haygood and Alice Maude Tanner, usually called "Nell," is living at this date (1944). She was married in New Orleans at 1525 Clio Street, the home of her parents, by the Methodist minister, on January 21, 1908, to Dr. John William Macune, son of Charles William and Sarah Macune. Dr. Macune was born in Texas on January 12, 1882. They have two children:—

a.—Donnell Haygood Macune, born October 24, 1908.
b.—Alida Taah Macune, born November 30, 1910.

a.—Donnell Haygood Macune was born in New Orleans at 1525 Clio Street, and married Bessie Thelma Unsell in Abeline, Texas, on August 30, 1930. She was born in Winters, Texas, on August 7, 1910. They have no children.

b.—Alida Taah Macune was born in Dallas, Texas, and is unmarried at this time.

v.—George Bettison Haygood married August 17, 1919, Paula Marie Faucon who was born in New Orleans April 2, 1885, and was a daughter of Xavier Octave Faucon and Amelie Reboul. Mr. Faucon was born in Nye, France, and his wife in New Orleans. One child was born of this marriage:—

a.—Doris Nell Haygood, born December 24, 1920.

a.—Doris Nell Haygood was married to Carlyle Joseph Clement, son of Gaston Clement and Leona Bergeron. He was born on Greenwood plantation, near Thibodaux, La., on February 19, 1919.

viii.—Theoda Caroline Haygood, youngest child of George Louis Haygood and Alice Maude Tanner, is living in New Orleans at this time and has never married. It was she who kindly furnished most of this information on the Haygood branch of the family. In mentioning herself she wrote, "still single," then added, "thanks be"———. What a blessing it is to be contented with one's station in life!

7.—Horace Tanner, seventh child of Peter Tanner and Eunice Rebecca Bettison, was born in 1845 and died young.

8.—Providence Tanner, eighth child of Peter Tanner and Eunice Rebecca Bettison, was born near Cheneyville, Rapides parish, La., on June 9, 1847.She was educated in New Orleans and is said to have been a very versatile conversationalist, a splendid letter writer, and was particularly noted for her quick wit. She was married on July 29, 1869, to David McClure

Lyle. An announcement of their marriage in THE LOUISIANA DEMOCRAT, an Alexandria newspaper, reads as follows:—

MARRIED:—On the 29th of July, 1869, by the Rev. Fred White, Mr. David M. Lyle to Miss Provie Tanner, both of Avoyelles parish.

Mr. Lyle was a native of Shelbyville, Kentucky, where he was born September 26, 1834, his parents being John Newton Lyle and Mary Malvina Allen. After their marriage Mr. and Mrs. Lyle moved to Cheneyville where Mrs. Lyle had inherited a cotton plantation from her father, and their children were born there. About 1879 they moved to New Orleans where Mr. Lyle became a Cotton Commission Merchant. Due to failing health he moved over on the Mississippi gulf coast and died there at Handsboro on April 1, 1886. Mrs. Lyle lived many years after the death of her husband and died in New Orleans on January 13, 1927. She was buried in Handsboro, Miss., beside her husband. Four children were born of this marriage:—

    i.—Robert Tanner Lyle, born July 5, 1871.
    ii.—Mary Eunice Lyle, born March 6, 1873.
    iii.—David Reed Lyle, born March 25, 1875.
    iv.—Alice Kathrine Lyle, born September 13, 1877.

    i.—Robert Tanner Lyle was born in Cheneyville, Rapides parish, La. He married Vernie Kilborn of Sacramento, California, and died at Biloxi, Miss., on December 26, 1934. They had one child, Agnes Kilborn Lyle, born in July, 1910, and who married in 1934, Ray Brail of Davis, California, and has a son, born in October, 1940.

    ii.—Mary Eunice Lyle was born in Cheneyville, Rapides parish, La., and was married in New Orleans on April 29, 1897, to Orcenith G. Swetman of Biloxi, Miss., where they now live. They have had four children:

        a.—Hugh Lyle Childress Swetman.
        b.—Kathryn Bettison Swetman.
        c.—Glenn Lyle Swetman.
        d.—Dora Eunice Swetman.

    a.—Hugh Lyle Childress Swetman was born in 1898 and died in 1899.

b.—Kathryn Bettison Swetman was born in Biloxi, Miss., on November 1, 1899. She was married to Luther Morse Page of Vivian, La. They have one son, Lyle M. Page.

c.—Glenn Lyle Swetman was born in Biloxi, Miss., on July 4, 1901. He married Eleanor June Reid and they have three children: — Nancy Louise, Robin, and Eleanor June Swetman.

d.—Dora Eunice Swetman was born in Biloxi, Miss., on August 9, 1903. She was married to Archie Maloy Bongé of Nebraska and they have one child, Lyle Bongé.

iii.—David Reed Lyle married Sadie Dudley of Wilmington, North Carolina, on March 12, 1931, and she died August 17, 1940, leaving no issue.

iv.—Alice Kathryne Lyle, youngest child of David McClure Lyle and Providence Tanner, was born in Cheneyville, Rapides parish, La. She has never married and at this time is living in Biloxi, Miss.

9.—David Tanner, ninth child of Peter Tanner and Eunice Rebecca Bettison, was born near Cheneyville, Rapies parish, La., in 1849. Our information about him is very sparse and hazy. We understand that he went to the Klondike during the Alaska gold rush. Since then it is said he lived in Lafayette, La., and there married a Miss Mouton and had two sons and a daughter.

10.—Charles Tanner, tenth child of Peter Tanner and Eunice Rebecca Bettison, was born near Cheneyville, Rapides parish, La., on March 9, 1851, and died at Cheneyville, La., on April 2, 1933, at the advanced age of eighty-two. He married on June 20, 1878, Dora Tillman of Hazelhurst, Miss., where she was born August 1, 1855. She survived her husband five years and died at Cheneyville, La., on October 20, 1938, having reached the age of eighty-three. THE ALEXANDRIA TOWN TALK of that date contained the following notice of her death:—

CHENEYVILLE, LA., October 20, 1938.—Mrs. Dora I. Tanner, 83, died at her home here at 1 a. m. today following a heart attack she suffered yesterday. Mrs. Tanner was born in Hazelhurst, Miss., August 1, 1855. She had lived in Cheneyville most of the time since 1877 when she was married to the late Charles Tanner. Surviving are one son, Tillman Tanner, Cheneyville; five grandchildren and four great-grandchildren.

Charles Tanner and Dora Tillman had only one child:—
i.—Charles Tillman Tanner.

i.—Charles Tillman Tanner was born in Cheneyville, Rapides parish, La., on December 17, 1879. He married in 1903 Lenora Blanche Hetherwick, daughter of Clarence Hetherwick and Mary N. Rusk. She was born in Avoyelles parish, La., on February 25, 1884. Mr. Tanner died at his home in Cheneyville on Sunday morning, April 25, 1943. Besides his wife he left five children. The latter are:—

a.—Blanche Tanner.
b.—Charles Tillman Tanner, Jr.,
c.—Dora Tanner.
d.—Harold Hetherwick Tanner.
e.—Vernon Sidney Tanner.

a.—Blanche Tanner was born in Cheneyville, La., on September 27, 1904, and was married to Joseph Scott Ewell on September 8, 1924. They have one son:—Joseph Scott Ewell, Jr., born July 29, 1925.

b.—Charles Tillman Tanner, Jr., was born in Cheneyville, La., on November 23, 1906. He is unmarried at this time.

c.—Dora Tanner was born in Cheneyville, La., on February 10, 1909, and was married on May 28, 1928, to Madison Earnest. They have three children:—Gwendolyn, born September 3, 1929; Bobby Madison, born April 3, 1932; Douglas Tanner, born October 2, 1933.

d.—Harold Hetherwick Tanner was born in Cheneyville, La., on August 2, 1910. He married Lalla Dean Randolph of Corpus Christi, Texas, on November 2, 1937. They live in Bryan, Texas, and have no children.

e.—Vernon Sidney Tanner was born in Cheneyville, La., on August 10, 1914. He married Ruby Nell Martin of Beaumont, Texas, on August 20, 1938. They have a son, Sidney Erle Tanner, born Saturday, April 12, 1941, and a daughter, Jerry Lynn Tanner, born Tuesday, July 27, 1943.

N.

ROSALIND HARLEY TANNER.

Rosalind Harley Tanner, fourteenth child of Robert Tanner and Providence Robert, was born near Cheneyville, Rapides parish, La., on April 7, 1813, and died there on December 28, 1834, being only twenty-one years of age. She was married at the age of fifteen, on June 19, 1828, to William Bray Pearce, son of Stephen Pearce, and his first wife, Sallie Goodwin Bray. He was born in Rapides parish, La., on October 14, 1807, and died there on July 1, 1837. Three children were born of this marriage:—

          1.—Sarah Providence Pearce.
          2.—Matilda Ann Pearce.
          3.—Rosalind Josephine Pearce.

A full account of these children and their descendants will be found in Part Four.

O.

MARY MATILDA TANNER.

Mary Matilda T. uner, fifteenth and youngest child of Robert Tanner and Providence Robert, was born near Cheneyville, Rapides parish, La., on October 1, 1815. She was married in 1835 to William Hetherwick. We are not certain of the ancestry of Mr. Hetherwick but know definitely that he was closely related to the Hetherwicks of Alexandria, La., who were descendants of William A. Hetherwick who came to America from Aberdeen, Scotland, with his three sons, James, Robert Cecil, and John. James, it is said, settled in Chicago, John returned to Scotland but many years later came back to America, and Robert Cecil located in Alexandria, La. It is also said that Robert Cecil Hetherwick served in the Confederate Army and was captured at Gettysburg. He married Elvira Leckie of Alexandria and was the father of James Murray Hetherwick who for many years was a prominent citizen of Alexandria and was the father of Robert Murray Hetherwick who is now a prominent business man there. Our William Hetherwick who married Mary Matilda Tanner was probably a brother of the William A. Hetherwick who came from Aberdeen, Scotland. After their marriage Mr. and Mrs. Hetherwick lived near Cheneyville for a number of years and then moved to the Atchafalaya river and settled somewhere between the present towns of Melville and Simmesport. Both of them died there, she in 1864 and he in August of the same year.

They were members of the Beulah Baptist church in Cheney-ville in the early days of its establishment and were among the dissenters in that organization who withdrew and formed the Christian or Campbellite church there. In Paxton's History of the Louisiana Baptists on page 168 we find the following item taken from the book of records of Beulah Baptist church:—

Saturday before the first Lord's Day in October, 1843.—After praise and prayer by Brother B. C. Robert, the state of the church was inquired after, when it was found that some members of this church had joined churches of a different faith.

Resolved, that the following members and others who may come under the knowledge of the clerk between now and our next meeting, be cited to appear to answer this church for having joined different churches; viz:—William Hetherwick, Matilda Hetherwick, Andrew Jackson, Ella Jackson, and N. C. Chambers.

Saturday before the first Lord's Day in November, 1843, the church met according to rule.

Said Hetherwick failing to come or render any excuse for the conduct complained of, it was moved and carried that the fellowship of this church be withdrawn from him and that he be no longer a member of this church. The cases of Matilda M. Hetherwick, Andrew Jackson, and Nancy C. Chambers were severally taken up, and decided that the church withdraw fellowship, and that they be no longer members of the church for the same offences and under the same circumstances with William Hetherwick.

William Hetherwick and Mary Matilda Tanner had sixteen children, seven of whom died in infancy. Those reaching maturity were:—

       1.—Mary Hetherwick.
       2.—Elizabeth Hetherwick.
       3.—Providence Hetherwick.
       4.—Emma Hetherwick.
       5.—Esther Hetherwick.
       6.—Franklin Hetherwick.
       7.—William Hetherwick, Jr.
       8.—Jefferson Hetherwick.
       9.—Clarence Hetherwick.

1.—Mary Hetherwick was married to Thomas Toller. They moved to Galveston, Texas, where they resided until they died. It is said they left a large family, some of whom were lost in the great Galveston storm of 1900.

2.—Elizabeth Hetherwick was married to Frank Kennedy. They emigrated to Brazil and died there. From the best available information it would seem that they left a large family in that country.

3.—Providence Hetherwick was married to Richard Ratcliff. They moved to Texas and there died leaving four children:—Annie, Maude, Cornelia, and Richard Ratcliff, Jr.

4.—Emma Hetherwick was married to Simpson Boykin. They lived in Avoyelles parish, on the Atchafalaya river, where she died leaving one daughter, Mattie Boykin.

5.—Esther Hetherwick was never married.

6.—Franklin Hetherwick moved to Texas and married there. It is said he left two daughters.

7.—William Hetherwick, Jr., lived in Pointe Coupee parish, La., and there married Mattie Rogers. Both died there leaving seven children:—Peter, Moses, John, Ernest, Frank, Mary, and Jennie Hetherwick.

8.—Jefferson Hetherwick died young, unmarried.

9.—Clarence Hetherwick, youngest child of William Hetherwick, Sr., and Mary Matilda Tanner, was born in Avoyelles parish, La., about 1852. He married Mary N. Rusk, better known as "Minnie," on Bayou des Glaises, La., on January 27, 1875. She was born November 30, 1856, in Kentucky, and was educated at Shelbyville, in that State. Shortly after 1893 Mr. Hetherwick moved to Rapides parish and settled on Bayou Bouef a short distance below Cheneyville. He died at his home there in April, 1913. His wife lived ten years longer and died in Shreveport, La., on February 22, 1923, at the home of her son, Henry Sidney Hetherwick. They had eleven children, the youngest of whom died in infancy and was not named. The other ten were: —

    i.—Mary Katherine Hetherwick.
    ii.—Clarence Hetherwick, Jr.
    iii.—Hettie Harmanson Hetherwick.
    iv.—Clara Hetherwick.
    v.—Jefferson Hetherwick.
    vi.—Lenora Hetherwick.

vii.—Septimus Severus Hetherwick.
viii.—Minnie Pearl Hetherwick.
ix.—Henry Sidney Hetherwick.
x.—Edwin Campbell Hetherwick.

i.—Mary Katherine Hetherwick, better known to her friends as "Kate," was born at the home of her parents on the north bank of the Atchafalaya river, in Avoyelles parish, La., on December 20, 1875. She was married on August 30, 1893, to Walter Irion Tanner, eldest son of Robert Linn Tanner, Jr., and his wife, Matilda Sannie Calloway. Walter Tanner and his wife are cousins, both being great-grandchildren of Robert Tanner and Providence Robert. They now reside in Cheneyville and are the parents of three children:—Robert Clarence, Mary Cornelia, and Charles Hetherwick Tanner. A full account of these children may be found on page 252.

ii.—Clarence Hetherwick, Jr., was born in Avoyelles parish, La., on February 2, 1877. He married May McGinnis on July 16, 1904. They now reside in Thibodaux, La., and have three children:—Louis, Roy, and Ray Hetherwick.

iii.—Hettie Harmanson Hetherwick was born in Avoyelles parish, La., on August 25, 1878. She was married to Ed Campbell and they have one daughter, Sylvia Campbell, who was married to John Barbre and has four daughters.

iv.—Clara Hetherwick was born in Avoyelles parish, La., on February 12, 1880, and died on August 10, 1897. She was unmarried.

v.—Jefferson Hetherwick was born in Avoyelles parish, La., on August 23, 1881. He married Mary Laborde and they have four daughters.

vi.—Lenora Hetherwick was born in Avoyelles parish, La., on February 25, 1884. She was married on January 14, 1903, to Charles Tillman Tanner. They had five children. See a previous page in this section.

vii.—Septimus Severus Hetherwick was born in Avoyelles parish, La., on September 27, 1885. He married Addie Gilbert and they now reside in Shreveport, La., and have two children: —Gilbert and June Hetherwick.

viii.—Minnie Pearl Hetherwick was born in Avoyelles parish, La., on April 22, 1887. She was married twice: first to Henry Laborde and second to Louis Brewerton. She has one son by her first marriage, Edward Laborde.

ix.—Henry Sidney Hetherwick was born in Avoyelles parish, La., on June 19, 1893. He married Gladys Swords of St. Landry parish, La., a daughter of Ewell Swords of Opelousas who died in January, 1942, at the age of ninety, and was a brother of the late Marion Swords, sheriff of St. Landry parish for more than a quarter of a century. Mr. and Mrs. Hetherwick live in Shreveport, La., and have three children:—Marion, Gladys and James Hetherwick.

x.—Edwin Campbell Hetherwick was born in Rapides parish, La., on November 9, 1898. He married Alice Brooks and they now reside in Jackson, Michigan. They have one son, Freddie Hetherwick.

BIBLIOGRAPHY:—

New England Genealogical Dictionary by James Savage, Vol. IV, page 253.
New England Historical and Genealogical Register, Vol. 47, page 354.
Records of Chesterfield county, Virginia, Deed Book 12, page 404.
Inscriptions on tombstones of Robert Tanner and Providence Robert in family graveyard near Cheneyville, La.
Letter from Linn Tanner to Mrs. Leora Robinson of Louisville, Kentucky.
Records from Robert Tanner family Bible.
Data furnished the compiler by the late Walter Lodowick Tanner, grandson of Robert Tanner.
Data from the Hetherwick family Bible furnished by Mrs. Walter Irion Tanner of Cheneyville, La.
Inscriptions on tombstones in the Henry Jackson graveyard, near Cheneyville, La.
Data furnished the compiler by the late Robert Henry Jackson, Jr., of Lecompte, La., grandson of Henry Jackson and Esther Elvira Tanner.
Inscriptions from tombstones in the Christian cemetery at Cheneyville, La.
Personal interviews and correspondence between the compiler and numerous members of the Tanner famliy now living in Louisiana and elsewhere.

History of the Baptists of Louisiana, by Rev. Wm. E. Paxton, pages 144, 146, 149, 157, 169,. 172, 186, 196, 211, 235, 495, 520.

Records furnished by Mrs. Thomas Hewes Hewes of Pointe Coupée parish. La.

Records furnished by Miss Theoda Caroline Haygood of New Orleans, La.

Records furnished by Mrs. J. G. Delesdernier of San Antonio, Texas.

Records from the family Bible of Mrs. Irene Ethel (Tanner) Johns, now owned by Mrs. Blanchard Iles of Oakdale, La.

Records furnished by Mrs. David Cathcart Bettison of Belle Chasse, La.

Data furnished by Mrs. Samuel C. Lipscomb of Beaumont, Texas.

Data furnished by Mrs. Stuart Graves of Tuscaloosa, Alabama.

Data furnished by Miss Alice Kathrine Lyle of Biloxi, Miss.

Records from the "Notary Books" of Silas Talbert, William Pearce, J. J. Robert, M. R. Marshall and George Benoist Marshall, all holding the office of Notary Public for the Cheneyville section of Rapides parish, La., between the years 1825 and 1870.

PART FOUR

THE PEARCE FAMILY

The Pearce family—one of the most prominent and prolific in central Louisiana—traces its origin back to Virginia
in the first quarter of the seventeenth century. Imbued with
courage and rugged pioneer spirit, some of the members of it
followed the tide of emigration to the great southwest, and we
find the indelible stamp of their footprints in North and South
Carolina, Georgia, Mississippi, and Louisiana. Our Louisiana
Pearces are all descendants of William Pearce, Sr., and his
wife, Sarah Bray. We have attempted to render that portion
of this genealogy dealing with them as complete as possible,
and we do not hesitate to state that all dates of birth, death and
marriage contained herein are authentic.

We are indebted to Mrs. Ettie Tidwell McCall of Atlanta,
Georgia, for some very essential data on the Pearces before
they came to Louisiana. Every present and future generation
of this family should ever be grateful to her for her splendid
work, McCALL-TIDWELL and ALLIED FAMILIES. we
learn there for the first time that the names *Pearce* and *Pierce*
are synonymous, and we are told that the progenitor of this
sturdy stock came from England and settled in Virginia in
1631. We believe, from information listed below, that he came
seven years earlier. In J. C. Hotten's LISTS OF EMIGRANTS
TO AMERICA we find that a "Captain William Peerce
patented 200 acres of land nere Mulbery Iland in the corpora-
cion of James Cittie in 1636." In this work of Hotten we also
find the name variously given as *Pearce, Pearse, Peerce,*
Peerse, Peirce, Peirse, and *Pierce.* This author also tells us
that on August 1, 1635, "Steeven Pierce, aged 30, was licensed
to go beyond the seas on the ship ELIZABETH of London,
Christopher Browne, Master."

This same author on page 224 gives us the muster of
Captain William Pierce taken in 1624, which recites that he
came over in the ship SEAVENTURE, and that his wife, "Mrs.
Jone Pierce came in the BLESSING." This muster likewise
shows that Captain Pierce was at James Cittie and at that time

had four servants there, one of whom was a Negro wo
He also had a plantation at "Mulbury Iland," according to
same authority, and the muster taken there on January
1624, shows that he had thirteen servants at that place
gives their names.   In Stanard's Colonial Virginia Regis
page 32, we learn that William Pierce of James City Cour
Virginia, was a member of the Council in 1631.   All this wo
indicate that our Captain Pierce or Pearce was one of 1
prominent men of the colony in its infancy.

There has always been a William and a Stephen Pearce
the branch of the family in which we are particularly intereste
and we feel that it does not take an unusual stretch of th
imagination to believe that either the Stephen or William men
tioned in Hotten's valuable work was the ancestor of our Louis
iana Pearce family.   The earliest of the name on whom we car
place our finger with any degree of certainty is a Stephen
Pearce who was born in Virginia towards the close of the
seventeeth century or in the early part of the eighteenth.   He
emigrated to North Carolina where he permanently settled
and married.   It is claimed that his wife was a Lanier.   We
do know that he had three sons:—Stephen, Joshua, and William.   We have been unable to trace any descendants of
Stephen, the eldest.   However, the records show many Pearces
in North Carolina about this period and later, and some of
them may have been his progeny.   William Pearce, the youngest of the three brothers, appears to have been the most famous.
He was born about 1740 in North Carolina and served with
distinction in the Revolutionary Army.   At one time he held
the rank of a captain in the First Continental Artillery, and
later was an aide on the staff of General Nathanael Green with
the rank of major.   He is recorded as being a member of the
Sons of Liberty in Savannah, Georgia.   In 1781 Congress presented him with a sword for gallant services.   He was a member of the Continental Congress in 1786, and died on December 10, 1789.   In 1783 he married Charlotte Fenwick, daughter of Edward Fenwick and Mary Drayton of Charleston,
South Carolina.   They had no issue.

Joshua Pearce, the second son of the Stephen Pearce who
emigrated to North Carolina from Virginia, was the father of
William Pearce, Sr., the immediate ancestor of the Louisiana

Pearces. He (Joshua) was born in North Carolina about 1735. We later meet him in Georgia where his name first appears on the records in July, 1768, when he applies for 150 acres of land on Buck Creek, in St. Matthews Parish. In his application he stated that he came from North Carolina to Georgia four months previously, had a wife and six children, and owned slaves. He received a Royal grant from King George III, in St. Matthews Parish in 1769. On that land the original Pearce home was built. It was in Effingham county and there, so we learn from "THE BEVILL FAMILY," by Agnes White Tedcastle, it was that President George Washington paid a visit on his way from Savannah to Augusta in 1791. We are told also that in 1825 when Steven Pearce (son of this Joshua) lived there he entertained the Marquis de La Fayette when that distinguished gentleman made his famous tour of the United States.

Joshua Pearce soon became one of the leading men in the vicinity of his new home in Georgia. In 1777 he was appointed Surveyor of Roads for Effingham county, and in 1778 when the Georgia Legislature passed an act under the provision of which five commissioners were appointed from each county as representatives for the colony, one of the commissioners from Effingham county was *Joshua Pearce, Sr...* He was here for the first time officially recorded as *Senior* in order to distinguish him from his son Joshua who was likewise a prominent man in Georgia at that period. Joshua Pearce, Sr., married Hannah Green in North Carolina about 1752. He died in Georgia (probably Screven county) on April 17, 1810—so says the family Bible of his son Stephen, now the property of a descendant, Mrs. Cora Cheney (Pearce) Bailey of Opelousas, Louisiana. His will was dated September 10, 1807, and was probated in Screven county, Georgia, in 1816. He mentions his wife and four children. The children were:—William, Joshua, Stephen and Sarah Pearce.

In his application for a grant of land in 1768 he stated that he had six children. It is therefore probable that two of them had died before he signed his will. His second son, Joshua Pearce, Jr., was a Revolutionary soldier and moved to Mississippi in 1807 where he died, leaving children, one of whom, Mary Pearce, married William McCall and lived in

Screven county, Ga. Stephen Pearce, the third son of Joshua, Sr., remained in Georgia and there married Mary Mills. Their daughter, Mary, married Paul Bevill, Jr. This Stephen Pearce's will is dated May 4, 1829, and is on file in Screven county. The only daughter of Joshua Pearce, Sr., Sarah, married a McRea.

William Pearce, Sr., eldest son of Joshua Pearce, Sr., and Hanna Green, was the forebear of the Pearce family of Rapides and Avoyelles parishes, Louisiana. He is usually designated as *William Pearce, Sr.,* in order to distinguish him from his son of the same name. That he was a soldier in the Revolutionary Army is proven by a certified list of the Troops of the Georgia Line on which his name is found (see page 621 in "The Story of Georgia and the Georgia People," by Smith). A certificate that he was a soldier in the First Battalion, Georgia Line, was signed by Gen. Elijah Clark in 1784 (see page 481, McCall-Tidwell and Allied Families). This William Pearce, Sr., was the first of his name to come to Louisiana, arriving here about 1808. He was born in North Carolina in 1754 and went to Georgia with his parents in 1768. His name appears in White's Statistics of Georgia in 1793 as being one of the early settlers of Screven county. He was a Justice of the Peace in 1773 and Judge of the Inferior Court of Screven county in 1794. We find the following mention of him in his father's will:—

> Secondly:—I give and bequeath unto my beloved son William Pearce, whom I appoint executor, two tracts of land, ... Also 1,075 acres of land which shall be used for the mill, to be equally divided between my sons William and Stephen.

William Pearce, Sr., came to Rapides parish, Louisiana, about 1808, and settled on the right descending bank of Bayou Boeuf about two miles above the present town of Cheneyville. His home is said to have been somewhere near Lloyd's Bridge. He was killed there on November 6, 1813, by a chimney falling on him. There is some myth in the family about his having buried a lot of money near his home, and having died suddenly no one ever knew the where-about of the "golden sepulchre." It is said that much "digging" has been done in the vicinity in the vain hope of finding it. The place of his burial is not known.

William Pearce, Sr., married Sarah Bray in Georgia about 1781 and she died there on June 6, 1801—so we are told by the family Bible. Six children, as far as we know, were born of this marriage. They were:—

A.—William Pearce, Jr.
B.—Stephen Pearce.
C.—Delia Pearce.
D.—Mary Pearce.
E.—James Pearce.
F.—Joshua Pearce.

For numerous reasons we are inclined to believe that our William Pearce, Sr., father of the above children, was *at least* twice married, and probably three times. There can no doubt that the children named were the offspring of himself and his wife, Sarah Bray. But there appear to have been other children by the name of Pearce for whom we must account. We have no definite data with which to substantiate the statement that there were other marriages but the circumstances are so strong that we believe our position to be a tenable one. Mrs. A. C. Simmonds of Alexandria, Louisiana, is a descendant of Hugh Wilson Robinette whose wife was Hanna Pearce Bray. In her family it has always been understood that the *mother* of Hanna Pearce Bray was a *Pearce* and that she was *a half-*sister of William Pearce, Jr., and therefore a daughter of William Pearce, Sr. Now Hannah Pearce Bray was born in 1804, so if her mother was a *half-sister* of William Pearce, Jr., she must necessarily have been a daughter of William Pearce, Sr., by a marriage other than that with Sarah Bray in 1781. Had not the word *half-sister* been so definitely insisted on by tradition we might easily conclude that she was a daughter of William Pearce, Sr., and Sarah Bray, as there is plenty of space as to time between the dates of birth of several of their children for them to have had an other. It would therefore seem that the only logical conclusion (provided our information that "the mother of Hannah Pearce Bray was a half-sister of William Pearce, Jr.," is correct) is that William Pearce, Sr., was a widower when he married Sarah Bray in 1781.

Another problem of a similar nature has arisen in the Pearce genealogy which offers much latitude for speculation. We know that Leonidas Alonzo Robert, son of Joseph Robert and Mary Hyrne Jaudon, was first married to *Tuzette E. Pearce*. Who was she? Thus far none of the family seem able to place her on that branch of the Pearce tree where she properly belongs. In the old Dunwoody family Bible we find the following pertinent item:—

Tuzette Pearce, daughter of William and Elizabeth Pearce, was born September 17, 1811.

She could only have been a daughter of William Pearce, Sr., or his son, William Pearce, Jr. There was no one else of that name in central Louisiana at that time. But none of our records show either of them ever had a wife named *Elizabeth*. We know that Delia Pearce, daughter of William Pearce, Sr., and Sarah Bray, married John Dunwoody, and the Bible in question was hers. It would seem only natural for Mrs. Dunwoody to record the birth of a near relative in her Bible. Then what relation was Tuzette Pearce to Mrs. Dunwoody? She could have been either a half-sister or a niece. To have a half-sister Tuzette must have been a daughter of William Pearce, Sr., and since his wife Sarah Bray died in 1801, there must have been a later marriage. This is not at all improbable. William Pearce, Sr., died in 1813 at the age of fifty-nine and Sarah Bray died June 6, 1801, so he was only forty-seven when this wife died and lived twelve years longer. It is therefore not very "far-fetched" to say that Tuzette's mother, Elizabeth, may have been a third wife of William Pearce, Sr., and in that case she herself would have been a half-sister of Mrs. Dunwoody.

Since Tuzette Pearce's father is definitely given in the Dunwoody Bible as *William Pearce*, there is only one other person than that given above who could have been her father, and that was *William Pearce, Jr.*, and in this case she would have been a niece of Mrs. Dunwoody. But to have been a daughter of William Pearce, Jr., she must have been born of an earlier marriage than the one we have on record for him. We know that he was born in 1782 and therefore twenty-nine years old at the time Tuzette was born. We also know that he married Frances Tanner about 1812, being nearly thirty years old at that time. Marriages occurred much earlier in those days than now, and it was rare that a man waited until he was thirty years old before establishing a home of his own. Consequently it is not improbable that William Pearce, Jr., had been married prior to his union with Frances Tanner in 1812 and that his first wife left a daughter named Tuzette. Both of these explanations of the parentage of Tuzette Eliza Pearce who married Leonidas Alonzo Robert are purely speculations on the part of the compiler, but to him they seem quite feasible.

A.

WILLIAM PEARCE, JR.

William Pearce, Jr., eldest child of William Pearce, Sr., and his wife, Sarah Bray, was born in Screven county, Georgia, in 1782, just at the closing days of the Revolutionary War. Through his mother he was connected with many of the pioneer families of North Carolina. The Brays seemed to have lived principally in Pasquotank county. We find the will of William Bray there dated August 23, 1725, and that of Henry Bray dated September 20, 1745. There was a Thomas Bray in that section who appeared to be prominent and who married Mary Pollock, daughter of Thomas Pollock. The latter name is very prominent in the early settlement of North Carolina.

William Pearce, Jr., came to Louisiana with his father in 1808. He probably lived for a while in Wilkinson county, Mississippi. He established his home on Bayou Boeuf, in Rapides parish, La., and there spent the remainder of his days in planting. He married about 1812 Frances Tanner, daughter of Robert Tanner and Providence Robert, and a granddaughter of Captain Peter Robert and Anne Grimball, all early pioneers to Wilkinson county, Miss., and then to Rapides parish, La. This marriage probably took place in Woodville, Wilkinson county, Miss. Frances Tanner was born in St. Peter's Parish, Beaufort District, South Carolina, on January 11, 1795, and died near Cheneyville, Rapides parish, Louisiana, on April 13, 1821. We have no record of the death of Mr. Pearce but know from official documents of that period that he was living as late as January, 1830. On November 13, 1829, we find the following record of him:— "I, William Pearce, for and in consideration of the good will and affection that I bear my daughter, Providence Taliaferro, do hereby give unto her, etc." Then on January 23, 1830, we find a deed in which William Pearce sells land on Bayou Boeuf to Robert Tanner.

William Pearce, Jr., and Frances Tanner had three children:—

  1.—Eliza Pearce.
  2.—Sarah Providence Pearce.
  3.—Alanson Green Pearce.

  1.—Eliza Pearce, eldest child of William Pearce, Jr., and Frances Tanner, was born in Rapides parish, Louisiana, in 1813. She was married in 1830 to Septimus M. Perkins. As far as we know they had no children.

  2.—Sarah Providence Pearce, second child of William Pearce, Jr., and Frances Tanner, was born in Rapides parish, Louisiana, in 1814. She was married to Robert Leckie Taliaferro, a native of Culpeper county, Virginia, who had emigrated to Louisiana. He was a nephew of Robert Leckie, a prominent Virginian who had come to Louisiana in the early days of the nineteenth century and located near Alexandria.

EXCURSUS—TALIAFERRO.

  The Taliaferro family came to Virginia soon after the revocation of the Edict of Nantes in 1685, and have been prominent there ever since. There is a family legend handed down through many generations as to the origin of the Taliaferros. It is most interesting and carries back to the year 58 B. C. According to this tradition Julius Caesar in his famous campaign in Gaul went unattended late one evening on a tour of inspection of his camp. While unsuspectingly strolling between two distant outposts he was suddenly surrounded by a horde of Gallic barbarians. In spite of his heroic efforts at defence he was overcome and was about to be killed when one of his assailants, struck with admiration by his bravery, intervened and saved his life. Caesar, in gratitude for this protection, made him one of his personal attendants and gave him a permit to carry arms within the Roman camp. This was quite an honor as all outsiders were forbidden to be armed within certain limits. Hence the Latin derivation of the name Taliaferro—*telum, a dart*, and *ferro, to bear*.

  Some of the descendants of the first Taliaferro, centuries later, settled in Normandy and were the forebears of those of that name who followed William the Conqueror into England. We are told of a Baron Taliaferro who was proclaimed "the hero of Hastings." To him the Conqueror made large grants of land in Kent, and his progeney became the Earls of Pennington. In the 9th century we find where a Taliaferro was created Duke of Angouleme by Charles the Bold of France. Hume in his history of England tells us that Isabelle Taliaferro, daughter of the Count d'Angouleme, married King John of England, from whom descended many kings and queens. They were also Dukes of the Plantagenet line.

After the revocation of the Edict of Nantes two brothers, James and John Taliaferro, left France and came to the colony of Virginia. They purchased a large tract of land there having a front of 40 miles on the James river. Of these John Taliaferro became the ancestor of the Virginia Taliaferros. He settled near Williamsburg and called his estate "POWHATAN." His eldest son, John, inherited "POWHATAN"; his second son, William, settled in King George county and named his place "HAGLEY"; his third son, Philip, established his residence in King and Queen county and called it "HOCKLEY." Richard Taliaferro, son of John the eldest son of John the emigrant, went to Georgia and left descendants there. A county in Georgia yet bears his name. A younger son of John the emigrant moved to Ohio and left descendants in Cincinnati.

The Virginia Taliaferros have always occupied foremost places in the political and social life of their native State. The name is symbolic of Virginia aristocracy. Intermarriages with the Garnet, Hooe, Brent, Tyler, Mason, Barbour, Armistead, Baytops, Carter, Throckmorton, and other noted families of the "Old Dominion" have only added prominence to this already prominent family.

Robert Leckie Taliaferro and his wife, Sarah Providence Pearce, lived for a while at Evergreen, in Avoyelles parish, Louisiana, and later moved to a large plantation which Mr. Taliaferro owned on Bayou des Glaises in the same parish. There they spent the remainder of their lives. We have been unable to ascertain the dates of their death. They had six children:—

       i.—William Robert Taliaferro.
      ii.—Alanson Perkins Taliaferro.

       iii.—Francis Alcott Taliaferro.
       iv.—Henrietta Taliaferro.
       v.—Sidney Leona Taliaferro.
       vi.—Warren Taliaferro.

     i.—William Robert Taliaferro was born in Avoyelles parish, Louisiana, on March 21, 1831, and died there on February 24, 1905. In 1852 he married Louisa Hatfield who was born February 22, 1833, and died October 25, 1907. They had three children:—

       a.—Leona Louisa Taliaferro.
       b.—Virginia Taliaferro.
       c.—A daughter who died in infancy.

     a.—Leona Louisa Taliaferro was born March 18, 1853, and died January 19, 1939. She was married to William Nicholas Price and had five children:—Eva, Emmett, Sophronia, Albert, and Henrietta. The last mentioned was married to O. E. Hodnett and is the only one of them living at this date.

     b.—Virginia Taliaferro was born March 3, 1858, and died at her home in Bunkie, Louisiana, on Friday, February 21, 1941. The funeral services were held at the White Chapel Methodist Church, Gold Dust, St. Landry parish, Louisiana, and she was buried in the cemetery there. Surviving her at the time were three sons, three daughters, sixteen grandchildren and five great-grandchildren. She was married on October 24, 1876, to Dennis Oliver Nugent who died December 3, 1897. They had seven children:—

       az.—Jessie Sue Nugent.
       bz.—Bertie Cornelia Nugent.
       cz.—Ludie Nugent.
       dz.—Robert Matthew Nugent.
       ez.—Marshall Oliver Nugent.
       fz.—Noel Wynn Nugent.
       gz.—Alonzo Lee Nugent.

     az.—Jessie Sue Nugent was born August 11, 1879, and was married May 16, 1912, to A. P. DeLaune. They have no children.

     bz.—Bertie Cornelia Nugent was born December 19, 1880, and was married March 30, 1904, to Toleman Tarleton Sandefur who died June 16, 1937. Two children were born of this marriage:—Virginia Inez Sandefur, born September 11, 1909, and married December 21, 1932, to Richard Layhae—they have one daughter, Aline Louise Layhae, born February 3, 1934; Alvin Tarleton Sandefur, born June 2, 1913, and yet single.

cz.—Ludie Nugent was born July 25, 1883, and was married June 25, 1908, to Daniel Sandefur, a brother of Toleman Tarleton Sandefur who married his sister Bertie Cornelia. These Sandefur brothers were sons of Daniel Sandefur and Emily McCrory, and were born near Whiteville, Louisiana. Daniel Sandefur and Ludie Nugent have six children:—Marshall Nugent Sandefur, born August 12, 1909, who married Grace Christian on July 3, 1938, and has one son James Daniel Sandefur, born December 9, 1941; Daniel Dennis Sandefur, born December 2, 1912, who married Ida Mae Gil on March 19, 1942; Laura Laverne Sandefur, born July 4, 1915, who was married on July 17, 1940, to Henderson Gregory Garnett, Jr.; Herschel Myron Sandefur, born November 22, 1916, who married Elsie Mae Parker on March 6, 1938; Mary Lorena Sandefur, born November 18, 1919, who was married October 25, 1941, to Leonard Conrad Tobin; Robert Duke Sandefur, born February 10, 1925, and as yet unmarried.

dz.—Robert Matthew Nugent was born February 18, 1885, and married on December 1, 1909, Lise Milburn Morrison who died November 28, 1926. They had six children:—Aline Nugent, born October 3, 1910, who was married to Jerome Butcher and has two children, Lise Ann Butcher, born October 3, 1934, and Kenneth Louis Butcher, born February 20, 1942; Philip Morrison Nugent, born December 26, 1911, who married Helen Harper and has three children, Joy Dale, Philip, and Jerry Nugent; Myrtle Leona Nugent, born February 17, 1913 who was married to Clyde Bear; Elizabeth Virginia Nugent, born October 23, 1914, who was married to Clarence Derousselle and has one son, Edgar Derousselle; Robert Oliver Nugent, born November 28, 1917, unmarried as yet; Eloise Nugent, born November 2, 1919, who was married to Curtis Mitchel and has one son, Richard Mitchel.

ez.—Marshall Oliver Nugent was born November 25, 1886, and died February 4, 1907, unmarried.

fz.—Noel Wynn Nugent was born July 29, 1890, and has been twice married: first in 1915 to Ada Wells, and second in

October, 1930, to Lucye Grillett. He has two children by his 1st marriage:—Noel Wynn Nugent, Jr., born August 20, 1917, now unmarried; Muriel Alice Nugent, born January 14, 1924, married to Jack Werner, and has a daughter born March 9, 1942. By the second marriage Mr. Nugent has a daughter, Nancy Sue Nugent, born October 20, 1937.

gz.—Alonzo Lee Nugent was born January 27, 1896, and married Essie Dear on October 5, 1917. They have five children:—Alonzo Lee Nugent, Jr., born September 15, 1921; Malcom Eddie Nugent, born October 28, 1923; Westley Oliver Nugent, born July 13, 1925; Ruth Elaine Nugent, born November 2, 1927; Virginia Ann Nugent, born July 22, 1938.

ii.—Alanson Perkins Taliaferro, second child of Robert Leckie Taliaferro and Sarah Providence Pearce, was born in Avoyelles parish, Louisiana, in 1833. He married Elizabeth Hudson of Evergreen, Louisiana, and they had four children:—

  a.—Charles Taliaferro.
  b.—Clifton Taliaferro.
  c.—Alanson Perkins Taliaferro, Jr.
  d.—Loula Taliaferro.

a.—Charles Taliaferro married Desirée Wells Burges, daughter of John Mortimer Burges and Bettie Desirée Tanner. She was a grand-daughter of Branch Tanner and Desirée wells, and a great-grand-daughter of Willing Wells and Rosalie Meuillon, and was born in Avoyelles parish, Louisiana, on June 28, 1868. Charles Taliaferro has been dead for many years but his widow is yet living. They had no children.

b.—Clifton Taliaferro married Rowena Fisher. They had no children. After his death she married Z. T. Perry of Lecompte, Louisiana.

c.—Alanson Perkins Taliaferro, Jr., never married.

d.—Loula Taliaferro was married to a Mr. Price. We have been unable to obtain any further information about her.

iii.—Francis Alcott Taliaferro, third child of Robert Leckie Taliaferro and Sarah Providence Pearce, never married.

iv.—Henrietta Taliaferro, fourth child of Robert Leckie Taliaferro and Sarah Providence Pearce, was born in Avoyelles parish, Louisiana, about 1837. She was married about 1857 to the Rev. Frederich White, a Methodist minister who came to Louisiana from Tennessee a few years before the Civil War and settled on Bayou des Glaises. Being a minister and a man of peace he entered the Confederate Army as a chaplain but in the midst of so much tumult and fighting he soon became dissatisfied with his peaceful duties and resigned. He had scarcely done so when we find him enlisting in the ranks as a private soldier. There he fought to his heart's content and with such ferocity and gallantry that when the war ended he came out of it as captain of a company of infantry. Now that the fighting was over this brave old soldier who had so long been influenced by what the Bible calls "just anger" and who had led his men into many a fierce battle, sheathed his sword, hung it placidly on the wall and betook himself once more to his ministerial labors. He was a highly respected and much loved Christian gentleman, and was ever afterwards an earnest worker in the Lord's vineyard.

Rev. Frederich White and Henrietta Taliaferro had eight children, so we are informed by a member of the family, but the list furnished us shows only seven. It is probable that one died at birth or in early infancy. Those given us by a grand-daughter are as follows:—

> a.—Mozella Elmina White.
> b.—Sarah Edelene White.
> c.—Frederich Redding White.
> d.—Frances Leona White.
> e.—Henrietta May White.
> f.—Flavilla White.
> g.—Charles Kavanaugh White.

a.—Mozella Elmina White was born February 10, 1858, and died April 11, 1858, when but two months old.

b.—Sarah Edelene White was born April 9, 1860, and died November 3, 1887, at the age of twenty-seven. She never married.

c.—Frederich Redding White was born September 13, 1863, and married Emma Augusta Huff who was born at Cheneyville, Rapides parish, Louisiana, on February 18, 1872. They had ten children, eight of whom are now living. Those living are:—Walter D., R. Wallace, Horace C., Virgil D., Charles N., Frederich C., Sarah and Nanee. Mr. White died on August 9, 1910, and his wife died in Alexandria, Louisiana, on December 24, 1941. Besides her eight children she was survived by nineteen grandchildren and three great-grandchildren.

d.—Frances Leona White, fourth child of Rev. Frederich White and Henrietta Taliaferro, was born February 5, 1870, and was married to Walter Seals, a native of Mississippi. She died on December 23, 1895, leaving the following children: Mary, Irma Corinne, Helen, Annie and Leona Seals. Some years after her death Mr. Seals married her sister, Henrietta May White.

e.—Henrietta May White was born May 15, 1872, and was married to Walter Seals, her sister's widower. She died on September 6, 1936, leaving two children:—Sidney Lee and Walter Hayes Seals.

f.—Falvilla White was born October 7, 1875, and was married to W. Columbus Townsend of Bunkie, Louisiana. They had three children:—Frederich, May and Mildred Townsend. Flavilla (White) Townsend died on March 13, 1938. The following notice of her death appeared in the BUNKIE RECORD at the time:—

> DIED:—At the family residence, Bunkie, Louisiana, Sunday afternoon, March 13, 1938, Mrs. W. C. Townsend, aged 63 years. Deceased is survived by her husband, one son, Fred Townsend of Portland, Indiana; two daughters, Mrs. W. B. Nettles and Miss Mildred Townsend; one brother, Mr. C. K. White, and several grandchildren. Funeral services were held at the Methodist Church at 4:30 p. m., March 14, conducted by Rev. J. J. Rasmussen of Mansfield, her former pastor, assisted by Rev. R. M. Bentley, her present pastor, Rev. S. C. Rushing and Rev. T. T. Trimble. Interment was made in Pythian cemetery in Bunkie.

g.—Charles Kavanaugh White, youngest of the children of Rev. Frederich White and Henrietta Taliaferro, was born in Avoyelles parish, Louisiana, on August 9, 1877, and died at his home at Gold Dust, St. Landry parish, Louisiana, on Thursday,

January 26, 1939. The following account of Mr. White's death appeared in the ALEXANDRIA DAILY TOWN TALK:—

> DIED:—At the family residence, Gold Dust, La., Thursday, January 26, 1939, Charles K. White, 61. The deceased is survived by his widow, Mrs. Charles K. White; three sons, Otey White of Alexandria, C. K. White, Jr., of Houston, Texas, Roy White of Gold Dust; two daughters, Mrs. Robert Hemphill of Beaumont, Texas, and Mrs. J. A. Bordelon of Kentucky. There are also four grandchildren. Funeral services will be held sometime tomorrow at the family residence in Gold Dust. Interment will be made in the Evergreen cemetery under the direction of Hixson Bros. of Bunkie.

Charles Kavanaugh White married on October 25, 1899, Susan Eliza Prosser, daughter of Otey S. Prosser of Milledgeville, Georgia, and his wife, Mary E. Roberts of Norfolk, Virginia. She was born on November 12, 1878, and is living at this date (1944). Five children were born of this marriage:—

> az.—Otey L. White.
> bz.—Mary Lucille White.
> cz.—Gladys Henrietta White.
> dz.—Charles Kavanaugh White, Jr.
> ez.—Roy William White.

az.—Otey L. White, eldest of the above children, was born on October 2, 1900, and has resided in Alexandria, Louisiana, for many years where he has been for some time one of the efficient assistant cashiers of the RAPIDES BANK AND TRUST COMPANY. He married Jessie Hudson of Alexandria who was born on December 14, 1900. They have three children:—Otey L. White, Jr., born August 9, 1927, Jack Kavanaugh White, born July 14, 1933, Alice White, born November 2, 1935.

bz.—Mary Lucille White was born in Avoyelles parish, Louisiana, on August 24, 1902. She was married to Robert Hemphill of Houston, Texas. They now reside in Beaumont, Texas, and have no children.

cz.—Gladys Henrietta White was married to J. Alva Bordelon of Bowling Green, Kentucky. They have no children at this time.

dz.—Charles Kavanaugh White, Jr., married Sylvia Minen of Houston, Texas, where they now reside.

ez.—Roy William White resides at Gold Dust, Louisiana, and is as yet not married.

v.—Sidney Leona Taliaferro, fifth child of Robert Leckie Taliaferro and Sarah Providence Pearce, was born on Bayou des Glaises, in Avoyelles parish, Louisiana, about 1849. Her father's home was a stately and commodious edifice of the Southern ante-bellum type of architecture, and was on a large plantation near the present town of Moreauville, in Avoyelles parish, Louisiana. Mr. Taliaferro was one of the rich men of that community before the Civil War, but his fortune, like that of many other Southerners, was swept away in the storm of civil strife, and what was left was soon devoured by the flock of carpet-bag vultures who followed in the wake of a conquering army.

Soon after the war Sidney Leona Taliaferro was married to Charles Lafayette Robinson, son of Andrew Jackson Robinson and Elizabeth Ann Jones. He was born on his father's plantation in Amite county, Mississippi, on June 1, 1840. He was an energetic and enterprising young man, and though reared in affluence and ease was not afraid of the hard work he plunged into after the war, and as a result soon made himself independent. He first accepted a position as manager for Mr. Joel Matthews on the "Chaseland" plantation below Lecompte, Louisiana. Later he managed an adjoining plantation known as "Coco Bend," and some time later he purchased "Quantico" plantation on Bayou Boeuf, above Lecompte. He and his bride were married at "Jessamine Hill," the elegant summer home of Governor James Madison Wells in the beautiful pine hills near Lecompte, which the Taliaferro family were renting at the time. The ceremony was performed by the Rev. Benjamin Franklin White, Methodist minister and father of Hon. Horace H. White of Alexandria, on December 9, 1867. Mr. Robinson died in Alexandria, Louisiana, on May 28, 1905. We have no record of the date of his wife's death. Six children were born of this marriage:—

        a.—Frances Temperance Robinson.
        b.—Levi Wells Robinson.
        c.—Frederich Charles Robinson.

d.—John Andrew Robinson.
e.—Lucius Albert Robinson.
f.—Edwin Mercer Robinson.

a.—Frances Temperance Robinson was married to J. Stucky and had three children:—Frances who married Cleveland Richerson of Richland, Louisiana; Jehu who never married; Howell who married a Miss Voorhies of Richland, Louisiana.

b.—Levi Wells Robinson married his first cousin, Sarah Tarver McDonald. They had no children.

c.—Frederich Charles Robinson married Eula Jackson from the southern part of the state. Their five children are:— Sidney Leona Robinson who married Alto Parker of Battle Creek, Michigan, and has one child, Floyd Parker; Werdner Robinson who married Fred McWright of Glenmora, Louisiana, and has one child, Beverley Ray McWright; Bessie Robinson who married Albert Sumler and has one child, Eula Lou Sumler; Bertha Lou Robinson who never married; Frederick Robinson, Jr., as yet unmarried.

d.—John Andrew Robinson never married.

e.—Lucius Albert Robinson married Irma Corinne Seals, daughter of Walter Seals and his first wife, Frances Leona White. They were cousins. Four children were born of this union:—Charles, Edwin, Lucius Albert, Jr., Helen Lois, and Walter Seals Robinson. After the death of his wife (Irma Corinne Seals) Lucius Albert Robinson married Noami McBride. There are no children by the second marriage.

f.—Edwin Mercer Robinson married Minerva Whittington (better known as "Minnie"), daughter of Robert Holt Whittington and Eugenia Hamilton. They have two children: —Robert Whittington and Charles Lafayette Robinson.

vi.—Warren Taliaferro, sixth child of Robert Leckie Taliaferro and Sarah Providence Pearce, never married. He served in the Confederate Army during the Civil War and was later shot and killed by "Jay-Hawkers."

3.—Alanson Green Pearce, third child and only son of William Pearce, Jr., and his wife, Frances Tanner, was born near Cheneyville, Rapides parish, Louisiana, December 14, 1816, and died near Evergreen, Avoyelles parish, Louisiana, on January 13, 1863. He married in 1837 Sidney Elizabeth

Kay, daughter of Richard Wioatte Kay and Emily Wells, and grand-daughter of Willing Wells and Rosalie Mouillon (daughter of Dr. Ennemond Meuillon and Jeannette (Poiret) La Mothe). Sidney Elizabeth Kay was born in Rapides parish, Louisiana, on May 21, 1821. We have no record of the date of her death. Ten children were born of this marriage:—

> i.—Virginia Ann Pearce.
> ii.—William Oscar Pearce.
> iii.—Sarah Ophelia Pearce.
> iv.—Eugenia Pearce.
> v.—Ella Pearce.
> vi.—Emily Octavia Pearce.
> vii.—Clara Pearce.
> viii.—Wioatte Kay Pearce.
> ix.—Lillinia Eliza Pearce.
> x.—Alva Green Pearce.

i.—Virginia Ann Pearce, eldest child of Alanson Green Pearce and Sidney Elizabeth Kay, was born in Evergreen, Avoyelles parish, Louisiana, on November 29, 1838, and died on Sunday, January 10, 1904. She was married on February 23, 1857, to Henry Clay Kemper, son of Burdette Kemper and his wife, Jemima Thompson of Garrard county, Kentucky. Burdette Kemper was a Baptist minister of note in his time. He died in his native State in 1876 in the 89th year of his age. His father, John Kemper, was a native of Virginia and of German origin. According to family tradition his first forebear in America came to this country in 1712 and settled in Fauquier county, Virginia. Jemima Thompson, the mother of Henry Clay Kemper, was a daughter of James Thompson who was born in Edinburgh, Scotland, and came to this country when a young man. He was a surveyor and was commissioned by the Governor of Virginia to survey and locate lands in Kentucky.

Henry Clay Kemper was born in Garrard county, Kentucky, on December 27, 1831. He graduated from Georgetown (Kentucky) College in 1856 and the following year came to Evergreen, Avoyelles parish, Louisiana. His mission there was to take charge as principal of the Evergreen Home Institute, one of the early notable seats of learning in central Louisiana. It was there that he met and married Miss Virginia Ann Pearce.

He taught school one year after his marriage and then devoted his energies to planting. In 1862 he enlisted in Company H, Sixteenth Louisiana Infantry of the Confederate Army, which was assigned to the Army of Tennessee. He took part in the battles of Shiloh and Perryville, and other important engagements in Tennessee and Mississippi. In 1863 he was called home to look after the affairs of his wife's father, Alanson Green Pearce, who died during that year. Mr. Kemper spent the remainder of his life on his plantation near Evergreen and was one of the prosperous planters of his community. He died at his home on Wednesday, April 22, 1896, and was buried in the Evergreen cemetery. He and his wife had three children:—

> a.—Sidney Jemima Kemper.
> b.—Ann Eliza Kemper.
> c.—Burdette Kemper.

a.—Sidney Jemima Kemper, eldest child of Henry Clay Kemper and Virginia Ann Pearce, and grand-daughter of Alanson Green Pearce and Sidney Elizabeth Kay, was born near Evergreen, Avoyelles parish, Louisiana, on December 7, 1859, and was married on Thursday, January 22, 1885, to Dr. Porter Bagley Wright who was born July 30, 1849, at Darien Center, near Alden, New York. Dr. Wright practiced dentistry in and around Evergreen for many years and died there Thursday, December 4, 1924. His wife survived him more than twelve years, dying at Evergreen on April 22, 1937. They had four children:—

> az.—John Sidney Wright.
> bz.—Henry Clay Kemper Wright.
> cz.—George Burdette Wright.
> dz.—Alva Pearce Wright.

az.—John Sidney Wright, eldest son of Dr. Porter Bagley Wright and Sidney Jemima Kemper, was born at Evergreen, Avoyelles parish, La., on November 8, 1885, and on Wednesday, October 2, 1912, he married Kate Orme Brunson, born November 26, 1890, a daughter of John Burns Brunson and Sarah Metcalf Tanner, and a grand-daughter of Robert and Anna Tanner. Five children were born of this marriage:— John Brunson Wright, born July 16, 1915; Henry Clay Wright, born April 9, 1917; Robert Lynn Wright, born December 1, 1919; Alanson Burns Wright, born January 8, 1922; William Daniel Wright, born January 9, 1924.

John Brunson Wright married Kathleen Bourland of Mississippi in November, 1939. They have one daughter, Susan Bourland Wright, born June 29, 1944. Henry Clay Wright married Marjorie Escudé on December 23, 1939. She is a daughter of Arthur Escudé and Martha Regard and was born in Mansura, Avoyelles parish, La., on October 19, 1916. They now reside in Baton Rouge, La., and have two children:— Martha Kay Wright, born September 9, 1941, and Constance Lynn Wright, born December 27, 1944.

Robert Lynn Wright is as yet unmarried and at this time is serving in the United States Army.

Alanson Burns Wright enlisted in the U. S. Marines in World War II and on December 12, 1942, the Navy Department notified his family that he had been "killed in action" somewhere in the South Pacific.

William Daniel Wright is as yet unmarried and is now serving in the U. S. Navy.

bz.—Henry Clay Kemper Wright, second son of Dr. Porter Bagley Wright and Sidney Jemima Kemper, was born January 28, 1887, and died January 6, 1889, at the age two years.

cz.—George Burdette Wright, third son of Dr. Porter Bagley Wright and Sidney Jemima Kemper, was born at Evergreen, Avoyelles parish, La., on Thursday, September 6, 1888, and married Wednesday, November 11, 1909, at Richmond, Virginia, Willie Chapman Crutchfield, daughter of Judge John Jeter Crutchfield and Rosa Alice Brown of that city. She was born in Richmond on September 26, 1887, and died at Evergreen on March 23, 1935. Four children were born of this marriage:—Sidney Kemper Wright, born September 24, 1910; Alice Crutchfield Wright, born January 5, 1913; Porter Bagley Wright, born October 3, 1919; John Jeter Crutchfield Wright, born March 7, 1922. The eldest of these, Sidney Kemper Wright, was married September 6, 1942, to James Edward McNamara who was born at Thibodaux, Louisiana, on July 25, 1905. They are now living in Santo Domingo where Mr. McNamara has been employed as a sugar chemist for many years. His wife met him when she went there to teach school. Alice Crutchfield Wright, the second daughter, was married to Captain Irwin M. Porter of Raleigh, N. C., who was a member of the 82nd Airborne Division and participated in the invasion of France where he was killed in action on June 15, 1944. Porter Bagley Wright is in the U. S. Navy at present and married at Newark, N. J., Saturday, July 29, 1944, Jean Frances, daughter of Mr. and Mrs. Raymond Francis Cleary. John Jeter Crutchfield Wright is now serving in the U. S. Marines.

dz.—Alva Pearce Wright, fourth son of Dr. Porter Bagley Wright and Sidney Jemima Kemper, was born at Evergreen, Avoyelles parish, La., on Sunday morning, March 15, 1891, and married at Birmingham, Alabama, on Thursday, June 20, 1913, Louise Esten Oliver, daughter of James McCarty Oliver and Ada Shepard. She was born at Dadeville, Alabama, on May 11, 1890. They have three children:—Olivia Louise Wright, born April 10, 1914; Henry Kemper Wright, born July 17, 1915; Alva Shepard Wright, born June 7, 1919. The eldest, Olivia Louise Wright, was married to Lionel Atz Folse on Tuesday evening, March 6, 1934, a son of Raphael James Folse and Pauline Rosenberg. They have one son, Raphael James Folse, III, born March 6, 1936. Henry Kemper Wright is now an aviator in the U. S. Army. He married Martha Mahoney October 14, 1941. No issue as yet. Alva Shepard Wright is now serving in the U. S. Navy. He married Helen Margarette Berthelot on July 27, 1940. They have one daughter, Marlene Helen Wright, born April 25, 1941.

b.—Ann Eliza Kemper, second daughter of Henry Clay Kemper and Virginia Ann Pearce, was born near Evergreen, Avoyelles parish, La., on December 13, 1868. She was married in 1889 to William Usery Perkins, son of Hardeman Perkins and Elizabeth Jackson Barham, both natives of Tennessee. He was born in Rusk county, Texas, on May 13, 1856, and he and his wife are both dead at this time (1944). She died April 22, 1936. They had four children:—

> az.—Louise Kemper Perkins.
> bz.—Samuel Joseph Perkins.
> cz.—Henry Clay Perkins.
> dz.—Virginia Elizabeth Perkins.

az.—Louise Kemper Perkins, born September 1, 1890, was married September 25, 1917, to Jesse Rodman Wilson of Fort Worth, Texas. They now reside in Westfield, New Jersey, and have four children:—William Daniel born March 11, 1919; Anne Kemper, born April 4, 1921; Jesse Rodman, Jr., born April 4, 1921; George Mickle, born July 30, 1923.

bz.—Samuel Joseph Perkins was born May 13, 1892, and died March 18, 1914.

cz.—Henry Clay Perkins was born December 8, 1896, and married September 15, 1927, Dorothy Monroe Benners of Dallas, Texas, who died June 17, 1932, leaving no issue. He is a physician and now resides in Austin, Texas.

dz.—Virginia Elizabeth Perkins, born April 8, 1902, was married September 21, 1923, to Dr. Albert Langston Nelson, son of Dr. and Mrs. Albert A. Nelson of Nacogdoches, Texas. He was born October 2, 1900, and is a prominent physician in his native city. Dr. and Mrs. Nelson have no children. They reside at 721 North Street, in Nacogdoches.

ii.—William Oscar Pearce, second child of Alanson Green Pearce and Sidney Elizabeth Kay, was born in Evergreen, Avoyelles parish, Louisiana, March 24, 1840. He was twice married. His first wife was Minerva Frith, daughter of Thomas Poindexter Frith and Sarah Cullom. The Friths are an old family in Avoyelles parish, almost as old as the parish itself. Archibald Frith left Virginia in the early days of the nineteenth century and emigrated to the Mississippi Territory. A little later, and prior to the battle of New Orleans (1815), he crossed the Mississippi river and went into Louisiana, settling permanently in Avoyelles parish on Bayou Huffpower. There at this date (1944), and on the same property, lives his great grand-daughter. After his death his son, Thomas Poindexter Frith, succeeded to his vast estate. This son married Sarah Cullom, daughter of Francis Cullom and Maria Prewett. Sarah Cullom was a sister of Judge E. North Cullom, a famous jurist and lawyer in central Louisiana half a century ago. William Oscar Pearce and Minerva Frith had three children:—

a.—Alanson Green Pearce.
b.—Mary Frith Pearce.
c.—Thomas Frith Pearce.

Some years following the death of his first wife, William Oscar Pearce remarried, his second wife being Ida Rice. They had one child:—

d.—Augustus Rice Pearce.

a.—Alanson Green Pearce, eldest child of William Oscar Pearce and his first wife, Minerva Frith, was born near Evergreen, Avoyelles parish, Louisiana, in 1867. He was a prominent and popular physician in his section of his native parish, and married June 25, 1890, Mary H. Winn, a daughter of Dr. William H. Winn. Both are long since dead. They left five children:—Lucille Pearce who married P. H. Harrison, Maudrie Pearce who married Carl Bancroft, Sadie Pearce who married William Reid, and Malcolm and Winn Pearce who, as far as we have been able to ascertain, never married.

b.—Mary Frith Pearce, second child of William Oscar Pearce and his first wife, Minerva Frith, was married to A. Byron West of Avoyelles parish, La., son of Isham West and Eliza Catherine O'Quin, and grandson of Rev. John O'Quin and Anna Allen. His grandfather (Rev. John O'Quin) was a son of Rev. Ezekial O'Quin and Mary Brockston, and Ezekial O'Quin was a son of John O'Quin and Gracey Spivey of North Carolina. A. Byron West was born in Avoyelles parish, La., on September 28, 1868, and he and his wife now reside in Bunkie and have one daughter, Sarah Frith West.

c.—Thomas Frith Pearce, third child of William Oscar Pearce and his first wife, Minerva Frith, was born in Avoyelles parish, La. He now resides in Bunkie where he is a prominent business man. He married Addie Smyth, a daughter of Hervy Smyth and Ann Rebecca Irion (daughter of Robert Richardson Irion and Ann Bernard Audebert). They have no children.

d.—Augustus Rice Pearce, son of William Oscar Pearce and his second wife, Ida Rice, is now living in or near Prescott, Arizona. He has been twice married but we have been unable to get any very definite information on the subject. We are told that his first wife's name was Alma and his second Ruth, and that there are children by both marriages.

iii.—Sarah Ophelia Pearce, third child of Alanson Green Pearce and Sidney Elizabeth Kay, was born in Evergreen, Avoyelles parish, La., on March 16, 1842, and died on April 10, 1919. She was married on Aug. 17, 1859, to David Maunsel

Bennett, son of Ezra Bennett and his wife, Sarah Providence Eldred (daughter of Randal Eldred, Jr., and Esther Susannah Robert). Mr. Bennett was born in Rapides parish, La., on September 24, 1837, and died there on June 13, 1884. His father, Ezra Bennett, was a native of the State of New York where he was reared and educated. He came to Louisiana when a young man in the capacity of a school teacher. Soon after reaching here he married Sarah Providence Eldred who was born in Rapides parish whither her father had emigrated from his native State of North Carolina. Ezra Bennett and his wife were the parents of seven children and three of their sons were soldiers in the Confederate Army. His wife's father (Randal Eldred, Jr.) died in Rapides parish at the age of seventy. Ezra Bennett died at his home on Bayou Boeuf in 1878 at the age of sixty-five, and his wife ten years previously, in 1868, at the age of fifty-six.

David Maunsel Bennett served in the Confederate Army throughout the Civil War and at the ending of it held the rank of a captain. He was a civil engineer by profession and was actively engaged in surveying during the greater part of his life. Of his marriage with Sarah Ophelia Pearce four children were born:—

> a.—Sarah Ophelia Bennett.
> b.—Mary Virginia Bennett.
> c.—Susie Bennett.
> d.—Paul Jones Bennett.

a.—Sarah Ophelia Bennett, eldest child of David Maunsel Bennett and Sarah Ophelia Pearce, was born in Rapides parish, La., on September 20, 1862, and died in October, 1912. She was married in 1887 to Dr. William Griffin Branch, son of Dr. Leroy Kilpatrick Branch and his second wife, Laura E. Griffin (daughter of William F. Griffin). Dr. Branch was born in Avoyelles parish, La., on December 18, 1860. He graduated in medicine from the University of Louisville, Kentucky, in February, 1884. He first located in Karnes county, Texas, but a few years later returned to Louisiana and located at Bunkie in the parish of his birth. We have no record of the date of his death. He and his wife had no children.

b.—Mary Virginia Bennett, second child of David Maunsel Bennett and Sarah Ophelia Pearce, was born in Rapides parish,

La., on March 22, 1866. She was married on April 13, 1898, to Frank Pearce, son of Silas Franklin Pearce and his second wife, Frances Tanner (daughter of Asa Tanner). Silas Franklin Pearce was a son of Stephen Pearce, and his first wife, Sally Goodwin Bray. Frank Pearce and his wife had four sons, all of whom are living at this date (1944). They are:—John Silas, Maunsel Bennett, Walter Francis, and Frank Pearce, Jr. (See "Silas Franklin Pearce.")

c.—Susie Bennett, third child of David Maunsel Bennett and Sarah Ophelia Pearce, was born in Rapides parish, La., on August 13, 1869. She was married on February 18, 1892, to Beauregard Pearce, son of Silas Franklin Pearce and his second wife, Frances Tanner. They had three children:— Fannie Ophelia, William Branch, and Sidney Bennett Pearce. (See "Silas Franklin Pearce.")

d.—Paul Jones Bennett, fourth child of David Maunsel Bennett and Sarah Ophelia Pearce, was born in Rapides parish, La., on July 12, 1873. He was a prominent business man in Cheneyville and later in Alexandria, La. He married Ruth Branch, daughter of Dr. Leroy Kilpatrick Branch and his second wife, Laura E. Griffin. They had no children. Mr. Bennett died April 11, 1927. His widow now resides in Bunkie, La.

iv.—Eugenia Pearce, fourth child of Alanson Green Pearce and Sidney Elizabeth Kay, was born in Evergreen, Avoyelles parish, La., July 26, 1846. She was married to Joshua Burdette Kemper, son of Burdette Kemper and his wife, Jemima Thompson of Garrard county, Kentucky. He was a brother of Henry Clay Kemper who had married Virginia Ann Pearce. We have no records of the dates of death of Mr. and Mrs. Kemper. They had one child, Octavia Kemper, who married William Anderson, now deceased, and had three children:— Paul, Eugenia, and William Anderson. We regret our inability to obtain any information on these children.

v.—Ella Pearce, fifth child of Alanson Green Pearce and Sidney Elizabeth Kay, was born in Evergreen, Avoyelles parish, La., April 19, 1848. She was married to Andrew Kendrick Jackson (usually recorded as "Ken" Jackson), son of Andrew Jackson and Eliza Chambers (daughter of William Woodson Chambers and Sarah Ann Pearce). We find Andrew Jackson and his wife frequently mentioned by Rev. W. E. Paxton in his "History of the Baptists of Louisiana." On page 169, in writing of the trouble which occurred in the Baulah Baptist Church at Cheneyville, Paxton says:—

> The seceding members organized a church in Cheney-ville, which they denominated the "Church of Christ," and they called themselves Disciples or Christians. This was done in May, 1843. By January, 1844, this body, at first organized with eight members, had grown to fifty members. At this time they chose Jabez Tanner and Andrew Jackson as deacons, and John W. Pearce as bishop, and these were ordained by Rev. W. P. Ford, an ordained minister of the Spring Hill Baptist Church.

This seceding church was known during the early days of this compiler as the Campbellite Church and the brick columns of the old edifice are yet standing. Andrew Jackson, his wife, W. P. Ford and others were tried by the local Baptist Church and their membership in it taken from them. Kendrick Jackson and Ella Pearce, his wife, died many years ago. They had four children:—

    a.—Eliza Jackson.
    b.—Oscar Jackson.
    c.—Alanson Green Jackson.
    d.—Stephen Rushing Jackson.

a.—Eliza Jackson was married to Aubry L. Johnston. They had three children:—Louise Johnston who married R. Stump; Mary Johnston who married a Mr. Shirley; Caro Johnston (probably Caroline) who married J. B. Mackey.

b. and c.—Oscar and Alanson Green Jackson died young and unmarried. The latter was murdered by a Negro.

d.—Stephen Rushing Jackson was engaged in the mercantile business in or near Cheneyville, La., most of his life. He first married Alice Robert, daughter of John Pearce Robert and Mary Sandefur, and a grand-daughter of James Bordeaux Jaudon Robert and Martha Esther Pearce (daughter of Stephen Pearce, and his first wife, Sally Goodwin Bray). One son, Stephen Rushing Jackson, Jr., was born of this marriage, who is now postmaster of Cheneyville, and who married on November 6, 1924, Helen Davis Barstow, daughter of George

Baham Barstow and Helen Keary Stafford. They had three children:—Helen Alice, Constance Elise, and Blanche Catherine Jackson. Stephen Rushing Jackson, Jr., and his wife were divorced a few years ago and on Saturday, December 6, 1941, he married Elise Tanner, daughter of Early Tanner and Grace Miles.

Stephen Rushing Jackson, Sr., after the death of his first wife, Alice Robert, married Blanche Casin Doherty. They had no children. Mr. Jackson died at his home near Cheneyville, La., on Wednesday, February 5, 1941, at the age of sixty-seven years, eleven months and eighteen days. He was buried in the Cheneyville Baptist cemetery.

vi.—Emily Octavia Pearce, sixth child of Alanson Green Pearce and Sidney Elizabeth Kay, was born in Evergreen, Avoyelles parish, La., December 12, 1845. She lived to an advanced age and died January 17, 1933, unmarried.

vii.—Clara Pearce, seventh child of Alanson Green Pearce and Sidney Elizabeth Kay, was born in Evergreen, Avoyelles parish, La., on February 16, 1850. She was married there on February 23, 1869, to Jesse James Toon, and died on August 5, 1931, at the advanced age of eighty-one years. Jesse James Toon was born in Memphis, Tennessee, on April 10, 1845, and died on August 20, 1885. Three children were born of this marriage:—

> a.—Sidney Caroline Toon.
> b.—Eugenia Kemper Toon.
> c.—John Lewis Toon.

a.—Sidney Caroline Toon, better known to her family and and friends as "Caro," was born in Avoyelles parish, La., on May 8, 1870, and died on November 30, 1937. She never married. It is said she was very interested in genealogy and had accumulated much data on the Pearce family.

b.—Eugenia Kemper Toon was born in Avoyelles parish, La., on March 15, 1873, and was married to James Steele Barker on February 4, 1897. Mr. Barker is now dead and his widow resides in Bunkie, La., at this time. Three children were born of this marriage:—

> az.—Jesse Barker.
> bz.—Clarence Barker.
> cz.—Anna Caroline Barker.

az.—Jesse Barker married Rosalie Eliff on February 1, 1935, They have a son, Jesse Barker, Jr.

bz.—Clarence Barker married Hester Beene on February 3, 1927. They have three children:—Anna Marie, Betty,and Nancy Barker.

cz.—Anna Caroline Barker was married to Homer Morris on September 17, 1928. One daughter was born of this marriage, Anna Carolyne Morris.

Mrs. Morris kindly furnished the compiler with much of this data on Alanson Green Pearce and his descendants, for which he wishes here to express his gratitude.

c.—John Lewis Toon married Lillian Lyons. They now have three daughters:—Catherine, Barbara, and Mary Ruth Toon.

viii.—Wioatte Kay Pearce, eighth child of Alanson Green Pearce and Sidney Elizabeth Kay, was born in Evergreen, Avoyelles parish, La., on October 21, 1852, and died on December 19, 1910. He was twice married. His first wife was Anna Pollard and his second was Mary Bennett West. As far as we can ascertain there were no children by the first marriage. He married his second wife, Mary Bennett West, on December 27, 1899. She was a daughter of Isham West and Eliza Catherine O'Quin, and a grand-daughter of Rev. John O'Quin and Anna Allen, and was born in Avoyelles parish, La., on October 14, 1876. She is living at this date (1944). Wioatte Kay Pearce and his second wife, Mary Bennett West, had three children, all of whom are living at this time. They are:—

a.—Mary Anna Pearce, born August 15, 1901
b.—Lula Eliza Pearce, born July 14, 1904.
c.—Sidney Anita Pearce, born November 25, 1906.

a.—Mary Anna Pearce, was married in 1924 to John Webster Hickman. He was born in Rapides parish, La., on June 28, 1898, and was a son of Taylor Sanford Hickman and Fannie Fee Taylor. His father's parents were John Webster Hickman and Alice Sanford, and his mother's parents were Waverley Emmett Taylor and his first wife, Rosa Manidue (Dawson) Johnson (a daughter of James H. Dawson and his first wife, Louisa A. Bonner, and widow of William Hunter

Johnson). Mr. and Mrs. Hickman reside in Alexandria, La., and have four daughters:—

Mary Elizabeth Hickman, born June 19, 1925.
Evelyn Taylor Hickman, born October 20, 1927.
Shirley Sanford Hickman, born November 4, 1928.
Joan Pearce Hickman, born February 2, 1932.

b.—Lula Eliza Pearce was married at the Highland Baptist Church, Shreveport, La., on Tuesday, November 14, 1944, by the Rev. John C. Caylor, to Staff Sergeant Joseph Melville Kincaid, son of Windall Philip Kincaid and Minnie Beard of St. Petersburg, Florida. Sergeant Kincaid is now with the 4th Air Force, stationed at Santa Maria, California.

c.—Sidney Anita Pearce was married in Alexandria, La., on March 13, 1943, to George Washington Shannon of El Dorado, Arkansas, son of Henry Heywood Shannon.

ix.—Lillinia Eliza Pearce (better known as Lily), ninth child of Alanson Green Pearce and Sidney Elizabeth Kay, was born in Evergreen, Avoyelles parish, La., June 15, 1854. She was married in June, 1883, to Alvin Thomas Allen who was born in Plaquemine parish, La., on August 24, 1852, and came to Bunkie, La., in 1882 as agent for the Texas & Pacific Railway Company. He was reared and educated in New Orleans where he learned telegraphy when quite a young man and began working for the Western Union Telegraph Company. Mr. Allen was a son of A. D. Allen and Mary A. Neal, the the former a native of Buffalo, New York, and the latter of Louisiana. Paternally his grandparents were Germans and maternally they were natives of Liverpool, England. His father (A. D. Allen) was reared in New York State and for many years was an ocean sailor. He later became a pilot at the port of New Orleans. He went to England for his health and died at Liverpool on July 4, 1859. Alvin Thomas Allen and his wife, Lillinia Pearce, had three children:—

a.—Mary Kemper Allen.
b.—Octavia Pearce Allen.
c.—Anna Wioatte Allen.

a.—Mary Kemper Allen was married to Christopher Columbus Robinson. They had two children:—Christopher Columbus Robinson, Jr., and Mary Allen Robinson.

b.—Octavia Pearce Allen was married to Levi Patrick Carter, Sr. She was his second wife. They reside in Bunkie, La., and have a son, Henry Allen Carter, born in 1930.

c.—Anna Wioatte Allen never married and has been teaching in the public schools of Louisiana for many years.

x.—Alva Green Pearce, tenth child of Alanson Green Pearce and Sidney Elizabeth Kay, was born in Evergreen, Avoyelles parish, La., November 27, 1856. He married Josie Horn who yet survives him and who after his death was married to a Mr. Coates. One child was born of the first marriage, Alva Pearce, and sne was married to Walter J. Dunn and has one child, Eleanor Dunn.

B.

STEPHEN PEARCE.

Stephen Pearce, second son of William Pearce, Sr., and his wife, Sarah Bray, was born in Screven county, Georgia, on December 19, 1783, and died near Cheneyville, Rapides parish, La., on October 16, 1833. He came to Rapides parish, La., about 1808 and settled on the left descending bank of Bayou Boeuf about a mile above the present town of Cheneyville. His plantation was known as "Magnolia," and there he spent the remainder of his days in peace and plenty, rearing a large family. He was twice married. His first wife, whom he married in Screven county, Georgia, on September 13, 1805, shortly before he left there for Louisiana, was Sally Goodwin Bray—very probably a relative of his mother. She was born in Georgia on February 15, 1790, and was less than fifteen years of age when she married. She died in Rapides parish, La., on October 25, 1829, being the mother of eleven children. In a copy of THE ALEXANDRIA GAZETTE, one of the early newspapers of central Louisiana, we find the following notice of her death:—

Sally G. Pearce, consort of Stephen Pearce, died on Sunday, October 25, 1829, in her 40th year.

Her eleven children were:—

1.—William Bray Pearce.
2.—Susan Heddingrant Pearce.
3.—Eliza Caroline Pearce.
4.—Sally Ann Pearce.

5.—John Washington Pearce.
6.—Mary Talbert Pearce.
7.—Martha Esther Pearce.
8.—Delia Melvina Pearce.
9.—Silas Franklin Pearce.
10.—Amelia Tuzette Pearce.
11.—Charles Lafayette Pearce.

The second wife of Stephen Pearce, was Anne Grimball (Tanner) Brown, widow of William Brown and daughter of Robert Tanner and his wife, Providence Robert. She had one son by her former marriage, William Robert Brown (see Part Three). Her marriage to Mr. Pearce took place on September 30, 1830. He died three years later leaving one son by the second marriage:—

12.—Stephen Samuel Pearce.

Mrs. Anne Grimball (Tanner-Brown) Pearce died July 27, 1852. As both Mr. Pearce and his second wife had issue by their first marriages it became necessary for the protection of the inheritance of those children to have an inventory taken of their possessions at the time of their marriage. We are fortunate in having the notary book kept by William Bray Pearce in which the inventory and appraisment of the property of Stephen Pearce and Anne Grimball (Tanner) Brown was recorded. We will here insert an abbreviated copy of both of the documents:—

STATE OF LOUISIANA,
PARISH OF RAPIDES:

I, W. B. Pearce, Notary Public in and for the Parish aforesaid, together with Silas Talbert and Winder Crouch, yeoman of the Parish and State aforesaid, repaired to the last place of residence of the late Sarah G. Pearce, dec'd., for the purpose of making an inventory and appraisment of the gains and acquits of Stephen Pearce and his wife Sarah G. Pearce, dec'd. Wherefore it stands stated as follows, to-wit:

Tract of land on left bank of Bayou Boeuf in descending, 380 acres,	$ 6,000.00
Negro slaves	11,925.00
Stock, farming implements, household furniture, notes,	3,170.87
	$21,095.87

We the appraisers of the foregoing property after being qualified according to law have appraised it as it stands stated. Given under our hands this 21st day of March, 1831.

Witnesses: Silas Talbert
Henry Jackson   Winder Crouch.
C. D. Brashear.   Done before me,
                       W. B. Pearce, Notary Public.

STATE OF LOUISIANA,
PARISH of RAPIDES:

I, W. B. Pearce, Notary Public in and for the Parish aforesaid, together with Silas Talbert and Winder Crouch yeomen of the State and Parish aforesaid, have this day proceeded to make an inventory and appraisment of the goods and effects, rights and credits of Anne G. Brown, alias Ann G. Pearce. Wherefore it stands as follows, to wit:

Tract of land on right bank of Bayou Boeuf in
    descending, containing 400 arpents, ... $4,800.00
Negro slaves 2,050.00
Stock, household furniture, accounts, etc., ... 1,144.00
                                                        _____
                                                         $7,994.00

We the appraisers of the foregoing property after being qualified according to law have appraised it as it stands stated. Given under our hands this 12th day of March, 1831.

Witnesses: Silas Talbert
Henry Jackson   Winder Crouch.
C. D. Brashear.   Done before me,
                       W. B. Pearce, Notary Public.

1.—William Bray Pearce, eldest son of Stephen Pearce, and his first wife, Sally Goodwin Bray, was born October, 14, 1807, probably in Screven county, Georgia. He died in Rapides parish, La., on July 1, 1837. He was twice married. His first wife, whom he married on June 19, 1828, was Rosalind Harley Tanner, fourteenth child of Robert Tanner and Providence Robert. It is a unique incident that she and the second wife of her husband's father (Stephen Pearce,) were sisters. Rosalind Harley Tanner was born near Cheneyville, Rapides parish,

La., on April 7, 1813, and died there on December 28, 1834, at the age of twenty-one, leaving three daughters:—

      i.—Sarah Providence Pearce.
      ii.—Matilda Ann Pearce.
      iii.—Rosalind Josephine Pearce.

In 1836 William Bray Pearce married his second wife and died the following year, leaving no issue by her. She was Jane Sophronia Grimball, a cousin of his first wife, and a daughter of Paul Grimball and Esther Jaudon. The Grimballs were early pioneers to Rapides parish, La. from South Carolina. After the death of Mr. Pearce his widow married Otho L. Pumphrey and moved with him to Franklin, La., where both died many years later. She had one daughter by her second marriage, Annette, who married a Mr. Trasteur and died without issue.

      i.—Sarah Providence Pearce, eldest daughter of William Bray Pearce and his first wife, Rosalind Harley Tanner, was born near Cheneyville, Rapides parish, La., on June 14, 1829. She married on January 27, 1847, to Newton McCluskey Proctor who was born February 8, 1814, at Pea Ridge, Lincoln county, Tennessee, about ten miles from Fayetteville which was the county seat, and was a son of James Newton Proctor and Elizabeth McCluskey. In 1854 Mr. and Mrs. Proctor left Louisiana and moved to Texas, settling about five miles southwest of Belton, the county seat of Bell county. Mr. Proctor died there on September 5, 1885, and his wife on November 30, 1914. They had fifteen children, five of whom were born in Louisiana and all the others in Texas. Those children were:—

      a.—William James Proctor.
      b.—Newton McCluskey Proctor, Jr.
      c.—Charles Proctor.
      d.—Mary Elizabeth Proctor.
      e.—Henry Proctor.
      f.—Jefferson Proctor.
      g.—Infant daughter, un-named.
      h.—Sally Pearce Proctor.
      i—Silas Talbert Proctor.
      j.—Louis Calvin Proctor.
      k.—Rosalind Proctor.
      l.—Robert Lee Proctor.

m.—Maggie Proctor.
n.—Julia Proctor.
o.—George A. Proctor.

Five of these children died in infancy, viz., e.—Henry, born September 16, 1853, died January 18, 1857; f.—Jefferson, born December 7, 1854, died June 21, 1855; g.—Infant daughter, un-named, born April 10, 1856, died April 11, 1856; h.—Sally Pearce, born January 28, 1864, died November 15, 1864; m.—Maggie, born August 24, 1867, died December 18, 1870.

a.—William James Proctor, eldest child of Newton McCluskey Proctor and Sarah Providence Pearce, was born near Cheneyville, Rapides parish, La., on January 22, 1848, and died in Texas on November 7, 1882. He married Fannie Elizabeth Law on October 16, 1873. They had seven children:—

az.—Henry Keys Proctor.
bz.—Newton McCluskey Proctor, III.
cz.—Robert Hughes Proctor.
dz.—William McKey Proctor.
ez.—Rosa Alice Proctor.
fz.—Jarrett Law Proctor.
gz.—Sallie Elizabeth Proctor.

az.—Henry Keys Proctor was born July 26, 1874, and married Ettie Smith on May 10, 1911. They have no children.

bz.—Newton McCluskey Proctor, III, was born July 20, 1875, and died on December 1, 1894.

cz.—Robert Hughes Proctor, the elder of twins, was born July 11, 1877, and married Zilpah Bailey Allen on August 31, 1911. We have been unable to get a record of any descendants.

dz.—William McKey Proctor, the younger of twins, was born January 11, 1877, and married Lou Henry Jarnigin on December 18, 1898. They have one son, Lester Earl Proctor, who married Gladys Sutton and they have a daughter, Mary Lou Proctor.

ez.—Rosa Alice Proctor was born October 5, 1879, and was married to Robert Henry Law on May 22, 1902. They have five children:—Robert Henry Law, Jr., born May 17, 1903, married Verna Ellis on July 3, 1936; Leyland Hunter Law, born August 9, 1905, married Mertie Marie Fowler on February 28, 1941; Lovick Law (one of twins), born September

30, 1908, married Sarah Elizabeth Weaver on December 31, 1938; Fannie Law (the other twin), born September 30, 1908, married Herbert Voss on June 21, 1936, and they have one daughter, Margaret Ann Voss; Wallace William Law, born August 21, 1911, unmarried.

fz.—Jarrett Law Proctor was born March 17, 1881, and died July 27, 1882.

gz.—Sallie Elizabeth Proctor was born May 16, 1883, and was married on December 26, 1906, to Arthur Wade Capps. They had four children:—William Clinton Capps, born October 9, 1908, and died November 15, 1908; Sallie Agnes Capps, born August 12, 1910; Arthur Proctor Capps, born March 20, 1914, married Prudie Hodge on December 26, 1938, and they have one son, Arthur Wade Capps, Jr., born July 11, 1940; Clyde M. Capps, born October 1, 1921.

b.—Newton McCluskey Proctor, Jr., second child of Newton McCluskey Proctor and Sarah Providence Pearce, was born near Cheneyville, Rapides parish, La., on May 1, 1849, and died in Texas on February 7, 1937. He married Laura Wilson Shanklin of Goliad, Texas. They had eight children:—

az.—Sarah Maude Proctor.
bz.—Mary Katherine Proctor.
cz.—Margaret Summers Proctor.
dz.—Charles Luther Proctor.
ez.—Calvin Farris Proctor.
fz.—Roy L. Proctor.
gz.—Eleanor Proctor.
hz.—Samuel Shanklin Proctor (died in childhood).

cz.—Margaret Summers Proctor, third daughter of Newton McCluskey Proctor, Jr., and Laura Wilson Shanklin, was married to James Philip Cogdell of Winters, Texas. They have two sons:—Alfred Banfield and James Newton Cogdell. The elder married Syble Rose of Wink, Texas, and they have a son, Alfred Banfield Cogdell, Jr., three years and three months of age at this date (March, 1944).

dz.—Charles Luther Proctor, fourth child of Newton McCluskey Proctor, Jr., and Laura Wilson Shanklin, married Arline Osterhout of Belton, Texas. They have one child, Charline Osterhout Proctor, who married Alton L. Strieber of San Antonio, Texas.

ez.—Calvin Farris Proctor, fifth child of Newton Mc-
Cluskey Proctor, Jr., and Laura Wilson Shanklin, married
Irene Rosalind Harward of Brownwood, Texas, who died five
years ago. No issue.

fz.—Roy L. Proctor, sixth child of Newton McCluskey
Proctor, Jr., and Laura Wilson Shanklin, married Ruby Chris-
teen Spence of Salado, Texas. They have a son, Richard Lee
Proctor.

c.—Charles Proctor was born July 19, 1850, near Cheneyville, Rapides parish, La., and died in Texas on April 2. 1897.
He never married.

d.—Mary Elizabeth Proctor, fourth child of Newton Mc-
Cluskey Proctor and Sarah Providence Pearce, was born near
Cheneyville, Rapides parish, La., on March 10, 1852, and died
in Texas on November 16, 1936. She was married May 26,
1870, to John Watson Shanklin who was born November 21,
1842, and died November 28, 1891. They had three sons:—

> az.—Newton William Shanklin.
> bz.—Nal L. Shanklin.
> cz.—John Watson Shanklin, Jr.

az.—Newton William Shanklin was born October 4, 1871,
and died June 5, 1898. He never married.

bz.—Nal L. Shanklin was born March 9, 1875, and married Ruth Barton on April 29, 1903. They have one son, Nal
L. Shanklin, Jr., born December 23, 1909.

cz.—John Watson Shanklin, Jr., was born December 9,
1879. He married Felda Louise Davis on October 14, 1903.
They have three children:—Louise Lane Shanklin, born September 19, 1904, married Ira C. Jenkins on June 15, 1927, and
has two children, Gale Jenkins, born April 18, 1934, and Robert
Ferrel Jenkins, born April 3, 1940; John Harold Shanklin,
born July 16, 1907, married Ruth Vernon LaFon on June 25,
1938; Evelyn Lorraine Shanklin, born February 14, 1911,
married Eugene L. Seastrand on February 13, 1937.

i.—Silas Talbert Proctor, ninth child of Newton McCluskey
Proctor and Sarah Providence Pearce, was born in Bell county,
Texas, on April 16, 1857, and married Estelle Black of Belton,
Texas, on December 1, 1889. They had four sons:—William,
born September 6, 1890, married, no issue; Lee, born August

13, 1892, married and had eight children; Wallace, born June 16, 1894, married and has two sons; Charlie, born April 23, 1896, married, no children, and is now dead.

j.—Louis Calvin Proctor, tenth child of Newton McCluskey Proctor and Sarah Providence Pearce, was born in Bell county, Texas, on January 3, 1859, and married Rita Hutchinson on November 1, 1891. He died on January 11, 1937, leaving two sons:—Leonard C. Proctor, born September 23, 1892, married Evelyn Scruggs of Georgia; Troy Proctor, born September 28, 1895, married Hahle Mitchel of New Mexico. The elder of these sons, Leonard C. Proctor, had a daughter, Jo Ann Proctor, born July 9, 1925.

k.—Rosalind Proctor, better known as "Rose," eleventh child of Newton McCluskey Proctor and Sarah Providence Pearce, was born in Bell county, Texas, in 1861, and married on January 13, 1886, Dr. A. C. Enochs of Crystal Springs, Mississippi. Dr. Enochs died May 17, 1933, and his wife on July 25, 1938. They had six children:—

az.—Un-named boy, born May 19, 1887.
bz.—Maggie Lee Enochs, born July 17, 1888.
cz.—Rosa Capers Enochs, born October 15, 1889.
dz.—Laura Estelle Enochs, born August 24, 1891.
ez.—Newton Edgar Enochs, born October 27, 1894.
fz.—Julia Elizabeth Enochs, born July 8, 1899.

az.—Un-named boy died May 26, 1887.
bz.—Maggie Lee Enochs was married October 28, 1908, to Richard Griffith. They have one daughter, Rosalind, born March 16, 1910.
cz.—Rosa Capers Enochs has never married.
dz.—Laura Estelle Enochs was married November 12, 1919, to Edwin D. Minteer. They have one son, Edwin Drew Minteer, Jr., born February 18, 1927.
ez.—Newton Edgar Enochs died January 13, 1896, aged fifteen months.
fz.—Julia Elizabeth Enochs was married March 23, 1922, to William C. Boyce. They have one child, Barbara, born October 15, 1925.
l.—Robert Lee Proctor, twelfth child of Newton McCluskey Proctor and Sarah Providence Pearce, was born in Bell

county, Texas, about 1866. He married Docia Bourne on
uary 22, 1900. Five children were born of this union:—

    az.—William Newton Proctor, born November 3, 1901
    bz.—Mary Estelle Proctor, born November 2, 1903.
    cz.—Hattie Rose Proctor, born January 8, 1906.
    dz.—Tolbert Lee Proctor, born July 15, 1908.
    ez.—Julia Alice Proctor, born August 4, 1916.
    az.—William Newton Proctor died September 19, 1904

    bz.—Mary Estelle Proctor was married to Elmer Hollaı
They have one child, Mary Sue Holland.

    cz.—Hattie Rose Proctor was married to Dr. Martin]
Densen. They have three children:—Mary Lee, Shirley Louis
and Martin H. Densen, Jr.

    dz.—Tolbert Lee Proctor marred Margerie Hollimon.The
have no children as yet.

    ez.—Julia Alice Proctor was married to Ed V. Lancaster.
They have one child, Shirley Ann Lancaster.

    n.—Julia Proctor, fourteenth child of Newton McCluskey
Proctor and Sarah Providence Pearce, was born in Bell county,
Texas, on August 13, 1870, and was married there on May 5,
1901, to David Ramsey Pendleton who was born in Ellis
county, Texas, on January 21, 1861. They now reside in
Tyler, Texas, and have five children:—

    az.—Hall Proctor Pendleton, born September 8, 1902.
    bz.—Enochs Lee Pendleton, born October 27, 1904.
    cz.—Sarah Pendleton, born April 3, 1907.
    dz.—Julia Pendleton, born September 30, 1909.
    ez.—Elizabeth Pendleton, born April 1, 1912.

    az.—Hall Proctor Pendleton married Velma Densen of
Spur, Texas, on September 11, 1926. They have two daughters:—Julia Ann, born April 28, 1930; Sandra, born December 29, 1937.

    bz.—Enochs Lee Pendleton is unmarried and lives in
Austin, Texas, where he is connected with a prominent Audit-
ing Company.

    cz.—Sarah Pendleton is unmarried and now teaches in the
public schools of Tyler, Texas.

    dz.—Julia Pendleton was married to Vernon Otis Magrill
on September 29, 1935, who was born and reared in Smith

county, Texas. They have one child, Madelyn, born November 28, 1938,

ez.—Elizabeth Pendleton was married to John Redd Penn of Martinsville, Virginia, on October 2, 1937. They have one child at this time, Elizabeth Caroline, born January 10, 1939.

o.—George A. Proctor, fifteenth and youngest child of Newton McCluskey Proctor and Sarah Providence Pearce, was born in Bell county, Texas, on July 13, 1872. He married Callie Pope Baker on December 6, 1899. They reside in Belton, Texas, and have three sons:—

az.—Robert Lynn Proctor, born September 8, 1900.
bz.—Clifford Eugene Proctor, born April 3, 1908.
cz.—William Freeman Proctor, born March 11, 1910.

az.—Robert Lynn Proctor married Corine Northan and they have two sons:—Billie Gene, born May 18, 1926, and Bobbie George, born August 27, 1928.

bz.—Clifford Eugene Proctor married Minnie Lee Warrenkin. They have two children:—a daughter born November 18, 1932, and a son born October 17, 1940.

cz.—William Freeman Proctor married Winnie Stringer. They have no children as yet.

ii.—Matilda Ann Pearce, second child of William Bray Pearce and his first wife, Rosalind Harley Tanner, was born near Cheneyville, Rapides parish, La., on July 25, 1831, and her death occurred there on April 7, 1911. She was married to William Franklin Cheney, son of William Fendon Cheney and Elizabeth Bealer. His father was the founder of Cheneyville. William Franklin Cheney was a veteran of the Mexican War and one of the outstanding citizens of the Cheneyville neighborhood, where he was born in 1818. We have no record of his death but it occurred many years before that of his wife. Six children were born of this marriage:—

a.—Rosa Jennie Cheney who married Marshall Pearce (son of John Washington Pearce and Eliza Jane Bray and grandson of Stephen Pearce). See page 388.

b.—Charles Cheney who died young.

c.—William F. Cheney who also died young.

d.—Elizabeth Ann Cheney who married James H. Cocks, and had two children:—Selser and Susie. The elder of these lived most of his life at Tioga, Rapides parish, La. He was twice married but had no children. Susie Cocks married Ed Pittman and had two daughters, Hartwell and Fay Bess.

e.—Sarah Elizabeth Cheney was married to Selser Cocks, a brother of James H. Cocks. They lived in Crosby, Texas, and after Mr. Cocks' death she married a Mr. Brown and lived in Dallas, Texas, until her death sometime after 1930. Mr. and Mrs. Selser Cocks had two children, William and Gussie. We know nothing further of the son. The daughter, Gussie, married a Dr. Crocker of Crosby, Texas, and they had several children among whom are Will and Cheney Crocker. The elder, Will Crocker, was postmaster when last heard of at Goose Creek, Texas, where all of them were living.

f.—George Morgan Cheney, the only son of William Franklin Cheney and Matilda Ann Pearce, married Fannie Marshall, daughter of Dr. Francis Wioatte Marshall and Mary Eleanor Chambers. He and his wife have been dead for many years. They left three children, William Franklin, II, Eleanor, and George Morgan Cheney, Jr. All are now living in New Orleans. See page 385.

iii.—Rosalind Josephine Pearce, youngest child of William Bray Pearce and his first wife, Rosalind Harley Tanner, was born near Cheneyville, Rapides parish, La., on May 4, 1834, and died in Alexandria, La., on September 29, 1917. She was buried in the old Cheney graveyard near Cheneyville. On November 20, 1850, she was married to Thomas Jefferson Stafford, born in Rapides parish, La., August 6, 1830, and died there November 1, 1911, son of Leroy Stafford and his second wife, Elizabeth Susan Calliham, and grandson of Seth Stafford and Amanda Maner. They had one son:—

a.—Leroy Stafford, II, born October 1, 1851.

a.—Leroy Stafford, II, was three times married. His first wife, whom he married March 12, 1878, was Henrietta Berlin. She died at the birth of their only son:—

az.—Henrie Leroy Stafford, born January 13, 1879.

His second wife, Henrietta Louise Cheney, whom he married February 9, 1885, was a daughter of Oscar Bailey Cheney and his first wife, Ellen Judith Wright. They had two sons:—

    bz.—Thomas Jefferson Stafford, II, born
           November 25, 1885.
    cz.—Oscar Cheney Stafford, born October 8, 1887.

His third wife, whom he married on February 28, 1892, was Priscilla Allen, daughter of Roland Allen and Joanna O'Neal. She was born September 22, 1873, and is living at this date (1944). Leroy Stafford died at his home near Cheneyville, La., on March 15, 1933, and was buried in the old Christian cemetery. There were fourteen children by his third marriage:—

    dz.—William Roland Stafford, born April 16, 1893.
    ez.—Rosalind Pearce Stafford, born November 30, 1894.
    fz.—Allen Stafford, born August 18, 1896.
    gz.—Manila Dewey Stafford, born June 12, 1898.
    hz.—David May Stafford, born February 13, 1900.
    iz.—James McWaters Stafford, born August 13, 1901.
    jz.—Alma Augusta Stafford, born October 27, 1903.
    kz.—Kate Tanner Stafford, born April 20, 1905.
    lz.—Joanna Stafford, born October 19, 1906.
    mz.—Julia Harmoline Stafford, born September 27, 1908.
    nz.—Ettie Gertrude Stafford, born May 11, 1909.
    oz.—Byron Lee Stafford, born October 6, 1910.
    pz.—Ruth Gayle Stafford, born February 16, 1912.
    qz.—Ralph Kilpatrick Stafford, born May 10, 1913.

    az.—Henrie Leroy Stafford, only child of Leroy Stafford and his first wife, is now living in Alexandria, La. He first married Annie May Jordan of Cheneyville, La. (at that time she was the widow Worthy), who died in Alexandria, La., on November 22, 1916. A few years later he married Lola Whitley. There were no children born of either marriage.

    bz.—Thomas Jefferson Stafford, II, and cz.—Oscar Cheney Stafford, the two children of Leroy Stafford by his second marriage, went to Texas to reside many years ago and little has been heard of them since. The elder is now living in Fort Worth, Texas. He has never married. The younger entered the U. S. Army many years ago and is now a sergeant stationed at Fort Sam Houston, San Antonio, Texas.

dz.—William Roland Stafford, son of Leroy Stafford, II, and his third wife, Priscilla Allen, now resides in Cheneyville, La., where he is engaged in the seed business. He married on November 3, 1915, Ione Hulsey. They have three children:—

Kennie Lee Stafford, born July 25, 1919.
Amelia Fay Stafford, born January 20, 1923.
Beverly Louise Stafford, born January 7, 1928.

The eldest of these, Kennie Lee Stafford, was for several years employed in the business office of the Louisiana State University. She was married in the Cheneyville Baptist church at 4 o'clock in the afternoon of Saturday, April 12, 1941, to Eben McBurney Stubblefield, son of Rev. and Mrs. E. Stubblefield of Slaughter, La. They now reside in Baton Rouge where Mr. Stubblefield is employed by the du Pont Company. The second daughter, Amelia Fay Stafford, was married at the Baptist Church at Cheneyville, La., on Saturday evening, August 5, 1944, to Lieutenant Robert Clark Jackson, son of Mr. and Mrs. Robert Clark Jackson of Lecompte, La. For the present they will reside at Laredo, Texas, where Lieutenant Jackson is stationed with the U. S. Army Air Corps.

ez.—Rosalind Pearce Stafford was married on October 14, 1915, at Cheneyville, La., to Alvin Hamilton May whose father was for many years presiding elder for the Methodist church in the Alexandria district. They resided for some time at Hattiesburg, Miss., but have recently moved to Baton Rouge, La. They have three children:—

Alvin Hamilton May, Jr., born July 24, 1917.
Leroy Stafford May, born February 29, 1920.
Priscilla Jean May, born March 26, 1928.

Alvin Hamilton May, Jr., is now a Captain in the U. S. Air Corps and is presently stationed at Calsstorm Field, Arcadia, Florida. He married Mary Dyer Teague on Saturday, July 18, 1942, at St. Francisville, La., a daughter of Mrs. Carrie Ledden Teague and the late Thomas Lewis Teague of Fayette, Miss. They have a son, Alvin Hamilton, III, born September 26, 1944, at Buckingham Hospital, Fort Myers, Florida.

Leroy Stafford May, the second son, is a Lieutenant in the U. S. Army Anti-Tank Corps, 86th Division, and is at present stationed in California, preparatory to a "Pacific voyage."

fz.—Allen Stafford resided for many years at Cheneyville, La., where he was engaged in business. A few years ago he moved to Baton Rouge, La., where he is employed by a large construction company. He married on October 1, 1921, Mary Haw, and they have two children:—

> Mary Juanita Stafford, born July 23, 1922.
> Allen Stafford, Jr., born January 16, 1928.

Mary Juanita Stafford was married Saturday, July 8, 1944, in the first Baptist Church at Baton Rouge, La., to Lieutenant Burdette E. Nygren who is stationed at Harding Field there. He is a son of Mr. and Mrs. Albert Nygren of Wayne, Nebraska.

gz.—Manila Dewey Stafford, generally known to her family as "Nell," received her name in response to an outburst of her father's patriotic enthusiasm during the Spanish-American War, her birth having occurred about the time of Admiral Dewey's famous victory over the Spanish fleet in Manila Bay. She was married on June 6, 1923, to Albert Tally Browne, son of Dr. Albert Roe Browne and his wife, Emma Reitzell. He was born on August 15, 1896, and was for several years Principal of the Lecompte High School in Rapides parish. Later he was made Assistant Superintendent of Education for the schools of Rapides parish, with headquarters in Alexandria. He then moved to Crowley, La., where he served for several years as Parish Superintendent of Education for Acadia parish. He then taught for a while at the State Normal College at Natchitoches. At present he resides in Baton Rouge where he is Assistant Superintendent of the schools of East Baton Rouge parish. Mr. and Mrs. Browne have two children:—

> Gwendolyn Nell Browne, born October 31, 1929.
> Jo Ann Browne, born April 3, 1932.

hz.—David May Stafford married Lucille Clopton of Morrow, La., in January, 1924, a daughter of B. W. Clopton and Dora Havard. He died in New Orleans on Friday, July 13, 1928, from an abscess of the brain, and was buried in the Christian church cemetery in Cheneyville, La. He left no children.

iz.—James McWaters Stafford was a teacher in the public schools of Louisiana for a number of years and at the time of his death was Principal of a school in Tangipahoa parish, near Pontchatoula. He married on January 12, 1935, Mertie Cunningham of Pontchatoula, La. They had one child, James McWaters Stafford, Jr., born September 24, 1936. James McWaters Stafford had been a sufferer for many years from rheumatism which evidently effected his heart, and he died from that complication at Cheneyville, La., while visiting his mother there, on March 24, 1939. He was buried in the Christian church cemetery at Cheneyville on Sunday morning following his death.

jz.—Alma Augusta Stafford is not married at this date —says she never expects to change her present status. Maybe she will not, but that is not the way the Staffords usually do. She is at present teaching in the public schools at Cheneyville, La.

kz.—Kate Tanner Stafford was married on August 6, 1930, to Edwin Burges Murphey, son of James Herbert Murphey and Lilla McDowell. They are distantly related, her great-grandmother and his great-great-grandmother were two sisters—daughters of Robert Tanner and Providence Robert. Mr. and Mrs. Murphey have resided for a number of years in Ann Arbor, Michigan, where Mr. Murphey is a prominent business man. They have two children:—Edwin Stafford Murphey, born in Detroit, Michigan, on March 22, 1941, and Catherine Allen Murphey, born May 25th, 1944, at St. Joseph's Hospital, Ann Arbor, Michigan.

lz.—Joanna Stafford, and nz.—Ettie Gertrude Stafford both died in infancy.

mz.—Julia Harmoline Stafford was married on December 31, 1935, to Arthur Everette Kloch, son of John C. Kloch, a resident for many years of Cheneyville, La., but a native of Nebraska. They have had two children:—Julia Harmoline Kloch, born Saturday, July 10, 1937, and died in November of the same year, and John Leroy Kloch, born Sunday, July 7, 1940.

oz.—Byron Lee Stafford, familiarly known to his family as "Jake," has been connected with the public schools of Rapides parish, La., for many years. For some time he was a member of the faculty of the Tioga High School, then he was transferred to the Bolton High School in Alexandria. He is now Principal of the High School at Forest Hill, La. He married on Tuesday, June 22, 1937, Marie Cleo David, daughter of John Poussin David and Ethma Ellington of Alexandria, La. They have two children, Marie Cleo Stafford, born at the Baptist Hospital in Alexandria, La., on Saturday, March 25, 1939, at 1 p. m., and Sally Ann Stafford, born at Baptist Hospital, Alexandria, La., on Saturday, January 20, 1945.

pz.—Ruth Gayle Stafford was married at Cheneyville, La., on September 6, 1936, to Hope Philip Wemple. They have two children at this time, Ruth Hope Wemple, born at Cheneyville, on Friday, September 9, 1938, and Priscilla Nan Wemple, born Sunday, October 22, 1944, at Alexandria, La.

qz.—Ralph Kilpatrick Stafford married on Sunday, December 29, 1940, Ruth Robert, daughter of Samuel Henderson Robert and Mattie Wall. They now reside in Cheneyville, La., and have a son, Samuel Leroy Stafford, born at Bunkie, La., Sunday, January 17, 1943.

2.—Susan Heddingrant Pearce, second child of Stephen Pearce, and his first wife, Sally Goodwin Bray, was born in Rapides parish, La., on January 24, 1809, and died in July, 1833. She was married in 1826 to R. Milligan. We have been unable to find any record of any descendants.

3.—Eliza Caroline Pearce, third child of Stephen Pearce, and his first wife, Sally Goodwin Bray, was born in Rapides parish, La., on May 15, 1811. She was married on February 5, 1829, to Charles Duvall Brashear, son of Belt Brashear and Amelia Duvall of Prince George county, Maryland. THE ALEXANDRIA (La.) GAZETTE of February, 1829, verifies this marrige with the following item:—

Charles D. Brashear married Eliza Caroline Pearce, daughter of Stephen Pearce, on Thursday, February 5, 1829.

Mr. Brashear was of splendid lineage—his father's and mother's families being very prominent in Maryland. A history of the Brashear family has been written and published by Mr. Henry Sinclair Brashear of Texarkana, Tex. The early progenitors of the Louisiana Brashears were two brothers, Ignatius and Jeremiah Brashear. Ignatius was familiarly known as "Nacy" Brashear and his son, Dr. Walter Brashear, settled in Morgan City, St. Mary's parish, La. He was probably the most distinguished of his name in this State. As an outstanding member of the medical profession of his day he has been accorded the credit of being the first surgeon to successfully perform a hip joint amputation. He was also a prominent and wealthy planter and took a leading part in political matters. He served a term as U. S. Senator from Louisiana and in 1844 was a delegate to the Whig Convention held in Baltimore to nominate a candidate for President of the United States., Dr. Brashear left several children and we heard of a grandson living in Louisiana as late as 1929 who bore his full name.

According to Mr. Henry Sinclair Brashear of Texarkana, Texas, the first known ancestor of the Brashear family was John de Brassier, a gentleman of the city of Rheims, France, who lived in the 15th century. In 1653 two Huguenot refugees, Benois and Robert Brassier (brothers), came to Virginia, but finding their surroundings unpleasant there they moved to Maryland in 1658 and settled in Calvert county. There Benois Brassier was commissioned a Justice in 1661. In 1663 he was naturalized and his name Anglicized as *Benjamin Brashear*... He died during that year. His wife Mary, whom he had married in France, later married Thomas Starling. She recorded her will at the time, as a prenuptial contract, and named her children by her first husband, Benjamin Brashear. They were:—Robert, John, Benjamin, Mary, Ann, Susanna, Martha and Elizabeth. The eldest of these children, Robert Brashear, married and left three sons:—Robert, Jr., Samuel, and Benjamin.

Samuel Brashear, the second of these three sons, married Ann Jones, daughter of William Jones and his wife, Dorothy. Their children were:—Basil, William, Ann, Elizabeth, Mary, Robert, and Samuel, Jr. Samuel Brashear, Jr., the last mentioned of these children, and probably the youngest, was born January 2, 1696, and married his cousin, Elizabeth Brashear, a daughter of Benjamin Brashear (son of Robert, Sr.) and Mary Jones (sister of Ann). They had many children, twelve or more, among whom were Jeremiah and Ignatius Brashear, progenitors of the Louisiana Brashears. Jeremiah Brashear was born in Prince George county, Maryland, on November 5,

1731, and Ignatius ("Nacy") Brashear was born there in 1734. The latter married Pamelia ————— and had thirteen children among whom was Dr. Walter Brashear, born in Prince George county, Maryland, on February 11, 1776. Our Charles Duvall Brashear who married Eliza Caroline Pearce was a son of Belt Brashear and a grandson of Jeremiah Brashear. Belt Brashear came to the Red river country in central Louisiana with his family in the early days of the nineteenth century. As before stated, he married before he left Maryland Amelia Duvall. We only know that he had two sons, Charles Duvall and Dr. Thomas B. Brashear. There may have been other children but we are unable to get any definite information on the subject.

Doctor Thomas B. Brashear married his cousin, Marie Crow, on December 8, 1818. They had many children, among whom was a daughter, Frances. This daughter was married on January 27, 1846, to Dr. Euclid Fontenel Beauchamp, and had six or seven children, all of whom died young except three:—Jennie, Clara, and Edwin. Mrs. Beauchamp died in Liberty, Texas, and was buried in the Brashear cemetery there. After her death the family moved to Lafayette, La. Jennie Beauchamp married a Mr. Latiolais; Clara married William Irwin; Edwin married Elodie Ollée. The last mentioned were the grandparents of Mr. Thomas C. Earman of 1820 S. Dupre street, New Orleans, La., who is much interested in genealogy and has accumulated much data on his branch of the Brashear family.

The compiler of this data has been most fortunate in securing from Mrs. Bert (Albert) Joseph Jackson of Beaumont, Texas, a copy of the records in the Charles Duvall Brashear family Bible, and also those in the Basil Crow Brashear family Bible, and all the names and dates connected with the descendants of Charles Duvall Brashear and Eliza Caroline Pearce which are given in the following pages are taken from these records.

Charles Duvall Brashear lived at Florida Bend on Red river, in Avoyelles parish, La., and was an outstanding man in the business, social and political circles of that community. During the first years of his married life we are inclined to believe he lived in the vicinity of Cheneyville, in Rapides parish, as his name quite frequently appears in the notarial records of that community, particularly as a witness. We find him recorded as sheriff of Avoyelles parish in 1837, and as mayor of Marksville in 1843. We have no exact record of his death but know that it occurred after 1850. His wife, Eliza Caroline (Pearce) Brashear, died in West Liberty, Texas, on May 13, 1860, at the age of forty-six. Ten children were born of this marriage:—

  i.—Sarah Amelia Brashear, born August 26, 1830.
  ii.—Stephen Belt Brashear, born September 16, 1832.
  iii.—William Ralph Brashear, born February 17, 1836.
  iv.—Melvina Rebecca Brashear, born January 14, 1838.
  v.—Charles Duvall Brashear, Jr., born March 22, 1840.
  vi.—Lucy Brashear, born April 4, 1842.
  vii.—Basil Crow Brashear, born December 2, 1843.
  viii.—Sophia Eliza Brashear, born December 22, 1845.
  ix.—Mary Maxim Brashear, born July 22, 1848.
  x.—Henry Alfred Brashear, born September 9, 1850.

  i.—Sarah Amelia Brashear, eldest child of Charles Duvall Brashear and Eliza Caroline Pearce, was born in Rapides parish, La. This record of the place of nativity is in accordance with that transcribed in the Charles Duvall Brashear family Bible, and from this we are substantiated in a previous statement that Mr. Brashear and his wife lived for a while in Rapides parish, probably near Cheneyville where Mrs. Brashear's people resided. We are told by the same good book that Sarah Amelia Brashear was married at the home of her parents in Avoyelles parish, La., on June 5, 1849, to Henry A. Cairnes of New Orleans. The date of this marriage is further verified by an item appearing in the New Orleans Picayune of Wednesday morning, June 13, 1849, which reads as follows:—

  MARRIED:—At Florida Bend, Parish of Avoyelles, on the 5th instant, by the Rev. W. J. Therber, Mr. Henry A. Cairnes of this city to Miss Sarah Amelia, eldest daughter of Charles D. Brashear, Esq.

  There is little data to be recorded of this couple and their descendants. The Brashear family Bible shows the birth in New Orleans on July 2, 1850, of one child, Annie P. Cairnes. We understand that there was also another child born later. A member of the family recently informed the compiler that

Mr. and Mrs. Cairnes moved to Ireland some years after their marriage. For a while there was a correspondence kept up with them by relatives in Louisiana but all contact has now been lost for many years.

ii.—Stephen Belt Brashear, second child of Charles Duvall Brashear and Eliza Caroline Pearce, was born in Rapides parish, La. He married on June 13, 1860, Saline Corbello who died in West Liberty, Texas, on December 3, 1871, at the age of twenty-nine years. We have little knowledge of Mr. Brashear after his marriage, but it would appear that he moved to Texas about the time of the commencement of the Civil War, or probably a little earlier. He settled in Liberty county, that rich delta country lying between Beaumont and Houston. There were three daughters born of this marriage. The family Bible thus records their marriages:—

Effie G. Brashear married J. M. Tilton on February 9, 1882. Lucy M. Brashear married Philip M. Green on December 6, 1882; Eva Duvall Brashear married Washington Stubbs on October 17, 1883.

iii.—William Ralph Brashear, third child of Charles Duvall Brashear and Eliza Caroline Pearce, was born in Rapides parish, La. He married on September 1, 1859, Amanda Melvina Pruitt. They had six children:—Amanda Josephine Brashear who married D. F. Smith; Charles Beasley Brashear; Rebecca Zee Brashear who married J. D. Dunks; Mary Sophia Brashear who married 1st Willie Brazil, and 2nd Roy Robinson; Eulalie Brashear who married Tom Warren; Alcina Pruitt Brashear.

iv.—Melvina Rebecca Brashear, fourth child of Charles Duvall Brashear and Eliza Caroline Pearce, was born in Avoyelles parsh, La. She is the first of the Brashear children recorded as having been born in Avoyelles parish and we are therefore justified in concluding that her parents moved there about 1837. She was married on November 18, 1856, to her first cousin, Dr. Neville D. Brashear, a son of Dr. Thomas B. Brashear and Marie Crow. They had one daughter, Fanny Brashear, born December 23, 1857. Whether she died early or lived to adult life we are unable to say.

v.—Charles Duvall Brashear, Jr., fifth child of Charles Duvall Brashear and Eliza Caroline Pearce, was born in

Avoyelles parish, La. He never married and was killed in battle during the Civil War.

vi.—Lucy Brashear, sixth child of Charles Duvall Brashear and Eliza Caroline Pearce, was born in Avoyelles parish, La. She was married to her first cousin, Dr. Tom Brashear, a son of Dr. Thomas B. Brashear and Marie Crow. They had several children among whom were Henry and Fred Brashear.

vii.—Basil Crow Brashear, seventh child of Charles Duvall Brashear and Eliza Caroline Pearce, was born in Avoyelles parish, La., and was named for Basil Crow who married Maxim Brashear, a sister of Charles Duvall Brashear. Basil Crow and Maxim Brashear have descendants now living in Lafayette, La., among whom are Judge Charles Duvall Caffery and Mrs. P. D. Beraud. Basil Crow Brashear settled in Refugio county, Texas, when a young man. He was twice married, his wives being first cousins. He first married on February 22, 1866, Julia E. Dugat, the daughter of Joseph Leonar Dugat and Sidney Pamela Duncan. They had twins and in giving birth to them Mrs. Brashear forfeited her life. The first, Mary Emma Brashear, was born January 19, 1867, and the second was born dead three days later on January 22, 1867, at which time Mrs. Brashear died. Mary Emma Brashear lived to be two years of age and died in 1869. The following item in the family Bible tells us of Basil Crow Brashear's second marrage:—

The Rite of Holy Matrimony was celebrated between B. C. Brashear of Refugio county, Texas, and M. J. Dugat of Refugio county, Texas, on April 26, 1871.

The full name of the second Mrs. Brashear was Mary Jane Dugat. She was born on May 10, 1849, and was the daughter of Charles Edward Dugat and Mary Ann Fear. She died January 31, 1912, and Mr. Brashear died March 18, 1924. They had seven children who are recorded in the family Bible as follows:—

a.—Julia E. Brashear, born February 3, 1872.
b.—Sarah Brashear, born February 10, 1874.
c.—Mattie E. Brashear, born October 15, 1875.
d.—Charles D. Brashear, born February 5, 1878.
e.—Stephen T. Brashear, born June 13, 1880.
f.—Libbie Elma Brashear, born May 1, 1882.
g.—Irene E. Brashear, born April 12, 1888.

On the next page of the famly Bible the following deaths among these children are recorded:—

b.—Sarah Brashear died on February 10, 1874.
c.—Mattie E. Brashear died on May 9, 1877.
e.—Stephen T. Brashear died on November 9, 1880.
f.—Libbie Elma Brashear died on March 21, 1905.

a.—Julia E. Brashear, eldest child of Basil Crow Brashear and his second wife, Mary Jane Dugat, was marred on November 9, 1902, to Henry S. Jirou of Beaumont, Texas. Three children were born of this union:—

az.—Edyth Jennie Jirou, born March 28, 1904.
bz.—Kydie Rae Imogene Jirou, born May 4, 1906.
cz.—Morene Merle Jirou, born June 18, 1908.

az.—Edyth Jennie Jirou was born at Skidmore, Texas, and was married at Beaumont, Texas, on May 1, 1930, to Maurice Joseph Boudreaux who was born in Louisiana on February 28, 1905. At this writing they have three children all of whom were born in Beaumont. They are:—

David Ross Boudreaux, born January 27, 1933.
Kathryn Celeste Boudreaux, born August 19, 1934.
Ann Boudreaux, born September —, 1935.

bz.—Kydie Rae Imogene Jirou was married on September 21, 1927, to Victor Edwards, a native of Canada. They have three children at this time:—

Keith Lane Edwards, born November 4, 1928.
Mary Glee Edwards, born June 10, 1930.
Jane Henry Edwards, born July 29, 1938.

cz.—Morene Merle Jirou was married in March, 1930, to Edward Pierce of California, and died on July 19, 1934. She left one child, Gale Monroe Pierce, born January 26, 1931.

d.—Charles Duvall Brashear, fourth child of Basil Crow Brashear and his second wife, Mary Jane Dugat, was born at St. Marys, Refugio county, Texas. He married on July 1, 1899, Jessie Eliza Dugat (his third cousin), daughter of Wilbur Meredith Dugat and Emma Cassandra Duncan. She was born on November 30, 1875. They had three children:—

az.—Celima Agnes Brashear, born January 18, 1901.
bz.—Wilbur Elma Brashear, born March 11, 1903.
cz.—Walter Everett Brashear, born May 4, 1905.

az.—Celima Agnes Brashear was born at Skidmore, Texas, and was married at Beaumont, Texas, on June 6, 1925, to Bert (Albert) Joseph Jackson. He was a son of Lewis Jackson and Louisa Lavinia Lamarsh, and was born at Iron River, Wisconsin, on June 10, 1900. They now reside on Route No. 1, Beaumont, Texas. It was Mrs. Jackson who so kindly and willingly furnished the compiler with all the data on the descendants of Charles Duvall Brashear and Eliza Caroline Pearce. We wish here in a most special and grateful manner to thank her for this invaluable service. Mr. and Mrs. Jackson have four children, all born in Beaumont, Texas.

Edna Yvonne Jackson, born September 21, 1927.
Rae Mignonne Jackson, born October 5, 1928.
Basil Bert Jackson, born January 13, 1933.
Lavinia Meredith Jackson, born July 10, 1936.

bz.—Wilbur Elma Brashear was born at Skidmore, Texas, and as far as we know is not married at this date.

cz.—Walter Everette Brashear was born at Corpus Christi, Texas, and was married at Beaumont, Texas, on March 17, 1926, to Evelyn Winberg, daughter of George Winberg and Belle Wallace. She was born in Mobile, Alabama, on October 21, 1908. They have two children, both born in Beaumont, Texas:—

Walter Everett Brashear, Jr., born January 19, 1927.
Virginia Faye Brashear, born July 26, 1932.

f.—Libbie Elma Brashear, sixth child of Basil Crow Brashear and his second wife, Mary Jane Dugat, died at Beaumont, Texas, on March 21, 1905, at the age of twenty-three. She was unmarried.

g.—Irene Ethel Brashear, seventh child of Basil Crow Brashear and his second wife, Mary Jane Dugat, was born at St. Marys, Refugio county, Texas. She never married.

viii.—Sophia Eliza Brashear, eighth child of Charles Duvall Brashear and Eliza Caroline Pearce, was born in Avoyelles parish, La., She probably died young or unmarried, as the Bible makes no further reference of her.

ix.—Mary Maxim Brashear, ninth child of Charles Duvall Brashear and Eliza Caroline Pearce, was born in Avoyelles parish, La. She was married on November 19, 1868, to S. J. Abshire. After his death she was married to a Mr. Simpson. It is said that she left children but we have been unable to get any information about them.

x.—Henry Alfred Brashear, tenth child of Charles Duvall Brashear and Eliza Caroline Pearce, was born in Avoyelles parish, La. He probably died young as there is no further record of him.

4.—Sally (Sarah) Ann Pearce, fourth child of Stephen Pearce, and his first wife, Sally Goodwin Bray, was born in Rapides parish, La., near the present town of Cheneyville, in 1813. She was married about 1828 to William Woodson Chambers, an early settler on Bayou Boeuf in Rapides parish, La., and probably a son of James Chambers on Ninety Six District, South Carolina. In the same vicinity on Bayou Boeuf also settled Josias Chambers who was very likely a brother. We have seen the grave of Josias Chambers in Mount Olivet cemetery in Pineville, La., which tells us that he was born in 1782 and died in 1858. In the same lot is the tomb of his son, Josiah Chambers, who died in 1917 at the age of ninety-seven. The compiler of this volume remembers him very distinctly. He was a veteran of the Mexican War, having been a member of the company commanded by the compiler's maternal grandfather. There seems to have been some connection between the Chambers and Pearce families besides the marriage already mentioned, but we are unable to throw any light on the subject at this time. It may be that the Chambers connection was with Silas Talbert who married Mary Pearce. It has been said that Mrs. Talbert reared Josiah Chambers. An item in an old Alexandria newspaper tells of the death of a grandchild of this Josiah Chambers at the home of Silas Talbert. This would indicate at least very close friendship, if not relationship.

We find the name of William Woodson Chambers occurring very frequently in the early business transactions of Rapides parish. On August 6, 1825, he was appointed one of the appraisers of the estate of David Bettison, and in many instances we see his name as a witness to deeds passed before the notaries of that day and place. In 1832 he and his wife sign a transaction before a notary in which they mortgage certain property to the Bank of Louisiana to secure a loan of $20,000.00. We are glad to note that it was later cancelled. To further substantiate the fact of their marriage we will here quote the first paragraph from this legal document:—

> Be it known that on this 21st day of March, 1832, before me William B. Pearce, Notary Public in and for the parish of Rapides and State of Louisiana, personally appeared William Woodson Chambers of the parish of Rapides and State of Louisiana, and Sarah Ann Chambers his wife, she being of the age of majority, by him authorized, who declared, etc. . . . . .

Mr. Chambers died some time between 1833 and 1836. In this latter year we find his widow married to L. F. Ardrey, as will appear from the following transaction:—

> Before me W. B. Pearce, Notary Public in and for the parish of Rapides and State of Louisiana, and the undersigned witnesses, personally appeared Alexander Comton on the one part and Sarah Ann Ardrey by and with the advice and consent of her husband L. F. Ardrey on the other part, ...

Sally Ann Pearce died August 7, 1843. She had no children by her second marriage, as far as we can learn, but by her marriage to William Woodson Chambers she had three daughters:—

       i.—Eliza Ann Chambers.
      ii.—Sarah Goodwin Chambers.
    iii.—Mary Eleanor Chambers.

i.—Eliza Ann Chambers was born in Rapides parish, La., near the town of Cheneyville, about 1829. She was married to Andrew Jackson, son of Stephen Jackson and Nancy Tanner. Stephen was probably a brother of Henry Jackson who married Esther Elvira Tanner (daughter of Robert Tanner and Providence Robert), and they were sons of Reuben Jackson and Susannah Richardson of Camden District, South Carolina. Nancy Tanner was a daughter of Joseph Tanner and his first wife, Elizabeth Lanier. This Joseph Tanner was related to Robert Tanner who married Providence Robert but we do not know the exact degree of kinship. Nancy Tanner and Stephen Jackson had four children:—Susan who married Lemuel Miles,

Reuben who married Emily Ann Sutton (daughter of Joshua and Rachel Sutton), Joseph who married Caroline Carson, and Andrew who married Eliza Ann C hambers. This last mentioned couple, Andrew Jackson and Eliza Ann Chambers, had five children:—Andrew Kendrick, Laura, Sallie, Helen, and Joseph Jackson. We have been unable to obtain data on any of them except the first, Andrew Kendrick Jackson, better known as "Ken Jackson." We find him signing as a witness on September 19, 1867, as "A. Ken Jackson." Andrew Kendrick Jackson married Ella Pearce, daughter of Alanson Green Pearce and Sidney Elizabeth Kay. See a previous page.

ii.—Sarah Goodwin Chambers was born in Rapides parish, La., about 1831. She first married Joseph Willing Tanner about 1848, a son of Branch Tanner and Desirée Wells (daughter of Willing Wells and Rosalie Meuillon). He was familiarly known to his friends as "Toby Tanner" and died in 1853 leaving no children. A few years later his widow was married to James Lemuel Pearce, son of James Pearce and Rhoda Tanner (sister of Branch). James Lemuel Pearce and his wife were second cousins, and he was a first cousin of Toby Tanner on his mother's side. They had six children, a full account of whom will be found on a subsequent page.

iii.—Mary Eleanor Chambers was born in Rapides parish, La., on December 12, 1832. She was married May 22, 1851, to Dr. Francis Wioatte Marshall, born in Avoyelles parish, La., on February 16, 1821, son of William C. Marshall and his second wife, Rosalie (Meuillon) Wells—widow of Willing Wells and daughter of Dr. Ennemond Meuillon and Jeannette (Poiret) La Mothe. Dr. Marshall was for many years a prominent planter and physician in the Cheneyville neighborhood of Bayou Boeuf. He died at the home of one of his daughters in Alexandria, La., on November 7, 1908. Mrs. Marshall died in New Orleans on October 30, 1901. William C. Marshall, father of Dr. Marshall, came to Louisiana prior to 1815 as it was in that year he married Rosalie (Meuillon) Wells. We find his name on the records of East Feliciana parish, La., some years earlier than that date. It is said that he came from Fredericksburg, Virginia, and with him came his son by a former marriage, Roger Banks Marshall. In 1831 we find both of them living in Avoyelles parish. Robert H. Marshall

was another member of the family in Rapides parish as early
as 1825. Whether he was a nephew or a son of William C.
Marshall we are unable to say with any degree of certainty,
but we are inclined to believe he was a nephew. Mark Richards
Marshall, son of Horace Marshall and Elizabeth Heiskell of
Fredericksburg, Va., and a nephew of William C. Marshall,
came to Louisiana from Tennessee soon after the Civil War
and settled in Avoyelles parish where he died May 9, 1898, at
the age of seventy-three. Elizabeth Marshall, a sister of Mark
Richards Marshall, married Dr. Samuel Slaughter of Cheneyville but left no descendants. We have endeavored to locate
the graves of William C. Marshall and his second wife, hoping
an inscription on his tombstone would give us additional data
as to his antecedents, but without avail. Recently a daughter
of Dr. Marshall told the compiler that she believed her grandparents were buried in the Rapides cemetery in Pineville, La.,
as she had heard her father express the desire to be buried
there near them.

Dr. Francis Wioatte Marshall and his wife, Mary Eleanor
Chambers, had ten children, four of whom died in infancy.
The six reaching adult life were:—

> a.—Emily Marshall.
> b.—Florence Marshall.
> c.—Frances Wioatte Marshall.
> d.—Rose Marshall.
> e.—John Wioatte Marshall.
> f.—Eleanor Marshall.

a.—Emily Marshall was married to Berthier Mordella
Pearce (familiarly known as "Buck Pearce"), son of Joshua
Pearce and Esther Tanner (sister of Branch and Nancy Tanner, mentioned above, and daughter of Joseph Tanner and his
first wife, Elizabeth Lanier). Nine children were born of
this marriage, a full account of whom may be found on a subsequent page.

b.—Florence Marshall, who was a registered nurse, married her brother-in-law, Berthier Mordella Pearce, and reared
the nine children of her deceased sister, some of whom were
"little tots" at the time and found a true mother in her. She
never had any children of her own and died March 26, 1935.

c.—Frances Wioatte Marshall, better known to her family and friends as "Fannie," was married to George Morgan Cheney, son of Captain William Franklin Cheney and Matilda Ann Pearce. Mr. Cheney's maternal grandfather and his wife's maternal grandmother were brother and sister, and therefore he and his wife were third cousins. He died several years before his wife of pneumonia, and she died November 27, 1924, leaving three children:—William Franklin, Eleanor, and George Morgan, Jr. The eldest, William Franklin Cheney, now resides in New Orleans. He married Hazel Brothers and they have two children:—Frances Elise and Hazel Cheney. Eleanor Cheney was married to Arthur Henry Vignes, a native of Pointe Coupee parish, La. They now reside in New Orleans and have three children:—Arthur Henry, Jr., Mary Eleanor, and Marshall Kingston Vignes. George Morgan Cheney, Jr., lives in New Orleans and is unmarried at this time.

d.—Rose Marshall, probably named for her grandmother, Rosalie Meuillon, was a registered nurse. She never married and died in New Orleans on May 23, 1935.

e.—John Wioatte Marshall married Daisy Dean and had several children, but we regret our inability to obtain any further data on him. He is living at this date (1944). His marriage was recorded in THE ALEXANDRIA TOWN TALK of Saturday, February 4, 1893, as follows:—

MARRIED:—Miss Daisy Dean to Mr. John W. Marshall, at the residence of the bride in Greensburg, La., last Wednesday. Miss Dean is the daughter of A. C. Dean, Clerk of Court of St. Helena parish, La. They will reside at Cheneyville.

f.—Eleanor Marshall, youngest child of Dr. Francis Wioatte Marshall and Mary Eleanor Chambers, is residing in New Orleans at this date (1944). She is a registered nurse, is actively engaged at this time in her profession, and has never married.

5.—John Washington Pearce, fifth child of Stephen Pearce, and his first wife, Sally Goodwin Bray, was born in Rapides parish, La., on June 15, 1817, and died at his home there on January 25, 1872. He married March 19, 1839, Eliza Jane Gray who was born in 1826 and died April 5, 1898. Mr. Pearce was a notary public for Rapides parish in the Cheneyville neighborhood for several years and kept a meticulous record of all his legal transactions. We have the original book of his notarial records beginning February 17, 1853, and ending December 24, 1856. These records have been invaluable to us in compiling this work. He was an active member of the Beulah Baptist Church of Cheneyville in its early days, but later was among the *objectors* to some of the "articles of faith" of that denomination and took a prominent part in the organization of the Campbellite or Christian Church in that section. Rev. W. E. Paxton in his History of the Louisiana Baptists reports the following item from the church minutes relative to Mr. Pearce and his wife:—

> Saturday before the first Lord's Day in September, 1843, by the request of brother J. W. Pearce that the names of himself and sister E. J. Pearce be erased from the church book, the church do hereby withdraw their fellowship from them.

Soon after this the Christian Church at Cheneyville was organized and Mr. Pearce was chosen bishop and ordained by Rev. William Prince Ford. He was ever afterwards a staunch member of his new church. Mr. Pearce inherited his parents' family Bible and passed it on to his descendants. It is now the proud posession of his great-grand-daughter, Mrs. Robert Lee Bailey, Jr., of Opelousas, Louisiana. The vital statistics items in it are of such great value that we will here insert them in full:—

MARRIAGES

Stephen Pearce and Sally Goodwin Bray were married Sept. 13, 1804.

Stephen Pearce and Ann Grimball Brown were married Sept. 30, 1830.

R. Milligan and Susan H. Pearce were married Apr. 13, 1826.

W. B. Pearce and Rosalind H. Tanner were married June 19, 1828.

C. D. Brashear and Eliza C. Pearce were married Feby. 5, 1829.

John W. Pearce and Eliza Jane Gray were married Mch. 19, 1839.

Marshall Pearce and Rosa Jennie Cheney were married Nov. 10, 1869.

Marshall Pearce, Jr., and Jennie Louise Bridenthal were
married Feb. 7, 1906.
Cora Cheney Pearce and Robert Lee Bailey, Jr., were
married in Alexandria, La., Aug. 24, 1929.

BIRTHS

William Pearce, Sr., was born 1754 in North Carolina.
William Bray Pearce was born October 14, 1807.
Susan Heddingrant Pearce was born Jany. 24, 1809.
Eliza Caroline Pearce was born May 15, 1811.
John Washington Pearce was born June 15, 1817.
Mary Talbert Pearce was born Aug. 28, 1818.
Stephen Pearce, Jr., was born Dec. 19, 1783.
Sally Goodwin Pearce was born Feby. 15, 1790.
Martha Esther Pearce was born Aug. 11, 1820.
Delia Melvina Pearce was born October 16, 1822.
Silas Franklin Pearce was born January 20, 1825.
Amelia Tuzette Pearce was born March 18, 1827.
Charles Lafayette Pearce was born May 14, 1829.
Stephen Samuel Pearce was born October 18, 1833.
Eliza Jane Gray, wife of John Washington Pearce, was
born 1826.
Clinton Pearce was born October 17, 1859.
Ella Pearce was born October 25, 1843.
Frank Pearce was born November 30, 1868.

(John W. Pearce family)

Helen Elizabeth Pearce was born July 7, 1840.
Eleanora Pearce was born October 25, 1843.
Marshall Pearce was born Dec. 23, 1844.
Rosa Jennie Cheney was born Dec. 18, 1848.
Betty Maud Pearce was born July 22, 1871.
John William Pearce was born Nov. 8, 1874.
Marshall Pearce (i) was born Dec. 5, 1876.
Marshall Pearce (ii) was born Sept. 16, 1881.
Rosa Jane Pearce was born Jany. 10, 1885.
Jennie Louise Bridenthal, wife of Marshall Pearce (ii),
was born Oct. 25, 1881.
Cora Cheney Pearce was born April 16, 1907.
Marshall Pearce Bailey was born Sept. 24, 1931.
Robert Lee Bailey, III, was born Dec. 12, 1933.

DEATHS

William Pearce, Sr., departed this life Nov. 6, 1813.
Sarah (Bray) Pearce, his wife, died June 6, 1801.
Joshua Pearce, Sr., departed this life April 17, 1810.

Mary Talbert Pearce departed this life Sept. 12, 1819.
Sarah Bray departed this life Sept. 26, 1820.
Susan Liefer Pearce departed this life Sept. 21, 1820.
Eliza Chambers departed this life October 7, 1822.
Delia Chambers departed this life Sept. 4, 1825, aged 2
years and 3 months.
Sally Goodwin Pearce departed this life Oct. 25, 1829,
aged 39 years and 8 months.
Stephen Pearce departed this life Oct. 16, 1833, aged 49
years and 10 months.
Susan H. Milligan departed this life July, 1833.
Rosalind H. Pearce departed this life Dec. 28, 1834.
William B. Pearce departed this life July 2, 1837.
Sarah Ann Ardrey departed this life Aug. 7, 1843.
Eliza Jane Pearce departed this life April 5, 1898.
Amelia T. Scott departed this life May 25, 1844.
Tuzette Robert departed this life July, 1839.
John W. Pearce departed this life January 25, 1872.
Silas F. Pearce departed this life Feby. 25, 1873.
Helen Elizabeth Pearce departed this life July 10, 1878.
Marshall Pearce departed this life April 5, 1890.
Marshall Pearce (i) died December 10, 1876.
John Pearce died October 1, 1878.
Rosa Cheney Pearce died August 5, 1925.
Marshall Pearce (ii) died October 25, 1937.

John Washington Pearce and Eliza Jane Gray had seven
children:—

> i.—Helen Elizabeth Pearce.
> ii.—Judith Ann Pearce.
> iii.—Eleanora Pearce.
> iv.—Marshall Pearce.
> v.—Silas Talbert Pearce.
> vi.—Esther Pearce.
> vii.—Dewitt Clinton Pearce.

i.—Helen Elizabeth Pearce was born July 7, 1840, and
died July 10, 1878. We can find no record that she ever married.

ii.—Judith Ann Pearce was born in 1842 and married a
Mr. Murdock. They had no children.

iii.—Eleanora Pearce was born October 25, 1843, and died
in 1909. We have been unable to get any futher data on her.

iv.—Marshall Pearce, fourth child of John Washington
Pearce and Eliza Jane Gray, is the only one of the seven chil-

dren we have been able to get a complete record of. He was born December 23, 1844, and died April 5, 1890. He married on November 10, 1869, Rosa Jennie Cheney, daughter of William Franklin Cheney and Matilda Ann Pearce, and granddaughter of William Fendon Cheney, the founder of the town of Cheneyville, La. Mr. Pearce and his wife were second cousins. She was born near Cheneyville, Rapides parish, La., on December 18, 1848, and died in Bunkie, La., on August 5, 1926. Five children were born of this marriage:—

> a.—Betty Maud Pearce.
> b.—John William Pearce.
> c.—Marshall Pearce (i).
> d.—Marshall Pearce, (ii).
> e.—Rosa Jane Pearce.

The second child, b.—John William Pearce, died when four years old, and the third child, c.—Marshall Pearce (i), died when five days old.

a.—Betty Maud Pearce, the eldest child, was born on July 22, 1871, and was married to A. N. Mann. They now reside in Dallas, Texas, and have three children:—Maud, Rosa Lillian, and Alice Mann. The last mentioned was married to C. B. Philbrick and has one child, Doris Philbrick. Mr. Mann assumed the name of his foster parents—his true name was Pearson.

d.—Marshall Pearce (ii), usually recorded as Marshall Pearce, Jr., the fourth child of Marshall Pearce and Rosa Jennie Cheney, was born on September 16, 1881, and died in a hospital at Vicksburg, Mississippi, on Monday, October 25, 1937. He was for more than thirty years an engineer of the Texas and Pacific Railway, was a Master Mason, and was highly respected in the community where he resided. He spent most of his life in Bunkie, La. His body was brought back to his home there and buried in the Pythian cemetery in that town. Mr. Pearce married on February 7, 1906, Jennie Louise Bridenthal, daughter of James P. Bridenthal and Cora Keller. His wife was born on October 25, 1881, and is living at this date (1944). Mrs. Bridenthal (Cora Keller) came from one of the pioneer families of central Louisiana. She had t hree sisters and a brother:—Martha Ada Keller who married

David Rutledge Bettison (see page 149), Medora Keller who married Lemuel Culpepper, Alice Keller who never married, and Thomas Keller who never married. Marshall Pearce, Jr., and Jennie Louise Bridenthal had one child:—

az.—Cora Cheney Pearce.

az.—Cora Cheney Pearce was born April 16, 1907, and was married in Alexandria, La., on August 24, 1929, to Robert Lee Bailey, Jr., son of Robert Lee Bailey, Sr., and Mary Stokes. Mr. Bailey was born August 25, 1905. They now reside in Opelousas, La., and have two children:—Marshall Pearce Bailey, born September 24, 1931, and Robert Lee Bailey, III, born December 12, 1933.

e.—Rosa Jane Pearce, fifth child of Marshall Pearce and Rosa Jennie Cheney, was born on January 10, 1885, and is at this date (1944) living in Birmingham, Alabama. She was married in 1905 to Maunsel Bennett Bridenthal. They have two children:—

az.—Elizabeth Bridenthal.
bz.—Jane Bridenthal.

az.—Elizabeth Bridenthal was born in 1905 and was married to Samuel B. Valentine. They have two children:—Jane and Anne Valentine.

bz.—Jane Bridenthal was born in 1907 and was married to Lou A. Henry. They have one child, Jane Henry.

v.—Silas Talbert Pearce, vi.—Ether Pearce (recorded as "Ettie"), and vii.—Dewitt Clinton Pearce, the last three children of John Washington Pearce and Eliza Jane Gray, probably died young. The family Bible shows the youngest, Dewitt Clinton, was born October 17, 1859.

6.—Mary Talbert Pearce, sixth child of Stephen Pearce and his first wife, Sally Goodwin Bray, was born in Rapides parish, La., on August 28, 1818, and died September 12, 1819.

7.—Martha Esther Pearce, seventh child of Stephen Pearce and his first wife, Sally Goodwin Bray, was born in Rapides parish, La., on August 11, 1820. She was married about 1838 to James Bordeaux Jaudon Robert, son of Joseph

Robert and Mary Hyrne Jaudon. They had twelve children. (See page 122).

8.—Delia Melvina Pearce, eighth child of Stephen Pearce and his first wife, Sally Goodwin Bray, was born in Rapides parish, La., on October 16, 1822, and died near Evergreen, Avoyelles parish, La., in 1847. She was married to William H. Duvall, scion of a noted family in Prince George county, Maryland. Three children were born of this marriage:—

     i.—Flavilla Jemima Duvall.
     ii.—William Emmett Duvall.
     iii.—Charles Winchester Duvall.

i.—Flavilla Jemima Duvall was born near Evergreen, Avoyelles parish, La., on September 27, 1841, and died in Alexandria, La., on June 13, 1903. She was married in 1857 to Dr. Stephen Harris Rushing, a prominent physician in central Louisiana for nearly half a century. He was born near Wadesboro, Anson county, North Carolina, on October 25, 1830, and was a son of Col. James Madison Rushing and Susan Rushing. His parents, though bearing the same family name, were not related. In 1832 the family moved to Sumter county, Alabama, and there Stephen Harris Rushing grew to manhood. He graduated in medicine from the University of Pennsylvania in 1853, and in 1856 emigrated to Louisiana, locating at Evergreen, in Avoyelles parish. At the outbreak of the Civil War he entered the Confederate Army and first served in Virginia. He was later transferred to The Army Of The Tennesse and there served until the close of the war as Staff and Field Surgeon. In 1880 he moved to Alexandria, La., and there practiced his profession until his death on April 20, 1905. He was elected coroner of Rapides parish in 1900 and served a term of four years. It is a coincidence that the present compiler of these notes, then a young physician, opposed Dr. Rushing in the race for coroner in 1904 and defeated him. Both the doctor and his wife are buried in Mt. Olivet cemetery in Pineville, La. Three daughters were born of this marriage:—

     a.—Inez May Rushing.
     b.—Mary Eliza Rushing.
     c.—Flavilla Duvall Rushing.

a.—Inez May Rushing was born at Evergreen, Avoyelles parish, La., on May 1], 1860, and was married to Lucius Campbell of Avoyelles parish in 1904. Mr. Campbell died about 1912, and she died on February 26, 1943. They had no children.

b.—Mary Eliza Rushing was married to Thomas Moore Biossat, member of one of the oldest families of Alexandria, La.. They resided in Lafayette, La., and had three children:—

az.—Thomas Moore Biossat, Jr.
bz.—Stephen Rushing Biossat.
cz.—Inez Rushing Biossat.

az.—Thomas Moore Biossat, Jr., first married Annie Skipwith and had one child who died in infancy. He then married Anna Harris. There was no issue by the second marriage. He died in 1928.

bz.—Stephen Rushing Biossat married Norma Joret on November 19, 1913. They had three children:—Doris, Mary Rushing, and Stephen Rushing Biossat, Jr. Mr. Biossat died of influenza on April 19, 1919. The second child, Mary Rushing Biossat, was married to George O'Brien.

cz.—Inez Rushing Biossat was married to Vernon Griffin and lives at Lafayette, La. They have no children.

c.—Flavilla Duvall Rushing, youngest daughter of Dr. Stephen Harris Rushing and Flavilla Jemima Duvall, was born in Avoyelles parish, La., and was married on March 5, 1896, to Frederick William Bradt who was born in Toledo, Ohio, on June 30, 1873. They spent all of their married life in Alexandria, La., and there Mr. Bradt died on Sunday, August 3, 1941. They had one child, Flavilla Bradt, who is as yet unmarried. The compiler can not close this paragraph without expressing his gratitude to Mrs. Bradt for her kindness in putting the records of the Dunwoody Bible at his disposal and furnishing him with other valuable data on the Pearce family.

ii.—William Emmett Duvall, second child of William H. Duvall and Delia Melvina Pearce, was born near Evergreen, Avoyelles parish, La., in 1843. He was never married and died in 1865. Although a mere boy at the outbreak of the Civil War he joined Company H (Cheneyville Rifles), 8th Louisiana Infantry, and served four years in Virginia.

iii.—Charles Winchester Duvall, third child of William H. Duvall and Delia Melvina Pearce, was born near Evergreen,

Avoyelles. parish, La., in 1844. He served in the Louisiana Cavalry during the greater part of the Civil War. In 1883 he married Nellie Jackson of Evergreen, La., a daughter of Dr. Jackson and his wife who was a Miss Cason. Mr. Duvall died in 1889 and his wife in 1926. They had one daughter:—

    a.—Robena Jeannette Duvall.

    a.—Robena Jeannette Duvall was born in Avoyelles parish, La., in 1885. She was twice married. First to Ed Griffith by whom she had two children:—Jeannette who married a Daigle, and Gertrude who married but we have been unable to obtain her husband's name. Her second husband is Frank Silas Brown, a son of Henry Jackson Brown and Hettie Bailey. There are two children by the second marriage:— Frank Silas Brown, Jr., and Audry Brown.

    9.—Silas Franklin Pearce, ninth child of Stephen Pearce and his first wife, Sally Goodwin Bray, was born in Rapides parish, La., on January 20, 1825. In 1847 he married Penelope Desirée Wells, daughter of Benoist Willing Wells and Janetta Gordon. She died in April, 1853, leaving no issue. About 1860 Mr. Pearce married his second wife who was Frances Tanner, daughter of Asa R. Tanner and Caroline Williams. Asa R. Tanner was a son of Joseph Tanner and his first wife, Elizabeth Lanier and a brother of Branch and Lodowick Tanner. Caroline Williams was a daughter of Thomas Williams and Joyce Thomas, natives of South Carolina. Joyce Thomas was a daughter of Capt. James Thomas and Elizabeth Calliham of Edgefield county, South Carolina. Elizabeth Calliham was a daughter of David Calliham, Sr., and his wife Elizabeth, and a sister of John and David Calliham, Jr., who left South Carolina after the Revolution and came to Wilkinson county, Mississippi, where David, Jr., remained permanently but John came to Rapides parish, La., and died sometime before 1825. John Calliham was a Revolutionary soldier and so was his brother-in-law, Capt. James Thomas. Silas Franklin Pearce and his second wife had three children, two boys and a girl. The girl was the second chlid and died young of scarlet fever. The boys were:—

    i.—Beauregard Pearce.
    ii.—Frank Pearce.

i.—Beauregard Pearce was born in 1862 about the time that General P. G. T. Beauregard of the Confederate Army was very popular in the South and was named for that distinguished leader. He married on February 18, 1892, Susie Bennett, daughter of David Maunsel Bennett and Sarah Ophelia Pearce (daughter of Alanson Green Pearce). Beauregard Pearce lived all of his life in Cheneyville, La., and died there in 1933. His wife's death occurred some years prior to that date. Three children were born of this marriage:—

a.—Fannie Ophelia Pearce.
b.—William Branch Pearce.
c.—Sidney Bennett Pearce.

a.—Fannie Ophelia Pearce was born in Cheneyville, La., on June 8, 1893. She was married in September, 1919, to Robert Bolling Miles, son of Charles S. Miles and Lulie Clark. They resided for many years in and near Alexandria, La., and Mr. Miles died at the Baptist Hospital there on Sunday, December 19, 1943, at the age of fifty-one. He was buried in the Greenwood Memorial Park in Pineville, La. Two children were born of this marriage:—

az.—Ruth Frances Miles.
bz.—Robert Pearce Miles.

az.—Ruth Frances Miles was born December 3, 1920, and was married March 27, 1944, at the post chapel, Langley Field, Virginia, to Sergeant Charles J. Buckley, son of Mr. and Mrs. Edward J. Buckley.

bz.—Robert Pearce Miles was born July 15, 1923, and is now in the military service of his country.

b.—William Branch Pearce was born at Cheneyville, La., on March 27, 1895, and died on October 12, 1918, unmarried.

c.—Sidney Bennett Pearce was born in Cheneyville, La., on September 11, 1897. For many years he was the efficient Superintendent of the Electric Light and Water Works System of the City of Alexandria. He married Lena Burch in 1926. They have no children.

ii.—Frank Pearce, second son of Silas Franklin Pearce and his second wife, Frances Tanner, was born in Rapides parish, La., on November 30, 1868. He married on April 13,

1898, Mary Virginia Bennett, daughter of David Maunsel Bennett and Sarah Ophelia Pearce. Frank Pearce spent most of his life in the vicinity of Cheneyville where he was reared. He died at the Touro Infirmary in New Orleans, La., on Sunday morning at 9:50, May 26, 1940, and was buried in the cemetery at Evergreen, La., beside his wife who had died on June 2, 1931. They had four sons, all of whom are living and married at this date (1944). They are:—

> a.—John Silas Pearce.
> b.—Maunsel Bennett Pearce.
> c.—Walter Francis Pearce.
> d.—Frank Pearce, Jr.

a.—John Silas Pearce was born February 16, 1899, and is a prominent business man in Bunkie, La. He married on June 20, 1919, Cora Frank Lincoln of New Orleans, who was born on June 5, 1900. They have one son, Charles A. Pearce, born September 7, 1921, now serving in the U. S. Air Corps.

b.—Maunsel Bennett Pearce was born April 3, 1902. He graduated in medicine from Johns Hopkins University, Baltimore, Maryland, and after practicing his profession for several years in Monroe, La., moved to Alexandria where he has been a prominent member of the firm of McBride, Pearce and Hardy. Doctor Pearce is recognized as a very skillful surgeon. He is at present serving in the U. S. Army Medical Corps and is stationed at Camp Claiborne, La., where he is executive officer of the large general hospital there. He married on December 28, 1929, Mildred Morton of Monroe, La., daughter of Oliver Morton, prominent business man in that city. Mrs. Pearce was born there on July 12, 1906. Dr. and Mrs. Pearce have one son at this time:—Maunsel Bennett Pearce, Jr., born August 5, 1938.

c.—Walter Francis Pearce was born December 7, 1903. He married on November 11, 1929, Isabel Contois of Alexandria, La. She was born there on December 22, 1904, and was a daughter of the late C. F. Contois, at one time a prominent business man of Alexandria. They have three daughters:—Isabel Contois Pearce, born May 28, 1932; Jane Louise Pearce, born March 20, 1937; Sue Bennett Pearce, born December 14, 1938.

d.—Frank Pearce, Jr., was born January 15, 1906. He married on June 30, 1928, Leila Musgrove, who was born on October 31, 1906. They have three children:—Mary Virginia Pearce, born July 21, 1929; Gene Ann Pearce, born December 14, 1930; Frank Pearce, III, born October 16, 1932.

10.—Amelia Tuzette Pearce, tenth child of Stephen Pearce and his first wife, Sally Goodwin Bray, was born in Rapides parish, La., on March 18, 1827, and was married in 1843 to Rev. Josiah Scott, son of Joseph John Scott and Harriet Sarah Gray. She died May 26, 1844, leaving no issue.

11.—Charles Lafayette Pearce, eleventh child of Stephen Pearce and his first wife, Sally Goodwin Bray, was born in Rapides parish, La., on May 14, 1829. He married in 1853 Mary Tuzette Robert, daughter of Polhill Ware Robert and Caroline Amanda Rowley. He and his wife eloped to Natchez, Miss., and were married there. Her father was very much opposed to her marriage (see page 105). Polhill Ware Robert was the second son of Joseph Robert and Mary Hyrne Jaudon, and a grandson of Captain Peter Robert and Anne Grimball. Charles Lafayette Pearce and Mary Tuzette Robert lived all of their lives in Rapides parish and had nine children:—

      i.—Silas Pearce.
      ii.—Oscar Pearce.
      iii.—Rowley L. Pearce.
      iv.—Carrie Pearce.
      v.—Jeffie Pearce.
      vi.—Anna Pearce.
      vii.—Eddie Walter Pearce.
      viii.—Ewell Pearce.
      ix.—Samuel Pearce.

It is very much to be regretted that we have so little information about this extensive branch of the Pearce family, but it has seemed impossible to obtain more than the meager data we present below. Four of the above children were living in 1940, all of whom resided in Houston, Texas. The third in order of birth, Rowley L. Pearce, and the eighth, Ewell Pearce, are the male members who were living at that date. The fourth, Carrie Pearce, was born in 1865 and married S. C. Bailey, and the sixth, Anna Pearce, married W. B. Archer.

They are the two females who were living at the date mentioned.

vii.—Eddie Walter Pearce, seventh child of Charles Lafayette Pearce and Mary Tuzette Robert, was born in Rapides parish, La., on August 31, 1871, and died at Cheneyville, La., at 7 p. m. on Friday, June 16, 1939. He was buried in the Episcopal cemetery there. Mr. Pearce was twice married. His first wife was Winifred Gertrude Lyman. They had three children:—

        a.—Paul Reed Pearce.
        b.—Ruth Pearce.
        c.—Eddie Winifred Pearce.

Mr. Pearce lived for many years in Texas where he was connected with the Southern Pacific Railway. After the death of his wife he returned to the scenes of his early life near Cheneyville, La., and there married Miss Medora Marshall, daughter of Captain George Benoist Marshall and Margaret Dawson Cureton. They had no children and she yet survives him.

a.—Paul Reed Pearce was born on July 2, 1893, and married on October 23, 1922, Cornelia Elizabeth Fullilove, daughter of Charles Thomas Fullilove (born in De Soto parish, La., February 12, 1854—died June 29, 1916) and Ella Butler (born August 12, 1860—died September 9, 1928). Mr. and Mrs. Fullilove were married in Rapides parish, La., on Nov. 23, 1883, and their daughter, Cornelia Elizabeth, was born at Keachi, De Soto parish, La., on May 18, 1894. Paul Reed Pearce and his wife had three children, all born at Cheneyville, La. They were:—Charles Edward Pearce, born December 14, 1923; Elizabeth Winifred Pearce, born September 4, 1925, and died March 6, 1926; Virginia Elizabeth Pearce, born June 21, 1927. Paul Reed Pearce and his wife were divorced some years ago and on Saturday, November 9, 1940, he was married at the Baptist Church in West Monroe, La., to Viola Elizabeth Green, daughter of the late Mr. and Mrs. C. A. Green of that place.

b.—Ruth Pearce was married to P. G. Longmire and lives in Houston, Texas. They have one daughter, Kathleen, who married Carroll Clements and has a son.

c.—Eddie Winifred Pearce lives in Houston, Texas, and has been twice married. By his first wife he has two daughters, Ruth and Evelyn Pearce.

12.—Stephen Samuel Pearce, only child of Stephen Pearce and his second wife, Anne Grimball (Tanner) Brown, was born near Cheneyville, Rapides parish, La., on October 18, 1833, two days after the death of his father. He received his education at Centenary College, Jackson, La., then one of the outstanding institutions in Louisiana. This college is yet functioning and has been moved to Shreveport, La. Mr. Pearce established himself on a plantation near Evergreen, Avoyelles parish, La., and became one of the leading agriculturists in the central part of the State and one of the most prominent citizens. He served in the Louisiana Legislature 1880-82. In 1854 he married Mary Ellen Bennett, daughter of Ezra Bennett and Sarah Providence Eldred. She was born in Rapides parish in 1839. We have been unable to obtain the record of the deaths of Mr. and Mrs. Pearce but know they were living as late as 1890. They had eight children, three of whom are living at this date (1944). Their children were:—

> i.—Sarah Annie Pearce.
> ii.—Claudia Ellen Pearce.
> iii.—Maunsel Kemper Pearce.
> iv.—Jennie Maude Pearce.
> v.—Addie Gertrude Pearce.
> vi.—Stephen Samuel Pearce, II.
> vii.—Heber Livingston Pearce.
> viii.—Algeron B. Pearce.

i.—Sarah Annie Pearce was married to her cousin, Sidney Tanner, son of Paul Jabez Tanner and Esther Providence Bettison. They were third cousins. Both have now been dead for many years. They had four children:—

> Mary Esther Tanner.
> Annie Laurie Tanner.
> Pauline Tanner.
> Sidney Otis Tanner.

All of these children are living at this date. See page 304.

ii.—Claudia Ellen Pearce was married to Charles W. Owen, a native of Alabama. He was a son of John Owen and Susannah Frasier. He received his education in New Orleans and became agent for the Southern Pacific Railway at Cheneyville, La. It was there that he met and married his wife. He later enterd the mercantile business at Cheneyville and became a successful business man there. Two children were born of this marriage:—Claudia P. Owen who married C. U. Johnson, and Chauncey H. Owen who married Mollie McGehee. Charles W. Owen died many years ago and his wife in 1938. In an Alexandria newspaper we found the following notice of her death:—

> DIED:—At Monroe, La., Friday, May 20, 1938, Mrs. Claudia Pearce Owen, aged 74. The deceased was the wife of the late Charles W. Owen. She is survived by the following children:—Chauncey H. Owen, son, of Houston, Texas; Mrs. C. U. Johnson, daughter, of Monroe, La. Funeral services will be held at Evergreen, La., at 5 p. m. today under the direction of Hixson Bros., at Bunkie.

iii.—Maunsel Kemper Pearce was born in Avoyelles parish, La., on November 6, 1867, and was one of the prominent and successful merchants of that section of Louisiana. He died in 1924 in Shreveport, La. He first married Nannee Snellings and they had three children:—Sarah, John Snellings, and Nannee Pearce. His second wife was Bessie Pouriefoy was a grand-daughter of David C. Paul a prominent citizen of Rapides parish in the post Civil War period and for many years sheriff of that parish. There were two children by the second union but we have been unable to obtain their names.

iv.—Jennie Maude Pearce was born near Evergreen, La., on February 24, 1869, and was married to Dr. Herbert Kilpatrick, son of Andrew Milton Kilpatrick and Margery Eliza Cushman, and a grandson of Andrew Conger Kilpatrick and Janes Sophronia Tanner. Dr. Kilpatrick practiced his profession for many years at Washington, La., and died there on October 30, 1930. Mrs. Kilpatrick still resides in that vicinity. They had four children:—Mary Margery Kilpatrick, Stephen Milton Kilpatrick, Lizzie Caffery Kilpatrick, and Ralph Cushman Kilpatrick. (See page 276).

v.—Addie Gertrude Pearce, fifth child of Stephen Samuel Pearce and his wife, Mary Ellen Bennett, was born near Evergreen, La., in 1870. She never married and died at the Baptist Hospital in Alexandria, La., on Friday, November 19, 1943.

vi.—Stephen Samuel Pearce, II, sixth child of Stephen Samuel Pearce and Mary Ellen Bennett, was born near Evergreen, La., on July 22, 1871. He yet resides there and is one

of the outstanding men of his community. On January 12,
1892, he married Eura Voorhies, born October 13, 1871, daughter of Gradni Peter Voorhies and Mary Virginia Griffin.
Three children were born of this union:—

        a.—Gradni Voorhies Pearce.
        b.—Samuel Edwin Pearce.
        c.—Eura Voorhies Pearce.

    a.—Gradni Voorhies Pearce was born at Evergreen,
Aovyelles parish., La., on August 17, 1893. He was one of the
most enterprising young business men of central Louisiana.
For several years he was prominent in the automobile industry
in Bunkie, and then he came to Alexandria where he organized
and became president and general manager of the PEARCE
CHEVROLET COMPANY, INC. He was a very popular
young man and was familiarly known to his many friends as
"Red Pearce." He was a director of the Guaranty Bank and
Trust Co. of Alexandria, and of the Pan-American Petroleum
Corporation of that city, and also of the Pearce Syrup Co. of
Bunkie. In 1937-38 he was president of the Alexandria Cham-
ber of Commerce. Mr. Pearce married on June 17, 1918,
Annie West, daughter of Rufus A. West and Annie Gill. He
died suddenly at his home in Alexandria, La., from heart
trouble at 1:30 a. m., Friday, November 17, 1939, and was
buried in the Greenwood Memorial Park in Pineville, La.
Besides his wife he left three daughters:—

        az.—Eleanor Virginia Pearce.
        bz.—Marjorie Claudia Pearce.
        cz.—Wilma West Pearce.

    az.—Eleanor Virginia Pearce was born November 30,
1919, and was married at the First Presbyterian Church in
Alexandria, La., on Thursday, November 28, 1940, to Dr. Herman Celestian Quantz, a prominent young physician of Bunkie,
La. Dr. Quantz is a son of the late Mr. and Mrs. Albert Theodore Quantz of Rockhill, South Carolina, where he was born,
and is a grandson of the late Mr. and Mrs. Herman Celestian
Quantz, early settlers of South Carolina. Dr. Quantz is at
present an officer in the Medical Corps of the U. S. Army. He
and his wife have two children:—Virginia Ann Quantz, born
at the Baptist Hospital in Alexandria on Wednesday, February

1, 1942, at 5 p. m., and Katherine Patterson Quantz, born at Touro Infirmary in New Orleans on Friday, September 22, 1944, at 4:40 p. m.

bz.—Marjorie Claudia Pearce was born July 14, 1921, and was married in the First Presbyterian Church at Alexandria, La., by the Rev. John R. Richardson, on Tuesday evening, October 7, 1941, at 7:30 o'clock, to John Wallace Beasley, Jr., son of Mr. and Mrs. John Wallace Beasley of Alexandria, La. Paternally he is a grandson of the late Mr. and Mrs. John Wallace Beasley of Evergreen, La. Maternally his grandparents were Mr. and Mrs. John Allen Cargill of Jonesville, Texas. Mr. Beasley is a vice-president of the Garanty Bank and Trust Co., of Alexandria of which his father is president. At present he is serving in the U. S. Army. They now have a little daughter, Elizabeth Pearce Beasley, born at the Baptist Hospital in Alexandria on August 15, 1944, at 4:03 a. m.

cz.—Wilma West Pearce was born January 27, 1924, and was married at the First Presbyterian Church in Alexandria on Friday, February 4, 1944, by the Rev. John R. Richardson, to Lieutenant Patrick Hayes Johnson, U. S. Army, a son of the late Governor Paul Burney Johnson of Mississippi.

b.—Samuel Edwin Pearce was born at Evergreen, Avoyelles parish, La., on August 4, 1895, where he now resides and is a prominent business man. He married in 1917 Bella M. Quarles, born in Galveston, Texas, October 1, 1894, daughter of David William Quarles and Louise M. May. Her grandfather was a pioneer settler of Houston, Texas, and belonged to the noted Virginia family of that name. Mr. and Mrs. Pearce have four children:—

az.—Mary Louise Pearce.
bz.—Virginia Quarles Pearce.
cz.—Barbara May Pearce.
dz.—William Stephen Pearce.

az.—Mary Louise Pearce was born December 25, 1918, and is as yet unmarried.

bz.—Virginia Quarles Pearce was born November 28, 1921, and was married at the Evergreen Baptist Church on Saturday, May 23, 1942, to James Arthur Person of Louisburg, North Carolina. They have a son, Arthur Edwin Person, born December 16, 1943.

cz.—Barbara May Pearce was born September 6, 1925, and was married at the Evergreen Baptist Church on August 26, 1944, to William Paul Wilson, U. S. Naval Reserve, son of Mr. and Mrs. Oscar Glendon Wilson of Alexandria, La.

dz.—William Stephen Pearce was born July 25, 1927, and is yet unmarried.

c.—Eura Voorhies Pearce, only daughter of Stephen Samuel Pearce II and his wife, Eura Voorhies, was born at Evergreen, La., on November 6, 1907, and was married in 1929 to Jennings Gordon Kavanaugh, born March 19, 1902, son of James R. Kavanaugh and Mattie Hinton. They reside in Bunkie, La., and have two children:—Amy Carolyn Kavanaugh, born December 29, 1930, and Martha Ann Kavanaugh, born in 1934.

vii.—Heber Livingston Pearce, seventh child of Stephen Samuel Pearce and Mary Ellen Bennett, was born near Evergreen, La., on January 25, 1874. He is familiarly known to his family and friends as "Livy Pearce," and now resides at Denham Springs, La. He married Ellen Esther Brown, daughter of Henry Jackson Brown and Martha Esther Bailey. They have six children:—Mary Ellen, Heber Livingston, Jr., Martha Aline, Alice Marr, Edward Joseph, and Claud Bennett Pearce. (See page 239).

viii.—Algeron B. Pearce, youngest child of Stephen Samuel Pearce and Mary Ellen Bennett, was born near Evergreen, La., and died unmarried at the age of nineteen.

C.

DELIA PEARCE.

Delia Pearce, third child of William Pearce, Sr., and Sarah Bray, was born in Screven county, Georgia, on January 15, 1787, and died near Cheneyville, Rapides parish, La., on March 24, 1829. From information at hand it appears that her father located on Bayou Boeuf above the present town of Cheneyville. His plantation was somewhere in the vicinity of the property now known as "Lunenburg" plantation. Family tradition intimates that he brought a quantity of gold with him when he left Georgia and buried it near his new home in Rapides parish. He was accidentally killed by a chimney falling on him in 1813. His sudden and unexpected death caused the secret of his buried gold to remain hidden forever. But the lure of it has continued until the present day to fascinate all those who have heard of it, and there have been frequent attempts to unearth it. The site of the plantation, so it is said, has been well dug up for the past century but no gold has yet been found. Some of the present generation still discuss it and dream of the time when they will find it.

Delia Pearce was married on January 1, 1807 (in Rapides parish, La., it is said), to John Dunwoody, a native of Georgia who had likewise emigrated to Louisiana. He was born in Georgia on November 18, 1782, and died near Cheneyville, La., on September 8, 1862. His name frequently appears on the early maps and land records of Rapides parish, in the Cheneyville neighborhood, where it is said he was a large land owner. Three children were born of this marriage:—

> 1.—William R. Dunwoody.
> 2.—Mary L. Dunwoody.
> 3.—Sarah Ann Dunwoody.

We have obtained this record of Mr. and Mrs. Dunwoody from their family Bible now in the possession of a member of the family. William R. Dunwoody, the eldest child, was born July 9, 1809, and died September 3, 1819. The youngest child, Sarah Ann Dunwoody, must have died in infancy as we find no further record of her.

2.—Mary L. Dunwoody, second child of John Dunwoody and Delia Pearce, was the only one of the children to reach maturity. She was born near Cheneyville, Rapides parish, La., on September 9, 1814, and died there July 7, 1834, in her twentieth year. She married about 1831 James Dickson McCoy who died September 16, 1834, in the 28th years of his age. They had two children:—Charles McCoy who died October 5, 1849, at the age of seventeen, and Mary Dunwoody McCoy who was born June 16, 1834. The second, Mary Dunwoody McCoy, not only lived to adult life but was three times married. Her first husband was Dr. Dewitt Clinton Rhodes who came to Rapides parish from Texas. They were married in 1853.

A letter from Frank Myers, Jr., to his father who was in California, dated May 13, 1854, contains the following item:—

"Miss Mary McCoy is married to a Dr. Rhodes from Texas. It is said that Dr. Rhodes is worth $60,000.00."

Dr. Rhodes died prior to 1860, leaving his wife with two children:— John Talbert Rhodes, born November 8, 1855, and Roberta A. Rhodes, born October 6, 1857. The latter died May 12, 1859, when less than two years of age.

John Talbert Rhodes married Lucy Marshall, born in 1859, youngest daughter of Thomas Douglas Marshall and Joyce Hoggatt. He died September 29, 1911. He and his wife had five children:—Banks Marshall Rhodes born in 1878 and died in 1893; John Talbert Rhodes, Jr., now living at Bunkie, La., who married Nora Miller; Nannie Rhodes who married Dr. Holloway; Maude Rhodes who married a man named Egan and is now a widow living in Pueblo, Colorado; Hattie Rhodes who married Gus Sideris.

Mary Dunwoody McCoy, after the death of her first husband, Dr. Dewitt Clinton Rhodes, was married in 1860 to Austin Willis Burges, son of Lovatt Samuel Burges, Sr., and Frances Cocke. He was born in Avoyelles parish, La., on June 16, 1829, and was educated in Georgetown, Kentucky. He first married Sarah Evolina Tanner, daughter of Lodowick Tanner and Ann Martha Eldred, and she died January 21, 1859, without issue. Mr. Burges resided in Rapides parish after his second marriage where he was extensively engaged in planting. He died there on June 26, 1870.

EXCURSUS—BURGES

The Burges family is so frequently mentioned in connection with other families in Rapides and Avoyelles parishes that a short disgression here is not inappropriate. We are told that there was a John Burges in Staffordshire, England, who married there on October 1, 1707, and was the sire of fourteen children. The third in order of birth of these children was Thomas Burges who emigrated to America and settled in North Carolina. He was born in Staffordshire, England, on September 6, 1712, and died in North Carolina in 1779. He was twice married. By his first wife, Miriam ————, he had six children.

Whether he married his first wife in England or America, we are unable to say. On May 21, 1760, he married Mary Haywood in North Carolina. As far as we know there was but one child of this second marriage, Lovatt Burges. He was born in North Carolina on January 31, 1762, and died there on October 10, 1807. We are told that Lovatt Burges was three times married:—1st to Elizabeth Irwin, by whom he had three children; 2nd to Priscilla Manny on July 11, 1790, by whom he had one child; 3rd to Mrs. Sallie (Lucas) Black on September 1, 1793, in Halifax county, N. C., by whom he had seven children. These seven children were:—

Elizabeth Ann Burges, born July 19, 1794.
Melissa Jane Burges, born January 25, 1797.
Augustine Willis Burges, born November 22, 1798.
John Burges, born March 24, 1801.
Mary Haywood Burges, born March 8, 1803.
Sallie Burges, born April 14, 1805.
Lovatt Samuel Burges, Sr., born March 19, 1807.

All of our Louisiana branch of the Burges family spring from the third and seventh of the above mentioned children of the third marriage, viz., Augustine Willis Burges and Lovatt Samuel Burges, Sr. The elder, Augustine Willis Burges, married Harriet Terrell, daughter of Halcot Terrell and Martha Cocke. Halcot Terrell Burges, a son of Augustine Willis Burges and Harriet Terrell, married Mary Elizabeth Wells, daughter of Gov. James Madison Wells of Louisiana. Lovatt Samuel Burges, Sr., married Frances Cocke (sister of Martha Cocke who married Halcot Terrell), and their son, Lovatt Samuel Burges, Jr., married Mary Elizabeth Wells, a daughter of General Montfort Wells. Thus two first cousins of the Burges family married two first cousins of the Wells family— the latter bearing identically the same name.

Lovatt Samuel Burges, Sr., and his wife, Frances Cocke, were both born, reared and educated in Warren county, North Carolina, where they married about 1827. Soon afterwards they moved to Louisiana and during the remainder of their lives resided in Avoyelles and Rapides parishes. They had six children:—

Austin Willis Burges, born June 16, 1829.
Joseph Lovatt Burges, born December 7, 1830.
Sallie Lucas Burges, born August 9, 1832.
John Mortimer Burges, born October 18, 1834.
Mary Elizabeth Burges, born April 1, 1837.
Lovatt Samuel Burges, Jr., born August 27, 1839.

Lovatt Samuel Burges, Sr., was killed by his brother-in-law Collin Cocke in a difficulty which occurred between them while both were under the influence of liquor. Collin moved to Arcola, Fort Bend county, Texas, where he married and had one daughter. Our source of information tells us that he was later assassinated there by his enemies, but failed to tell us anything as to who those enemies were.

John Mortimer Burges, fourth child of Lovatt Samuel Burges, Sr., and Frances Cocke, was a gallant Confederate soldier. He served under Stonewell Jackson and held the rank of a lieutenant when mustered out of the army at the end of the war. He married on January 25, 1866, Bettie Desirée Wells. They had five children:—

Frances Alice Burges, born November 15, 1866.
Desirée Wells Burges, born June 28, 1868.
Bettie Tanner Burges, born July 6, 1870.
Edward Lanier Burges, born February 3, 1872.
Eugene M. Burges, born March 11, 1874.

Mary Elizabeth Burges, fifth child of Lovatt Samuel Burges, Sr., and Frances Cocke, was married to James Harris Fitts of Tuscaloosa, Alabama. They had eight children.

Lovatt Samuel Burges, Jr., sixth child of Lovatt Samuel Burges, Sr., and Frances Cocke, married Mary Elizabeth Wells, daughter of General Montfort Wells and Jeannette Dent. They had two children, one of whom died in infancy. The other married Russell Rogers and died young without issue.

Halcott Terrell Burges, son of Augustine Willis Burges and Harriet Terrell, married Mary Elizabeth Wells, daughter of Gov. James Madison Wells and Mary Ann Scott. They had nine children, five of whom are living at this date. (1944).

Mary Dunwoody (McCoy) Rhodes and her second husband, Austin Willis Burges, had three children:—Charles Dunwoody Burges, born October 2, 1861, and died August 7, 1863; Lovatt Francis Burges (see below), born August 17, 1863; Judith Burges, born February 28, 1866, and died on January 29, 1867.

Lovatt Francis Burges, second child of Austin Willis Burges and Mary Dunwoody (McCoy) Rhodes, only one of the three children to survive childhood, was born in Avoyelles parish, La., and educated at the University of the South, at Sewanee, Tennessee, and at Roanoke College, Virginia. He graduated in medicine at Tulane University, New Orleans, La., after which he married Mrs. Annie (Grace) Didlake. They had two children:—Austin Earl Burges, born August 7, 1891, and Mary Dunwoody Burges, born in August, 1893. Dr. Dr. Burges died of tuberculosis on July 31, 1896.

Mary Dunwoody (McCoy-Rhodes) Burges married as her third husband Silas H. Cooper, a prominent Methodist minister, in 1876. They had one child, Helen Compton Cooper, born September 22, 1877. She was married in 1900 to James Lemuel Helm, son of Thomas Benjamin Helm and his first wife, Jane Wells Tanner (daughter of Branch Tanner and Desirée Wells). He was born near Cheneyville, Rapides parish, La., on February 13, 1865, and died at his home there on March 10, 1907. Mr. Helm's father died July 19, 1880, at his home near Cheneyville, La. Helen Compton (Cooper) Helm is living at this date (1944). She had five children, two of whom died in infancy. The two infants were Thomas Lovatt Helm, born January 7, 1901, and died March 29, 1901; Desirée Wells Helm, born October 18, 1902, and died September 29, 1904. The other three, living at this date, are:—

az.—Mary Jeannette Helm, born March 5, 1898.
bz.—Newton Cooper Helm, born March 28, 1899.
cz.—James Lemuel Helm, Jr., born January 2, 1905.

az.—Mary Jeannette Helm was married at Baton Rouge, La., on January 16, 1919, to Burton Paul Dupuy who was born at Marksville, La., on January 29, 1898. They now reside in Bunkie, La., and have two sons:—Burton Paul Dupuy, Jr., born September 27, 1919, and James Alfred Dupuy, born November 27, 1925.

bz.—Newton Cooper Helm married Corinne Adeline Gaiennie, daughter of George Washington Gaiennie and Martha Carnal, of Lecompte, La. They now reside in Eunice, La., and have two sons:—Robert Newton Helm, born March 18, 1926, and John Cooper Helm, born January 24, 1938.

cz.—James Lemuel Helm, Jr., is a prominent attorney in New Iberia, La. He married Sarah Land Jastrempski, daugh-

ter of Henry Jastrempski and grand-daughter of General Leon
Jastrempski, gallant Confederate soldier and at one time Ad-
jutant General of Louisiana. They have three children:—
Sarah Frances Helm, born October 26, 1935; John Henry
Helm, born August 7, 1938; James Lemuel Helm, III, born
August 7, 1938.

D.

MARY PEARCE.

Mary Pearce, fourth child of William Pearce, Sr., and his
wife, Sarah Bray, was born in Screven county, Georgia, about
1790. She was married to Silas Talbert, but just when and
where we are unable to say. The Talbert (or Talbot) family
originated in England. The progenitor of it in this country
seems to have been Matthew Talbert. He was in Maryland
first, then in Amelia and Bedford counties, Virginia. He died
in the latter about 1758. Some of the family later moved to
East Tennessee and finally to Wilkes county, Georgia. It is
quite likely that our Silas Talbert was of the Georgia branch
and it was probably there that he first met the Pearce family.
It is not unreasonable to suppose that he came to Louisiana
with them. We find another Talbert on Bayou Boeuf who was
apparently of the same generation as Silas, his name was
Abner. There is nothing to indicate that they were related
except that Abner also seems to have been on very close terms
with the Pearce family. In 1832 he owned property in com-
mon with John G. Pearce on Bayou Boeuf. However, just who
this John G. Pearce was or what relationship he bore to the
others of that name in Rapides parish, we have been unable
to determine. He was undoubtedly of the same generation as
the children of William Pearce, Sr., with whom we are here
dealing. Their paternal grandmother was Hannah *Green* and
it may even be that this John G. Pearce's middle name was
Green. This is purely suggestive. But it is strange that we
find no mention of him in the various family records and
Bibles at our disposal. He was a property and slave owner in
the community where he resided but we do not find that he
was married or left children. It was stated in the first part
of this chapter that Joshua Pearce, Jr., a brother of William

Pearce, Sr., settled in Mississippi and died there in 1810 leaving children. It is possible that John G. Pearce may have been his son.

Silas Talbert was a Notary Public for the parish of Rapides in the Bayou Boeuf neighborhood and we have been fortunate in locating his record book. It covers the period from February 10, 1825, to May 28, 1830. Below the last entry in it we find the following:—"Silas Talbert resigned July 1, 1830." The LOUISIANA DEMOCRAT of Wednesday, November 7, 1866, carried the following notice of his death:—

DIED:—On the 31st ult., at his residence on Bayou Boeuf, in this parish, Silas Talbert, in the 80th year of his age.

Silas Talbert signed his will March 13, 1866. There is nothing in it to indicate that he left children. He gives the usufruct of everything to his wife and after her death all his possessions are to go to "John Talbert Rhodes, minor son of Dewitt Clinton Rhodes, deceased, and Mary D. McCoy, now wife of A. W. Burges." His wife, Mary (Pearce) Talbert, died in the early part of December, 1867, and her will was admitted to probate on December 16, 1867. She also left everything she died possessed of to John Talbert Rhodes, whose mother, Mary D. McCoy, was her niece.

Silas Talbert had accumulated extensive holdings in Rapides parish during his residence there, and an inventory and appraisement of his effects made shortly after his death showed a total value of $100,763.00. That was quite a large fortune at that period. On December 22, 1865, he and his wife executed a deed before George B. Marshall, Notary Public, which is of interest. It is as follows:—

Personally came and appeared Mr. Silas Talbert, a resident of the said State and Parish, and with him also came and appeared Mrs. Mary Talbert, his wife, who intervened and became a party to this act, who declared to me Notary that in consequence of their high regard, esteem and affection for Mrs. Eliza Jane Gray, wife of John W. Pearce, residents of said State and Parish of Avoyelles, they do by these presents jointly and severally bequeath, donate and deliver unto the said Mrs. Eliza Jane Pearce two several tracts of land

E.

JAMES PEARCE.

James Pearce, fifth child of William Pearce, Sr., and his wife, Sarah Bray, was born in Screven county, Georgia, in 1792. He came to Rapides parish, La., with his father sometime after 1804 when he was a mere boy. After reaching adult life he established his home on Bayou Boeuf just above the present town of Cheneyville and married Rhoda Tanner, daughter of Joseph Tanner and his first wife, Elizabeth Lanier, and sister of Lodowick, Branch and Asa Tanner. The following notarial act found in the notary book of William Bray Pearce establishes definitely the fact that James Pearce married Rhoda Tanner.

STATE OF LOUISIANA,
PARISH OF RAPIDES:

> Know all men by these presents that I, Rhoda Pearce, of the State and Parish aforesaid, by and with the authority and consent of my husband James Pearce, do by these presents release and relinquish unto William H.Cureton all my right, title and interest in and unto a certain tract of land situate on the left bank of Bayou Boeuf in descending, being the same tract of land sold by the said James Pearce to Josias Chambers on the 20th day of April, 1827. In testimony whereof the said Rhoda Pearce and her husband James Pearce here present have signed these presents in presence of W. B. Pearce, Notary Public, and the undersigned witnesses, this 22nd day of October, 1832.

Witnesses:—   Rhoda Pearce,
S. Talbert,   James Pearce.
James D. Loyd.   Done before me
                        W. P. Pearce, Notary Public.

We regret that our information about James Pearce and his wife is so sparse. It appears very likely that they died in early adult life as we find no further mention of either of them in any of the transactions of that period which are now extant. As far as we can ascertain they left but one child:—

1.—James Lemuel Pearce.

1.—James Lemuel Pearce, only child of James Pearce and Rhoda Tanner, was born near Cheneyville, Rapides parish, La., about 1834. He is usually recorded and spoken of as *Lemuel*

Pearce. His mother's eldest brother was Lemuel Tanner and it was probably from him that the name came. From that time until the present day the name of *Lemuel* has been handed down among his descendants.

The following is from a deed passed June 12, 1856:—

Appeared James Lemuel Pearce of Rapides parish, La., and with him his wife, Mrs. Sarah Goodwin Pearce.

In this transaction they sell land to Mrs. Desiree Tanner (widow of Branch Tanner). The following item from it is of interest:—

Being the same land purchased by Joseph W. Tanner, deceased, and inherited by the said Mrs. Sarah G. Pearce from her former husband, deceased, the said Joseph W. Tanner, deceased.

On December 4, 1859, James Lemuel Pearce and Sarah Goodwin Pearce, his wife, sell Silas Talbert 830 acres of land on Bayou Boeuf "seven miles below the village of Cheneyville, bounded above by land of said vendee." It seems quite evident that James Lemuel Pearce was at one time an extensive land owner.

It was through this only son that the James Pearce branch of the family was perpetuated. In 1856 he married the widow of his first cousin, Joseph Willing Tanner (son of Branch Tanner). She was Sarah Goodwin Chambers, daughter of William Woodson Chambers and Sarah Ann Pearce (daughter of Stephen Pearce and Sally Goodwin Bray). James Lemuel Pearce and his wife were second cousins. They had six children:—

     i.—Desiree Pearce.
     ii.—Nellie Pearce.
     iii.—George Chambers Pearce.
     iv.—James Lemuel Pearce, Jr.
     v.—Newton Pearce.
     iv.—Francis Wioatte Pearce.

We find Mr. Pearce's death recorded in THE ALEXANDRIA TOWN TALK of Saturday, April 28, 1894, as follows:—

DIED:—In Cheneyville ward, Rapides parish, La., on Thursday night, April 19, 1894, Lemuel Pearce, aged 60 years, a native of Rapides parish.

i.—Desirée Pearce was born near Cheneyville, Rapides parish, La., in 1859, and died in Winston-Salem, North Carolina, on Saturday, September 7, 1929. Her body was brought to Alexandria, La., where she had lived for many years, and buried in the Rapides cemetery in Pineville beside her husband. She was married to Jesse Robert Ford, Jr., son of Jesse Robert Ford and Lida Calaway, and a grandson of William Prince Ford and his first wife, Martha P. Tanner (daughter of Robert Tanner and Providence Robert). See Part III, section K for Ford data.

Jesse Robert Ford, Jr., was well known to the compiler who can testify that he was a good and true man. He died in Alexandria, La., ten or twelve years prior to the death of his wife. They had four children:—Louis, Ruth, Edith and William Branch Ford. All of these children are living at this time (1944) and the youngest is married and has two children, a boy and a girl.

ii.—Nellie Pearce, second daughter of James Lemuel Pearce and Sarah Goodwin Chambers, first married William Branch Helm, son of Thomas Benjamin Helm and his first wife, Jane Wells Tanner (daughter of Branch Tanner and Desirée Wells). There was one son born of this union, William Branch Helm, Jr., who died at the age of fifteen. After the death of Mr. Helm, Nellie Pearce was married to Oscar S. Powell, a citizen and prominent business man of Alexandria, La. He was shot and killed a few years after their marriage while traveling on a railroad train. They had one son, Oscar S. Powell, Jr., who is now married and has a son.

iii.—George Chambers Pearce, son of James Lemuel Pearce and Sarah Goodwin Chambers, was born in Rapides parish, La., about 1865, and died on July 5, 1930. He was twice married. He married his first wife, Clara Middleton Glaze, on December 30, 1891, daughter of Middleton Glaze and Clarissa Eugenia Eldred (daughter of Peter Robert Eldred and Evolina Griffin). Middleton Glaze was the fourth child of John Adams Glaze and Mary Cocke, and was born in Avoyelles parish, La., on November 7, 1836. His father, John Adams Glaze, died on May 30, 1858. Mary Cocke (his mother) was the daughter of Joseph Cocke and Winifred Alston, and was born in Warren county, North Carolina, on May 6, 1808.

Joseph Cocke and Winifred Alston were married about 1783 in Warren county. Winifred Alston was the daughter of Philip Alston and Winifred Whitmel, and was born in North Carolina on November 28, 1764. Winifred Cocke, a sister of Mary (Cocke) Glaze, married Tacitus Gaillard Calvit, Sr., of Rapides parish, La., in 1827, and they were the parents of Tacitus Gaillard Calvit, Jr., who married Jeannette Dent Wells, daughter of General Montford Wells and Jeannette Dent.

George Chambers Pearce and his first wife, Clara Middleton Glaze, had three sons:—

        a.—George Middleton Pearce.
        b.—James Pearce.
        c.—Eric Pearce.

After the death of his first wife, George Chambers Pearce married Eugenia McPhitter. They had one daughter:—

        d.—Mary Pearce.

a.—George Middleton Pearce, eldest son of George Chambers Pearce and his first wife, Clara Middleton Glaze, married Lony Hatfield, daughter of Mr. and Mrs. Charles Hatfield, and they have three children:— George Middleton Pearce, Jr., Charles Hatfield Pearce, and Clara Elain Pearce. The eldest of these, George Middleton Pearce, Jr., is at this time a captain in the aviation corps of the U. S. Army. He has been almost continuously in the South Pacific for the past two years. While serving with a troop carrier squadron of the Fifth Air Force he was awarded the air medal for "Meritorious Achievement." Later he was awarded the "Distinguished Flying Cross" for taking part in at least fifty roundtrip missions. Then Lieut. Gen. George C. Kenny, Commander of the Allied Air Forces in the South Pacific, awarded him the Oak Leaf Cluster in lieu of a second award of the "Distinguished Flying Cross."

The second son, Charles Hatfield Pearce, is an aviation machinist-mate in the U. S. Navy.

b.—James Pearce, second son of George Chambers Pearce and his first wife, Clara Middleton Glaze, married Mabel Keller. They have no children.

c.—Eric Pearce, third son of George Chambers Pearce and his first wife, Clara Middleton Glaze, married Belle Escudé of Mansura, La. They have no children.

d.—Mary Pearce, only child of George Chambers Pearce and his second wife, Eugenia McPhitter, was married to Simmie Deville of Alexandria, La. They have two children:—Jessie Nell and Donald Ray Deville.

iv.—James Lemuel Pearce, Jr., son of James Lemuel Pearce and Sarah Goodwin Chambers, was born in Rapides parish, La., about 1867, and now resides in Pineville, La. He married Mattie Catherine Pearce (better known as "Kate Pearce"), daughter of William Eugene Pearce and Charlcie Emma Leadbetter. Mr. Pearce and his wife are cousins—he being a grandson of James Pearce and she a great granddaughter of Joshua Pearce, two brothers. They have four children:—

    a.—Charlcie Sarah Pearce.
    b.—William Francis Pearce.
    c.—Mary Catherine Pearce.
    d.—James Lemuel Pearce, III.

a.—Charlcie Sarah Pearce was married to James Edwin Davis. They have one daughter, Catherine Louise Davis, born December 18, 1933.

b.—William Francis Pearce married Inez Guidros. They have one son, Louis Francis Pearce, born on January 11, 1928.

c.—Mary Catherine Pearce was married to Leo Earl Maricella. They have no children at this time.

d.—James Lemuel Pearce, III, born May 31, 1907, in Alexandria, La., married Beatrice Pierce. They have two children:—Lemuel Eugene Pearce, born March 18, 1932, and Jimmie Beatrice Pearce, born August 9, 1933.

v.—Newton Pearce, fifth child of James Lemuel Pearce and Sarah Goodwin Chambers, now resides in California. He married Maude Roberts and they have two daughters, Nellie Maude and May Agnes Pearce. Both of these daughters are married but we have been unable to obtain any additional information about them.

vi.—Francis Wioatte Pearce (better known as "Frank"), youngest child of James Lemuel Pearce and Sarah Goodwin Chambers, lived to maturity but died unmarried. We find in the ALEXANDRIA TOWN TALK of Tuesday, December 17, 1901, the following notice of his death:—

> DIED:—At Bunkie, Louisiana, at the residence of his sister, Mrs. Desiree Ford, on Sunday, December 5, 1901, Francis Wioatte Pearce, aged 32 years. Interment was made at Trinity Church graveyard, Cheneyville, on Monday, at 4 P. M. The deceased was a brother of Mrs. O. S. Powell of Alexandria.

F.

JOSHUA PEARCE.

Joshua Pearce, sixth child of William Pearce, Sr., and his wife, Sarah Bray, was born in Screven county, Georgia, on June 5, 1795, and died near Cheneyville, Rapides parish, La., on December 30, 1879. He came to Rapides parish with his father as a young boy in the first decade of the nineteenth century. He married about 1824 Esther Tanner, daughter of Joseph Tanner and his first wife, Elizabeth Lanier, and sister of Lodowick, Branch and Asa Tanner. She was born on August 4, 1806, probably in South Carolina. She died in Rapides parish, La., on February 2, 1858. She and her husband were buried in the Christian graveyard in Cheneyville, La., where their tombs may be seen today, and on marble slabs are carved the dates of their birth and death. Joshua Pearce married as his second wife the widow of Leonidas Alonzo Robert, Sarah H. Coffeen. She outlived him several years. They had no children. According to information furnished the compiler by one of their grandchildren Joshua Pearce and his first wife, Esther Tanner, had seventeen children, most of whom died in early infancy. Only four reached adult life. They were:—

1.—Eliza Eugenia Pearce.
2.—William Lodowick Pearce.
3.—Joseph M. Pearce.
4.—Berthier Mordella Pearce.

1.—Eliza Eugenia Pearce, daughter of Joshua Pearce and his first wife, Esther Tanner, was born near Cheneyville, Rapides parish, La., on April 8, 1826, and died near Evergreen, Avoyelles parish, La., on December 6, 1893. She was married about 1848 to James Horace Marshall who was born in Avoyelles parish, La., on March 2, 1817, and died at his home there on February 13, 1896. He was a son of William C. Marshall and his second wife, Rosalie (Meuillon) Wells, daughter of Dr. Ennemond Meuillon and Jeannette Poiret, and widow of Willing Wells. James Horace Marshall and his wife are buried at Evergreen, La., where we find recorded on marble slabs the dates of their birth and death. They had seven children:—

      i.—James Horace Marshall, Jr.
     ii.—Desirée Marshall.
    iii.—Rose Marshall.
    iv.—Alzine Marshall.
     v.—Ada Marshall.
    vi.—Robert Hiram Marshall.
   vii.—Esther Marshall.

     i.—James Horace Marshall, Jr., was born at Evergreen, Avoyelles parish, La., on September 2, 1852, and died August 29, 1942, at the age of ninety. He married Annie Clara Rush on February 9, 1876, daughter of Charles Conrad Rush and Ann Irion. Mr. Rush was a native of Tennessee and came to Avoyelles parish, La., shortly before the Civil War. He married before coming to Louisiana and his wife was a daughter of John Poindexter Irion of Paris, Tennessee. Mrs. Rush was related to the descendants of Rev. George Anderson Irion who were living in central Louisiana. Mrs. Marshall was born at Big Bend, Avoyelles parish, La., on August 19, 1857, and died July 16, 1938, at the age of eighty-one. She and her husband were married at Big Bend by the Rev. Adolph J. Terry and the ceremony was witnessed by T. A. Spurlock, Howard Irion, and Robert H. Marshall (brother of the groom), Mr. and Mrs. Marshall had eleven children:—

    a.—Charles E. Marshall, born November 9, 1876.
    b.—Robert John Marshall, born March 29, 1878.
    c.—Royal Branch Marshall, born December 2, 1879.
    d.—Durwood Horace Marshall, born October 6, 1881.
    e.—Esther Nean Marshall, born November 14, 1883.
    f.—Lester Boyd Marshall, born April 1, 1885.
    g.—Earl Wendell Marshall, born May 20, 1887.
    h.—Thomas James Marshall, born April 9, 1889.
    i.—Clarence C. Marshall, born July 10, 1892.
    j.—Otis Clyde Marshall, born May 10, 1894.
    k.—Pearl Marshall, born April 12, 1896.

a.—Charles E. Marshall was born at Evergreen, La., and died September 27, 1882.

b.—Robert John Marshall was born at Big Bend, La., and died September 1, 1943. He never married and was for many years cashier of the Planters Bank at Bunkie, La.

c.—Royal Branch Marshall was born at Big Bend, La., and is now living at Evergreen, La. He never married.

d.—Durwood Horace Marshall was born at Big Bend, La., has never married and now resides at Evergreen, La.

e.—Esther Nean Marshall was born at Evergreen, La., and died there on June 6, 1884.

f.—Lester Boyd Marshall was born at Evergreen, La., and married Minnie West on February 8, 1910, who is now dead. They had one son, Ralph, also dead at this time.

g.—Earl Wendell Marshall was born at Evergreen, La., and married Ida Martin on August 2, 1912. They now live at DeRidder, La., and have five sons, two of whom, Sidney and Horace, are now married. Two of their sons are in the U. S. Army during this great world war.

h.—Thomas James Marshall was born at Evergreen, La., and married Nora Cole about 1921. They have a son, Thomas James Marshall, Jr.

i.—Clarence C. Marshall was born at Evergreen, La., and died March 22, 1893.

j.—Otis Clyde Marshall was born at Evergreen, La., and married Eugenia Frank about 1923. They have no children.

k.—Pearl Marshall was born at Evergreen, La., and married February 8, 1920, Early Andrew Sharpe. One daughter, Elulia Sharpe, was born of this union, who is yet unmarried. Pearl Marshall was married a second time on November 20, 1941, to Louis H. Johnson.

ii.—Desirée Marshall, born at Evergreen, Avoyelles parish, La., about 1854, married George Henry Irion, son of Robert Richardson Irion and Ann Bernard Audebert. We will disgress here to give a brief summary of the Irion family.

EXCURSUS—IRION

The first of the Irion family in America came over about 1763. He was Philip Jacob Irion and was born in Leichmar, Germany, in 1733. He settled in Culpeper county, Virginia, and there on August 12, 1765, married

Sarah Poindexter, daughter of John Poindexter an
Christian Anderson of Louisa county. She was a grand
daughter of Thomas Poindexter and a great grand-daugh
ter of George Poindexter. She died October 12, 1794
having been the mother of ten children. We have a recor
of only one of these children, George Anderson Irion, whо
was the ninth in order of birth. He was born in Culpepe:
county, Va., on August 12, 1782, and died in Avoyelle:
parish, La., on December 16, 1849. Early in life he be
came affiliated with the Baptist church and was ordaine
to the ministry before leaving Virginia. He marriе
Rebecca Hunt in Halifax county, Va., a daughter of Elijal
Hunt who was a son of James Hunt of Charlotte county
During the war of 1812 Rev. Irion put aside his peacefu
calling and entered the U. S. Army. He was advanced tо
the rank of major before the end of hostilities. Aftеr
peace was declared he moved to Williamson county, Tenn.
and later to Woodville, Miss. After a few years in thе
latter state he came to Louisiana, first settling in Rapidеs
parish and then in Avoyelles. Paxton's History of thе
Baptists of Louisiana has the following to say abouf
him:—

> Elder George A. Irion was a native of Virginia, where
> he was ordained to the ministry. He first settled in
> Wilkinson county, Miss., and in 1825 came to Louis-
> iana and became pastor at Cheneyville. John O'Quin
> says of him that "he was a very logical and zealous
> preacher. He possessed great versatility of talent.
> He was an apothecary, and very active in business."
> He ceased to preach about 1840, and spent some
> time in West Tennessee. He then returned to Louis-
> iana, and died at the residence of his son, Robert R.
> Irion, in Avoyelles parish.

George Anderson Irion and Rebecca Hunt had three
children:—Marion Hervery, William Hunt, and Robert
Richardson Irion. The eldest Marion Hervery (better
known as "Mary Ann"), married Robert Lynn Tanner—
see page 251.

William Hunt Irion was born in Halifax county, Va.,
on October 2, 1807. He married Nancy Gay of Virginia
who died leaving two daughters. One of these, Rebecca
Hunt Irion, married John Clark Griffith of Chicot, St.
Landry parish, La., and had quite a large family. The
other never married. William H. Irion later went to
Texas where he is said to have re-married and raised another family.

Robert Richardson Irion, second son of George Anderson Irion and Rebecca Hunt, was born in Halifax county, Va., on August 22, 1808. He became a prosperous and wealthy planter in Louisiana and his plantation included the site of the present town of Bunkie. He married on January 6, 1831, Ann Bernard Audebert, daughter of John Audebert and Henrietta Polhill. Mr. Irion died at the home of his son, Alfred Briggs Irion, in 1888. His wife died three years previously. She was of Huguenot descent, her father being a son of John Audebert and Judith Robert (daughter of Jacques Robert and Sarah Jaudon and a great grand-daughter of Rev. Pierre Robert, first Huguenot preacher in South Carolina). Henrietta Polhill was a daughter of Major Thomas Polhill of Burke county, Georgia, and a grand-daughter of Rev. Nathaniel Polhill who came to Savannah, Georgia, from Bedfordshire, England. Robert Richardson Irion and Ann Bernard Audebert had five children:—

1.—Alfred Briggs Irion.
2.—Charles Richardson Irion.
3.—George Henry Irion.
4.—Robert Howard Irion.
5.—Ann Rebecca Irion.

1.—Alfred Briggs Irion, born in Avoyelles parish, La., on February 18, 1833, and better known as "Judge Irion," graduated from the University of North Carolina in 1855. He was admitted to the bar in Opelousas, La., in 1857. Later he located at Marksville, La., was elected to Congress in 1884, and in 1889 was elected Circuit Judge. He married Caroline King, born 1836, daughter of Valentine and Nancy King of Opelousas. She was a grand-daughter of General John Edward King and Sallie Clifton, and a great grand-daughter of William King and Elizabeth Edwards of Virginia. She was also a great grand-daughter of Richard Bland—her grandmother, Letitia Bland being a sister of Theoderick Bland, "The Cato of the American Revolution." Caroline King died in 1878 leaving nine children. In 1879 Judge Irion married Alice Mort of New Orleans and they had one daughter who died young. The children by the first marriage were:—

Annie Winn Irion who married Judge Adolphe J. Lafargue and died leaving two children:—Sidney and Walter.

Clifford Hill Irion, prominent physician and President of the Louisiana State Board of Health 1904-1908, who married 1st Kate Keary Stafford and 2nd Mary Clint Egan. There were three children by the 1st marriage:—Alfred Briggs, Caroline King, and Leila Havard; and three by the 2nd:—Clifford Hill, James Valentine, and Mary Clint.

Valentine King Irion, outstanding in the dental profession and for several years Conservation Commissioner for the State of Louisiana, now living in New Orleans. He was born in Marksville, La., July 31, 1862, and married on September 18, 1889, Helen Lastrappes, daughter of Leonce F. Lastrappes and Mary King. They have four children:—Mary Caroline, Alfred King, Alice, and Albert Moore.

Robert Richardson Irion, prominent planter of Eola, La. Married Katherine French Boyd and had four children:—Dorothy, Annie, Katherine King, and Robert Richardson, Jr.

Percy Irion who married Emma Providence Bennett and had one child, Gladys.

Emma Irion who after the death of her elder sister married her brother-in-law Judge Adolphe J. Lafargue. They had three children:—Irion, Valentine, and Annie.

Henry Audebert Irion, prominent Alexandria dentist, now dead, who married Sadie Hunter—no issue.

Eola Irion, yet living and unmarried.

2.—Charles Richardson Irion. See page 469.

3.—George Henry Irion. See below.

4.—Robert Howard Irion married Mattie Baker and had one son, Robert Howard Irion, Jr.

5.—Ann Rebecca Irion married Hervy Smyth and had four children:—Addie who married Thomas Frith Pearce, Lena, Hervy who married Bessie Hogan and had eight children, Clarence Rhodes who married Mabel Kurtz and is now dead.

(The following Irion ancestors participated in the American Revolution:—Philip Jacob Irion, Elijah Hunt, John Audebert, Thomas Polhill, John Edwards, William King, Richard Bland).

Desirée Marshall and George Henry Irion lived in Avoyelles parish all of their lives and died there sometime prior to 1913, as is shown by the Rapides parish court records of that year. They had six children, two of whom, Kitty and Eugene Henry, died in infancy. Those reaching adult life were: Herbert Carlisle Irion, now deceased, who married Bertha Pearce (see page 431); Lucy Marshall Irion who married Charles Catlin Carver (died in 1938) and she now lives in Rayne, La.; Daisy Lee Irion, unmarried and now living in Rayne, La.; John Hollingshead Irion, married twice, and living in Shreveport, La. His first wife was Aletha Neal of Richmond, Texas. They had one child, Marie, who married Howard Turner on February 19, 1938, and they have a daughter, Memory, born August 17, 1943. Aletha Neal Irion died in 1928 and her husband married Tinye Davis of Dubberly, La., in 1934. They have no children.

iii.—Rose Marshall, born about 1856, was married to Charles Richardson Irion, second son of Robert Richardson Irion and Ann Bernard Audebert. They lived in Avoyelles parish, La., all their lives. We have no record of the date of death of either of them but know from the court proceedings of Rapides parish for the year 1913 that they were dead before that year. They had four children:—Horace, now dead; Caroline (usually called "Callie") who married John Moss Marshall (now dead, a son of Robert Harden Marshall and Sarah Elizabeth Moss) and had three daughters and a son:—Rose who married Dahl Dewees and has no children, Florence who married Herbert Smith and has no children, Esther who married John Green and has one child, Nancy, and Albert who married Jean ———— and has a son—all live in San Antonio, Texas, except Esther who lives in Hollywood, California; Alfred Wade who married Pearl ———— and has two sons and three daughters; Henry Bennett who married Bertha Hays of Woodville, Mississippi, in 1904, and has a son, William Bennett Irion, who married Aimee Primeau in 1927 and has three children, Dolores and twins—Benton and Bennett.

iv.—Alzine Marshall, born about 1860, was married to Isaac Cureton Johnson, son of Charles Lewellyn Johnson and Martha Rachel Cureton. Mr. Johnson was a prominent planter and citizen of his community and was sheriff of Avoyelles parish for several years. Alzine (Marshall) Johnson died at Evergreen, La., on Sunday, September 10, 1893, leaving six children:—Eliza, Esther, Frank, Rose, Nora, and Isaac Cureton Johnson, Jr. Eliza Johnson was married to Harry Sneed who died about fifteen years ago. She is yet living. They had three children:—Harry Johnson, Alzine and Isaac Cureton.

Esther Johnson was married to Elihu Kilpartick Branch son of Dr. Leroy Kilpatrick Branch and his second wife, Laura Griffin. Mr. Branch lived at Cheneyville, La., for many years where he was engaged in the mercantile business. He and his wife had four children:—William, Henry, Alzine and Laura.

Frank Johnson married Lilly Rusk. They had no children

Rose Johnson was married to Ed. Middleton. They had no children.

Nora Johnson died young.

Isaac Cureton Johnson, Jr., graduated from the U. S. Naval Academy at Annapolis, Maryland, and is now a retired rear admiral. He was twice married but has no children.

v.—Ada Marshall, born about 1862, was married to William Franklin Everett, son of John Everett and Letitia Spurlock (sister of Thomas Andrel Spurlock who married Cornelia Rush). John Everett and his wife are buried in the Evergreen cemetery in Avoyelles parish, La., and according to the inscriptions on their tombstones he was born February 9, 1827, and died March 17, 1897, and she was born September 7, 1833, and died May 21, 1896. William Franklin Everett and Ada Marshall had five children:—Corry, Walter, William Franklin, Jr., Floyd, and Katie. The eldest of these, Corry Everett, married George Ford who died in January, 1927. They had five children:—Frank, Gertrude and Arthur (twins), Katie May, and George. Frank is in the army at present, is married and has one child. Gertrude married Walter Patrick and has two children, Martha and Brenda. Arthur, the younger of the twins, married and died March 6, 1944, leaving two children. Katie May married Foster Grimball and is now dead, leaving no children. George is unmarried and is now in the U. S. Army.

vi.—Robert Hiram Marshall, second son of James Horace Marshall and Eliza Eugenia Pearce, was born in Avoyelles parish, La., on November 6, 1866. He graduated in dentistry and is now (1944) living at Gibsland, Bienville parish, La., where he is still practicing his profession. He married Daisy Helm, born September 16, 1866, a daughter of Thomas Benjamin Helm and his first wife, Jane Wells Tanner (daughter of

Branch Tanner and Desirée Wells). They had three children:—

    a.—Esther Maude Marshall, born November 29, 1887.
    b.—Nellie Helm Marshall, born January 22, 1889.
    c.—Bessie Marshall, born April 30, 1891.

The youngest of these children, Bessie Marshall, died at the age of 15. In the Alexandria Town Talk of Saturday, December 16, 1893, the following item tells of the death of Mrs. Marshall:—

DIED:At Evergreen, Louisiana, on Wednesday morning, December 13, 1893, at 1 o'clock, Daisy Helm, wife of R. H. Marshall, aged 27 years. Cause of death, pneumonia.

Dr. Robert Hiram Marshall married as his second wife Josephine Schneider. They had eight children:—Daisy, Joseph Schneider, Annie, Carrie, Jewell, Robert, William, and Paul Koenig Marshall. After the death of his second wife Dr. Marshall married a third time in 1941. We have been unable to ascertain this lady's name.

    a.—Esther Maude Marshall, eldest child of Dr. Robert Hiram Marshall and his first wife, Daisy Helm, was married November 3, 1909, to Thomas Jefferson Spurlock, son of Thomas Andrel Spurlock and Cornelia Rush. Mr. Spurlock died October 29, 1940, and his wife is now living in Baton Rouge, La. They had six children:—Nell Marshall Spurlock who was married to Dr. Denzel Leigh Gill of the Agricultural Department of the Louisiana State University and at present serving in the United States Army with the rank of captain —they have one daughter, Caroline, born January 6, 1941; Thomas Jefferson Spurlock, Jr., who married Lucille Lakin and has a daughter, Margaret Lucille, born August 26, 1944; Edward Marshall Spurlock* as yet unmarried and now a chief

---

* NOTE:—The following is taken from the Baton Rouge *State-Times* of March 24, 1945:—Mrs. T. J. Spurlock, 2846 Lockwood street, has a son and a daughter in the service. Warrant Officer E. M. Spurlock, recently returned from the Pacific theater of operations, is now visiting his mother for a few days. Lieut. (j. g.) Daisy Spurlock, a Navy nurse, was recently promoted to that rank. She is with the evacuation air corps and is stationed at the Alemeda Air Base, Calif. Lieut. Spurlock is a graduate of the Baton Rouge General hospital nursing school here, and did private duty in Baton Rouge before enlisting in the Navy.

petty officer in the U. S. Navy; Daisy Maude Spurlock, a graduate nurse and now serving as an ensign in the U. S. Naval Nursing Corps; Donald Helm Spurlock, unmarried and a 1st lieutenant in the U. S. Army; Joyce Lynn Spurlock, at present a senior high school student.

b.—Nellie Helm Marshall, second daughter of Dr. Robert Hiram Marshall and his first wife, Daisy Helm, was married December 17, 1913, to Ernest Percivil Spurlock, brother of Thomas Jefferson Spurlock, Sr., and son of Thomas Andrel Spurlock and Cornelia Rush. They have three children:— Clyde, unmarried and now in the U. S. Army; Alton, married to Mary Smiley and has a daughter, June Elaine; Lucille, unmarried and teaching English in the Tioga High School in Rapides Parish, La.

vii.—Esther Marshall, youngest child of James Horace Marshall and Eliza Eugenia Pearce, was born about 1868. After the death of her sister Alzine she married her brother-in-in-law Isaac Cureton Johnson. They had no children and both are now long since dead.

EXCURSUS—MARSHALL

The close association of the Marshall family with several of the branches of the various families dealt with in this work merits a more extensive consideration than has already been accorded here. We will therefore devote a little space to the descendants of the two brothers of James Horace Marshall who married Eliza Eugenia Pearce. These brothers were George Benoist Marshall and Francis Wioatte Marshall. They were sons of William C. Marshall and his second wife, Rosalie (Meuillon) Wells. Rosalie Meuillon's father was Dr. Ennemond Meuillon who came from France in 1770 and first settled in Pointe Coupee parish, La., then went to Opelousas where he met and married Jeannette Poiret, daughter of Andre Claude Baptist Poiret, the Chevalier de Brie, and his wife, Francoise Le Kintreck. At the time she was the widow of Col. Jacques La Mothe, by whom she had four children. Dr. Meuillon served in the army of Governor Bernado Galvez as a lieutenant in that famous campaign against the British in 1779. He later moved to Rapides parish where he remained until his death in 1820. Rosalie, born in Rapides parish November 2, 1782, first married in 1798 Willing

Wells, son of Samuel Levi Wells, I, and Dorcas Huie, by whom she had five children. In 1815 she married as her second husband, William C. Marshall, and had three sons.

George Benoist Marshall, second son of William C. Marshall and Rosalie (Meuillon) Wells, was born in Avoyelles parish, La., on December 20, 1818. He is better known as "Captain Marshall," which title dates from the Civil War. He first married Phoebe Tippett and had one daughter who died in early life, unmarried. He married secondly, Margaret Dawson Cureton, daughter of William H. Cureton and Mary Boaz Dawson. She was born near Cheneyville, in Rapides parish, La., in 1824, and died in 1886, and he ten years later, in 1896. Both are buried in the Episcopal cemetery at Cheneyville. They had twelve children:—Margaret, Hardin, Mary Margaret, Martha, George Cureton, James Horace, Wioatte, Virginia Annette, Edward Cullom, Medora, Lemuel Pearce, Richard Taylor. The eldest child, Margaret, died in infancy. Hardin Marshall, the second child, died many years ago. He married Belinda Cullom, daughter of Judge E. North Cullom, and left one son, Aubrey, who is now living in New Orleans. Mary Margaret Marshall married 1st. John Lodowick Compton, and 2nd. R. Layson Walker (see page 153). Martha Marshall never married and died a few years ago when past middle life. George Cureton Marshall moved to the southern part of the State, married and probably left descendants but have been unable to get any data on them. James Horace Marshall married Rosalind Stafford, daughter of General Leroy A. Stafford. He was killed soon afterwards in a difficulty with William F. Jackson. Wioatte Marshall married Emma Butler. They had no children. Virginia Annette Marshall, better known as "Luna," married Norton R. Roberts who moved to New Orleans where he practiced law for many years and was prominent in his profession. We find the following item in the Alexandria Town Talk of Saturday, March 22, 1890:—

Died:—At the residence of her son, Norton R. Roberts, in New Orleans, La., on Wednesday, March 12, 1890, at 3 o'clock p. m., Margaret V. Roberts, aged 65 years, relect of the late Roger Roberts of Rapides parish.

Norton Roger Roberts and his wife, Virginia Annette Marshall, had two sons, George Marshall and Horace Norton Roberts. Both are living in New Orleans at this time and neither have ever married.

Edward Cullom Marshall, born November 30, 1859, died June 1, 1923. He married twice: 1st Anna Liddle Wheeler and 2nd Emma Brooks. His first wife was born in New Orleans on October 1, 1861, and died at Abbeville, La., on December 8, 1905. They were married in 1885 and had eight children:—John Wheeler, Margaret, Mattie Cushman, Susannah Bein, Virginia Annette, Alice Gertrude, Edward Cullom, Jr., Joseph Ewell. The third of these, Mattie Cushman Marshall, was born November 1, 1889, and maried November 21, 1916, George M. Eldredge, born August 11, 1883. They now reside in Abbeville, La., and have two children:—Janie Pond Eldredge, born February 3, 1919, and married December 2, 1942, Marcel Joseph Languirand and has a son, Marcel Joseph, Jr., born June 3, 1944; George M. Eldredge, Jr., unmarried at this time and serving in the U. S. Army. By his second wife Mr. Marshall had four children:— Brooks, Annie, Dolly, and Richard. All of his children are living at this date except the second child by the first marriage who died young. Medora Marshall married Eddie Walter Pearce who is now dead. They had no children. Lemuel Pearce Marshall, born on June 21, 1862, is now dead. He married Elizabeth Compton Meeker, daughter of Dr. Samuel F. Meeker and Elizabeth Compton. He left seven children:—Samuel Meeker, George Benoist, Lemuel Pearce, Jr., Margaret Dawson, Mathilda Meeker, Wioatte Cureton, and Elizabeth Meeker. Richard Taylor Marshall was a physician and was twice married. He left children but we regret our inability to obtain information on them.

Francis Wioatte Marshall, third son of William C. Marshall and Rosalie (Meuillon) Wells, was born in Avoyelles parish, La., on February 16, 1821. He was a prominent physician and was well known in central Louisiana in professional circles. On May 22, 1851, he married Mary Eleanor Chambers, daughter of William Woodson Chambers and Sarah Anne Pearce (daughter of Stephen Pearce and his first wife, Sally Goodwin Bray). For their descendants see page 358.

There was another branch of the Marshall family in central Louisiana represented by Mark Richards Marshall who was a nephew of William C. Marshall. See pages 157 and 161. in this book.

2.—William Lodowick Pearce, son of Joshua Pearce and Esther Tanner, was born near Cheneyville, Rapides parish,

La., about 1830. He married about 1851 Martha Frances Meadeariss. A letter from Thaddeus Sobieski Robert to his brother-in-law, Francis Myers, dated at Robinson's Ferry, Stanislaus River, California, July 15, 1851, contains the following paragraph:—

> They are marrying off quite fast at last at home. I suppose you have seen in the "Delta" where William L. Pearce (Joshua's son) and Miss Meadeariss have been married—she is gone at last. Toby Tanner and Miss Sarah Chambers, and I presume ere this that Dr. F. W. Marshall and Miss Eleanor Chambers are married—and John Marshall and. Miss Eldred (Peter Eldred's daughter).

We have no record of the dates of death of William Lodowick Pearce and his wife. They had six children:—

> i.—William Eugene Pearce.
> ii.—Esther Pearce.
> iii.—Austin Pearce.
> iv.—Sally Pearce.
> v.—Joshua Pearce.
> vi.—Catherine Pearce.

i.—William Eugene Pearce was born in Rapides parish, La., near the town of Cheneyville, in 1852, and died at his home in Alexandria, La., on Wednesday, March 16, 1932, at the age of eighty. He married on January 12, 1876, Charlcie Emma Leadbetter, who was born on March 24, 1854, and died October 15, 1942. She was buried in Greenwood Memorial Park in Pineville, La. It was this dear old lady who about two years before her death furnished the compiler of these notes with all information here given about the descendants of James and Joshua Pearce. Two daughters were born of this marriage:—

> a.—Mattie Catherine Pearce.
> b.—Charlcie Emma Pearce.

a.—Mattie Catherine Pearce (better known as "Kate") was married to her cousin, James Lemuel Pearce, Jr. They now reside in Pineville, La., and have four children. See page 414.

b.—Charlcie Emma Pearce is unmarried and now resides in Pineville, La.

ii.—Esther Pearce, eldest daughter of William Lodowick Pearce and Martha Frances Meadeariss, was married to Dr. T. M. Brentz. They had four children:—James, Mattie, Daisy, and Ruby Brentz.

iii.—Austin Pearce, second son of William Lodowick Pearce and Martha Frances Meadeariss, married Mattie Ready. They had three children:—Mary Martha, Carrie Meadeariss, and William Robert Pearce.

iv.—Sally Pearce, second daughter of William Lodowick Pearce and Martha Frances Meadeariss, was married to James Calton and they had five children:—

> a.—Josie Calton.
> b.—Frances Meadeariss Calton.
> c.—William Calton.
> d.—Samuel Hardison Calton.
> e.—Clarence Calton.

b.—Frances Meadeariss Calton was married to Everard Hamilton Tanner, son of Robert Linn Tanner, Jr., and Matilda Sannie Calloway. They had three children. See page 281 Part Three.

d.—Samuel Hardison Calton was born in 1881 and died in Alexandria, La., on Saturday morning, June 21, 1941. He married Carrie Brown who survives him. They had two children:—Donald Watson Calton and Inez Calton. Sam Calton was a good, upright, honest man, and a true friend, as the compiler of these notes, who knew him well, can testify.

e.—Clarence Calton lives in Fort Worth, Texas, but we have been unable to get in touch with him for data on himself and family.

v.—Joshua Pearce, third son of William Lodowick Pearce and Martha Frances Meadeariss, married Esther Hymes. They have a daughter, Inez Pearce.

vi.—Catherine Pearce, third and youngest daughter of William Lodowick Pearce and Martha Frances Meadeariss, died at the age of sixteen, unmarried.

3.—Joseph M. Pearce, son of Joshua Pearce and Esther Tanner, was born near Cheneyville, Rapides parish, La., on January 8, 1835. He married Anne Mackall Chilton Weems (known to her family as "Nannie"), born August 16, 1936, daughter of Dr. Nathaniel Chapman Weems and his wife, Annie Eliza Chilton Mullikin. She died on September 3, 1926, at the advanced age of ninety. Mr. Pearce died on May 14, 1866. We find the following notice of his death in the Louisiana Democrat of Wednesday, May 30, 1866:—

DIED:—In this parish, at the residence of his father, on the 14th inst., Joseph M. Pearce, aged 31 years, 4 months, and 6 days.

Joseph M. Pearce and his wife had two daughters, both of whom were living at a recent date in Ennis, Texas. They were:—

i.—Mary Elizabeth Pearce.
ii.—Corrie Weems Pearce.

i.—Mary Elizabeth Pearce was twice married; first to Charles Kidwell, and second to a Mr. Huffhines. There were no children by the second marriage, but by the first there were three:—

a.—Charles Weems Kidwell.
b.—Rollo C. Kidwell.
c.—Henry Graber Kidwell.

a.—Charles Weems Kidwell was born June 18, 1879. He is unmarried and now lives in Dallas, Texas.

b.—Rollo C. Kidwell is living at this time and has never married.

c.—Henry Graber Kidwell is yet unmarried and lives in Texas.

ii.—Corrie Weems Pearce was married to Edward C. Meredith and had two children, both of whom are now dead. They were Addison and Laura Meredith. Addison married but left no children.

4.—Berthier Mordella Pearce, son of Joshua Pearce and Esther Tanner, was born near Cheneyville, Rapides parish, La., in 1848. He was familiarly known to his family and friends as "Buck Pearce." He married Emily Marshall, daughter of Dr. Francis Wioatte Marshall and Mary Eleanor Chambers (daughter of William Woodson Chambers and Sarah Anne Pearce). They had nine children:—

    i.—Esther Pearce.
    ii.—Bertha Pearce.
    iii.—Malcolm Mordella Pearce.
    iv.—Claud Pearce.
    v.—Emily Pearce.
    vi.—Henry Munson Pearce.
    vii.—Fred William Pearce.
    viii.—Florence Pearce.
    ix.—Chester Pearce.

Mrs. Pearce died on June 24, 1903, and Mr. Pearce later married her sister, Florence Marshall, who became a true mother to the orphan children of her departed sister, as the compiler of these notes can well testify. There were no children born of the second marriage. Berthier Mordella Pearce died in Baton Rouge, La., on April 19, 1931, at the age of eighty-three years. His second wife, Florence Marshall, died in March, 1935.

i.—Esther Pearce, eldest child of Berthier Mordella Pearce and Emily Marshall, was born in Rapides parish, La., and was married December 17, 1903, to Jasper Gray Ewing of Baton Rouge, La., where they now reside. They have six children:—

    a.—Elizabeth Ewing.
    b.—Catherine Ewing.
    c.—Marshall Brookshire Ewing.
    d.—Margaret Ewing.
    e.—Jasper Gray Ewing, Jr.
    f.—Malcolm Pearce Ewing.

a.—Elizabeth Ewing was married to Charles Walter Carlton, Jr., who is at this time serving in the United States Army with the rank of captain. He was stationed in England for some time but is now probably across the channel. They have two children:—Charles Walter Carlton, III, and Robert Marshall Carlton.

b.—Catherine Ewing was married to Robert Taylor Pickett and they have three children:—Robert Taylor Pickett, Jr., James Marshall Pickett, and Martha Elizabeth Pickett.

c.—Marshall Brookshire Ewing married Scott Jolly of Shreveport, La. They have no children at this date.

d.—Margaret Ewing was married to Victor Leander Roy, Jr., son of Victor Leander Roy who for many years was prominent in the field of education in Louisiana, and who at one time was President of the State Normal College at Natchitoches, La. Mr. and Mrs. Roy reside in Baton Rouge and have three children:—Margaret Lucille, Catherine, and Victor Leander Roy, III. The last was born August 22, 1942.

e.—Jasper Gray Ewing, Jr., married Mary Gayden. They have two children:—Jasper Gray Ewing, III, and Georgie Chance Ewing.

f.—Malcolm Pearce Ewing married Marshall Reymond of Baton Rouge, La., on December 17, 1940. He was commissioned an ensign in the U. S. Navy on August 22, 1942, and is now on active duty.

ii.—Bertha Pearce, second daughter of Berthier Mordella Pearce and Emily Marshall, was married to Herbert Carlisle Irion, son of George Henry Irion and Desirée Marshall, and they had one son, Norman Carlisle Irion. Mrs. Irion died of pneumonia when her son was about one year old, and Mr. Irion has since died. The son, Norman Carlisle Irion, married Catherine Fox in Greenwich, Connecticut, and they had one daughter, Catherine Bertha Irion. His wife died and he then married May McMillan by whom he has three sons:—Norman Carlisle, Jr., Herbert, and Robert Irion.

iii.—Malcolm Mordella Pearce, eldest son of Berthier Mordella Pearce and Emily Marshall, was born in Rapides parish, La., on February 21, 1879, and now resides in Baton Rouge, La., where for many years he has held a responsible position in the Pearce Foundry and Machine Works. He married on June 25, 1907, Marion Irma Carver, a native of Red Wing, Minnesota. She was born August 24, 1887, and was a daughter of Charles Catlin Carver and Anna Maria Secor. Mr. and Mrs. Pearce have eight children:—

    a.—Malcolm Marshall Pearce.
    b.—Mildred Anna Pearce.
    c.—Evalyn Lucille Pearce.
    d.—Ray Douglas Pearce.
    e.—Marion Emily Pearce.
    f.—Robert Louis Pearce.
    g.—Jesse Lawrence Pearce.
    h.—Charles Allen Pearce.

a.—Malcolm Marshall Pearce died at the age of eighteen months.

b.—Mildred Anna Pearce was born on July 15, 1911, and was married June 23, 1928, to Charles Franklin Learner, son of Leavitt C. Learner and Cora Goodwine. He was born in Cocomo, Indiana, on March 31, 1908, and at this time is serving in the United States Army, having recently been promoted to the rank of Lt.-Colonel. He is at present on duty somewhere in the South Pacific. He was wounded there a short while ago but is now "back on the job again." They have three children:—

Evalyn Marie Learner, born October 27, 1929.
Donald Franklin Learner, born June 30, 1931.
Emily Ann Learner, born February 2, 1936.

c.—Evalyn Lucille Pearce, third child of Malcolm Mordella Pearce and Marion Irma Carver, was married June 23, 1944, to Donald Wade of Grand Rapides, Ohio. He is in the military service of his country and is at present stationed at Harding Field, Baton Rouge, La.

d.—Ray Douglas Pearce is unmarried and is in the Medical Corps of the U. S. Army, being presently stationed at Camp Stoneman, California.

e.—Marion Emily Pearce is at present unmarried and living with her parents.

f.—Robert Louis Pearce is in the Navy and is at present stationed at the Navy Aerial Technical Training School at Norman, Oklahoma. He there married on November 18, 1944, June Olander of Waterloo, Iowa.

g.—Jesse Lawrence Pearce is unmarried at this time and is serving in the U. S. Army. He is at this date following General George S. Patton in his famous drive on Coblenz, Germany.

h.—Charles Allen Pearce is unmarried at this time. He is in the U. S. Navy and is at present with the fleet operating around the Philippines.

iv.—Claud Pearce, second son of Berthier Mordella Pearce and Emily Marshall, is one of the best known men in hotel circles in Louisiana. He married Katie Lou Ryan in 1939 and is at present manager of the Rex Hotel in Shreveport, La. He has no children.

v.—Emily Pearce, fifth child of Berthier Mordella Pearce and Emily Marshall, was married to Shelton Meng and now lives in San Francisco, California. She has no children.

vi.—Henry Munson Pearce, sixth child of Berthier Mordella Pearce and Emily Marshall, married Annie Ashley. They have two children:—Doris and Henry Munson Pearce, Jr.

vii.—Fred William Pearce, seventh child of Berthier Mordella Pearce and Emily Marshall, has been twice married but has no children. He is living in Texas.

viii.—Florence Pearce, eighth child of Berthier Mordella Pearce and Emily Marshall, was married to Whitley Davenport in California. They have no children.

ix.—Chester Pearce, youngest child of Berthier Mordella Pearce and Emily Marshall, is married, lives in New Orleans, and has one daughter.

BIBLIOGRAPHY:—

List of Emigrants to America, by J. C. Hotten, pp. 118, 224, 240, 271.

McCall-Tidwell and Allied Families, by Mrs. Ettie Tidwell McCall, pp. 479-80-81.

The Story of Georgia and the Georgia People, by George Gillman Smith, D.D., p. 621.

Will of Joshua Pearce, Sr., on file in Screven county, Ga.

Records from the Stephen Pearce, family Bible, now property of Mrs. Robert Lee Bailey, Jr., Opelousas, La.

Official transcript of the descendants of Alanson Green Pearce, furnished by Mrs. Anna B. Morris of Bunkie, La. Pearce family records furnished by Mrs. Robert Bolling Miles of Alexandria, La.

Data on the Pearce family furnished by Mrs. Fred W. Bradt of Alexandria, La.

Records from the family Bible of William Bray Pearce furnished by his grand-daughter, Mrs. Julia Proctor Pendleton of Tyler, Texas.

Records from the Dunwoody family Bible, now the property of Mrs. James L. Helm of Bunkie, La.

Obituary of Mrs. W. C. Townsend, Bunkie Record of March 16, 1938.

Obituary of Charles K. White, Alexandria Daily Town Talk of January 28, 1939.

Kemper data furnished by Mrs. Albert L. Nelson of Nacogdoches, Texas.

Tombstone records from the cemetery at Evergreen, La., and the Christian cemetery at Cheneyville, La.

History of the Brashear Family, by Henry Sinclair Brashear of Texarkana, Texas.

Data on the descendants of Eliza Caroline Pearce and Charles Duvall Brashear, furnished by Mrs. Albert Joseph Jackson of Beaumont, Texas.

Obituary of Eddie Walter Pearce, Alexandria Daily Town Talk of June 17, 1939.

Data on the descendants of Joshua Pearce and Esther Tanner, contributed by Mrs. William Eugene Pearce of Pineville, La.

Data on the descendants of James Horace Marshall, Jr., furnished by his daughter, Mrs. Louis H. Johnson of Alexandria, La.

Data on the descendants of Dr. Robert Hiram Marshall, furnished by his daughter, Mrs. Thomas Jefferson Spurlock, Sr., of Baton Rouge, La.

Important family data furnished by Mrs. Malcolm Mordella Pearce of Baton Rouge, La.

Important family data furnished by Heber Livingston Pearce of Denham Springs, La.

INDEX

Tanner, Percy 301
Peter, 76, 150
Peter (ii), 306
Peter (ii), children of, 307
Peter E., 316
Providence, 319
Providence Tuzette, 48, 71,
112, 277
Ralph St. Clair, 314-15
Randal, 153-57
Randal Glaze, 158
Rhoda, 410
Robe Ann, 229
Robert, 47, 92, 131, 220, 224,
231-2-3-4, 307
Robert Barnes, 311
Robert, children of, 234-5, 307
Robert Clarence, 252
Robert Cromwell, 311
Robert Harris, 314
Robert Harris, Jr., 314
Robert Linn, 47, 245-6-7
Robert Linn, Jr., 247-51
In the Revolution, 221
Roger Lloyd, 314-15
Roger Irving, 316
Rollie, 296
Rosalind Harley, 322-3, 360
Rufus Clarence, 314
Sadie Guice, 317
Sallye, 313
Sarah, 132
Sarah Adeline, 258-9
Sarah Evalina, 153, 161
Sarah Frances, 302
Sarah Metcalfe, 308
Sidney, 304-6, 398
Sidney Erle, 322
Sidney Norman, 305
Sidney Otis, 304-5, 398
Stanley, 316
Thirza Caroline, 153-55
Thomas, 223
Thomas Gregory, 318
Tom Otis, 305
Vernon Sidney, 322
Villa, 313
Virgil, 316
Virgil Genin, 311-13
Virgin Genin, Jr., 313
Wade Hampton, 294
Wade Hampton, Jr., 295
Walter Irion, 252, 326
Walter Lodowick, 247-56
William (ii), 313
William, Jr., 313
William Lodowick, 256-7
William Lodowick, Jr., 257
William Peter, 314-15
Wills, 221

Tarpley, Lillie, 168
Nannie, 168
Tate, Gracie Magdoline, 69
Leon, 69
Taylor, Alice Havard, 116
George Mai, 177-9
Jane, 122
J. Clyde, 195
McCleland, 116
Shirley Jean, 195
Mary Sophronia, 179
Teague, Mary Dyer, 370
Tercy, Mary, 208
Terrell, Glenda Elizabeth, 204
Glenn, 204
Texada, Arnaud Preot, 183
Arnaud Preot, Jr., 183
Blanche Elizabeth, 182
Donald Edward, 198
Dorothy Rae, 198
Earnest Eugene, 198
Elizabeth Lucy, 202
Frank Neal, 198
Frank Neal, Jr., 198
Jacqueline, 184
James Louis, 198
James Parker, 198
John Augustin, Jr., 184
John Cary, 198
Lula Lorraine, 198
Patricia Ann, 198
Thomas Richard, 198
Welsh, 197
Thayer, Willie, 100
Thigpen, Benton, 69
Claudine, 69
Van E., 69
Thomas, Elizabeth, 27, 94
Fanny, 27
Florence, 27
James, 27, 94, 227
J. C., 228-9
Jane, 62
Jones, 27
Mary, 126
Thompson, Daisy Beatrice, 43
Ethel, 101
Roslyn Lambright, 110
Tillery, Gayle, 304
William, 304
Tillman, Dora, 321
Tilton, J. M., 377
Tobin, Leonard Conrad, 339
Toinette, Eugene A., 313
Sallye Gene, 313
Toler, Elmira, 237
Joel, 237
Toller, Thomas, 325
Toon, Eugenia Kemper, 355
Jesse James, 355

www.ingramcontent.com/pod-product-compliance
Lightning Source LLC
Chambersburg PA
CBHW050554270326
41926CB00012B/2050